MARK

PREACHING THE WORD
Edited by R. Kent Hughes

(((PREACHING *the* WORD)))

MARK

JESUS, SERVANT *and* SAVIOR

R. KENT HUGHES

WHEATON, ILLINOIS

Mark

Copyright © 2015 by R. Kent Hughes

Published by Crossway
      1300 Crescent Street
      Wheaton, Illinois 60187

Originally published as two volumes copyright © 1989 by R. Kent Hughes

Cover design: Jon McGrath, Simplicated Studio

Cover image: Adam Greene, illustrator

First printing 2015

Printed in the United States of America

Hardcover ISBN: 978-1-4335-3838-4
PDF ISBN: 978-1-4335-3839-1
Mobipocket ISBN: 978-1-4335-3840-7
ePub ISBN: 978-1-4335-3841-4

Library of Congress Cataloging-in-Publication Data

Hughes, R. Kent.
    Mark : Jesus, servant and savior / R.Kent Hughes.
       pages cm.— (Preaching the word)
    Includes bibliographical references and index.
    ISBN 978-1-4335-3838-4 (hc)
    1. Bible. Mark—Commentaries. 2. Bible. Mark—
Meditations. I. Title.
BS2585.53.H84   2015
226.3'07—dc23   2013043784

Crossway is a publishing ministry of Good News Publishers.

VP		31	30	29	28	27	26	25	24	23	22	21
15	14	13	12	11	10	9	8	7	6	5	4	3

For my mother

For even the Son of Man came not to be served but to serve, and to give his life as a ransom for many.

MARK 10:45

Contents

Acknowledgments

I must express appreciation to my secretary, Mrs. Sharon Fritz, for her patience and care in typing the manuscripts of these studies; also to Mr. Herb Carlburg for his cheerful, weekly proofreading, and Rev. Jeff Buikema, pastor of Covenant Presbyterian Church, LaCrosse, Wisconsin, for his reading of the manuscript and helpful suggestions. Lastly, special thanks to Dr. Lane Dennis, president of Crossway Books, for his vision for this undertaking and consistent encouragement.

A Word to Those Who Preach the Word

There are times when I am preaching that I have especially sensed the pleasure of God. I usually become aware of it through the unnatural silence. The ever-present coughing ceases and the pews stop creaking, bringing an almost physical quiet to the sanctuary—through which my words sail like arrows. I experience a heightened eloquence, so that the cadence and volume of my voice intensify the truth I am preaching.

There is nothing quite like it—the Holy Spirit filling one's sails, the sense of his pleasure, and the awareness that something is happening among one's hearers. This experience is, of course, not unique, for thousands of preachers have similar experiences, even greater ones.

What has happened when this takes place? How do we account for this sense of his smile? The answer for me has come from the ancient rhetorical categories of *logos*, *ethos*, and *pathos*.

The first reason for his smile is the *logos*—in terms of preaching, God's Word. This means that as we stand before God's people to proclaim his Word, we have done our homework. We have exegeted the passage, mined the significance of its words in their context, and applied sound hermeneutical principles in interpreting the text so that we understand what its words meant to its hearers. And it means that we have labored long until we can express in a sentence what the theme of the text is—so that our outline springs from the text. Then our preparation will be such that as we preach, we will not be preaching our own thoughts about God's Word, but God's actual Word, his *logos*. This is fundamental to pleasing him in preaching.

The second element in knowing God's smile in preaching is *ethos*—what you are as a person. There is a danger endemic to preaching, which is having your hands and heart cauterized by holy things. Phillips Brooks illustrated it by the analogy of a train conductor who comes to believe that he has been to the places he announces because of his long and loud heralding of them. And that is why Brooks insisted that preaching must be "the bringing of truth through personality." Though we can never *perfectly* embody the truth we preach, we must be subject to it, long for it, and make it as much a part of our ethos as possible. As the Puritan William Ames said: "Next to the Scriptures, nothing makes a sermon more to pierce, than when it comes out of the inward affection of the heart without any affectation." When a preacher's ethos backs up his logos, there will be the pleasure of God.

Last, there is *pathos*—personal passion and conviction. David Hume, the Scottish philosopher and skeptic, was once challenged as he was seen going to hear George Whitefield preach: "I thought you do not believe in the gospel." Hume replied, "I don't, but *he does*." Just so! When a preacher believes what he preaches, there will be passion. And this belief and requisite passion will know the smile of God.

The pleasure of God is a matter of *logos* (the Word), *ethos* (what you are), and *pathos* (your passion). As you *preach the Word* may you experience his smile—the Holy Spirit in your sails!

R. Kent Hughes
Wheaton, Illinois

1

The Purpose of Life

MARK 10:45

SOME YEARS AGO one of the world's renowned scholars of the classics, Dr. E. V. Rieu, completed a great translation of Homer into modern English for the Penguin Classics series. He was sixty years old, and he had been an agnostic all his life. The publisher soon approached him again and asked him to translate the Gospels. When Rieu's son heard this he said, "It will be interesting to see what Father will make of the four Gospels. It will be even more interesting to see what the four Gospels make of Father."[1] He did not have to wonder very long. Within a year's time E. V. Rieu, the lifelong agnostic, responded to the Gospels he was translating and became a committed Christian. His story is a marvelous testimony to the transforming power of God's Word. Experiences like this have been repeated time and time again.

Whenever I begin a fresh study of one of the Bible's books, I keep this story in mind, and especially the inviting questions: What will it make of me? What will it make of the people I influence? My own personal experience has been (and I think for many it has been the same) that when I have finished studies of sections in the Scriptures (for example, the Sermon on the Mount, the Lord's Prayer, or the book of Colossians), I was not the same person as when I began. Positive changes have taken place in my theology and my prayer life. The Sermon on the Mount has enhanced my understanding as no other Scripture as to what the Christian life is all about. The Lord's Prayer with its three upward petitions, three downward requests, and immense emphasis on God's Fatherhood has greatly enriched my prayer life. The towering Christology of Colossians has made me see, as never before, God in all his fullness. What is this in-depth study of the Gospel of Mark going to make of you and me?

Mark is the *oldest* of the Gospels. Matthew and Luke made such great use of it in writing their own Gospel accounts that between them they reproduced all but a few verses of Mark's! So in this Gospel we have for the very first time in history a systematic account of the life and words of Jesus. Mark was the beginning of a distinct and original literary form that we refer to as "Gospel."

Also intriguing is the background of this Gospel. Virtually everyone agrees that the author was John Mark, a young man who had a shaky beginning in the ministry when he abandoned Paul on the apostle's first missionary trip and decided to return home (Acts 13:13). Paul was so unhappy with Mark that he refused to take him on the second journey, thus beginning a bitter quarrel between Paul and Barnabas that ended with Paul and Silas going one way and Barnabas and Mark another (Acts 15:36–41). Although intimate details are lacking, Paul and John Mark later reconciled when Paul was in prison in Rome. Mark served as his aide and then as a delegate on an important mission to Asia Minor (see Philemon 24 and Colossians 4:10). Later Paul would ask Timothy to bring John Mark back with him to Rome because he was useful in service (2 Timothy 4:11). When the Apostle Peter was writing 1 Peter in Rome, he affectionately called Mark his son (1 Peter 5:13). It was Mark's close relationship with Peter that motivated and enabled him to write an intimate portrait of Christ.

The very earliest statement about the Gospel of Mark was written by Papias, Bishop of Hierapolis, about AD 140:

> Mark became Peter's interpreter and wrote accurately all that he remembered, not, indeed, in order, of the things said or done by the Lord. For he had not heard the Lord, nor had he followed him, but later on, as I said, he followed Peter, who used to give teaching as necessity demanded but not making, as it were, an arrangement of the Lord's oracles, so single points as he remembered them. For to one thing he gave attention, to leave out nothing of what he had heard and to make no false statements in them.[2]

What a recovery Mark made! He rose from failed follower of Christ, to devoted disciple, to premier biographer and honored martyr.

> They on the heights are not the souls
> Who never erred or went astray,
> Or reached those high rewarding goals
> Along a smooth, flower-bordered way.
> Nay, they who stand where first comes dawn
> Are those who stumbled but went on.[3]

After a promising start, some of us too have stumbled, and now our confidence is gone. For us, John Mark's triumph is an immense encouragement.

The context in which John Mark wrote was, to say the least, dramatic: Rome right after the death of Peter and the Neronian persecution, sometime between AD 60 and 70. According to the Roman historian Tacitus, Nero made the Christians scapegoats for his burning of Rome and butchered them wholesale, so that the Church was driven into the Catacombs.[4] It was during this time of misery that Mark wrote the Gospel.

The purpose of John Mark's writing was to encourage the Gentile church in Rome. He wanted them to see Christ as the Suffering Servant-Savior, and so arranged his material to show Christ as One who speaks and acts and delivers in the midst of crisis.[5] Mark has no long genealogy, no birth narrative, and only two of Jesus' long discussions.

Christ is all action in Mark! Mark used the historical present tense 150 times. Jesus *comes*, Jesus *says*, and Jesus *heals*—all in the present tense. There are more miracles recorded in Mark than in the other Gospels, despite its being far shorter. Everything is in vivid "Eyewitness Newsbriefs," brilliantly vivid and fast-moving. Mark uses the Greek word for "immediately" some forty-two times (there are only seven occurrences in Matthew and one in Luke). The conjunction "and" is unusually frequent (beginning twelve of Mark's sixteen chapters) and adds to the rush of action. Christ's life is portrayed as super-busy (he even had trouble finding time to eat—see 3:20 and 6:31).

It takes a slow reader about two hours to read Mark through at a single sitting; and if you take the time, you feel surrounded by crowds, wearied by demands, and besieged by the attacks of demons. You are also repeatedly brought face-to-face with the human emotions of Jesus and the astonishment of the multitudes. Mark is the "Go Gospel"—the Gospel of the Servant-Savior.

The acknowledged key verse, the one that summarizes the Gospel of Mark, is 10:45—"For even the Son of Man came not to be served but to serve, and to give his life as a ransom for many." This verse is part of the answer to the question, what will the gospel make of us? It will make us servants like the Master, effective servants who do not run on theory but on *action*. He was (and is) Christ for the crises! Power attended his every action. This same Christ brings power to life now, and a serious study of Mark will bring that power further to our lives.

The Disciples' Failure to Learn Jesus' Servant Approach (vv. 36–41)

The irony is this: though Jesus had been with the disciples for three years as the ideal Servant, though the end was near and he had just given them a detailed forecast of his death (10:32–34), though he had taught them that his way was to be the model for their lives, the disciples (represented by James and John) now made a request that revealed that their way of thinking was virtually the opposite of Christ the Servant.

The request was outrageous: "And James and John, the sons of Zebedee, came up to him and said to him, 'Teacher, we want you to do for us whatever we ask of you.' And he said to them, 'What do you want me to do for you?' And they said to him, 'Grant us to sit, one at your right hand and one at your left, in your glory'" (10:35–37). They dimly saw that the end was near and that it involved the possibility of thrones for the disciples. As part of the inner circle (Peter, James, and John), these two hoped to get the best thrones. Perhaps they wanted to ace Peter out, because he no doubt would try for the top. So they approached Jesus privately. Matthew tells us they even had their mother do the talking (Matthew 20:20, 21).

This all sounds pretty contemporary to me. "The Lord takes care of those who take care of themselves," some say.

> "Name it and claim it," that's what faith's about!
> You can have what you want if you just have no doubt.
> So make out your "wish list" and keep on believin'
> And you find yourself perpetually receivin'.[6]

Despite their association with Jesus and despite their piety, these disciples saw greatness according to the world's definition. A bit later (v. 42), Jesus described the world's viewpoint: "You know that those who are considered rulers of the Gentiles lord it over them, and their great ones exercise authority over them." James and John had fallen to the world's idea that seeking the place of authority and personal power was right for them.

It is so easy to succumb to such thinking, as Robert Raines mused:

> I am like James and John.
> Lord, I size up other people
> in terms of what they can do for me;
> how they can further my program,
> feed my ego,
> satisfy my needs,
> give me strategic advantage.
> I exploit people,
> ostensibly for your sake,
> but really for my own.
> Lord, I turn to you
> to get the inside track

and obtain special favors,
your direction for my schemes,
your power for my projects,
your sanction for my ambitions,
your blank check for whatever I want.
I am like James and John.[7]

The Lord, of course, was not going to leave James and John, or the rest of the disciples for that matter, in their delusion. So he began to dialogue with them, probing the shallowness and naivete of their thinking. Shortly the remaining ten got wind of what James and John had tried, and a major blowup ensued.

The Lord's Rebuke of His Disciples (vv. 42–45)

The Lord called all Twelve together and in a few brilliant moments set the record straight for all time and eternity: "But whoever would be great among you must be your servant" (v. 43). Then (v. 44) he told them that preeminence among God's people would go not to rulers but to slaves: "and whoever would be first among you must be slave of all."

Why is this so? Here he gave the ultimate rationale and the key verse of the Gospel: "For even the Son of Man came not to be served but to serve, and to give his life as a ransom for many" (v. 45).

Here we will do well to pay close attention to Christ's words. He called himself "the Son of Man." This was a self-proclaimed title that did not exist before he came. It means that he is human, but even more. By saying he was "*the* Son of Man," he meant that he was (and is) the unique representation of the human race. He is not merely a human being. He is *the* human being— *the* true man.

Now consider the second phrase: "came not to be served but to serve." Here "serve" and "served" refer to the most common service, as seen in the parallel section in Luke 22:27—"For who is the greater, one who reclines at table or one who serves? Is it not the one who reclines at table? But I am among you as the one who serves." Which is greater, the host and his guests, or the waiter? Jesus said, "I am among you as the waiter." These startling words were meant to shake up the disciples. The meaning is this: the Son of Man, the man who lived the truest human life, waited upon others instead of seeking others to wait on him.[8] The ultimate extension of this was "to give his life as a ransom for many," which he shortly did. The logic is: if the One who created both the supernova and the firefly and holds them together by the word of his power (Colossians 1:15–17) became our servant, our waiter, how can we do less?

> In 1878 when William Booth's Salvation Army had just been so named, men from all over the world began to enlist. One man, who had once dreamed of himself as a bishop, crossed the Atlantic from America to England to enlist. He was a Methodist minister, Samuel Logan Brengle. And now he turned from a fine pastorate to join Booth's Salvation Army. Brengle later became the Army's first American-born commissioner. But at first Booth accepted his services reluctantly and grudgingly. Booth said to Brengle, "You've been your own boss too long." And in order to instill humility into Brengle, he set him to work cleaning the boots of the other trainees. And Brengle said to himself: "Have I followed my own fancy across the Atlantic in order to black boots?" And then as in a vision he saw Jesus bending over the feet of rough, unlettered fishermen. "Lord," he whispered, "you washed their feet; I will black their boots."[9]

The "Son of Man," the Man for all of us, came not to be waited on, but to wait on us, and to give his life as a ransom. Therefore, how can we seek our own?

Jesus has thrown open for all of us a competition that has no charms for most. But the rewards are beyond imagination. We ought to go for it! The Gospel of Mark can bring profound servanthood and active power to our lives. It is the Gospel of miracles, the Gospel of power, the Gospel of service. May it rub off on us!

May the gospel of our Lord make something out of us. All of us have tremendous opportunities. If you are ruling in the community, your opportunities for service are infinite. If you are a student laboring through your books, or teaching a Bible class, or pastoring, or whatever you are doing, your opportunities to serve are more than you can possibly imagine.

The Ideal Man, the Man for all men, did not come to be waited on, but to wait tables and to live a life of sacrifice. May this sink into our minds so we can be used of God.

2

The Effective Witness:
John the Baptist

MARK 1:1–11

HAVING MADE IT MY BUSINESS as a preacher to acquaint myself with the stories of some of the great witnesses of church history, I have my favorites—events at which I would like to have been an invisible guest.

I would like to have been present when John Knox stood tall against Queen Mary. Witnesses said that even when the dangers were past and he was an old man, they would lift him into the pulpit and there he would stand tottering until he was caught up in the message. Then he would "ding the pulpit into balds"—break up the pulpit. A bit of hyperbole, no doubt, but I would like to have been there.

I would like to have been in Hampton Court the day Hugh Latimer preached to Henry VIII in such a way that it offended him. I would like to have been there the following Sunday when he was commanded by King Henry to preach again and make an apology. Hugh addressed himself as he began to preach:

> Hugh Latimer, dost thou know before whom thou art this day to speak? To the high and mighty monarch, the king's most excellent majesty, who can take away thy life if thou offendest; therefore, take heed that thou speakest not a word that may displease; but then consider well, Hugh, dost thou not know from whence thou comest; upon whose message thou art sent? Even by the great and mighty God! who is all-present, and who beholdest all thy ways, and who is able to cast thy soul into hell! Therefore, take care that thou deliverest thy message faithfully.[1]

He then gave King Henry the same sermon he had preached the week before—only with more energy!

I would like to have been at Worms on April 18, 1521, when Martin Luther stood against his world, *contra mundum*. There before him were arrayed the princes and theologians of the Church, and along with them, Charles, heir of a long line of sovereigns—of Maximillian, of Ferdinand the Catholic, of Isabelle—the orthodox-scion of the Hapsburgs, Lord of Burgundy, Austria, Naples, Spain, the Low Countries, Holy Roman Emperor! To the questioning of Johann Eck, Archbishop of Trier and his antagonist, Luther answered:

> I do not accept the authority of popes and councils, for they have contradicted each other—my conscience is captive to the Word of God. I cannot and I will not recant anything, for to go against conscience is neither right nor safe. God help me. Amen. Here I stand, I cannot do otherwise.[2]

And of course, I would like to have heard Peter on the day of Pentecost or perhaps before the Sanhedrin when he and John said, "Whether it is right in the sight of God to listen to you rather than to God, you must judge, for we cannot but speak of what we have seen and heard" (Acts 4:19, 20). What a day that was in the history of the Church. But if I really stop and think about it, there is one whom I would forego all the others to hear: *John the Baptist*. I say this for two reasons. First, Jesus said that "among those born of women none is greater than John" (Luke 7:28). And second, John was the herald, the primary witness, to the Lord Jesus Christ.

In Mark's Gospel, John jumps full-blown onto the front page of the story of Christ with a prophetic introduction made mostly from Malachi 3:1 and Isaiah 40:3: "Behold, I send my messenger before your face, who will prepare your way, the voice of one crying in the wilderness: 'Prepare the way of the Lord, make his paths straight'" (vv. 2, 3). John's story dominates the first eight verses of this Gospel. He is also mentioned extensively in each of the three other Gospels. Why? And why was he so effective? The answer will provide remarkable help to our own desire to witness.

The Character of the Messenger (v. 6)

Verse 6 gives us a visual introduction to his character: "Now John was clothed with camel's hair and wore a leather belt around his waist and ate locusts and wild honey." John definitely was not making a fashion statement. His camel's-hair robe was the kind worn by the very poor, and his belt, unlike the fancy belts so popular in those days, was simply a leather thong.

His food was not very exciting either. His idea of eating out was to catch a few grasshoppers and visit the local beehive for dessert.

Actually John was in perfect control of his lifestyle. He knew *exactly* what he was doing, for he had assumed the dress and style of the ancient prophet Elijah the Tishbite (described in 2 Kings 1:8) who called his people to national repentance. John's dress and lifestyle were a *protest* against the godlessness and self-serving materialism of his day. It amounted to a call to separate oneself from the sinful culture, repent, and live a life focused on God. Even his context, the desert wilderness, was meant to emphasize this, for it was originally to the wilderness that Israel came out of Egypt. The people's coming out to John in the wilderness was a subtle acknowledgment of Israel's history of disobedience and rebellion and a desire to begin again.[3]

What was beautiful was that John's life and actions bore out what he was. He lived a life of continual repentance and uncompromising devotion to God. He was fearless in his proclamation of the message, just as his ancient prophetic garb portrayed. He rebuked the Pharisees, saying, "You brood of vipers! Who warned you to flee from the wrath to come? Bear fruit in keeping with repentance" (Matthew 3:7, 8). For the common people, there was instruction in giving: "Whoever has two tunics is to share with him who has none" (Luke 3:11). He told the tax gatherers to be fair (Luke 3:13). He warned the soldiers to be content and not act high-handedly (Luke 3:14). John was as fearless as he looked! He was also, in keeping with his attire, *self-forgetting and humble.*

Later, when Jesus' star began to rise and John's ministry was being eclipsed, John's disciples came to him in alarm. John's response was impeccable: "A person cannot receive even one thing unless it is given him from heaven. . . . 'I am not the Christ'" (John 3:27, 28). John saw himself like a joyous friend of the bridegroom and concluded with these immortal words: "He must increase, but I must decrease" (John 3:30). He was a man of sublime *downward* mobility, just as his apparel suggested.

My point is this: the reason John was such an effective witness is that he embodied his message! In the 1877 Yale Lectures on Preaching, Phillips Brooks gave this foundational definition of preaching:

> Truth through personality is our description of real preaching. The truth must come through the person, not merely over his lips. . . . It must come through his character, his affections, his whole intellectual and moral being. It must come genuinely through him.[4]

Bishop Quail said almost the same thing by asking the question, "Preaching is the art of making a sermon and delivering it?" To which he answered,

"Why no, that is not preaching. Preaching is the art of making a preacher and delivering that!"[5]

That was precisely the case with John the Baptist. He was filled with the Spirit while yet in Elizabeth's womb. He was a Nazirite from birth, totally committed to God, never touching the dead or strong drink, never cutting his hair, all a sign that he was totally set apart for God's work (see Luke 1:15 and Numbers 6:1–8).

John the Baptist embodied his message. In this sense he *was* the message! Others could have said the same things, but to no avail. The fact that his words saturated his being and dominated his life—the fact that they were *true* in him—gave him immense power.

The same is true of us. Nothing will make our words penetrate more than that which is true in us and comes from the heart in total sincerity. If we want to have more effect, we must humbly ask God to make our lives demonstrations of the truth of our message.

The Nature of His Message (vv. 4–8)

What was John's message? To begin with, it was a message of baptism, of repentance, as verse 4 says: "John appeared, baptizing in the wilderness and proclaiming a baptism of repentance for the forgiveness of sins." The first thing we should note about this baptism is that it was totally radical. The notable Marcan scholar William Lane says that the baptism was wholly novel.[6] No one else had ever done it. The only thing that even came close was the fact that Gentile converts to Judaism were baptized. However, that baptism was a ritual washing from all the defilement of the past. The Jews were now being asked to do something they had *never* done before in their history! Jews being baptized? Unheard of! This was why John was called "The Baptizer." There had never been anyone like him.

The second thing we should note is that the baptism was focused on repentance from sin. Again, the wilderness location was very calculated because the Biblical concept of repentance was deeply rooted in the wilderness tradition. As Lane says:

> The summons to be baptized in the Jordan meant that Israel must come once more to the wilderness. As Israel long ago had been separated from Egypt by a pilgrimage through the waters of the Red Sea, the nation is exhorted again to experience separation; the people are called to a second exodus in preparation for a new covenant with God. Both John's call to repentance and his baptism are intelligible as aspects of the prophetic tradition which expected the final salvation of God to be unveiled in the wilderness.[7]

The Jews knew why they were coming out to the wilderness. When they came, John first sat them all down and then preached about their sin. Imagine the scene: hundreds, and later thousands at the height of John's ministry, seated along the Jordan, listening as John excoriated them, warning of judgment, speaking to individual sins, naming names, calling for social justice and repentance. Finally, when they were duly convicted, they formed endless lines to be baptized as a sign that they were repenting of their sins.

What a gift John gave to them by preaching on sin and judgment! This is a neglected gift in our day of the health-and-wealth, prosperity gospel. When men and women are awakened to the facts of judgment and their own sin, they become eager listeners to the good news of the Savior who brings forgiveness. There is grace in such preaching because any Christ whom men receive without being in the wilderness, without the stern preacher of sin and judgment, is but half a Christ, and the vital half is missing.[8]

The divine and proper preparation for the gospel of Jesus Christ is preaching about sin. That is why in the Sermon on the Mount Jesus said, "Blessed are those who mourn, for they shall be comforted" (Matthew 5:4). Those who mourn over their sin see their need for grace and for a Savior, and are thus in the place to receive and be "blessed."

The baptism of repentance for sin was the first part of John's message, but the second part spoke of a superior, ultimate baptism: "And he preached, saying, 'After me comes he who is mightier than I, the strap of whose sandals I am not worthy to stoop down and untie. I have baptized you with water, but he will baptize you with the Holy Spirit'" (vv. 7, 8).

He told them he had drenched them with water that was only *external*, but One would come who would drench them in the Holy Spirit, which was intrinsically *internal*. What a beautiful metaphor for the work of the Holy Spirit! When we are baptized with the Holy Spirit, he permeates every part of us. Christianity meets men and women in their radical need and provides a *radical* answer. If you do not know Christ, you are still in your sins. The Spirit's baptism is the answer. When he drenches your life with his, you are changed!

John's message was perfectly balanced: law and gospel. God's law condemned them in their sin and called for repentance. But repentance alone would not save them. There must be the gospel (God's grace) and the baptism of the Holy Spirit.

Why was John's witness so effective? First, because his character modeled his message. Therefore, what he said had the ring of truth. Second, his message was complete. It had both law and grace, and God's grace was (and is) infinite.

The Delivery of His Message (v. 5)

There is a third element that we note in passing: John's witness was also made effective by his passion. When he stood before the people in the wasteland, lean, gaunt, solitary, he preached with fire. We can be sure that, like the prophets of old, he wept. He wept like Jesus and Paul and Whitefield and Moody. Everything together—his character, his message, and his passion—reached the multitudes.

Verse 5 says, "And all the country of Judea and all Jerusalem were going out to him and were being baptized by him in the river Jordan, confessing their sins." Some say as many as 300,000 came out to John for baptism! John's *life*, John's *message*, and John's *passion* made him the greatest witness of history. *He had prepared the way for the Lord!* God was pleased with John's ministry, so he confirmed it, crowning his witness with the greatest of all honors—the baptism of Christ.

The Confirmation of His Message (vv. 9–11)

Verse 9 says, "In those days Jesus came from Nazareth of Galilee and was baptized by John in the Jordan." Why was Jesus baptized? That is a good question. In fact, Matthew says John asked it: "John would have prevented him, saying, 'I need to be baptized by you, and do you come to me?' But Jesus answered him, 'Let it be so now, for thus it is fitting for us to fulfill all righteousness.' Then he consented" (Matthew 3:14, 15). Because Jesus was sinless, he needed no baptism of repentance. But in his baptism he associated himself with us sinners and placed himself among the guilty—not for his own salvation but for ours—not for his guilt but for ours—not because he feared the wrath to come but to save us from it. His baptism meant the cross!

> My song shall be of Jesus,
> The precious lamb of God,
> Who gave himself my ransom,
> And bought me with his blood.

See and hear the beauty of the moment: "And when he [Jesus] came up out of the water, immediately he saw the heavens being torn open and the Spirit descending on him like a dove. And a voice came from heaven, 'You are my beloved Son; with you I am well pleased'" (vv. 10, 11). What did Jesus see? Literally, he saw the heavens tearing apart. Then he saw the Holy Spirit in the form of a dove descending *into* him, as the Spirit publicly entered Jesus for full empowerment for ministry. Jesus also saw the divine poetry, for this same Spirit brooded over the waters at the beginning of creation (Genesis 1:2).

What did Jesus hear? "You are my beloved Son; with you I am well pleased." God was pleased with his Son's commitment to be the humble Servant-Savior who would atone for the sins of the whole world (see Isaiah 53:11).

My song shall be of Jesus.

How I would like to have been with John Knox and Hugh Latimer and Martin Luther and Paul and Peter. But how much more I would like to have heard the greatest witness who ever lived! We all are called to emulate John's witness—to preach the whole message, both law and grace. We are to preach the radicalness of the gospel, that men and women might be drenched in the Holy Spirit through Christ. We are to have the character of our lives match the message we preach; to believe it so much, and with such sincerity, that others will sense the ring of truth. We are to passionately proclaim it, to weep for the world, and to exalt Jesus above all. "He must increase, but I must decrease."

To have a song, be a song, for Jesus!

Have you perhaps received water baptism but not the drenching in the Holy Spirit? That is the baptism you must have. All Christians are baptized into one Body in him. Unless Christ has filled your life, unless he has permeated your heart of hearts, you are not one of his. Regardless of how you have been dipped or sprinkled or dry-cleaned, or whatever has happened, you are not one of his unless you have received the regeneration of the Holy Spirit, his cleansing from sin, and his empowering to godliness. Is he that real to you? If so, then bless his name. If not, seek him today.

3

The Temptation of Christ

MARK 1:12, 13 AND MATTHEW 4:1–11

CHARLES COLSON, in his brilliant book of essays *Who Speaks For God?*, tells of watching a segment of television's "60 Minutes" in which host Mike Wallace interviewed Auschwitz survivor Yehiel Dinur, a principal witness at the Nuremberg war-crime trials. During the interview, a film clip from Adolf Eichmann's 1961 trial was viewed that showed Dinur enter the courtroom and come face-to-face with Eichmann for the first time since being sent to Auschwitz almost twenty years earlier. Stopped cold, Dinur began to sob uncontrollably and then fainted while the presiding judge pounded his gavel for order. "Was Dinur overcome by hatred? Fear? Horrid memories?" asked Colson, who answers:

> No; it was none of these. Rather, as Dinur explained to Wallace, all at once he realized Eichmann was not the godlike army officer who had sent so many to their deaths. This Eichmann was an ordinary man. "I was afraid about myself," said Dinur. "I saw that I am capable to do this. I am . . . exactly like he." Wallace's subsequent summation of Dinur's terrible discovery—"Eichmann is in all of us"—is a horrifying statement; but it indeed captures the central truth about man's nature. For as a result of the fall, sin is in each of us—not just the susceptibility to sin, but sin itself.[1]

It was not the horror of the man Eichmann that smote Dinur, but the horrible revelation of self and the predicament of mankind that made him faint. Eichmann is in all of us, because all of us are in Adam. This is proven by our susceptibility to temptation. We are tempted by theft because we *are* thieves, even though we may not in fact steal. We are tempted to kill because we *are* murderers, even if we do not literally slay our brother. We are tempted to adultery because we *are* adulterers, even though we may not commit adultery. James says, "Let no one say when he is tempted, 'I am being tempted by God,' for God cannot be tempted with evil, and he himself tempts no one. But each person is tempted when he is lured and enticed by his own desire" (James 1:13, 14). The fact that we are tempted proves that we are prone to evil—and it is terrible. Eichmann is in all of us.

Objecting to this shows that we have not yet fully grasped the Scriptures' teaching about our sin, nor have we come to grips with the realities about our own personalities.

What is our hope? As believers, it is the fact that we are in the second Adam, the last Adam, the Lord Jesus Christ who conquered temptation. Admittedly this is a wondrous mystery (cf. 1 Corinthians 12:13), as is the mystery of his being sinless and yet fully tempted (Hebrews 4:15). Because of our solidarity with him, we can have victory over the sin within us. In recognition of this, we are going to examine the great temptation of Christ in the wilderness—seeing the nature of his temptations and what he did to overcome them, and then seeing how this can be of help in our own struggles with temptation.

Mark 1:12, 13 provides the most descriptive introduction to our Lord's temptation found in any of the Gospels: "The Spirit immediately drove him out into the wilderness. And he was in the wilderness forty days, being tempted by Satan. And he was with the wild animals, and the angels were ministering to him." From this we understand that immediately after his baptism, when he saw the heavens tear apart and the Holy Spirit descend into him and heard the Father's voice pronounce, "You are my beloved Son; with you I am well pleased," he felt an inexorable compulsion from the Holy Spirit to plunge further into the wilderness to duel Satan. Heaven had opened. Now Hell opened. In Jewish thought the wilderness was viewed as a place of danger, gloom, and the abode of demons (Matthew 12:43; Luke 8:29; 11:24). The mention of "wild animals" underscores this idea—the wilderness was a place of loneliness and danger, the realm of Satan.[2]

Here amidst desolation, Matthew tells us, "And after fasting forty days and forty nights, he was hungry" (Matthew 4:2). It was a fast that was virtually impossible apart from intense spiritual absorption. Certainly his soul was given to innermost communication with the Father as he contemplated the immense and painful task that his baptism introduced and that would culminate in the cross. During this time he also repeatedly repulsed the attacks of Satan. Finally, in a weakened state, he faced the devil's greatest attack, as recorded in Matthew 4:3–11.

This encounter was supremely dramatic. The backdrop was a desolate,

monotonous wasteland like that in the forlorn surrealism of a Dali painting—
an anti-Eden. In the foreground sat the weary and desperately hungry Christ.
Before him glided the resplendent figure of Satan, radiating power and promise—elegantly beautiful. The first Adam fell to the gorgeous Satan in the
glories of Eden; now the second Adam faced Satan's deceptively beautiful
presence in trackless desolation. The encounter of Christ and Satan was the
greatest combat that has ever taken place on the face of the earth, and by far
the most important. If Christ had failed at any point, we would have no hope
of resisting temptation (the Eichmann in us) or of receiving salvation. Our
Lord was, of course, victorious. As we look at his victory, we look at ours.
What was the nature of Christ's three temptations? How did he resist them?

The First Temptation (Matthew 4:3, 4)

The initial temptation is described in Matthew 4:3—"And the tempter came
and said to him, 'If you are the Son of God, command these stones to become
loaves of bread.'" The first thing we must realize is that the temptation was
real. Christ was really and truly hungry! During the forty-day fast he had
undergone the characteristic reduction of appetite that goes with fasting. His
intense exchange with the Father had further removed his thoughts from his
physical needs. However, after forty days the physical realities naturally and
necessarily reasserted themselves with a vengeance. Jesus would die if he
did not soon eat!

It is probably safe to assume that few of us have ever known this kind
of hunger. Jesus' hunger was the hunger of starvation! Thus Satan's suggestion "If you are the Son of God, command these stones to become loaves of
bread" bore powerful appeal. The suggestion seemed so harmless. But it was
a temptation to sin, because in the Incarnation Christ had come to do the will
of the Father and nothing else. Moreover, in accordance with the Father's
will he had followed the Spirit's impulse to fast in the wilderness, and the
Father had not seen fit to provide him with food. Thus the temptation was for
Christ to provide for his own needs apart from the will of the Father.

The words, "If you are the Son of God" were meant to call into question
Christ's relationship with the Father who had called him his "beloved Son"
at the baptism. If Christ "proved" that he was the Son of God by turning the
stones into bread, he would betray his trust in his Father and create a breach
in the Holy Trinity! The temptation was insidiously real.

This was a temptation to which we, no doubt, would have fallen. History
proves that we naturally love the Father's bread more than him. After feeding the 5,000, and then being relentlessly pursued by the multitudes, Jesus in

bitter disappointment remarked that the people followed him not for spiritual reasons but because they "ate [their] fill of the loaves" (John 6:26).

Jesus was different. In that dreary wasteland, starving, he faced his brilliant tempter and replied, "It is written, 'Man shall not live by bread alone, but by every word that comes from the mouth of God'" (Matthew 4:4). He said in effect, "It is better to starve than to be fed apart from the will of the Father. As his Son I cannot act independently of my Father. I must live by my Father's word!" The will of the Father meant more to Christ than food and life.

Likewise, doing God's will should mean more to us than life or physical well-being, important as these may be. It meant more to Wycliffe martyr Chet Bitterman, who was murdered by Colombian hard-line N19 guerrillas. On the collar of the shirt he was wearing when he was killed, his wife had stitched: "His way is perfect." Bitterman and his wife knew and believed the truth.[3]

I hope we see the truth—that God's will is more important than a hamburger or a promotion or getting married or "success." To the first temptation Jesus gave a tremendous "No!" But the Tempter was not through and came back to Christ with another carefully constructed enticement.

The Second Temptation (Matthew 4:5–7)

"Then the devil took him to the holy city and set him on the pinnacle of the temple and said to him, 'If you are the Son of God, throw yourself down, for it is written, "He will command his angels concerning you," and "On their hands they will bear you up, lest you strike your foot against a stone"'" (Matthew 4:5, 6). Whether Satan took him in a vision or in reality to the pinnacle of the temple, we do not know. If he transported Christ physically, he probably took him to the "royal portico" of Herod on the south side, from which one could plunge down into the Kedron Valley. From here one could not fully see the depth of the abyss.[4] From this dizzy height Satan urged Christ to jump, slightly misquoting Psalm 91:11, 12, leaving out the phrase "to guard you in all your ways," which means "in all your *righteous* ways." Thus the devil suggested that God would protect Christ no matter what he did.[5]

Again Jesus faced a real temptation: to display miraculous power apart from the Father's will. The second temptation, like the first, was calculated to be psychologically beguiling. It was as though Satan said, "You have shown your trust in the Father in response to my first temptation. So now show the world how much you trust him by diving from the pinnacle of the temple. It's OK—the Scriptures promise you won't get hurt." Good things would surely come of this. It would be such a great act of faith on his part!

But would it? Jesus thought otherwise. He knew that he had no command to leap from the temple. He again recognized that as the Son he was never to do anything in his own power—that he would be putting God to the test, bringing "a moment of ineffable tension" between him and the Father.[6] So he responded by quoting Deuteronomy 6:16—"Again it is written, 'You shall not put the Lord your God to the test'" (Matthew 4:7). Even the very highest and best ends do not justify operating contrary to God's will.

Years before, the Israelites tempted God at Massah by requiring him to provide water to prove his promise that he would take care of them. On that occasion God told Moses to speak to the rock and it would bring forth water for all. But when confronted by the people, Moses' anger rose, and instead of speaking to the rock he *struck it twice*. In response, despite Moses' disobedience, God graciously provided water for the people (Numbers 20:8–11). But Moses was forbidden to enter the promised land. God does not appreciate being tested. Jumping from the pinnacle is never justified, even though it brings great "success," if God does not order it. We need to remember this in a day when the Church has enthroned pragmatics, when the Church says, "If it gets people saved it must be OK . . . If it gets people in the door it must be God's will!" External prosperity does not mean God approves of all we are doing. God approves *obedience*. Again Christ remained under the Father's word.

The Third Temptation (Matthew 4:8–11)

Satan then came with his third and final temptation: "Again, the devil took him to a very high mountain and showed him all the kingdoms of the world and their glory. And he said to him, 'All these I will give you, if you will fall down and worship me'" (Matthew 4:8, 9). Satan presented Christ with a vision of the world in which nations stood ready to abandon their idols and accept Christ as Lord. Christ could hear the rustling of flags as he enjoyed peace and power. He could win the world without pain—no weeping over Jerusalem, no crucifixion. Jerusalem, the mighty Roman Empire, young Britain would all open their gates singing, "The King comes!"[7]

All the Master would have to do would be to acknowledge in worship the limited sovereignty that Satan has been allowed to exercise on Planet Earth. The temptation was to take the easy way to kingship, apart from God's will, to be a "shortcut Savior." The choice was infinitely extreme: the long agony of the cross, or instant exaltation following a fleeting bow. The cross was the Father's will. So Christ rose high above the wasteland and his adversary and cried, "Be gone, Satan! For it is written, 'You shall worship the Lord your God and him only shall you serve'" (Matthew 4:10). Every creature must bow to the Father, including the Incarnate Son! At Christ's words the devil fled, leaving Christ alone in the desolation.

Then in the air above the desert and around Jesus on the wilderness stretches, angels glimmered, and soon the sky was filled with God's messengers ministering to him. Satan and Christ would meet again, but the first great battle was over and *Christ was victor!*

It is a terrible revelation when we see the truth about ourselves. We are easily *tempted* to sin because sin is *in* us.

> And all man's Babylons strive but to impart
> The grandeurs of his Babylonian Heart.
>
> Francis Thompson, "The Heart"

Our lives prove what we are. But we must take heart, for Christ has taken on our condition. He was "tempted as we are, yet [was] without sin" (Hebrews 4:15). This is an unfathomable mystery—that he could be sinless though truly tempted. But the fact is, he endured *real* temptation and came out utterly victorious. Because of that, he not only delivers us but sympathizes with our weaknesses.

Jesus' experience provides us with mighty wisdom. The most important factor in fighting temptation is to be filled with the Spirit of Christ, the Holy Spirit (Romans 8:9). Christ is the victor over temptation and sin. His very words to us are, "[T]ake heart; I have overcome the world" (John 16:33).

When Martin Luther was asked how he overcame the devil, he replied, "Well, when he comes knocking upon the door of my heart, and asks 'Who lives here?' the dear Lord Jesus goes to the door and says, 'Martin Luther used to live here, but he has moved out. Now I live here.'" When Christ fills our lives, Satan has no entrance.

The other factor in fighting temptation is to be filled with God's Word. In response to each of the three temptations, Christ answered with Scripture (Deuteronomy 8:3, 6:16, and 6:13). He knew the truth of, "I have stored up your word in my heart, that I might not sin against you" (Psalm 119:11). Why is this so? God's Word reveals God's mind, and God's mind cannot be subject to sin. Therefore, if we fill our hearts with his Word, sin and temptation cannot dominate.

These two things, the fullness of Christ and the fullness of the Word, will make us victorious, and the angels will minister to us to meet all our needs.

4

The Beginning of Christ's Ministry

MARK 1:14–20

LAST YEAR I CAME ACROSS an old black-and-white photo of me, age sixteen, standing in the pulpit of my home church as I preached my first sermon. I was a skinny boy, hair carefully slicked back with Brylcreem in a short fifties pompadour ducktail haircut, wearing an inch-wide tie and a sport coat that I had outgrown. I was preaching on Jonah and the whale, which was to become my favorite text the next few years—especially as I added little puns to my delivery: "God has a whale of a plan for your life," "Jonah's experience proves that you can't keep a good man down," "As Jonah fled, he was the original 'Chicken of the Sea.'" It was a sermon of doubtful quality and dubious wit! But on that first night my mind was not on anything but trying to get through the sermon. My cheek kept twitching, and I could feel my face flush red from time to time.

Probably most preachers have had shaky starts. I read of one, later to become one of Scotland's great preachers, who stood to preach the first time and instead ran out of the church! There are a few, only a few, who had very fine beginnings—like Chrysostom ("golden-throat," as his name translates). God develops his preachers in different ways, to his glory.

But there was One who had it all together—perfectly so—from the very first. That One was, of course, our Lord Jesus Christ. His *logos*, his word, was perfect. Whatever he said was absolutely true. His exegesis of Scripture was flawless. His application of spiritual truth was the most penetrating in all of history, as we see in such discourses as the Sermon on the Mount.

His *ethos*, the kind of person he was, was without parallel in the human race. The tone of his voice, the expression on his face, the integrity of his eyes flowed with truth. His *pathos* came from a heart absolutely convinced of man's need, absolutely loving, and absolutely determined. There never has been anyone as truly passionate as Christ in all human experience.

These three, his *logos*, *ethos*, and *pathos*, blended in Christ with such ineluctable force that he, from the beginning, was the greatest communicator the world has ever known!

Notwithstanding all we have said about John the Baptist being the greatest of preachers, the Baptist could not hold a candle to Christ the preacher. In fact, John's Gospel tells us that after Jesus was baptized, more people attended his preaching than that of the Baptist, causing great consternation among John's ignorant disciples. Ultimately we read that when John the Baptist was jailed by Herod, Jesus shifted his own ministry into high gear, for with the quenching of John's light it was right and proper for the unquenchable Light to burn even more brightly.

So stupendous was Jesus' preaching in Galilee that St. Matthew in the parallel passage in his Gospel (Matthew 4:12–16) quotes the appropriate passage from Isaiah 9:1, 2—"The land of Zebulun and the land of Naphtali, the way of the sea, beyond the Jordan, Galilee of the Gentiles—the people dwelling in darkness have seen a great light, and for those dwelling in the region and shadow of death, on them a light has dawned." Before Christ, the people in this region were paralyzed by the darkness, unable to find their way. They were subject to the "shadow of death." But then Christ came preaching, and the people saw a great light like the dawn of day! There had never been such preaching.

The Heart of Jesus' Preaching (vv. 14, 15)

Verses 14, 15 tell us what Jesus' preaching was like: "Now after John was arrested, Jesus came into Galilee, proclaiming the gospel of God, and saying, 'The time is fulfilled, and the kingdom of God is at hand; repent and believe in the gospel.'" Jesus' original preaching had three emphases: *the kingdom*, *repentance*, and *belief*. We will work our way back through these emphases for clarity.

Jesus' preaching called the Galileans to "believe in the gospel." Specifically he called them to believe the good news that the kingdom was about to happen. They were to believe that Messiah was coming posthaste. In a short time this call to belief would be transferred explicitly to him. Of course, with the cross the essential message would be, "Believe in the Lord Jesus, and you will be saved" (Acts 16:31). Jesus' original preaching contained the kernel of what we call today gospel preaching. We feel affirmed by this in our proclamation of Christ as evangelicals.

There is no doubt that this is the way salvation is to be preached. We must be committed with all our hearts to preaching faith alone. Sadly, it is easy in our existentialist, post-rational culture to be accorded the status of "believer" whether a person is born again or not. Display the right cultural traits and you will be accepted. Here are some of the most effective:

Vocabulary. Biblical history records that when the Gileadites and the Ephraimites were warring, the Gileadites developed a password to detect captured Ephraimites who pretended to be Gileadites. The word was *Shibboleth*, which the Ephraimites (who had trouble with the "sh" sound) could only pronounce *Sibboleth*. It worked perfectly on the unsuspecting enemy (Judges 12:4–7). We evangelicals have our Shibboleths, but unfortunately they are easy to pick up. Use passwords such as "fellowship" and "brother" and "born again" and you will fool most of the people most of the time.

Social conventions. Share the same social attitudes about alcohol and tobacco, modesty and style of clothing—share the same likes and dislikes (especially dislikes), and you will probably pass as a believer. The ease with which you can adopt the behavioral mores of professing Christianity has been greased by the gradual alignment of many believers with the materialism and hedonism of our secular culture.

Heritage. If your parents are respectable Christians—or even better, Christian workers—it will probably be assumed that you are a believer. By attending evening services and prayer meetings and practicing the tithe, you will place yourself beyond question. Some well-meaning parents have manipulated their children into bogus confessions, bogus baptisms, and bogus memberships.

For these and similar reasons, multitudes of unregenerate "believers" are comfortably ensconced in their churches and no one has the gracious temerity to question the authenticity of their faith. Belief is all that is necessary to become a Christian, but it must be a belief that changes the life. If you say that you believe, but there are no substantial changes in your life, you had better consider carefully whether you *truly* believe.

That is why in Jesus' preaching and indeed in the preaching of the Apostolic Church, repentance and belief are so closely bound together. Repentance plays like a musical refrain through the Book of Acts, where Paul sums up his teaching to the Ephesian elders by saying, "You yourselves know . . . how I did not shrink from declaring to you anything that was profitable, and teaching you in public and from house to house, testifying both to Jews and to Greeks of repentance toward God and of faith in our Lord Jesus Christ" (Acts 20:18–21). Gospel preaching involves preaching repentance! Sadly, repentance has been reduced to little more than a whisper in much of today's preaching.

David McKenna, who served with such distinction as president of Seattle Pacific University, once saw a prominent preacher walk out of a sermon in which a colleague insisted that the gospel included repentance from sin. Explaining his one-man protest march, the man said that "contemporary man needs a message of hope, not fear." That preacher spoke only half the truth. Man today needs hope, but he also needs to recognize that he is a sinner in need of forgiveness and repentance.[1] Unless sin is acknowledged and confessed, there is no hope.

Given our contemporary materialism and sensuality, we can be sure that if Jesus began his public ministry among us today he would begin by calling us to repentance. If he walked the streets of our town, he would call us to belief, but he would also call us to cease our adulteries, repent from our materialism, renounce our gossip and our jealousies, repent from our lying. Moreover, he would do it with urgency, just as he did then, calling out, "The time is fulfilled, and the kingdom of God is at hand." Our text literally says that Jesus *heralded* this truth, calling it out loudly.[2]

There was and is radical "nowness" to Jesus' preaching. *Now* is the time to believe, and *now* is the time to repent. How would Jesus urge you or someone else to believe if he were here now? Would he say, "I want to explain to you the hypostatic union," then say, "I would like you to consider this. It is up to you whether you want to believe"? How would he call you to repent? Would he say, "Sin is an abomination in my sight and in my Father's sight; it would be very nice if you would repent"? Or would he come with urgency and say, "Belief is the most important thing in life. You need to rest yourself in me." He would *plead* with you to do that. Then he would look at those of us who say we are believers and ask, "Have you repented? Is there a constant spirit of repentance? Now is the time to do it."

How do you think we would respond? We would fall flat on our faces in response to him. The fact is, *he is here*, and that is what he says to us. Are we responding?

As we have noted, the response to Jesus' preaching was remarkable. All were coming to him, the Scripture says (John 3:26). Among them were some fishermen named Simon, Andrew, James, and John. They believed the kingdom was imminent. They did not understand how, but they were sure. They had also come to believe that Jesus was the Messiah, though they had no idea how he would achieve ascendancy. They had repented, and they were beginning to see that their beliefs were making demands on their lives. As they fished, they talked and talked and talked. Whenever there was an opportunity, they were off to sit at Jesus' feet. They longed to be with him, and said so.

The Radical Effects of Jesus' Teaching (vv. 16–20)

And so it happened that one morning as they toiled along the shores of Tiberias, the Savior came. Verses 16 and following describe what happened. "Passing alongside the Sea of Galilee, [Jesus] saw Simon and Andrew the brother of Simon casting a net into the sea, for they were fishermen" (v. 16). Simon Peter and Andrew were repeatedly casting their circular nets from the sides of their boat and retrieving them when Jesus called to them with what Ernst Lohmeyer called a "sharp military command."[3] "Follow me, and I will make you become fishers of men" (v. 17).

As the call rang from the shore, one would have anticipated a lapse of time before a response came. But, as Mark tells us, having heard firsthand from Peter, there was no pause, not even a second look. "And immediately they left their nets and followed him" (v. 18). Amazing obedience! And if that was not enough, "And going on a little farther, he saw James the son of Zebedee and John his brother, who were in their boat mending the nets. And immediately he called them, and they left their father Zebedee in the boat with the hired servants and followed him" (vv. 19, 20).

In these few lines we have one of the most famous acts of obedience in history. Christ came with a radical message and then a radical call, and these four responded in radical obedience. Today wherever men and women think of obedience, they sing of these four. Let us think of what their obedience meant.

First, it meant an immensely expanded life. The horizon of these fishermen's lives was bound by the margins of Galilee. Once in a while they went down to Jerusalem for a festival. But by and large they knew little more than the deck of their boat, the currents of the lake, and the handful of people in the marketplace. Their conversation consisted of trade talk, local gossip, family affairs, and Galilean politics. In a word, they were remarkably provincial, even to the extent of having their own telltale accent.

Then Christ came, and how their world changed! In place of Galilee came the world! John was to become Bishop of Ephesus, Peter went to Rome, and Andrew went as far as the borders of Russia! Their hearts were enlarged to take in the whole world. Their minds, once circumscribed and committed to the smallest interests, now overflowed with deep thoughts.

They became theologians, thinkers, sociologists, psychologists, and strategists—all because of the gospel.

Following Christ eliminates the trivial and expands our hearts. I have seen people who had not read a book since high school come to know Christ and then go on to read twenty-five to thirty books the first year. Their mental and spiritual processes opened up as their hearts opened up. There is nothing that will make you grow more than following Christ.

Peter and Andrew and James and John grew to undreamed of heights because they made themselves special objects of Christ's love. Next, they made themselves special objects of Christ's attention by choosing to follow him. His promise was, and is, "Follow me, and I will make you become fishers of men." Christ committed himself to completing a miracle in them.

I am a good fisherman, but not great. To be great you have to fish and study so much that you mentally enter the great chain of life of the fish.[4] You must read and study and fish and talk about fish. How much more difficult it is to be good fishers of men! How much more sensitivity and how much more tenacity is needed! But Christ is able to equip us for the task. Because of their commitment to following Christ, these four opened themselves to his special attention, which he lavished on them.

Christ has not changed. He still expands lives that follow him. Reflecting on Christ's great message and call, and its effect on the lives of those who responded then, rings true to my experience now. I may yet be short-sighted in my thinking, but how much more would I be so if I had not responded to Christ. Without belief in him I would still be bound by the narrow sympathies of a heart that thinks only of self and would never have had my eyes opened to the needs of the world. Following Christ is the key to the expanding life!

Today he still extends his call. It is a call to *believe*. Do you believe? It is a call to *repent*. Do you need to repent? It is a call to *follow* him. Have you made this commitment?

5

The Authority of Christ

MARK 1:21–28

IN OUR LAST STUDY, in accounting for the success of Jesus' preaching ministry we reflected upon how he fulfilled the classic divisions of communication (*logos, ethos, pathos*) as no one had ever done before (or since). Jesus' *ethos*, what he was as a person, in his character, completely authenticated what he said, thus bringing the ring of truth to everything he uttered. Unfortunately this has not always been the case with those who preach the gospel, for by urging others to higher spiritual experience it is deceptively easy for a preacher to imagine that he himself has achieved it when in fact he has not.

Your life can become very much like that of the train conductor who comes to feel that he himself has been to all the towns whose names he has been shouting in passengers' ears and for which he has sold them tickets, when in fact he has never been off the train outside of his own station.[1] Put another way, your soul can become cauterized by handling the truth, so that you no longer *feel* it. Today many "Christians" do not back up what they say though they have been shouting the truth with apparent accuracy and fidelity for years.

Jesus was not like that. Neither are those who truly and fully follow him. Their sermons are like thunder because their lives are like lightning. Jesus' passion, his feeling, fired his message. So intense was his feeling that he wept over the impenitent city of Jerusalem (Matthew 23:37; Luke 19:41, 42). He was infused with a passionate *zeal* to communicate because he cared. This does not mean that he shouted like a loud, bawling orator (though we can be sure there were times when he shouted), but that there was *intense feeling* in what he said. Passion can be communicated as easily in a whisper as in a shout.

Jesus was the most truly passionate man in history because he believed more than any other in his message. He knew what was in the heart of man, and he knew the eternal issues that rest in moral choices. He was sublimely passionate, and this is why he was so supremely successful in his preaching of the gospel of repentance and belief. This is also why the four fishermen (Peter, Andrew, James, and John) followed him to become fishers of men and so transcended their provincial world and became apostolic in heart and life.

Christ's Authority: His Marvelous Preaching (vv. 21, 22)

Now in the text before us, with the four eager apostles in tow, Jesus intensified his ministry. What we have is Peter's eyewitness account as given to Mark. "And they went into Capernaum, and immediately on the Sabbath he entered the synagogue and was teaching. And they were astonished at his teaching, for he taught them as one who had authority, and not as the scribes." Capernaum was a small town on the upper northwest shore of the Sea of Galilee, about two miles from where the Jordan flowed into the lake. Those who visit Capernaum today can view the remains of a second-century synagogue that may well have been built on the sight of the original synagogue in which Jesus preached. Whatever the case, the congregation in Jesus' day was made up of humble townsfolk: fishermen, merchants, craftsmen, laborers and their wives. They participated in the praisings, the blessings, the prayers, and the reading of the Law and Prophets while they eagerly awaited the expected sermon from the Nazarene who had been causing such a stir in the countryside. And they were not to be disappointed. The text says in verse 22 that they "were astonished at his teaching." Literally the word means "to strike with panic or shock."[2] It means that his preaching struck them like a blow. Barclay renders it that they were left "thunderstruck."[3] Jesus' preaching carried a powerful punch.

Of course, much of this was due to his *ethos* and *pathos*. He was so real, so true, so utterly, passionately sincere. But as important as these factors were, the text places the responsibility for his success on his *logos*, his word: "for he taught them as one who had authority, and not as the scribes." The scribes, who were largely Pharisees, were in bondage to quotation marks— they loved to quote the authorities. "Rabbi Hillel says . . . But on the other hand Gamaliel says . . . Then there is Rabbi Eleazar's testimony . . ." It was secondhand theology! Their labyrinthine, petty, legalistic distinctions were boring, with no spontaneity, no joy!

When Jesus spoke, it was just the opposite. There were few quotation marks. His style was, "You have heard that it was said . . . But I say to you" (cf. Matthew 5:21, 22, 27, 28; 7:28, 29). He preached God's Word, not *about* God's Word. He explained the Law and the Prophets. He was clear and simple, as all great preachers of the Word have been (and are). He did not say, "I am the eschatological manifestation of the Ground of Being, the kerygma in which you will find your ultimate being, if you are supralapsarian, making no excuse, agreeing that God had decreed pre-cooking Adam's goose!"

Once Harry Ironside was greeted by a visitor who said he had enjoyed the service, although he did not think Ironside was a great preacher. Ironside replied, "I know that I'm not a great preacher. But what about my preaching brought you to that conclusion?" The man answered, "I understood everything you said." This was an unwitting confession of one of the reasons for Ironside's greatness. When Jesus preached the Word, he was clear and painfully direct in his application, as we see again and again in the Gospels. The conclusion there in Capernaum was that "he taught them as one who had authority." What would have been our conclusion if we were there? We would have been thunderstruck!

What a lesson to the four new fishers of men! To be sure, they did not sit down and analyze the situation in classical categories. But they learned by his example. They knew he was genuine. They knew he passionately cared. They saw how he handled God's Word, preaching it clearly. As they ministered in the name and example of Christ they would experience miraculous power, for the Holy Spirit is pleased to use such messengers.

Dr. Barnhouse told about riding in a car with a friend when the subject of music came up.

"What's your favorite symphony?" the friend asked.

"Brahams' First" was Dr. Barnhouse's reply.

"How does it go?"

Dr. Barnhouse began to whistle the main theme of the symphony.

"Then suddenly," he recalled, "I was overcome with how ridiculous it was that I should be trying to communicate that great musical composition with my weak whistle.

"But by the wonder of the human brain, my weak whistle was changed in my friend's mind into the strings and percussion and brass of the full symphony orchestra."

Then he applied the experience to his teaching.

"Every time I stand up to teach the Bible, I'm overcome with how ridiculous it is that I should be trying to communicate God's Word to the class.

"It would be hopeless, except for one thing: the Holy Spirit is in me, teaching through me; and He is also in the men and women in my class who listen. So He turns my weak little whistle into the full symphony of God's revelation in their minds and lives."[4]

If we want to communicate in our walk and talk, God's authority must be part of our life. We need not so much to possess the message, but rather to let the message possess us. If we want people to see that it is real, we need to be passionate about it and speak the Word clearly. Then there will be power, authority, and life in the communication between son and daughter, between parent and child, between teacher and student, between employer and employee.

Christ's Authority: His Miraculous Power (vv. 23–26)

We do not know when the opposition came or who the opposer was, but as the people sat thunderstruck by Jesus' teaching, "immediately there was in their synagogue a man with an unclean spirit. And he cried out, 'What have you to do with us, Jesus of Nazareth? Have you come to destroy us? I know who you are—the Holy One of God'" (vv. 23, 24). The light of Jesus' teaching was too much for the evil of a demonized life. Just as foul things scurry from the light when you lift a stone, evil spirits who love darkness recoil from the light. It is very possible to recognize Jesus for who he is and hate him all the more. This is what was happening here. This man wanted nothing to do with Christ. The demon's shriek was full of malevolent aggression. His opening burst, "What have you to do with us, Jesus of Nazareth?" was a common Old Testament formula that was roughly equivalent to, "You have no business with us yet!"[5] The evil spirit wanted Jesus to go away.

The next phrase, stated as a question ("Have you come to destroy us?"), was really a defiant assertion: "You have come to destroy us!"[6] The demon realized the menace of Christ and cried with an instinctive expression of dread. He wanted Jesus to disappear, for he knew that Jesus would destroy him. Note his dramatic, final cry: "I know who you are—the Holy One of God!" (v. 24). Rather than being a submissive attempt to palliate Christ, this was a frantic attempt to bring the Lord under his power. We know this because the idea was widespread at that time that "the exact knowledge of the other's name brought mastery or control over him."[7] This was an ill-informed attempt to control Christ.

From this encounter we know without doubt that whenever the authority of Christ, the Son of God, is invoked in preaching or teaching, there is a violent confrontation with the evil spirits who possess men's souls and rule their lives. This is what Billy Graham and other world evangelists experience as they minister around the globe, and will continue to experience as long as they hold Christ high. This is what those who are opposing pornography and other moral evils of our day as contrary to the good news of Christ will reap in the days and years to come. The foul creatures under the stones do not like to be disturbed.

I especially want us to see that this demonized man was completely under the sway of evil. His personality had been damaged to the point that the demonic spirit usurped the core of his self and even utilized his voice. Satan always tries to imitate God. Christ came to earth in human flesh and now dwells within us by the Spirit. Aping God, Satan fabricates incarnations through his spirits. This man was lost, a kennel for the malevolent spirits of fallen angels. He was literally "in an unclean spirit" (v. 23, Greek). The moral nature of the unclean spirit fused with his, so that he was coarse, filthy, and base within. So fully was he under the command of evil that he renounced all interest in Christ, saying, "You have no business with me yet! Go away!" Moreover, his religious and cultural associations had done him no good. He was absolutely helpless. This does not mean he was as *morally* evil as he could be or as some who were not demonized (men and women are quite capable of the deepest evil all by themselves!), but that he was completely under Satan's power.

Christ had been challenged. Very likely there was stone-silence for a moment in that synagogue by the sea. Perhaps the lapping water could be heard. Then Jesus responded. "But Jesus rebuked him, saying, 'Be silent [literally, be muzzled], and come out of him!' And the unclean spirit, convulsing him and crying out with a loud voice, came out of him" (vv. 25, 26). The poor man was racked with violent convulsions before the horror-stricken congregation, and the demon departed with an inarticulate howling, having been forbidden to say another word. The hopeless man who had rolled before them in dust and despair rose to wholeness, joy, and peace.

There is hope for the worst of us. You (or someone you know) may have the hardest heart in the nation. To you and everyone else it appears impenetrable, irredeemable, impossible. Chances are if you have the hardest heart in the city it is a *religious* heart. You may have the proudest will—a damned will in the full sense of the word—bloodied, unbowed, unbroken, condemned. Since you were a young child you have never given in to anyone, not even your parents or your mate. Yet there is great hope for you! Christ can free you from the evil that has you in bondage.

What we learn from Christ's action is that his gospel of love and power is for all, even the least and the worst of us. Do you think yourself least likely? Know this: Jesus rejoices to change your life with a word. And he will if you will come to him. Will you?

The text considered in this chapter shows four new fishers of men under the authority of Christ. These four recruits saw the people thunderstruck at his teaching, "for he taught them as one who had authority, and not as the scribes." As time progressed, they put this authority to use in their lives. Think of Peter at Pentecost! Think of his *ethos,* his *pathos,* and his *logos.* He preached in the authority of Christ and in the power of the Holy Spirit, and thousands were changed. These four recruits saw the demoniac healed and came to see that he was a symbol of the great things God would do through them.

We are the Church, the Body of Christ, which by definition has to do with those who have been indwelt by the Spirit of God. Our lives are to speak God's Word authoritatively. Not only that, but as the Church of Christ we are to be involved in deliverance from sin. Christ calls his followers to minister in his authority.

Among our Lord's final words were these: "All authority in heaven and on earth has been given to me. Go therefore and make disciples of all nations, baptizing them in the name of the Father and of the Son and of the Holy Spirit, teaching them to observe all that I have commanded you. And behold, I am with you always, to the end of the age" (Matthew 28:18–20).

Jesus is with us! His authority rests with his Church! Let us possess and use it with humility and energy.

6

The Heart of the Healer

MARK 1:29–39

I WOULD LIKE TO HAVE BEEN THERE that Sabbath day in Capernaum among the thunderstruck congregation in the synagogue. I would like to have been the synagogue mouse and heard Jesus speak with unparalleled authority: "You have heard that it was said . . . but I say to you . . ." I would like to have heard his intonation delicately nuanced so as to carry the greatest punch. I would like to have seen the changes of expression that played across his face as he spoke. I would like to have heard the startled gasps of the congregation as the preternatural voice of a demon challenged Jesus, and then was cast out with an imperial word. How I would like to have heard the conversations that followed in Capernaum that Sabbath afternoon.

Most of all, I would like to have spent the day with Jesus to see as much of his great ministry and heart as possible, for then my finite heart would have taken on some eternal dimensions. Fortunately, through the medium of Holy Scripture we can partially do this. In this chapter we are going to spend the Sabbath and the following Lord's day with Jesus—inside the heart of the Healer.

Jesus' Heart: The Healing of Peter's Mother-in-law (vv. 29–31)

The four new fishers of men must have nearly danced from the synagogue when they accompanied their Master to Peter's house for the Sabbath meal. They had been bowled over by what they had seen and heard. It was customary to take the main Sabbath meal immediately after synagogue, at the sixth hour (noon).[1] What they found is described in verses 29, 30: "And immediately he left the synagogue and entered the house of Simon and Andrew, with James and John. Now Simon's mother-in-law lay ill with a fever, and immediately they told him about her." Instead of a delicious, hot Sabbath feast, they found a sick cook. This is no way to return from church, especially if you are the preacher!

Peter probably had no idea she was ill when he invited the Master and his friends over. But there she was, sick with a fever. The woman most likely was not gravely ill, but incapacitated. A fever (or "fire" as the text literally says) made her feel too sick to do anything.

Verse 31 recounts what happened: "And [Jesus] came and took her by the hand and lifted her up, and the fever left her, and she began to serve them." Note the manner in which Jesus healed her. Luke says in the parallel account that he stood over her and rebuked the fever (Luke 4:39). Matthew (8:15) says he touched her. Here in Mark we read that he "took her by the hand." Thus, we have a composite picture of Christ standing close to her bed, taking her by the hand, rebuking the fever, and gently raising her up before Peter and his wide-eyed friends.

The point is, Jesus could have healed her any way he pleased. The Gospels reveal that at times he did miracles with a simple word or with something as complicated as clay made with spittle and the instruction to wash in Siloam. He could do them any way he wished. The reasons for the different ways in which he healed rested in the mental and moral condition of the people themselves and what he wanted to communicate. Here his reaching down and taking a dear woman by the hand was simply a natural, instinctive action springing from Jesus' sympathetic love. Later Jesus did virtually the same thing with a leper (1:41), something unheard of in his time.

Jesus' extended hand was simply an expression of his genuine love and his desire to tenderly meet the woman's need. It was "a condensation . . . of the very principle of the Incarnation."[2] Jesus' touch tells us volumes about what he is like and how much he loves us. To touch us in healing and in love—that is his instinctive way—the way of his healing heart. This is what he wants to do with each soul, both those who do not know Jesus and those who do, all who need a touch of grace. What a balm this ought to be to our hearts.

We see the woman's heart response too, in that she immediately got up and "began to serve them." This is the telltale sign of everyone who has truly received the healing touch of Christ. Our response to him should be like that of the talkative woman who received Christ under C. H. Spurgeon's ministry and said, "Oh, Mr. Spurgeon, Christ has changed my life—and he shall never hear the end of it!"

That must have been a great meal! It was great because she did her best with whatever she had. But it was also great because of the way it was served. Most of all, it was great because of the excitement. "Come here, my daughter, and you, my son-in-law. Feel my forehead. You too, James and John. I was on fire, burning up, and I became well. I've never felt better! The Lord be praised!" The shouts and laughter could be heard all around the Sabbath-quieted streets of Capernaum, and they continued all afternoon until the shadows began to lengthen.

Jesus' Heart: The Healings at Night (vv. 32–34)

As evening approached, an unmistakable air of anticipation settled over Capernaum, for with the conclusion of Sabbath, the ill and deranged could be carried to Jesus. A delectable tenseness blanketed the town and the countryside as they waited for nightfall. The law said the Sabbath ended when three stars came out in the night sky. So when the sun had set and the stars were blinking clearly above, the people came. Verses 32, 33 give us the picture: "That evening at sundown they brought to him all who were sick or oppressed by demons. And the whole city was gathered together at the door." The tenses indicate case after case arriving at the door, so that finally there was a surging mass of crippled and diseased with their friends. The press must have been threatening and the odor of the ill overpowering.

Jesus' heart naturally responded in healing power: "And he healed many who were sick with various diseases, and cast out many demons. And he would not permit the demons to speak, because they knew him" (v. 34). What a wonderful evening! The demons fled pell-mell from his presence, and the bed-ridden were tossing their mattresses and crutches into the air. The comatose were lucid and talking. The onlookers were in a state of frenzied joy. The sounds carried far out over the waters of the Sea of Galilee.

Marvelous as it was, we should not be naive about what was going on here: most of the people who came simply wanted something from Jesus. There is a reasonable sense in which we cannot blame them. Anyone who has an ongoing disability can certainly sympathize with them. At the same time, they tragically foreshadowed millions of people across the centuries who have only wanted Christ for what they hoped to receive from him. Jesus addressed those with this motive after he fed the five thousand, saying, "Truly, truly, I say to you, you are seeking me, not because you saw signs, but because you ate your fill of the loaves" (John 6:26). They cared little about the spiritual implications of Jesus' miracles and teaching, but much about the material and temporal. That is the way it was in Capernaum. How nice it would be to have a Jesus to heal us when we have a fever, to make us wealthy, and to give us prestige. Unfortunately, for every prayer that goes up in prosperity, ten thousand go up in adversity. It is natural to want a magic Jesus. But we must always remember that God is not someone to be used. He is to be loved, worshiped, and served regardless of what comes in this world.

Jesus was being used by man, but it is against this reality that we see his heart, for he genuinely cared about the physical plight of the people whatever their motivations. He hoped to direct some to spiritual reality through his touch. So he lovingly and gently healed them. Not only do we see this, but we also observe that the Savior's healing heart was tireless in its ministrations.

One of the most moving pictures of Jesus was when he sank in exhaustion by the well in Sychar. He had been ministering for days to increasingly demanding crowds in the wilderness of Judea. When he was away from the crowds, he was surrounded by his needy, ignorant disciples. He could barely find a minute to himself. When he came to the well, he was far more mentally and physically weary than his disciples. So he sent the Twelve into town for groceries and sat down by the well. How good it felt—the noonday sun, being *alone*, no questions to answer, no Peter! Then he heard the footfall of the needy Samaritan woman. How easy it would be to feign sleep, how easy to rationalize away the opportunity. But not Jesus, for he launched into one of the most beautiful cases of spiritual aggression ever recorded! This same heart beat far into the night in Capernaum. This same heart beats for us today. Jesus tirelessly ministers to his own and to those he seeks to woo to himself.

A young man responded to Christ at the conclusion of one of my sermons saying, "I am the one with the unbroken will. Jesus has been pursuing me for years, and I want to give up. I want Christ to have my life." Our tireless Jesus . . . that is the way he ministers to us. That is the kind of heart Jesus has.

Capernaum was exalted to Heaven that day, for deeds worthy of Heaven had been done in her. Children and unlearned parents would recount the deeds of this Sabbath with great detail in the years to come.

Jesus' Heart: The Pre-Dawn Prayer (vv. 35–39)

But the story does not stop there, because that wonderful evening was followed by an equally wonderful Sunday morning, as verse 35 reveals: "And rising very early in the morning, while it was still dark, he departed and went out to a desolate place, and there he prayed." Jesus had gotten as much sleep as he desired, and he awoke. It was dark, and everyone was asleep in the house. He noiselessly stole out of the room and found his way to the street.

Soon he was out of town and climbing a hillside to some remote spot, possibly a hidden hollow, where he lifted up his soul in ecstasy to the Father.

What did Jesus pray? To be sure, not exactly the same as we pray. Often many of us structure our prayer time with the acrostic ACTS (Adoration, Confession, Thanksgiving, Supplication). But not Jesus! There was never any confession, ever! But we can be sure there was plenty of adoration, thanksgiving, and petition. No doubt, Jesus prayed for *himself*. What lay before him was the greatest challenge ever conceived. He also prayed for *his disciples* one by one. Remember what he said to Peter? "Simon, Simon, behold, Satan demanded to have you, that he might sift you like wheat, but I have prayed for you" (Luke 22:31, 32). Before the devil ever made his move, Christ had already prayed for Peter. And then, as the context tells us, Jesus prayed for *the sinners* around him. He saw what was in Capernaum, and he knew what he would encounter in coming days. So he prayed accordingly. Above all, there was the joy of exchange of soul between him and the Father.

E. Stanley Jones once described prayer as a "time exposure to God."[3] He used the analogy of his life being like a photographic plate that, when exposed to God, progressively bore the image of God in keeping with the length of exposure.

Jesus exposed his humanity to God, even though he needed no more of the fullness of God (Colossians 2:8, 9), being already the exact representation of his nature (Hebrews 1:3). He was wonderfully refreshed as his light was exposed to the Father's light, his purity to the Father's purity and holiness, his life to Life.

But there was also a human reason for Jesus' prayers, for we must remember that though Jesus was God, he did not live his life as God apart from the Father, but rather as a man in dependence upon God. He said, "[T]he Son can do nothing of his own accord" (John 5:19) and "The words that I say to you I do not speak on my own authority, but the Father who dwells in me does his works" (John 14:10). Jesus depended upon the Father for his power!

One of the reasons Jesus did this was because he wants us to live our lives on the same basis. If Jesus prayed in order to live a godly life full of power, so must we! This is an overpowering argument. Jesus is the eternal God Incarnate, the Creator of all, who holds everything together by his power (Colossians 1:16). Yet, he still lived by and in prayer! I have heard people say they are so in tune with God that all of life is prayer, and therefore they do not need special times of prayer. But until they exceed the oneness of Christ with the Father, they cannot be right! Christ lived in the spirit of prayer, but he also needed regular times of prayer.

Prayer is the great necessity of our spiritual lives. We need to pray daily! We need to find times to get away alone. We need to get up early if necessary. Few of us are called to spend many hours in daily prayer, but *all* of us must spend *some* time. If it is impossible when the family is awake, pray before they get up. If you have no place you can do this at home, find a place to park your car on the way to work and pray in the anonymity of the passing traffic.

When I had small children, I had an office that was impossible to do anything in except greet people (it was in a trailer, and anytime the door opened, though the door was forty feet away, the floor of the trailer with its paper-thin walls shook). I could not think or pray in there, so daily I would get into my car and drive down to the local shopping center and park my car among the other cars. I would slouch down behind the wheel and pray. Or I would go to a local church, sit in the back, and pray. Nothing bothered me there. Or I would park my car along the way. We need to do this. It does not have to be hours and hours, but we need to pray! We must have that time exposure to God without interruption. Jesus did it, and we need to do it. Begin small, but do it.

Jesus was alone in his deserted place praying, but even there he was not safe. Like us, Jesus was interrupted: "And Simon and those who were with him searched for him, and they found him and said to him, 'Everyone is looking for you'" (vv. 36, 37). They pursued him, and when they found him they mildly reproached him.[4] The idea was, "Jesus, things are going great after last night. Let's get back and capitalize on it!" But our Lord was not interested. "And he said to them, 'Let us go on to the next towns, that I may preach there also, for that is why I came out.' And he went throughout all Galilee, preaching in their synagogues and casting out demons" (vv. 38, 39).

The healing heart of Jesus was not as interested in physical healing as in spiritual healing. He refused to let his disciples or the people own him as their healer in Capernaum, but went out in the country preaching the gospel of belief and repentance. Jesus did heal people and still heals today. I have seen people healed when the elders of the church have, in accordance with James 5:13–15, obeyed the call of the ill and anointed him or her with oil and prayed in faith. God heals! But physical healings are temporal at best. What Jesus emphasized was the healing of the spirit of men in salvation and then healing from bitterness, hatred, lust, anger, gossip, and the like. Ultimately, the healing of the human spirit is eternal! This is where Jesus' heart was!

That memorable Sabbath day and the Sunday following revealed wonderful things about the heart of the Healer, a heart of love and compassion. The outstretched hand to Simon's mother-in-law revealed the reflex of

Christ's loving heart. This heart labored tirelessly to bring healing to needy men and women. This is still true today. His healing heart was (and is) a heart that lived (and lives) in prayer. In respect to us, his heart desires above all else that we experience the ultimate healing of the gospel.

To those who do not know Christ we hold up his healing heart. If you are not a believer, can there be anything more attractive than a heart that beats for you? As believers we need to permit the Holy Spirit to produce Christ's heart in us. If you do not know the reality of the healing heart of Jesus, you can know it. Christ wants to bring his healing touch to your life.

7

The Master's Touch

MARK 1:40–45

AS WE NOTED WHEN WE began our study of the Gospel of Mark, the key verse for the entire book is 10:45—"For even the Son of Man came not to be served but to serve, and to give his life as a ransom for many." This verse capsulizes the dual themes of the book: first, Christ's *service*, which occupies the bulk of Mark; and second, Christ's *sacrifice*, which closes the book. With these themes, Mark's Gospel is preeminently a book of miracles. In fact, it records more of Christ's miracles than his sermons!

This does *not* mean that Mark is not a book of teaching. Far from it! All Christ's miracles were parables that visibly portrayed the effects of his Spirit's work among mankind. For instance, his healing the blind portrayed his illumination of darkened hearts; his calming the storm told of his power to bring peace to troubled hearts; raising the dead proclaimed his life-giving power; his feeding of the five thousand spoke of his being the Bread of Life.[1] Mark is a book of deep spiritual teaching.

Realizing, then, that Christ's miracles were parables, we must note that leprosy was especially symbolic of sin, and the healing of it especially a parable of deliverance from sin. R. C. Trench, the great Greek scholar and the inspiration for and first editor of the monumental *Oxford English Dictionary*, recognized this. Though the leper was not worse or guiltier than his fellow-countrymen, he was nevertheless a parable of sin—an "outward visible sign of innermost spiritual corruption."[2]

The nature of leprosy, with its insidious beginnings, its slow progress, its destructive power, and the ultimate ruin it brings, makes it a powerful symbol of moral depravity. If we see ourselves with spiritual eyes, we see that apart from the work of Christ we would be decaying forms of walking death.

Keeping this deeper meaning of leprosy before us, we are going to seek the lessons from the text under consideration.

The Leper's Cry (v. 40)

When news of Jesus' power reached the isolated huts of the lepers, hope began to stir in that wretched community, especially within one leper. In that poor soul courage welled so high, he was able to break through society's cruel conventions and cast himself at the feet of Jesus. From what we can learn from the other Gospels, this man suddenly appeared, plowing through an amazed crowd like the determined prow of a boat with its compass set on Jesus. When he arrived, he lay on the ground before Jesus, a mass of rotting flesh. Luke the physician, in a parallel account (Luke 5:12), describes him as "full of leprosy." The disease had run its course. None of us needs a detailed description of the poor man's loathsome appearance. If you have seen just one picture of someone *full* of leprosy, that one picture is enough.

What is important to note is that leprosy, or Hansen's disease as it is better known today (after the man who diagnosed its cause), is not a rotting infection as is commonly thought, nor are its horrible outward physical deformities imposed by the disease. In recent years, the research of Dr. Paul Brand and others has proven that the disfigurement associated with Hansen's disease comes solely because the body's warning system of pain is destroyed. The disease acts as an anesthetic, bringing numbness to the extremities as well as to the ears, eyes, and nose. The devastation that follows comes from such incidents as reaching one's hand into a charcoal fire to retrieve a dropped potato, or washing one's face with scalding water, or gripping a tool so tightly that the hands become traumatized and eventually stumplike.[3] In Third-World countries, vermin sometimes chew on sleeping lepers. Thus, Dr. Brand, after performing corrective surgery on a leper, would send a cat home with him as normal post-operative procedure. Dr. Brand calls the disease a "painless hell," and indeed it is. The poor man in our story had not been able to feel for years, and his body was *full* of leprosy, mutilated from head to foot, rotten, stinking, repulsive.

This poor leper was under no illusions about his miserable condition. If he suffered any lapses of reality, all he had to do was raise an infected stump before his browless eyes and all fantasy would flee. Moreover, the rest of the world was there to remind him of his plight. In Israel the lot of a poor leper was summed up in Leviticus 13:45, 46—"The leprous person who has the disease shall wear torn clothes and let the hair of his head hang loose, and he shall cover his upper lip and cry out, 'Unclean, unclean.' He shall remain unclean as long as he has the disease. He is unclean. He shall live alone. His dwelling shall be outside the camp."

We can hardly imagine the humiliation and isolation of this leper's life. He was ostracized from society because it was thought at that time that leprosy was highly contagious (which it is not). He had to assume a disheveled appearance and cry, "Unclean, unclean" whenever he came in range of the normal population. Think about how you would feel shouting this while entering a grocery store or a mall—the pervasive sense of worthlessness and despair.

By Jesus' time, rabbinical teaching, with its absurd strictures, had made matters even worse. If a leper even stuck his head inside a house, it was pronounced unclean. It was illegal to even greet a leper. Lepers had to remain at least 100 cubits away if they were upwind, and four cubits if downwind. Josephus, the famous Jewish historian, summarized by saying that lepers were treated "as if they were, in effect, dead men."[4] There were no illusions in this leper's life as to who he was and what his condition was.

The spiritual reality for all of us is that we are spiritual lepers! This is what the image is meant to teach us. But unlike the leper, we are often unconscious of our sin and the pervasiveness of our sinful condition.

Once the great Christian patroness Lady Huntington invited her friend, the proud Duchess of Buckingham, to hear George Whitefield preach. The duchess replied, "It is monstrous to be told, that you have a heart as sinful as the common wretches that crawl the earth. This is highly offensive and insulting; and I cannot but wonder that your Ladyship should relish any sentiments so much at variance with high rank and good breeding."[5] The less we know that there is anything wrong with us, the more full-blown our leprosy is! It is common to say, "Hey, I'm OK!" while we have the death of leprosy in our very souls.

That is why in preaching and sharing the good news it is our fundamental duty to alert people to their condition. Dr. Lloyd-Jones, who for years held forth in London's Westminster Chapel, said it is a spiritual necessity to have a sense of sin.

> What is more, unless you have experienced that, unless you have known that, you are not a Christian, you do not believe in Christ as your personal Saviour. Until you realise that you cannot possibly have felt the need of Christ; you may have felt the need of help and advice and comfort, but until you awake to the fact that your nature itself is evil, until you realise that your trouble is that you yourself are wrong, and that your whole nature is wrong, until you realise that, you will never have felt the need of a Saviour.

Christ cannot help or advise or comfort you until He has first of all saved you, until He has changed your nature. Oh, my friends, have you yet felt this? God have mercy upon you if you haven't. You may have been inside the church all your life and actively engaged in its work, but still I say (and I am merely repeating what is said repeatedly in the Bible) that unless you have at some time or other felt that your very nature itself is sinful, that you are, in the words of St. Paul, 'dead in sin' then you have never known Jesus Christ as a Saviour, and if you do not know Him as a Saviour you do not know Him at all.[6]

Jesus said it perfectly and with eternal economy: "Blessed are the poor in spirit, for theirs is the kingdom of heaven. Blessed are those who mourn, for they shall be comforted" (Matthew 5:3, 4). Can you see your leprosy? Can you say, "Unclean, unclean" and really mean it? I hope so, because if you can, you are on the threshold of the kingdom.

The leper knew how bad off he was, but he also had confidence in Christ, for he said, "If you will, you can make me clean" (v. 40). The leper believed Christ could cure him. He probably did not have a great theological understanding, but he was pragmatic: "If he can do it for others, he can do it for me."

Sin controls people with two exactly opposite lies. The first is, as we have already seen, that they are not sinners—that nothing is wrong with them. The second is that when they do see they are sinners, they think they are so bad they are beyond help. Over the years in my pastoral ministry I have talked to a number of people who felt this way. They have recited their sins to me with the naive supposition that I would be shocked. The fact is, I *cannot* be shocked! I have heard it all, and I can say that Christ is sufficient for all. One man told me, "I'm such a dirt bag—such scum. How could he ever forgive me?" He does not say that now, because he has experienced forgiveness!

To be accurate, the leper did voice some hesitation by saying, "If you will." Although he knew Christ *could* heal him, he did not know whether Christ *would* heal him. This was a reasonable hesitation. He did not know the Lord and could not know what eternally motivated his heart. But where the leper has hesitation, we have certainty. We know the gospel. We know Jesus' heart. "For even the Son of Man came not to be served but to serve, and to give his life as a ransom for many" (10:45). *Nothing is more in accord with the will of God than this!*

Hear God's Word: "The Lord is not slow to fulfill his promise as some count slowness, but is patient toward you, not wishing that any should perish, but that all should reach repentance" (2 Peter 3:9). "This is good, and it is pleasing in the sight of God our Savior, who desires all people to be saved and to come to the knowledge of the truth" (1 Timothy 2:3, 4).

We cannot say to Christ, "If you will, you can make me clean." But rather, "Since you are willing, I *will be clean.* Wash me now, Lord!" The leper was flat on his face before Christ in humble prostration. He was fully aware of his hopeless, leprous condition, and yet he believed Christ could heal him. From the leper's cry we turn to the Lord's answer.

The Lord's Answer (v. 41)

We see Jesus' answer in his *compassion*, his *touch*, and his *word.*

Verse 41 says our Lord was "moved with pity," which describes a visceral reaction on Jesus' part. He felt it in his stomach. Jesus' reaction went beyond pity and sympathy or even empathy. It was "not just mind for mind, hand for hand, or even heart for heart, but stomach for stomach, blood for blood, gut for gut, Jesus feels His way into the leper's needs."[7] We all understand this when we have a desperately sick brother or sister or child. It was gut-wrenching compassion.

What super-exalted revelation of the Son's and the Father's hearts we see here! Take this to *your* heart and hold it there with all you have. The Servant-Savior has compassion for your leprosy heart for heart, gut for gut. He does more than understand. He *felt* the full weight of your sins on the cross. Take heart! There is Someone who compassionately feels with you for the effects of sin in your life.

Then, of course, there was the Lord's touch, for Jesus "stretched out his hand and touched him" (v. 41). As we have already noted in part, it is very clear from Mark's Gospel that the Lord delighted in touching needy people. There are no less than eight touches recorded in the Gospel of Mark.

1. When Christ healed Peter's mother-in-law, he took her by the hand and raised her up (1:31).
2. He laid his hand on the leper (1:41).
3. When he healed Jarius's little daughter, he took her by the hand and said, "'Talitha cumi,' which means, 'Little girl, I say to you, arise'" (5:41).
4. Next "he laid his hands on a few sick people and healed them" (6:5).
5. When he encountered the deaf and dumb man, the Apostle Mark says, "And taking him aside from the crowd privately, he put his fingers into his ears, and after spitting touched his tongue. And looking up to heaven, he sighed and said to him, 'Ephphatha,' that is, 'Be opened'" (7:33, 34).
6. Later he did almost the same thing for the blind man at Bethsaida (8:23).

7. We see him raising up the formerly demonized boy (9:27).
8. Finally in the midst of his busy ministry, he repeatedly took little children in his arms (9:36; 10:16).

In all of this there was no need for Jesus to touch anybody. *He did so because he delighted to.* It is very natural, as we see the repeated parabolic/instructive nature of Christ's miracles, to think that he performed every miracle with a premeditated instructional motive, so that for us his actions have an unreal air. This simply is not so! Jesus' actions were always instinctive, spontaneous, and real. They were simply his human-divine heart in action.

Since this man was full of leprosy, we can reasonably assume that he had not been touched by a soft, healthy hand in years. If he had a wife, he had not known her touch, much less her embrace, for many long years. If he had children there had been no kiss, no touch, not even once—and now they were adults. Whatever his family status, he must have longed for a touch.

I once counseled a lonely man who was not a Christian. He had no family that cared. He belonged to no church. In describing his loneliness, he said that he had his hair cut once a week just to have someone touch him with no misunderstanding. Imagine that leper's longing for a touch or a caress. Time stood still as Christ touched him. As Bishop Westcott says, the word "expresses more than superficial contact."[8] It is often translated, "to take hold of." Jesus, at the very least, placed his hand firmly on the leper. We cannot attempt to adequately describe the ecstasy that coursed through the leper's body. The onlookers were shocked. The disciples were shocked. Jesus was now ceremonially unclean—and besides he might catch the disease, they thought.

Why did Jesus do this? Aside from the reason we have mentioned, that it was most natural for him, he wanted the leper to *feel* his willingness and sympathy. The touch said, "I'm with you, I understand, I love you." Those are the human reasons. But there was also an overshadowing theological reason: the touch of Christ's pure hand on the rotting leper is a parable of the Incarnation. Jesus in the Incarnation took on flesh, became sin for us, and thus gave us his purity. "For our sake [God] made him to be sin who knew no sin, so that in him we might become the righteousness of God" (2 Corinthians 5:21). Jesus laid hold of our flesh. He touched us and healed us. See Jesus bent over the prostrate leper, his holy hand resting on the decaying flesh of the foul-smelling leper, and you see what he did for him. What has he done for us?

There is a relevant application to all this. We will never affect others as Christ did unless there is contact and identification. We have to be willing to take the hand of those whom we would help. Sometimes a touch, caring involvement, will do a thousand times more than our theology. This is what all churches need to do. We are great in theory. We are careful about our doctrine. But we need to lay our hand on some rotting flesh in our neighborhood, in the executive towers where we work, in the city slums. We cannot expect this to be only the job of missionaries because a church that does not regularly place its hand on the rotting humanity around it will not be sending missionaries to do so either.

The Leper's Cure (vv. 42–44)

Now came the miracle. In describing it Mark used his favorite word (v. 42): "And *immediately* the leprosy left him, and he was made clean." The healing was *sudden* and *complete*. His feet—toeless, ulcerated stubs—were suddenly whole, bursting his shrunken sandals. The knobs on his hands grew fingers before his very eyes. Back came his hair, eyebrows, eyelashes. Under his hair were ears and before him a nose! His skin was supple and soft. Can you hear a thundering roar from the multitude? Can you hear the man crying *not*, "Unclean, unclean," but, "*I'm clean! I'm clean!*"

That is what Jesus Christ can do for you, for anyone in an instant, in a split second of belief. The healing of Christ in salvation from sin is *instantaneous* and *complete* ("the blood of Jesus his Son cleanses us from all sin," 1 John 1:7). All my confidence, everything I am, all I represent, all preaching rests in this!

If you realize that the leprosy of sin has infected your person, then you have no doubt that you are a sinner. If you believe that, there is no reason why you should not go immediately to him. He has compassion, he *feels* for you heart for heart, blood for blood. More, he will actually *touch* your leprosy. He will take hold of it. Even better, you will be immediately healed! Can you humble yourself to say, "I know you are willing, make me clean"? Then do it now.

8

The Capernaum Caper

MARK 2:1–12

ALPINE HIKERS HAVE TOLD ME that when caught in a brewing storm, they have seen the hair of their fellow-hikers stand straight out from their heads like radiant crowns, while the metal frames of their backpacks glowed with an eerie neon-like blue light called St. Elmo's Fire. The same phenomenon has been recorded by sailors from ancient times when they would see the tops of their ships' masts crowned with a ghostly aura of light. In all cases it means that the air is charged with electricity and that lightning is imminent. For the hiker it means it is time to discard the pack and take cover. I think this image conveys something of the atmosphere in Capernaum as described in our next text, 2:1–12.

There was a kind of interpersonal fire hovering over those who had jammed into a little home in Capernaum. Verses 1, 2 give us a feel for the situation: "And when he returned to Capernaum after some days, it was reported that he was at home. And many were gathered together, so that there was no more room, not even at the door. And he was preaching the word to them." Almost immediately the home in which Jesus stayed was packed with people. Some were just curious. Others were new, bright-eyed disciples who hung on his every word. As is always the case, crowds attract greater crowds, and soon it was impossible to even get to the door. Outside there was dust, noise, heat, disease, jostling, and crowding.

Yet, with all the great crush there were only two dominating presences. First, as the parallel account in Luke tells us, there were "Pharisees and teachers of the law" (Luke 5:17). To the unsuspecting crowd these theological heavyweights may have looked like a Spiritual Life Conference, but in actuality they were an investigative committee eager to find something wrong with the young rabbi. Though there was standing room only, the Pharisees were "sitting" (v. 6). We can picture them seated in honored positions, wearing suspicious looks and just waiting for a slip-up by Jesus. There was fire in the air!

The other presence was, of course, the Lord Jesus, who was calm, unperturbed, in control. He preached to them about the nearness of the kingdom and the necessity of faith and repentance (cf. 1:14ff.). I personally think the crowd sensed the tension, not that they knew exactly what it was, but they sensed something was going to happen. Luke says that "the power of the Lord was with him to heal" (5:17b). The room was charged, the atmosphere crackled, and a disturbance began.

Healing Faith (vv. 3, 4)

"And they came, bringing to him a paralytic carried by four men. And when they could not get near him because of the crowd, they removed the roof above him, and when they had made an opening, they let down the bed on which the paralytic lay" (vv. 3, 4).

Four men struggling with a litter on which lay a paralytic, prone and motionless, approached the fringe of the impossible crowd. Their few attempts to get through met with noisy rebuffs. So they rested the mat and mopped their perspiration as they glanced from the thin, worn face of the paralytic to the crowd. They conferred, picked up the stretcher, and moved around the crowd to the side of the flat-roofed house. Possibly there was an outside stairway leading to the roof, as some homes had, or perhaps they ascended the neighbor's roof and stepped across to the crowded house. Whatever the case, after much hauling and pushing they had their friend on the roof, where they rested long enough to catch their breath. Then they did an amazing thing: they began to tear a hole in the roof!

The typical Syrian roof was constructed of timbers laid parallel to each other about two or three feet apart. Then crosswise over the timbers, sticks were laid close to each other, thus forming the basic roof. Upon this was laid reeds, branches of trees, and thistles. The whole thing was overlaid with about a foot of earth, which was then packed down to resist water. All told, the roof was about two feet thick. During the spring, grass flourished on these primitive roofs. These men were digging through the roof!

Those inside the house heard the shoveling, then the pounding amidst loud conversation as the men dug away the dirt, tore the branches, and pried the roofing loose between the beams. Debris began to fall on those in the house, and then there was a crack of light that widened to the size of a man!

We can be sure there were some shouts exchanged between those inside and those on the roof, especially if this was Peter's mother-in-law's house!

Finally there was a warning from those above, and down came the paralytic's bed on ropes. What a picture! *Above*, with the light streaming past them in dusty beams, four sweaty, impish, determined faces; *below*, the Pharisees and scribes shaking dirt from their robes; and in the *midst*, the Prince and the paralytic. History would remember this Capernaum caper! We all know what happened, but for now let us concentrate on the four friends.

They really loved him, did they not? They would not be put off by the crowd. They even "vandalized" another's property to achieve their end. They ignored the protests and judgments of those around them for the sake of their friend. Perhaps he was "family"—a beloved brother or uncle or father. Maybe he was simply a neighbor with whom they had grown up and played together. Whatever the relationship, they loved him! And whatever happened that day—healing, rejection, whatever—the paralytic was a very rich man. He had something for which some people spend millions and yet never find. God was going to work in his life because his friends loved him. God is especially pleased to work when there is such love.

Along with great love, his friends had great faith. There was no way they would have gone to such outrageous extremes of action if they did not implicitly believe that Christ *could* and *would* heal their friend. A wavering faith would have demurred when they began hoisting the stretcher up to the roof or would have bolted when they began digging. "Hey, guys, this is embarrassing. You'll have to finish it yourselves." But the four truly believed! This kind of faith invites the Lord's miraculous power.

Their example teaches us about faith that makes the most of the Lord's power. *Their faith was persistent.* When they got their friend on the stretcher, there was no stopping them. When they came to an obstacle, none of them said, "Well, the door is closed. I guess this isn't the Lord's will." They did not leave it in committee either. They got going! Jesus lauded this type of action in the enigmatic saying, "From the days of John the Baptist until now the kingdom of heaven has suffered violence, and the violent take it by force" (Matthew 11:12). Those who really want something spiritually and "go for it" are the ones who get it. When the four tore through the roof, they took the kingdom by violent, determined force. Such faith unleashes God's power.

Their faith was also creative. Undoubtedly some were standing by who, seeing the others' success, said "Why didn't I think of that?" The answer is, they did not believe as passionately and love as much as the four. A faith that truly believes that Christ is the only way will be inventive!

This is the genius behind radio station HCJB, which sits smack on the Equator at 10,000 feet and broadcasts the gospel to virtually the entire globe seven days a week, twenty-four hours a day. The almost-legendary creativity of that ministry springs from the passionate, driving belief that Christ is the only hope for the world. Believing faith finds a way, whether in the home, the school, or the whole world.

Also, *their faith was sacrificial.* Somebody would have to pay for the roof or fix it, and that would take time, labor, and expense. A faith that brings Christ's power to the world is always willing to pay the price.

Few Christians have impacted the Church more in our day than did Francis and Edith Schaeffer, but it was with a cost. Schaeffer wrote in his book *The Church at the End of the 20th Century*:

> In about the first three years of L'Abri [Francis Schaeffer's Christian fellowship group] all our wedding presents were wiped out. Our sheets were torn. Holes were burned in our rugs. Drugs came into our place. People vomitted on our rugs. . . . How many times have you had a drug-taker come into your home? Sure it is a danger to your family, and you must be careful. But have you ever risked it?[1]

The Schaeffers risked it because they believed Christ was the only answer.

So we see in the lives of the stretcher-bearers how Christ's healing power is unleashed in the world—through *love* and through *faith.* Oh, how they loved their helpless friend! Oh, how the world must be loved by us—truly loved!

They *believed* Christ was the only way! Their belief wrought *persistence,* invincible determination. They would not be denied. It also brought *creativity,* so that they found a way. It was *sacrificial,* for it really cost them.

Do we believe Christ is the only way? Has our belief wrought *persistence* in our lives? Has it brought *creativity*? Has it brought *sacrifice*? Do we truly love our families, our neighbors, our weekday colleagues?

We have been looking at that which promotes Christ's healing power in the world. Now let's look at what hinders it.

Hindering Faith (vv. 5–11)

The real paralytics were the Pharisees and scribes! In marked contrast to the four stretcher-bearers, they were just "sitting there" (cf. v. 6 and Luke 5:17). As religious leaders, they should have been directing the traffic to Jesus and his free clinic. When the roof opened, they should have reached up to receive the poor cripple. But instead of love, there was indifference. Instead of faith, there was only criticism.

Of course, our Lord saw everything far more clearly than we do. So he decided to use this charged moment, with the paralytic before him, to make his point. Knowing that the Pharisees and scribes were looking for something to pin on him, he gave it to them, or so they thought. Verse 5 tells us, "And when Jesus saw their faith, he said to the paralytic, 'Son, your sins are forgiven.'" This was a calculatedly outrageous statement. From our perspective it seems cruel. Here is a wretched paralytic, barely able to raise his head, hoping for a cure, and Christ says, "Your sins are forgiven." From the Pharisees' perspective, this was blasphemy, for only God could forgive sins.

Why did Christ say it? First, the man may well have been a paralytic due to some personal or imagined sin. Many Bible scholars think so. We know from modern science that paralysis and many other diseases can have a moral base. Perhaps in order to effect a full healing, Jesus' words were necessary.

Second, regardless of the man's physical condition, his greatest need by far was forgiveness of sin. Forgiveness was a far greater work, for it cost Christ his very life. Thus he met the man's greatest need first and eternally.

Third, Jesus pronounced forgiveness first to trap the Pharisees with the implications of the healing he was going to perform. Verses 8–11 reveal his logic:

> And immediately Jesus, perceiving in his spirit that they thus questioned within themselves, said to them, "Why do you question these things in your hearts? Which is easier, to say to the paralytic, 'Your sins are forgiven,' or to say, 'Rise, take up your bed and walk'? But that you may know that the Son of Man has authority on earth to forgive sins"—he said to the paralytic—"I say to you, rise, pick up your bed, and go home." His *physical* miracle verified his *moral* miracle! What could the Pharisees say?

Now from the electricity came the lightning. Verse 12 continues, "And he rose and immediately picked up his bed and went out before them all, so that they were all amazed and glorified God, saying, 'We never saw anything like this!'" What a moment! The paralytic, illuminated by the dusty shafts of light from the hole, was leaping and whooping it up! His four friends were yahooing down through the opening. The crowd was oohing and aahing. The Pharisees and scribes were frowning.

Spurgeon wrote: "I think I see him! He sets one foot down to God's glory, he plants the other to the same note, he walks to God's glory . . . he carries his bed to God's glory, he moves his whole body to the glory of God, he speaks, he shouts, he sings, he leaps to the glory of God."[2]

What a display before the wondering crowd! Who is to say that the paralytic and his four friends did not dance down the street while the multitude clapped in rhythm? And as he went home, he bore something far more impressive than his bed. It was a clean heart, the greatest miracle of all—no guilt, no bitterness, no tension. Someday those newly restored limbs would wither. But there would remain in him a well of water springing up to everlasting life, for his sins were forgiven.

The Lord can do anything he wants. He can heal any disease he pleases. But the greatest miracle, the only one that is eternal, is that he forgives sin. Has he ever said to you, "Your sins are forgiven"?

As we noted earlier, Luke says of this event, "And the power of the Lord was with him to heal." That power was unleashed by the *love* and the *faith* of a helpless paralytic's four friends. And that is how it is unleashed today to a world paralyzed in sin. *We must love the world.* It begins by loving those we can see—our family members, our neighbors, our colleagues at work—and then extending that love to those we cannot see. We must begin where we are. Determine to love those in your circle of influence.

Finally along with love, *we must believe that Jesus Christ is the only One who can heal the paralyzed.* It is simply a matter of believing his own words: "I am the way, and the truth, and the life. No one comes to the Father except through me" (John 14:6). Do we, without qualification, believe this? If we do, then we will be *persistent*, *creative*, and *sacrificial* in bringing our friends to Christ.

9

Jesus, Friend of Sinners

MARK 2:13-17

ACCORDING TO THE *Congressional Quarterly Almanac for the Ninety-Eighth Congress*, our national budget for fiscal 1985 was 1.021 trillion dollars—a lot of money by anyone's estimation, and a lot of tax dollars. It is almost beyond comprehension. I asked Dr. Bob Brabanec, professor of mathematics at Wheaton College, to put this in more manageable form, and this is what he gave me in round figures:

> If you began at the birth of Christ spending $1,400,000 a day, every day, without any time off for weekends or holidays, and continued spending at that rate through the fall of Rome, the Dark Ages, the Middle Ages, the Renaissance, the Age of Enlightenment, the Industrial Revolution, right on into the Twentieth Century till today, you would have just now succeeded in having spent the $1,021 trillion. Or, putting it in a shorter time frame, say fiscal 1985, the fiscal year in which we succeeded in spending the $1,021 trillion, you would have to spend more than $32,000 a second, about $2,000,000 a minute, or more than $114,000,000 an hour![1]

Think of the energy it takes to spend this much money; or even better, think of the energy it takes to *collect* it. It seems almost impossible. But as we all know, Uncle Sam is capable of miracles! These are not political remarks, but simply an introduction to our passage. However necessary taxes are, none of us likes to pay them. Tax forms and the mention of the IRS go along with high blood pressure and heart medicine.

If it is any consolation, it has been this way for the last two thousand years in the Western world. Such were also the conditions in Palestine in Christ's own day, under Roman dominance. The Romans collected their taxes through a system called "tax farming" (similar to farming out franchises such as McDonald's fast-food restaurants). They assessed a district a fixed tax figure, and then sold the right to collect taxes to the highest bidder. The buyer had to hand over the assessed figure at the end of the year and could keep whatever he gathered above that. The obvious potential for extortion was compounded by the poor communication characteristic of ancient times, so that the people had no exact record of what they were to pay.

The system consisted of two categories of taxes.[2] First, there were stated taxes:

> There was a *poll tax* which all men ages 14 to 65 and women 12 to 65 had to pay simply for the reason of being alive.
> There was a *ground tax* which required one tenth of all grain and one fifth of all wine and oil produced. In some places, the Romans also exacted a tax on fish. Very possibly this was done in Capernaum where the fishing industry was so vital.
> Finally, there was an *income tax* which was one per cent of one's annual income.[3]

In these stated taxes there was not much room for extortion.

But in the second area of taxes, duties, there was ample opportunity for abuse. The people paid separate taxes for using roads and docking in harbors. There was a sales tax on certain items, as well as import and export duties. A tax was even paid on a cart; in fact, each wheel was taxed!

The system fostered exploitation by the arbitrary power of the tax gatherers. They could stop anyone on the road, make him or her unpack their bundles, and charge just about anything they wanted. If the person could not pay, the tax collectors sometimes would offer to loan money at an exorbitant rate, thus pulling the people further into their greedy hands. They were trained extortionists. Quite naturally, they attracted a criminal element of thugs and enforcers—the scum of society. So rare was honesty in the profession that a Roman writer said he once saw a monument to an honest tax collector![4]

The Jewish tax collectors were easily the most hated men in Hebrew society. They were considered to be despicable vermin. They were not only hated for their extortion, but also because they were the lackeys of the Romans—much as the French hated Nazi collaborators during World War II. These Jews could not serve as a judge or a witness in a court session and were excommunicated from the synagogues.[5] They were the lowest of the lowest!

All this made Jesus' dealing with Levi, the tax collector, remarkable. We want to examine for our own selves Christ's revolutionary social practices in these verses in Mark's Gospel. They will tell us how he relates to us, and how we ought to relate to the world.

Christ, the Friend of Sinners (vv. 13–15)

Verses 13, 14 describe what happened between Christ and the tax gatherer, Levi: "He went out again beside the sea, and all the crowd was coming to him, and he was teaching them. And as he passed by, he saw Levi the son of Alphaeus sitting at the tax booth, and he said to him, 'Follow me.' And he rose and followed him."

After the spectacular healings in Capernaum, Jesus went off by himself along the seashore. The people came after him in wave after wave, and he taught them. Then the Lord again returned to Capernaum, and as he was passing through the town he saw Levi, the local tax gatherer, sitting in his customs office. The rest is history!

Luke in his parallel description says, "And leaving everything, [Levi] rose and followed him" (Luke 5:28). This was a decisive act. He gave up his business—everything, and there was *no going back.*

In a few minutes the whole town knew about low-life Levi's decision, and they could not believe it! Would it last? they wondered. Little did they know. Levi, as he is called here, was Matthew, later to be a Gospel writer. "As Jesus passed on from there, he saw a man called Matthew sitting at the tax booth, and he said to him, 'Follow me.' And he rose and followed him" (Matthew 9:9). Whether he was then called Matthew, we do not know. Many believe that just as Simon was named Peter ("the rock") by the Lord, so Levi was likewise tagged Matthew ("gift of God") by Jesus. If so, this was divine poetry, because this covetous rip-off artist would become as his new name suggested: a gift of God to his people.

This is utterly amazing, for of all the people in Capernaum, Levi was the most unacceptable to be one of Christ's disciples! Jesus sought out the man no one else wanted, the one everyone else wished would fall under the immediate wrath of God. This, of course, was to become one of the trademarks of Jesus' ministry, as such notables as Mary Magdalene and many other nameless men and women would attest. Jesus saw a man in Levi, not a category, and he knew what that man could become.

Centuries ago a number of workmen were seen dragging a great marble block into the city of Florence, Italy. It had come from the famous marble quarries of Carrara and was intended to be made into a statue of a great Old Testament prophet. But it contained imperfections, and when the great sculptor Donatello saw it, he refused it at once. So there it lay in the cathedral yard, a useless block. One day another sculptor caught sight of the flawed block. But as he examined it, there rose in his mind something of immense beauty, and he resolved to sculpt it. For two years the artist worked feverishly on the work of art. Finally, on January 25, 1504, the greatest artists of the day assembled to see what he had made of the despised and rejected block. Among them were Botticelli, Leonardo da Vinci, and Pietro Perugino, the teacher of Raphael. As the veil dropped to the floor, the statue was met with a chorus of praise. It was a masterpiece! The succeeding centuries have confirmed that judgment. Michelangelo's *David* is one of the greatest works of art the world has ever known.

Christ saw in the flawed life of Levi (tax collector) a Matthew (writer and evangelist). He still sees men and women with his consummate artist's eye today. The Scripture says, "For we are his workmanship, created in Christ Jesus for good works" (Ephesians 2:10). He sees in us what no one else sees.

Levi's life was revolutionized. So he decided to sponsor a reception in Jesus' honor, as verse 15 describes: "And as he reclined at table in [Levi's] house, many tax collectors and sinners were reclining with Jesus and his disciples, for there were many who followed him."

Why the reception? Obviously to honor Christ. That is the natural reflex of the soul that has received his touch, as we see from Genesis to Revelation. Also, this was a spontaneous celebration of Levi's new life. Jesus was certainly all for this, for he described the prodigal's father as saying, "It was fitting to celebrate and be glad, for this your brother was dead, and is alive; he was lost, and is found" (Luke 15:32).

Levi also threw the party to share Christ with his friends. Luke says it was a "great feast" (Luke 5:29), and our text says "many" were there. Levi evidently had a big place, and it was packed out. The guests were "tax collectors and sinners"—"sinners" being a technical term for people who the Pharisees felt were inferior because they had no interest in scribal tradition. They were especially despised because they did not eat their food in a state of ceremonial cleanness.[6] These "sinners" even consorted with Gentiles. They were the offscouring of Capernaum—despised social pariahs. And there reclined pure Jesus in their midst—eating, drinking, and conversing with these lawless, materialistic compromisers.

Christ, the Enemy of the Self-Righteous (v. 16)

This was too much for the good citizens of Capernaum. "And the scribes of the Pharisees, when they saw that he was eating with sinners and tax collectors, said to his disciples, 'Why does he eat with tax collectors and sinners?'"(v. 16) The Pharisees (literally, "the separatists"),[7] though attending the banquets, carefully avoided ritual impurity from contact with others who did not keep the traditions. To them, it was an unforgivable disgrace for Jesus, who claimed to be a teacher of the Law, to disregard their time-honored customs.[8]

There are Christians who operate on similar unspoken suppositions. In nineteenth-century England, there was a poor woman who attended a church women's meeting. She had been living with a man of another race by which she had had a baby, and she brought the child with her. She liked the meeting and came back again and again. But then the vicar came to her and said, "I must ask you not to come to this meeting again." Seeing her questioning look, he continued, "The other women say that they will stop coming if you continue to come." Looking at him in poignant wistfulness, she asked, "Sir, I know that I'm a sinner, but isn't there anywhere a sinner can go?" Fortunately the Salvation Army found her, and she was claimed for Christ. That is precisely what Matthew was up against until he met Christ.

Perhaps none of us espouse such Pharisaical beliefs. In fact, we loathe them. But many of us live them out nevertheless. We come to Christ, and in our desire to be godly we seek out people "like us." Ultimately we arrange our lives so that we are with nonbelievers as little as possible. We attend Bible studies that are 100 percent Christian, a Sunday school that is 100 percent Christian, prayer meetings that are 100 percent Christian. We play tennis with Christians and eat dinner with Christians. We have Christian doctors, Christian dentists, Christian plumbers, Christian veterinarians, and even our dogs are Christian. The result is, we pass by hundreds without ever noticing them or positively influencing them for Christ. None of us are Pharisees philosophically, but we may be practically.

We need to reach out to the people with whom we work—go to dinner with them, attend sporting events together, have them over. We need to extend ourselves to those we know are hurting—provide a room for an unwed mother, minister to the multiple cultures around us, volunteer in the local prisons, get involved in the community, even if it means resigning a church job to do it. Jesus said, "I do not ask that you take them out of the world, but that you keep them from the evil one" (John 17:15).

The Pharisees were scandalized. So, brave men that they were, they approached Jesus' disciples, saying, "Why does he eat with tax collectors and sinners?" (v. 16).

Christ's Defense of His Socializing (v. 17)

Jesus heard what they were saying and, thoroughly disgusted with their small hearts, responded in two parts (verse 17). First he said, "Those who are well have no need of a physician, but those who are sick." This was a supremely common-sense answer that was known in both secular and religious proverbs.[9] The doctor needs to visit the ill; the whole should go to the fractured, the joyful to the mourning, the strong to the weak.

> History records that when Oliver Cromwell ruled England, the nation experienced a crisis: They ran out of silver and could not mint any coins. Cromwell sent his soldiers to the Cathedral to see if any silver was available. They reported back that the only silver was the statues of the saints, to which Cromwell replied, "Melt down the saints and get them back into circulation." Sometimes God must do that with us. We must be melted down so that we will get into circulation in the world for Him.[10]

This is only common sense!

Second, Christ completed his answer with a statement of his overall purpose: "I came not to call the righteous, but sinners." He spoke ironically and truthfully. The Pharisees were just as needy as the publicans and sinners, but tragically did not know it. Jesus was saying in effect, "To people who think they are righteous, I have nothing to say. But to those who know they have need, I have come."

Those who say, "I have no need"—who say, "There is no significant sin in me"—are beyond our help. All we can do is wait. Sooner or later life will go sour, and their dreams will collapse at their feet. Then they will know their need. That is why God so often allows trouble to come to men's and women's lives: to strip away the terrible delusion that they can make it by themselves and thus to open them to grace.

What do we learn from Christ at that party? Two things:

First, Christ and his followers did not (and still must not) isolate themselves from a needy world, nor did they assimilate it. They went out with Christ in mission. The Christian's life is not to be one of *isolation*, nor *assimilation*, but *mission*.

Second, Christ sat down (and sits down) with sinners. He dined with them and they with him. And he met their need.

As we close, we must confess all known sin to the best of our ability. But we must also come again as needy sinners saying, "The first link between my soul and Christ is not my goodness but my badness; not my merit but my misery; not my standing but my falling; not my riches but my need."

10

The New Wine of Christ

MARK 2:18—3:6

I AM CONVINCED THAT IF every man and woman of the literate population of the world would carefully read the Gospels through for himself or herself, we would witness a spiritual harvest beyond what the world has ever seen. I say this for two reasons:

First, most people have in their minds one of a number of distorted caricatures of Christ. These can include his being a thoroughly politicized opportunist who failed in a calculated power play, or a sweet, helpless Jesus whom the cruel tides of history abused. Though these caricatures are attractive to some, they have limited appeal to the millions in our lost world.

The other reason I believe a reading of the Gospels would bring a vast ingathering is that the Christ of the Scriptures, as portrayed in the Gospels, is radically winsome. That is, if people see him as he really was and is, they would by the millions find him absolutely irresistible.

If you have ever heard Becky Pippert share her experience in persuading nonbelievers to simply and seriously read the Gospels for themselves, you would be more convinced than ever of this truth.[1] Simply seeing Christ as he is in the Scriptures is life-changing. The more we and others see and respond to the Christ of Scripture, the more radically right our lives will become.

I think this is particularly true in relation to the second and third chapters of Mark, where we see Christ defining who he is and what he does in a series of collisions with the religious establishment. Each of the five collisions in 2:1—3:6 reveals something radically inviting about Jesus.

Jesus' Initial Collisions with the Religious Establishment (2:1–17)

First there was "The Capernaum Caper," when Jesus, illuminated in the dusty shafts of light beaming through a gaping hole in the roof, with a bedridden paralytic lying before him and the religious elite looking on, unexpectedly said, "Son, your sins are forgiven" (2:5). Shockingly, Jesus asserted his *power* to forgive sins, and thus proclaimed his divinity. The subsequent healing of the paralytic not only confirmed his power to forgive, but the *priority* he placed on spiritual healing. For all time, he called attention to the fact that the greater miracle, and by far his most important ministry, is the forgiveness of sins. In that initial collision, he put forth a vision of himself that was far superior to the false ideas of a politicized or sentimentalized Christ.

The other opening collision with the religious powers was over his enlisting the tax gatherer, Levi, as a follower, and then attending a party with Levi's "sinner" friends. Levi was a money-grabbing, *goyim*-loving, fornicating extortioner—everyone's candidate for "Scum of the Year." But Jesus called him and accepted him as a follower. When Jesus reclined at the table with the collected lowlife of Capernaum, the handwashing, exclusivist Pharisees went into orbit! But Jesus' unanswered words set the record straight for all time: "Those who are well have no need of a physician, but those who are sick. I came not to call the righteous, but sinners" (2:17). Christ has no time for spiritual elitists. He comes only for sinners. This means there is hope for my children and yours.

These initial head-on collisions with the religious establishment produced brilliant sparks that illuminated the character of Christ and the heart of God. The third collision, described in the present text, is equally revelatory of the divine heart, and even more revealing of our problem.

Jesus' Revealing Collisions with the Religious Establishment (vv. 18–22)

This time the collision was over fasting: "Now John's disciples and the Pharisees were fasting. And people came and said to him, 'Why do John's disciples and the disciples of the Pharisees fast, but your disciples do not fast?'" (v. 18). Many believe that the question came because at the exact moment Christ was feasting with Levi, the Pharisees and John's disciples were fasting. Actually the Scriptures commanded fasting only once a year (on the Day of Atonement, which was a national day of repentance and forgiveness, Leviticus 16:24). But by Jesus' time the Pharisees had decreed that godly people should fast twice a week (on the second and fifth days—Mondays and Thursdays). The Pharisees' attitude derived from, among other things, the false assumption that true religion was a solemn, joyless affair, an assumption that some people hold even today.

Erma Bombeck tells how she was sitting in church one Sunday when a small child turned around and began to smile at the people behind her. She was just smiling, not making a sound. When her mother noticed, she said in a stage whisper, "Stop that grinning—you're in church," gave her a swat, and said, "That's better!" Erma concluded that some people come to church looking like they had just read the will of their rich aunt and learned that she had given everything to her pet hamster!

I once knew a man who believed that Christians should be solemn. He was a young believer, full of zeal, but without the ability to keep things in perspective; so he would go off on self-righteous tangents. On one particular occasion he concluded that never once in the Scriptures does it say Jesus smiled or laughed—therefore, good Christians do not smile. Never mind that arguments from silence are patently dangerous. Never mind the repeated smiling wit of Christ. Good Christians do not smile. I can still see him sitting with his wife and a few like-minded friends through church—righteous but sober, holy but unsmiling. Absolutely absurd! Some of us have met clergy like this: formal, speaking in sepulchral tones, with their neckties twisted around their souls!

The Pharisees were like this too. They actually whitened their faces, put ashes on their heads, wore their clothes in shoddy disarray, refused to wash, and looked as forlorn as possible. You could not be spiritual unless you were uncomfortable. They thought spirituality makes you do things you do not want to do and keeps you from doing the things you want to do.

The fasting religious establishment had self-righteously put the question to Jesus. So Jesus answered them directly and brilliantly: "Can the wedding guests fast while the bridegroom is with them? As long as they have the bridegroom with them, they cannot fast. The days will come when the bridegroom is taken away from them, and then they will fast in that day" (vv. 19, 20).

After an ancient Jewish wedding, the couple did not honeymoon, but stayed at home for a week of open house in which there was continual feasting and celebration. For the hardworking, this was traditionally considered to be the happiest week in their lives. The bride and groom were treated like a king and queen that week (sometimes they even wore crowns). They were attended by chosen friends known as "guests of the bridegroom," which means literally, "children of the bride's chamber." Their guests were exempted from all fasting through a rabbinical ruling that said, "All in attendance on the bridegroom are relieved of all religious observances which would lessen their joy."[2]

For us believers on the other side of the cross and resurrection, the application for this is hugely encouraging. We are not just "guests of the bridegroom"—we are the Bride of Christ! This is more than metaphorical language—it is reality. It speaks of the deepest intimacy and exchange. We actually have "the Spirit of God" (Romans 8:9). Therefore, we are to outdistance the attendants of the bridegroom in the intensity and continuance of our joy.

Christianity brings perpetual joy for those who will take it and cultivate it. The early Christians were even accused of being drunk. The first Franciscans were reproved for laughing in church because they were so happy. The first convents of the Reformed Carmelites were most happy places, because St. Teresa insisted on musical instruments and a jolly time in the house of recreation. The first Methodists stole some of their hymn tunes from operas and set the songs of Zion to dance music. The first Salvationists jumped for joy because General Booth always told them that if they felt the Spirit move them, they could leap in a hymn or a prayer, and they did![3] There is perpetual wedding joy with Christ for those who will have it.

As Jesus continued to answer the Pharisees, he turned from this beautiful illustration to some parabolic analogies that diagnosed the problem. In verse 21 he said, "No one sews a piece of unshrunk cloth on an old garment. If he does, the patch tears away from it, the new from the old, and a worse tear is made." If you take an old sail, for instance, and patch one of its small holes with new sail cloth, as soon as it becomes wet and dries, you will have a far bigger hole. The new fabric that Christ brings cannot be interwoven with the tired fibers of old religion; it will simply tear it apart.

Jesus then used another, even more powerful illustration: "And no one puts new wine into old wineskins. If he does, the wine will burst the skins— and the wine is destroyed, and so are the skins. But new wine is for fresh wineskins" (v. 22). In ancient culture, the skins of goats were stripped off as nearly whole as possible and partly tanned, so they could be filled with new wine. Their natural elasticity and strength would allow the fermenting new wine to expand. However, if new wine was put into old wineskins, their brittle, inflexible condition would cause them to burst and both wine and wineskins would be lost. The new life that Christ brings is expanding.

Shortly after the Armistice of World War I, Dr. Donald Barnhouse visited the battlefields of Belgium. In the first year of the war, the area around the city of Mons was the scene of a great British retreat; in the last year of the war it was the scene of a great German retreat. For miles to the west of the city, the roads were lined with artillery, tanks, trucks, and other equipment of war that the Germans had abandoned in their hasty flight.

It was a lovely day in spring. The sun was shining, and not a breath of wind was blowing. As he walked along examining the German war material, he noticed that leaves were falling from the great trees that arched above the road. He brushed at a leaf that had blown against his breast; it became caught in the belt of his uniform. As he picked it out, he pressed it in his fingers, and it disintegrated. He looked up curiously and saw several other leaves falling from the trees. It was not autumn. There was no wind to blow them off. These were the leaves that had outlived the winds of autumn and the frosts of winter, yet now were falling, seemingly without cause. Then he realized that the most potent force of all was causing them to fall. It was spring. The sap was beginning to run, and the buds were beginning to push from within. From down beneath the dark earth, the roots were taking life and sending it along trunk, branch, and twig until that life expelled every bit of deadness that remained from the previous year. It was, as a great Scottish preacher termed it, "the expulsive power of a new affection."[4]

When Christ fills the wineskins of our lives, the swelling life within stretches us to new limits. The inner pressure expels unneeded things and fills every aspect of life. Those who have not yet had Christ take up residence in their life can scarcely imagine how fully they will be filled; how every aspect of their humanity from their intellect to their emotions will be changed. So dynamic is the new life that the old wineskins of previous religious structures must give way.

Practically speaking, our old selves (our previous experiences, our present level of growth, our intellectual formation, our cherished customs, our prejudices, the familiar, the comfortable) apart from Christ tend to be old wineskins.[5] We have to allow Christ to modify all these areas or we will burst. You may be one who needs to do this today—to say to Christ, "Take my intellect, my customs, my prejudices, the familiar, the comfortable, and renew them to hold your wine. I want all I can get."

Returning to the flow of our text, the reason the Pharisees were repeatedly colliding with Christ was that they were in effect old wineskins. They simply could not handle the real thing. This is what ultimately brought the fatal collisions over the Sabbath.

Jesus' Fatal Collisions with the Religious Establishment (2:23—3:6)

The Pharisees' domestication of real faith into humanly attainable standards made it impossible for them to fathom that Christ's disciples were not breaking the Sabbath when, as they walked through a wheat field, they broke off the heads of wheat, rubbed the grain out of their hands, blew away the chaff, and ate it. They could not handle Jesus' reasoning from Scripture that since King David ate forbidden consecrated bread to meet his need, so it was all right to meet one's need on the Sabbath: "The Sabbath was made for man, not man for the Sabbath" (2:27).

Nor could the petrified parameters of the Pharisees' lives handle Jesus' healing of the man's withered hand on the Sabbath. To them, healing was work, regardless of how necessary or beneficial it might be. So they began plotting Jesus' death. The wine he hoped to bring them burst their restricted skins and lay on the ground along with their broken lives.

What revelatory fire comes from the repeated collisions of Christ and the religious establishment. From them we see that Christ's great work is to heal us from our sin; that Christ comes to sinners who realize their need; that the new life he brings cannot be held in old religious structures or old lives. How these incendiary truths invite us. If many in the world could only see this Christ, they would find him irresistible.

People need to be exposed to the reality of God's Word, so the false caricatures of Christ will fall away. But they also need to be exposed to people full of his new wine.

A group of American Christians were on a tour of the Holy Land and had the opportunity to give Christian testimony to a Middle-Eastern audience. One woman in the group gave the translator a particularly difficult time because in explaining what her life was like before she came to Christ, she used a very uncomplimentary term to describe herself—a term her fellow-workers used for her: "old bag." She explained the name was used because she was unhappy and grim as she was trying to be a good person. At first the translator was confused, but in a moment he understood, for being an "old bag" has nothing to do with one's culture, age, or physical condition. It is spiritual.[6]

Is your life an old, petrified bag or a new, flexible wineskin? Only a new life can contain new wine. Not a religion, but a relationship. Have you experienced that?

Secondly, if you are a believer, if you were to characterize your life in Christ, is it an old, dried-up bag or is it a new wineskin? What is in your life? What is dominating—the new life of Christ, or cold, sour religiosity?

11

Jesus, Pressured Jesus

MARK 3:7–19

I HAVE CHOSEN for the title of this message a parody of a line from a favorite old hymn, "Jesus precious Jesus." The pressure in Jesus' life came from two sources: first, his repeated collisions with the religious establishment; and second, his popularity with the people.

In reviewing the head-on collisions, we see a mounting hostility toward Jesus. In Capernaum when he forgave the paralytic's sins, the scribes and Pharisees accused him of blasphemy, a sin punishable by death. Next, when he called the despicable tax gatherer Levi to be one of his disciples, and followed that by reclining at table with the low-life scum of Capernaum, the Pharisees were scandalized. Then they observed that he and his followers did not observe their ceremonial laws regarding fasting. This was incomprehensible to the Pharisees. From their perspective Jesus could not be a teacher of the Law, but only a dangerous fraud. Finally, there was the deadly collision over the observance of the Sabbath, because Jesus' disciples picked and ate grain on that day, and because Jesus healed a man's withered hand. Both of these acts were accounted unforgivable breaches of Sabbath law by the Pharisees. Now, maddened with hatred, the pious, separatist Pharisees formed an unholy alliance with the impious, worldly Herodians as together they plotted Jesus' extinction.

The pressure upon Christ was immense. Our Lord's every move, night and day, was observed by hostile interlopers. The worst interpretation was placed on everything seen and heard. Our Lord, being truly a man, felt the pain of hatred intensely with its emotional discomfort and pervasive alienation. Of course, Jesus knew what awaited him at their hands, but now was not the time. So he withdrew from Capernaum to the countryside along the seashore, where he would be less vulnerable to their strategies and pressure. But the move had only limited success because of his immense popularity.

The Demands of Popularity (vv. 7–12)

Now, if anything, the pressure was even more intense: "Jesus withdrew with his disciples to the sea, and a great crowd followed, from Galilee and Judea and Jerusalem and Idumea and from beyond the Jordan and from around Tyre and Sidon. When the great crowd heard all that he was doing, they came to him" (vv. 7, 8). The pressure came from two separate throngs. The Galilean multitude consisted of locals who had seen and heard of the recent miracles of his ministry. It was a "great crowd" because Galilee at this time was densely populated. Some commentators insist that tens of thousands were present. This was augmented by hundreds more who had come the hundred-mile journey from Jerusalem in Judea and many more who had come even farther, from Idumea. Add to this those who traveled from the Transjordan area and the coastal cities of Tyre and Sidon, and you have the picture.

It was a massive response. We must remember that people who have traveled far will not be denied. There were hordes followed by hordes, wave upon wave of needy people—all demanding attention. So great was the press that Christ was in physical danger: "And he told his disciples to have a boat ready for him because of the crowd, lest they crush him" (v. 9). One of his disciples hovered close by in a small boat (much the same way we would keep a car at hand with the engine running) in case Jesus needed to get away. Knowing the Apostle Peter, he was probably officiously manning the boat and formidably "staring down" the unruly multitude.

Our Lord's primary motivation at this time was to preach the gospel of the Kingdom—the necessity of repentance and belief (1:14, 15). Physical healing was only secondary. But the truth is, Jesus' words held little attraction for the multitudes. What they wanted to experience and see were healings and other attendant miracles that would benefit them personally. Jesus experienced a similar thing after feeding the five thousand, when a vast multitude pursued him around the perimeter of the lake. To them he sadly said, "You are seeking me, not because you saw signs [i.e., desire spiritual reality], but because you ate your fill of the loaves" (John 6:26).

Our Lord would allow nothing, not even popularity and "success," to divert him from his primary ministry. But it is not always the same for us. Success and popularity bring the crowds. Then keeping the crowds becomes all-important, so we do whatever will do that. Popularity can, and often does, seduce the ministry.

Jesus was under immense pressure, and the pressure came from two kinds of people: the sick and the demonized. Verse 10 describes the pressure from the sick: ". . . for he had healed many, so that all who had diseases pressed around him to touch him." The picture is one of wild disorder ("pressed around him to touch him" is literally, "to fall upon or jostle"). Add to this the pressure of the demonized, as described in verse 11: "And whenever the unclean spirits saw him, they fell down before him and cried out, 'You are the Son of God.'" The unclean spirits were drawn by a strange fascination to see Jesus, even though they knew he was their conqueror, the hated Son of God. Somehow "[t]error and malice drive them to His presence."[1] These "unclean spirits"—malevolent, obscene, sinister—had wrought bodily injury, psychological trauma, and immense spiritual harm to their victims.

Ray Stedman tells of talking with a girl who had fallen into the practice of using a Ouija board. He says:

> It eventuated in her hearing voices that demanded she write things down before she could sleep at night. Invariably, what she had to write was moral filth—obscenities, ugly, evil words. Sometimes she would have to write pages of them before the voices would cease and she could sleep. This is a mark of the kind of spirits these were.[2]

These filthy spirits would cast the bodies of their victims before Jesus, crying out with unearthly voices, "You are the Son of God" in futile attempts to render him powerless. This was in accordance with the ancient belief "that knowledge of the precise name or quality of a person confers mastery over him."[3] In response, Jesus forbade them to speak, and cast them out. There is tragic irony here, for the demons knew that Jesus was the Son of God, but the multitudes thought of him only as a miracle-worker whom they could use for their selfish ends.[4]

Putting it all together, the ill, the feverish, and the crippled were pushing and grabbing at Jesus and falling over him; the demonized were malevolently sizing him up and were howling his name in furtive combat; the jaundiced Pharisees were watching his every move, waiting for their chance. It is easy for us in the evangelical tradition to miss the point here because we have been so ready (rightly so!) to emphasize that Jesus was much more than the ideal man, being one hundred percent God. The truth is, he was also man, and he really did feel immense, inescapable stress and strain.

For us this means that Jesus was (and is) the unique man who understands modern-day mankind. In broadest terms, he understands the harried, frenetic lives of modern men and women. He understands, for example, what Anne Morrow Lindbergh meant when she wrote:

> The life I have chosen as wife and mother entrains a whole caravan of complications. . . . It involves food and shelter; meals, planning, marketing, bills and making the ends meet in a thousand ways. It involves not only the butcher, the baker, the candlestick maker, but countless other experts to keep my modern house with its modern "simplifications" (electricity, plumbing, refrigerator, gas-stove, . . . dish-washer, radios, car and numerous other labor-saving devices) functioning properly. It involves health; doctors, dentists, appointments, medicine . . . vitamins, trips to the drugstore. It involves education, spiritual, intellectual, physical; schools, school conferences, car-pools, extra trips for basketball or orchestra practice; tutoring; camps, camp equipment and transportation. It involves clothes, shopping, laundry, cleaning, mending, letting skirts down and sewing buttons on, or finding someone else to do it. It involves friends, my husband's, my children's, my own, and endless arrangements to get together; letters, invitations, telephone calls and transportation hither and yon.[5]

Jesus understands this! And he understands the pressured treadmill upon which most of us race day in and day out. He knows what it is like when the traffic light turns green and the car behind you immediately begins to honk. But more specifically, he understands the pressures that we feel when we try to reach out to others as he did. He knows that when you really care about others, you open yourself to troubles virtually incomprehensible to those who do not care. He understands that those who stand with him are assaulted by a demonized culture that tries to gain mastery. He understands the pressures of a life of faith.

We ought to take great solace in this. The more we care, the busier we are! Whenever we are "under it," we need to recall Jesus ministering to the crowd, so pressured that he had the car running and the doors open for a quick getaway!

How did our Lord manage to deal with the pressures of life and ministry? Our Lord's response gives us an unfailing model.

The Master's Management of the Demands (vv. 13–19)

Our Lord took three distinct steps to manage the demands and pressure of his ministry. The first step came immediately, for Jesus withdrew to be alone: "And he went up on the mountain" (v. 13a). Tradition says that he ascended the Horns of Hattin, the most prominent point on the west side of the lake. That is possible, though we cannot be sure. The point is, *he got away*, by himself. The Gospels make it clear that though he was man and God, he still needed to be alone. Though he came to save man, at times he needed to be away from man.

Though the world today celebrates its St. Francises and Thomas Mertons, it does not understand the need in men and women to be alone. Such a desire seems strange to many.

> Anything else will be accepted as a better excuse. If one sets aside time for a business appointment, a trip to the hairdresser, a social engagement, or a shopping expedition, that time is accepted as inviolable. But if one says: I cannot come because that is my hour to be alone, one is considered rude, egotistical or strange. What a commentary on our civilization, when one has to apologize for it, make excuses, hide the fact that one practices it—like a secret vice![6]

Actually these times are essential to wholeness and well-being. As Vance Havner said, "If we do not follow Christ's example to 'come apart,' we may, indeed, just come apart!" Too many of us wake up to a clock radio, shave to the news, drive through noisy traffic, work in the din of the office, listen to the rush-hour reports, relax to the evening news, and drift off to sleep surrounded by the base *thump, thump* of the family stereo. We need silence. To use the language of the mystics, we need a sanctuary, a hermitage. It is not that hard—a parked car in the park, a church sanctuary, a walk on a hiking path, a few minutes downstairs before the family wakes up. The pressures of life and the example of Christ demand that we do this every day for at least a few minutes, as well as during regular extended times.

Jesus got away—that was the first step. But he always took the second step—*he prayed*. The parallel passage in Luke 6:12 says, "In these days he went out to the mountain to pray, and all night he continued in prayer to God." Again the greater to lesser logic is overpowering: If Jesus had to do this, being the Eternal Son, how much more do we, adopted sons and daughters, need to follow his example.

Pressured people that we are—caring people, jostled not only by the regular demands of life, but by the needy, the ill, even the demonized, pressured almost beyond our limits—prayer to God is what we need most!

Someone once asked George MacDonald, if God loves us so much, and knows everything we need before we ask, why must we pray? MacDonald answered:

> What if He knows prayer to be the thing we need first and most? What if the main object in God's idea of prayer be the supplying of our great, our

endless need—the need of Himself? What if the good of all our smaller and lower needs lies in this, that they help to drive us to God? Communion with God is the one need of the soul beyond all other needs; prayer is the beginning of that communion, and some need is the motive of that prayer. Our wants are for the sake of our coming into communion with God, our eternal need.[7]

E. Stanley Jones describes the effect of prayer on us like this:

Prayer is not pulling God to my will, but the aligning of my will to the will of God. Aligned to God's redemptive will, anything, everything can happen in character, conduct, and creativeness. The whole person is heightened by that prayer contact. In that contact I find health for my body, illumination for my mind, and moral and spiritual reinforcement for my soul. Prayer is a time exposure to God, so I expose myself to God for an hour and a half to two hours a day, asking less and less for things and more and more for Himself. For having Him, I have everything. He gives me what I need for character, conduct, and creativeness, so I'm rich with His riches, strong in His strength, pure in His purity, and able in His ability.[8]

Jesus, our pressured Jesus, knew this and spent extended time exposing his human heart to that of his blessed Father.

The third and final step for our pressured Lord was that he shared the responsibility of his ministry with others, as verses 14–19 so memorably proclaim:

And he appointed twelve (whom he also named apostles) so that they might be with him and he might send them out to preach and have authority to cast out demons. He appointed the twelve: Simon (to whom he gave the name Peter); James the son of Zebedee and John the brother of James (to whom he gave the name Boanerges, that is, Sons of Thunder); Andrew, and Philip, and Bartholomew, and Matthew, and Thomas, and James the son of Alphaeus, and Thaddaeus, and Simon the Zealot, and Judas Iscariot, who betrayed him.

Though Jesus the man needed his time alone and carved it out of his impossible schedule, he also craved companions to serve with him and was strengthened by their "imperfect sympathy and unintelligent love."[9] If Jesus needed people to share his great work, so we in our imperfections need other men and women to share the load.

Our text is explicit about his method, for verse 14 says: "And he appointed twelve (whom he also named apostles) so that they might be with him." The result was, they really came to *know* Jesus. There was an exchange of soul, and ultimately a profound identification—word for word, breath for breath, emotion for emotion, volition for volition.

We all know the story: wavering, inconsistent Simon became Peter, the rock. John and James became Boanerges, the "Sons of Thunder"—dynamic apostles! Anonymous, average Andrew became the patron saint of three nations. Thomas the skeptic became a tenacious man of faith. Simon, the radical, subversive zealot, became a man truly zealous for God. The same happened to others outside the Twelve as well. Loathsome Levi became one of the writers of the Gospel of the Son of Man.

Christ's wisdom is still the same for those under the pressure of a caring life. "And what you have heard from me in the presence of many witnesses entrust to faithful men who will be able to teach others also" (2 Timothy 2:2).

What do we learn from our Jesus, our pressured Jesus, overwhelmed in Galilee? First, we sometimes need to get away. We need times of silence. We need a place. We need time for what is important: God and those closest to us.

> If I had only . . . forgotten future greatness
> and looked at the green things
> and reached out to those around me
> and smelled the air
> and ignored the forms and the self-styled obligations
> and heard the rain on my roof
> and put my arms around my wife
> . . . perhaps it's not too late.[10]

There is saving wisdom here for pressured men and women.

Second, we need to pray. What we are in the Lord wholly depends on what we receive from him. Those who are exposed to the Father's life find him bringing grace to their pressured lives.

Third, we need to share our ministry, to impart our lives to others. Collegial relationships defuse the pressure.

May we learn well from Jesus, our pressured Jesus.

12

A Third Opinion

MARK 3:20–30

The First Opinion: Jesus Is a Madman (vv. 20, 21)

There is no doubt about it: there came a time in Jesus Christ's ministry when his family "went out to seize him." The Greek text uses a very strong expression which means "*to arrest*."[1] Jesus' brothers came down to Capernaum with the sole intention of *forcibly* taking him under control and hauling him back to Nazareth!

Mark was absolutely clear as to why this was so: "for they were saying, 'He is out of his mind'" (v. 21).[2] Or as we would say, "He's crazy!" His own family, those for whom he had been caring as the eldest son since the death of Joseph, thought he had lost his mind and were trying to carry him off to some safe place in Nazareth where he could indulge his delusions without doing any harm to himself.

How was it that his own flesh and blood resorted to such extremes and such a humiliating plan of action? First, and to their everlasting credit, they loved him. It would have been so much easier just to let him go his own way. Keeping him "under wraps" at home would not be easy. But they risked trouble—they loved him and did what they thought best.

The second reason they went to such extremes was that they were afraid his religious fervor was going to ruin his health. This is clear from the way Mark structured his explanation in verses 20, 21: "Then he went home, and the crowd gathered again, so that they could not even eat. And when his family heard it, they went out to seize him." In a culture where meals were rituals and food was scarce, this was considered insane! Word also came that the press of the crowd along the shore was so great that he was in danger of being trampled and that he kept a small boat ready for a quick getaway. Besides, no sane man would give up a business that met his needs, set himself against the powers that be, and gather a motley group around him such as he had. They were afraid that his crazy life would kill him.

Lastly, his religious zeal was simply too radical. It was okay to be devout, but the extremes to which he went were not those of a balanced man. They had also heard reports of him staying up all night in prayer under the stars (cf. Luke 6:12). Moreover, it was clear to them that he was mistaken about who he was and his mission. John's Gospel tells us that even at the very end of his ministry his own brothers were *not* believing in him (John 7:5). Their brother was caught in a self-destruction megalomania and they had to save him! This was the opinion of Christ's family—those who loved him!

This has also become a model for the more *charitable* opinion of those who do not believe in Christ. They say Christ was a *good* man, perhaps even the greatest of men, but that he was mistaken about his own person and mission. They say he was a man to be admired for his teaching and his dedication, but he was "out of his mind." This is something of the position that Albert Schweitzer came to in his famous *The Quest for the Historical Jesus*, where he has Jesus, in messianic delusion, attempting to turn the wheel of history, only to have it turn and crush him.[3] The purest, noblest, most utterly self-oblivious and devoted life that ever was lived upon earth was (and is) disposed of in this way: "He is beside himself . . . he is crazy."

This is how those who have followed in his stead have been judged through the centuries. When the Apostle Paul preached before Festus, Festus cried out in response, "Paul, you are out of your mind; your great learning is driving you out of your mind" (Acts 26:24). Similar verdicts have been rendered over Luther[4] and Bunyan and Wesley and William Borden ("Borden of Yale"), who left his vast wealth and after attending Princeton Seminary traveled to Egypt in 1913 where he died the same year while preparing to reach the Muslims.

But let us note (and note well!) that given the truth of Christ and the truth of the gospel, such people are supremely sane! If the Apostles' Creed is sensible and true, then those who believe it have aligned themselves with sanity. If Christ is who he says he is, then the sanest thing in the world is to follow him. If Christ calls us to total commitment, anything else is crazy. *Christianity needs more of Christ's madness!*

The first opinion of an unbelieving world is that Christ was a madman. The second, and far less charitable, opinion is that he was a tool of Satan.

The Second Opinion: Jesus Is a Demoniac (vv. 22–30)

Those who rendered this opinion were "scribes," highly trained legal special-
ists sent out from Jerusalem to assay Jesus' miracles and see if Capernaum
was a "seduced" city.[5] They apparently came with their minds already made
up, as there is no evidence of interviews with Jesus and his disciples. Their
opinion had two parts.

First: "He is possessed by Beelzebul" (v. 22), Beelzebul being the lord
of evil spirits. This was a vicious attack. They were accusing Jesus of being
demonized and claimed that the demon that controlled him was the one that
ruled over the evil spirits.

The second accusation was that "By the prince of demons he casts out
the demons" (v. 22). Jesus was, according to them, a son of Satan. Some
think there was even a hint here that he used the name of Beelzebul, perhaps under his breath, to perform exorcisms.[6] This charge reduced Jesus to
a demonized sorcerer who majored in the black arts. The scribes perhaps
said this because he did perform *bona fide* exorcisms. They could not deny
this. In fact, the parallel rendering of this account in Matthew 12:22–24
indicates that he had just exorcised blind and dumb spirits from a man,
and this enraged the scribes. While they could not deny the power, they
would not accept it as being from God and therefore Christ had to be of
Satan. This made Jesus supremely evil, an archfiend, a horribly corrupt
tool of Satan.

Jesus answered in verses 23–27: "And he called them to him and said
to them in parables, 'How can Satan cast out Satan?'" Jesus illustrated this
obvious impossibility with two hypothetical examples: "If a kingdom is
divided against itself, that kingdom cannot stand. And if a house is divided
against itself, that house will not be able to stand." He then gave the only possible conclusion: "And if Satan has risen up against himself and is divided,
he cannot stand, but is coming to an end." The scribes' charges did not hold
water. Then, in verse 27, Jesus told them what had really happened: "But
no one can enter a strong man's house and plunder his goods, unless he first
binds the strong man." The "strong man" is Satan. His "house" is the kingdom that he dominates here on earth. His "goods" are the helpless victims
whom he holds in bondage through his demons.[7] Only one who is stronger
than Satan can free the victims, and this is what Jesus has done—entering
Satan's house, binding him, and loosing the hapless captive souls. Jesus appealed to logical argument to answer the scribes' accusations and left them
virtually speechless.

Then he gave them a chilling warning in verses 28–30: "'Truly, I say to you, all sins will be forgiven the children of man, and whatever blasphemies they utter, but whoever blasphemes against the Holy Spirit never has forgiveness, but is guilty of an eternal sin'—for they were saying, 'He has an unclean spirit.'" Here we have the so-called "doctrine of the unforgivable sin." There are few Scriptures so consistently misunderstood as this one, and so misapplied. Nearly everyone, even the most unchurched and Biblically illiterate, has heard of the unforgivable sin. I have even had Christians tell me they are afraid they have committed it.

The question is: what is this unforgivable sin, this unforgivable blasphemy against the Holy Spirit? First, let us note what it is not. It is not cursing the Holy Spirit. It is not taking the Lord's name in vain, though that is certainly a vile sin. It is not adultery or sexual perversion. It is not murder, even multiple murders, or genocide. Very simply it is the *ongoing, continual rejection* of the witness of the Holy Spirit to the divinity and saviorhood of Christ. It is the perversion in the heart that chooses to call light darkness and darkness light. It is continuing rejection of the witness of the Holy Spirit, whether that witness be a quiet witness in the conscience, the rational witness of the Word, or even miracles and wonders.

The scribes here were at the very brink of committing this sin, because they were saying that the Holy Spirit's witness to Christ through his exorcisms and miracles were really the work of Satan. Moreover, they were persisting in their blasphemy (verse 22 indicates they kept repeatedly saying it). If their attitude had become permanent, they would have crossed the line.

Have there been people who have committed the unforgivable sin? The answer is *yes*. There have been men and women who rejected the Spirit's testimony regarding their own condition and the person and work of Christ so consistently that their hearts became unable to believe. Such people have ranged from the gross sinner to the urbane "good" person.

Several years ago Ben Haden visited a hospital at 3:30 A.M. to see a man he had known for some years. The doctor had said the man was dying and knew it, so Pastor Haden asked him how it was between him and the Lord. "Oh," he said, "I've always believed in God, and I know everything is shipshape." "What do you believe about Jesus?" Haden asked him. "I've known God all my life," he said, "and I've tried to observe godly standards. I've been honest in business, and I've worked hard."

"My friend," said Pastor Haden, "and I wouldn't be here if I weren't your friend, answer a straight question: how is it between you and Jesus?" To which the man replied, "I've never made a place in my life for Jesus. I don't believe in Jesus. If I were to believe in Jesus, it would upset everything in my philosophy and my life, and I would have to rethink everything about me." "By the grace of God," Pastor Haden said, "you have that kind of time; rethink it." "No," he said, "I will die without Jesus." "Why then do you think Jesus died?" asked the pastor. "Oh, I understand he died for sins." "Your sins," said Haden. "Perhaps, perhaps, but it's too late in my life to rethink the place of Jesus." And he died.[8] This knowledgeable man died resolutely rejecting Christ.

We must add that the unforgivable sin—blasphemy against the Holy Spirit—is a sin that requires knowledge. C. E. B. Cranfield, the eminent New Testament scholar and theologian, notes that the "scribes" whom Jesus warned were the accredited theological teachers of God's people. He further notes that their daily business was the Scriptures and that they were therefore subject to the constant witness of the Holy Spirit who inspired the Scriptures. Then he concludes: "If we have been following the right clue, then it means that those who particularly should heed the warning of this verse today are the theological teachers and the official leaders of the churches."[9]

Cranfield is right. It is not the ignorant blasphemer on the street who is in danger of committing the unforgivable sin, but the man or woman in the church who knows the Scriptures, has heard the Word held forth with accuracy, has seen something of the miraculous power of God in changed lives, and yet rejects it all, even identifying what he has seen with the power of Satan. He calls light darkness and good evil, in testimony to a massive perversion of spirit (cf. Isaiah 5:20). The warning is particularly to those who have grown up in the church and may even have some theological education, but have willfully rejected it and in their heart of hearts attribute supposed Christian reality to evil.

To those who are afraid they have committed *the* sin, we can say with absolute confidence that their being so troubled is infallible testimony they have not committed it.[10] Note that as vile as the blasphemy of the scribes was, Jesus did not say they had committed this sin, but only warned them. Those who continue to blaspheme the Holy Spirit do not care a whit about what they have done. If someone cares at all, though his sins be the worst, there is hope and the possibility of grace.

Mark has showcased two unacceptable opinions regarding Christ. *The first, and most charitable, was that he was "out of his mind," that he was mad.* This was the opinion of those who appreciated him, who knew of his impeccable life, but did not believe he was God. This is the opinion of thousands today who believe that Jesus was a good man, a religious genius, but are deceived as to who he really was.

The second opinion, and least charitable, was, "He is possessed by Beelzebul," and "By the prince of demons he casts out the demons"—that he was satanic. This was (and is) the view of the utterly lost, those standing at the edge of the eternal Abyss from which there is no return.

This presents us with the Great Trilemma: either Jesus was a lunatic, or a demonic liar, or he was God. Regarding his being a liar, Philip Schaff, the eminent historian, wrote:

> The hypothesis of imposture is so revolting to moral as well as common sense, that its mere statement is its condemnation. How in the name of logic, common sense, and experience, could an imposter—that is a deceitful, selfish, depraved man—have invented, and consistently maintained from the beginning to end, the purest and noblest character known in history with the most perfect air of truth and reality? How could he have conceived and successfully carried out a plan of unparalleled beneficence, moral magnitude, and sublimity, and sacrificed his own life for it, in the face of the strongest prejudices of his people and ages?[11]

As to Jesus' sanity, we must realize that the historical difficulty of explaining his life, if he was a madman, has never been overcome. The incongruity of the immense sanity of his moral teaching and the massive megalomania that was his if he was not God has never been satisfactorily reconciled. Thus there is only one acceptable opinion: that Jesus was God.

In C. S. Lewis' oft-quoted words:

> I'm trying here to prevent anyone from saying the really silly thing that people often say about Him: "I'm ready to accept Jesus as a great moral teacher, but I don't accept His claim to be God." That's the one thing we mustn't say. A man who was merely a man and said the sort of things Jesus said wouldn't be a great moral teacher. He'd either be a lunatic—on a level with the man who says he's a poached egg—or else he'd be the Devil of Hell. You must make your choice. Either this man was, and is, the Son of God: or else a madman or something worse. You can shut Him up for a fool, you can spit at Him and kill Him as a demon; or you can fall at His feet and call Him Lord and God. But don't let us come with any patronising nonsense about His being a great human teacher. He hasn't left that open to us. He didn't intend to.[12]

Jesus Christ is King of kings and Lord of lords! As the eternal intelligence, as a framer of the universe, as the architect and vehicle of the Incarnation, *he is the supremely sane man!* All sanity resides in him.

It is an exercise in sanity to trust him. It is growing sanity to commit all of your life to him. In the light of his claims and the full revelation of Scripture, any other life is crazy. This is why Paul says: "I beseech you therefore, brethren, by the mercies of God, that ye present your bodies a living sacrifice, holy, acceptable unto God, which is your reasonable service" (Romans 12:1 KJV).[13] The supremely sane life is one that is totally committed to him.

Perhaps you need to step into spiritual sanity. You realize Jesus was not a madman, and neither was he an evil liar. He was, and is, God. If you believe, say it now to him:

> Lord Jesus Christ, I believe that you are who you say you are. I believe that you are God. I believe that you died for *my* sins. I rest my hope of eternal life in you.
>
> Gracious Lord, it is an upside-down world. It is insane. We thank you that when you stepped into history, sanity stepped into history; that when you stepped into life, sanity stepped into life. When I follow you, I do the sanest thing. The greater my commitment, the greater my sanity. Make me supremely sane, I pray. In Jesus' name, Amen.

13

Christ's Kinsmen

MARK 3:31-35

PICTURE THE SCENE WITH ME. Jesus was back in Capernaum where he had performed so many of his miracles—where the crowds had been so intense that some had even torn a hole in a neighbor's roof to get to him. And now even greater crowds, attracted by his subsequent miracles and his words (no man ever spoke as Jesus did), were pressing in on him.

This pressing multitude was a desperate mixture. At the center were the newly chosen apostles, the Twelve, admiringly hanging on Jesus' every word. In contrast to these eager faces, there leered in the press the pained visages of the scribes, also turning over his every syllable, having just accused Jesus of being in league with Satan. Some in the multitude were eager, some ecstatic, some quizzical, some perplexed, and some livid and blasphemous. Every extreme was represented: from nationalist Zealots to collaborationist tax collectors, from ignorant fishermen to the trained intelligentsia.

At the periphery of the surging throng, standing by nervously, was Jesus' family. "And his mother and his brothers came, and standing outside they sent to him and called him. And a crowd was sitting around him, and they said to him, 'Your mother and your brothers are outside, seeking you'" (vv. 31, 32). Unbeknownst to the crowd, Jesus' mother and his younger brothers hoped to lure him away so they could privately take him back to Nazareth where he could be protected from his mania (cf. 3:21). A message was passed from person to person. When it reached Jesus, many of the throng knew the nature of the request and expected Jesus to defer.

They certainly were not ready for his startling reply: "'Who are my mother and my brothers?' And looking about at those who sat around him [Here the idea is that he gave them a searching look.[1] Matthew adds that he gestured with his hand, 12:49], he said, 'Here are my mother and my brothers! For whoever does the will of God, he is my brother and sister and mother'" (vv. 33–35).

These would be startling words in any culture, but in Hebrew culture, where the family was so sacred, they were *shocking!* A murmur of amazement swept the multitude. Mary, who had nursed and dressed Jesus and loved him all the way into his magnificent manhood, and now had come for him in loving concern, was crushed. His brothers were likewise shocked, and perhaps angered. Though we have the advantage of Biblical perspective, we still, as parents and brothers and sisters, find his words difficult. This is one of Jesus' hard sayings, and Renan, the famous skeptic, used it to accuse Jesus of "trampling under foot everything that is human—love and blood and country."[2]

What then did Jesus mean by his shocking answer? First, he did not mean that he was severing family ties. In the final hours of his life, while he hung in agony on the cross, he thought of his mother and made provision for her (John 19:26, 27). Later his brother James would become a devoted father in the Church and a martyr. Jesus held parenthood in the highest regard and castigated those who failed to give honor to their parents, as in the disgraceful use of Corban (Mark 7:9–13). Jesus was not suggesting the breaking of family ties, though he did acknowledge that Christian commitment would sometimes bring division within the family (cf. 10:28–30).

What he did mean was that there is a deeper kinship than flesh and blood, a spiritual kinship that is characterized by obedience to the Father. For this reason he said, "Whoever does the will of God, he is my brother and sister and mother." Obedience does not originate relationship with God (faith does that), but obedience is a sign of it. Jesus was saying there is a new family that is far superior to the human family, for it is eternal. Its ties are far *stronger*. It is far more *satisfying*. It is far more *demanding*. Those who are in his spiritual family are *far more dear* to him than his human family, with whom he lived for thirty years! What Jesus said here has massive importance.

The Implications of Jesus' Statement for the Church

Put another way, obedience is the key to experiencing "family" with God. This was true even for Jesus. Early in his ministry Jesus told his followers, "My food is to do the will of him who sent me" (John 4:34). And in Gethsemane, in a bloody sweat, he cried to his Father, "Abba, Father, all things are possible for you. Remove this cup from me. Yet not what I will, but what you will" (14:36). Every beat of Christ's heart was given to performing his Father's will. This was essential to his experience of "family."

If this was so for Christ, how much more for us? We are children of God, but our subjective awareness of the sweetness of being in God's family is conditioned upon our obedience. Alexander Maclaren paraphrased this: "Whoever does God's will is [and feels himself to be] my brother and sister and mother."[3] It is no wonder that in the Lord's Prayer Jesus commanded us to pray, "your will be done," for in obeying God we open our souls to the fullness of being his family. Obey the Lord, and an unparalleled family experience awaits you.

But there is even more, for obedience is also the key to experiencing "family" with our brothers and sisters in Christ on earth. When we make our wills his will, we experience a dynamic relationship with others who are living in submission to him.

We have probably had the experience of meeting another Christian or Christian couple. You begin to converse, and soon you are talking about Christ and ministry for him. You quickly realize that you are experiencing a sense of "family" that transcends flesh and blood. One of my own dear memories of this is being in Austria at Schloss Mittersil, standing in the courtyard of the Castle surrounded by pink and white geraniums in the window boxes and talking to a missionary couple about our mutual ministries. This was followed by a cup of home-brewed coffee in their Volkswagen camper and an unforgettable sense of family. What a fellowship of mutual commitment and mutual obedience.

Jesus spoke of this rich experience later in 10:29, 30 when he said, "Truly, I say to you, there is no one who has left house or brothers or sisters or mother or father or children or lands, for my sake and for the gospel, who will not receive a hundredfold now in this time, houses and brothers and sisters and mothers and children and lands, with persecutions, and in the age to come eternal life." Jesus was talking about the sense of "family" that comes to the obedient.

Can there be any more positive call to do the will of God? Such are the implications of Jesus' statement about our *spiritual* sense of family. But there is more, because it has correspondingly wonderful implications for *our physical* husband-wife, parent-child families.

The Implications of Jesus' Statement for Our Families

We are often aware of the joys of our human families, perhaps particularly during Christmas and other holiday seasons. There is a special kind of family love or affection that courses through us. It is the kind of love, as C. S. Lewis has said, that makes us use "old" as a term of affection[4]—"good old Uncle Jim" who may in fact be only thirty, and "good old Larry" who is really forty! Such comfortable love develops with the years, like a favorite old slipper. At the same time, it is built upon and sustained by the other loves: *eros*, *agape*, and *phila*. Next to God and his will, our earthly families are of greatest importance.

Despite this, today we are witnessing the disintegration of the family all around us, even in the church. One reason for this is that societal pressures are hostile to the nuclear family. Some persons are even actively working for its dissolution.

The eminent sociologist Amitai Etzioni, in his book *An Immodest Agenda: Rebuilding America Before the 21st Century*, says:

> According to my calculations, if the nuclear family continued to be dismembered at the same accelerating rate, by the year 2008 there would not be a single American family left. I do not believe this will actually occur; I expect some major social force to change the present course of the American nuclear family, if only because no complex society has ever survived without a nuclear family. But one cannot ignore the fact that the present trend is over fifteen years old and has been accelerating. So a most obvious reason the family is in trouble is the negative tide of culture which is carrying many of the unwilling with it as hapless victims.[5]

But there is, especially among Christians, another reason why the family is in trouble: its *worship*. In a valiant effort to stem the tide, many Christians and non-Christians alike have made the family everything. Every moment of every day, every involvement, every commitment, every engagement is measured and judged by the question, how will this benefit my family? While this is generally commendable, it can degenerate into a *familial narcissism*. The four walls of the home become a temple, and only within and for those walls are any sacrifices made. *Thus we commit domestic idolatry!* This is an immense tragedy.

The tragedy is this: every earthly loyalty, if it is made central, becomes idolatry, and all idolatries eventually destroy their worshipers. The truth is, many of the psychological problems in our families can be traced to parents whose affections bind rather than release and liberate.[6] Avoiding the *permissive* destruction that is ravaging our society, some parents perpetrate a *possessive* destruction, which is equally devastating. Jesus warned about this when he said, "Whoever loves father or mother more than me is not worthy of me, and whoever loves son or daughter more than me is not worthy of me" (Matthew 10:37).

What can we do to preserve and elevate our families? The answer begins with the family putting love and obedience to Christ above everything else. What does this mean? For example: none of us can love our spouses as they ought to be loved. Only Christ can do that. However, "We love because he first loved us" (1 John 4:19). Thus, we are able to love him and others as we respond to his love. Most of us need to be better lovers, but being a better lover begins, for the believer, by loving him. Christ must be first!

The same is true for our children. Making them everything will not enable us to love them as we ought, or make it possible for them to love us as they ought. We must love and obey God first. Anything less is idolatry. Our children must also love and obey God. When our children come to Christ, there is a fellowship with them that transcends and eternalizes earthly kinship.

When St. Augustine finally came to faith in answer to the prayers of his mother, Monica, the two, according to his *Confessions*, stood in a window in Ostia realizing that they were more truly kindred than ever before. The family must be church!

Two thousand years ago when Jesus gave his startling answer, he shocked his mother and brothers, and all who heard him. The shock waves have reverberated down through the centuries. But it has been a therapeutic shock, for it teaches us that when we obey him we enjoy the blessed sense of being "family" with his devoted children here. This loving obedience to him is also the key to our earthly families, for when we please him first, we can love our wives, our husbands, our children, and our parents as they ought to be loved.

How about you? Do you have a growing sense of family with God? Is there a joyous sense of family with his servants? Is your own human family being elevated and perpetuated by the eternal sense of family? If not, or if you want it to be more so, commit yourself right now to doing his will.

14

Authentic Hearing

MARK 4:1–20

IT HAD BEEN a long and emotional day for Jesus. First his mother and brothers had come in an attempt to forcibly take him back to Nazareth to protect him from himself. Then he had been accused by the scribes of being in league with Beelzebul, to which he issued a solemn warning against unforgivable blasphemy. Lastly he had proclaimed the shocking fact that his true mother and brothers were not his earthly relations, but "whoever does the will of God" (3:35).

Now in the afternoon he left the house in Capernaum and went down to the refreshing shores of Galilee to preach.[1] Verses 1, 2 give us the setting: "Again he began to teach beside the sea. And a very large crowd gathered about him, so that he got into a boat and sat in it on the sea, and the whole crowd was beside the sea on the land. And he was teaching them many things in parables." The crowd was so great (some believe it was the greatest yet in his ministry) that Jesus was forced to preach from a fishing boat. The picture we have, then, is of a vast heterogeneous assembly sitting in a great arc on the rising shore,[2] all facing Christ, who was seated aboard the boat in rabbinical teaching posture, giving forth the parables of the kingdom as the sea gently lapped the shore.

As Jesus surveyed the sunlit multitude, he was aware not only of their diversity, but that a whole range of hearing and understanding was in operation. He was aware that the mystery of the kingdom was being worked out in their lives. Some were coming to faith, and others were hardening in their unbelief.

Jesus wanted all of them to listen with receptive hearts. He was the Word of God, and for this he had come. So he gave them a parable that if listened to and meditated upon would result in their opening themselves to life. The parable drew upon a rich agricultural image with which they were all familiar: a man with a seed bag tied to his waist, walking his field and rhythmically casting the seed.

The seed was a proper and powerful symbol of the Word of God springing into life. Within every seed there is almost infinite potential for life! God's Word is *the* seed *par excellence*! The sower is, of course, Christ and anyone else who puts forth God's Word, whether in preaching or in personal exchange. The soil represents the varying condition of human hearts on which the seed is tossed. As the sower hurls his seed, some falls on the roadside, and the birds flutter down and steal it away. He hurls again, and it lands on rocky soil, where it quickly sprouts, only to wilt under the Palestinian sun. The sower casts in another direction, and it falls among thorns, where it is choked and cannot grow. Other seed, cast on good soil, marvelously multiplies thirty, sixty, and a hundred times! End of parable.

Then Jesus began to repeat, "He who has ears to hear, let him hear" (v. 9). Jesus was the Word, God's ultimate communication. His every fiber longed for his hearers to comprehend.

Not everyone had ears to hear that day. Some understood, but many were perplexed. Some of his followers were in the dark themselves. Verse 10 tells us that they began asking him about the parable. Jesus responded with one of his famous "hard sayings": "To you has been given the secret of the kingdom of God, but for those outside everything is in parables, so that 'they may indeed see but not perceive, and may indeed hear but not understand, lest they should turn and be forgiven'" (vv. 11, 12).

What did Jesus' mysterious pronouncement mean? The parallel account (Matthew 13:12, 13) sheds some light: "For to the one who has, more will be given, and he will have an abundance, but from the one who has not, even what he has will be taken away. This is why I speak to them in parables, because seeing they do not see, and hearing they do not hear, nor do they understand." In essence Jesus was enigmatically saying that the condition of one's heart determines its receptivity to truth. The scribes had originally been given straightforward teaching that they rejected and thus they could ultimately lose the truth—it would be taken away from them.

Those who receive truth and act upon it receive more. Those who reject truth will ultimately lose the bit they have. The parables were full of truth, but for truth-rejecting people, they were inscrutable.

This principle is paralleled in other areas of life. Physically, if we fail to exercise a muscle, we will one day lose its use. It is the same with our intellectual powers. If we fail to use them, there will come a time when we will not be able to summon their full power. God confronts us with his truth, but if we do not positively respond to it, we will lose it. What a solemn reality for those who sit under the teaching of God's Word week after week and do not respond to it.

The writer to the Hebrews must have had these matters in mind when he said: "For if we go on sinning deliberately after receiving the knowledge of the truth, there no longer remains a sacrifice for sins" (Hebrews 10:26). If we repeatedly hear God's Word and refuse to respond time and time again, there will come a time when we become so hardened that we not only will not but *cannot* respond. If we are believers, we must set ourselves to always respond to God's truth as we read it or hear it from another believer or from the pulpit. An excellent spiritual discipline is to respond to truth by saying, "God, you have spoken to me, and I will do it." We *must* respond to truth!

Alone with his followers, having made this sobering pronouncement, Jesus graciously explained the parable. He wanted them to become better listeners to truth. What he said can open our ears and hearts too.

The Seed Cast on the Road: The Hard Heart (v. 15)

First the Lord explained about the seed cast on the roadside: "And these are the ones along the path, where the word is sown: when they hear, Satan immediately comes and takes away the word that is sown in them."

The farmers' fields in ancient Palestine were long, narrow, often serpentine strips divided by little paths that became beaten as hard as pavement by the feet, hooves, and wheels of those who used them.[3] The seeds merely bounced on these paths or were swept back and forth by the wind. These beaten paths represent the hardened hearts of some unsophisticated people who hear God's Word. Their own busy comings and goings and the frenetic traffic of life have so hardened them that nothing of God's truth stirs them. Life for them may be no more than the sports page and a beer, or a movie magazine and an hour at the beauty shop. There may be no gross sin, but there is no interest in God whatsoever. Life is crowded with other things.

Into this world to eat and to sleep,
And to know no reason why he was born.
Save to consume the corn,
Devour the cattle, flock and fish,
And leave behind an empty dish.

On the other hand the person may be more sophisticated. Screwtape describes one of his charges' experiences. The man is in the British Museum. He is reading, and his reading suggests a train of thought that sets him on the path of spiritual inquiry. But Screwtape, devil that he is, intervenes by making the man terribly hungry for lunch.

> Once he was in the street the battle was won. I showed him a newsboy shouting the midday paper, and a No. 73 bus going past, and before he reached the bottom of the steps I had got into him an unalterable conviction that, whatever odd ideas might come into a man's head when he was shut up alone with his books, a healthy dose of "real life" [by which he meant the bus and the newsboy] was enough to show him that "that sort of thing" just couldn't be true.[4]

Such people's lives are hardened with presuppositions, distortions, and prejudices that steel them to the truth. They may be hostile, but very often they are simply uninterested. God's truth has no relevancy for them.

The main emphasis of Jesus' metaphor was *busyness*. These people beat the ground of their own lives asphalt-hard with their frenetic feet. This was (and is) a warning to people on the go who had no time for contemplation, who rarely gave a second thought to the spiritual. What a powerful warning to the twenty-first century, which exhibits a busyness and a hardness that exceeds the first century. Many of us need to embrace Jesus' warning and pull it into our lives for our souls' sake.

As the truth bounces around on the surface of some lives, Satan comes with a fluttering, chirping interest, some busy excitement perhaps, maybe some gossip, and flies away with the life-giving seed. This ground needs to be broken up. Often the plowing that is needed is some pain or stress or trial to soften that hardened surface to the relevancy of God's truth. This is how grace came to some of our lives, isn't it? Life's hardships made us ready. "The hardness of God is kinder than the softness of man."[5] Difficulties made us quit our busyness, and then the Word of God fell powerfully into the plowed ground of our lives. Let us pray this for ourselves and for our hardened friends.

The Seed on Rocky Places: Shallow Hearts (vv. 16, 17)

Next our Lord explained about the seed sown in rocky places: "And these are the ones sown on rocky ground: the ones who, when they hear the word, immediately receive it with joy. And they have no root in themselves, but endure for a while; then, when tribulation or persecution arises on account of the word, immediately they fall away" (vv. 16, 17).

In Palestine much of the land is a thin two- or three-inch veneer of soil over a limestone bedrock. Here some of the seed falls, the warm sun quickly heats the seed in the shallow soil, and the seeds sprout in feverish growth. But then the sun beats down, the plant's roots meet the bedrock, and it withers and dies.

I have seen this tragically happen in a number of lives over the years. On one occasion I saw a young man make a dazzling profession of Christ. In a few weeks he was speaking everywhere, dominating testimony meetings, reproving older Christians for their coldness. But then he broke his leg, attempted vindictive litigation on the innocent property owner, cursed God for his hard luck, and abruptly fell away.

The problem was, he had a shallow emotional response to Christ that never penetrated his entire heart—his intellect and will. When affliction came, there was immediate rejection. I am convinced that this is where so many of the enemies of the faith come from. Too many, through their emotion, tasted something of God's power, but not true conversion. In falling away they became bitter and jaundiced and terribly lost. Affliction, like the sun, brings growth to roots in good soil, but withers the shallow profession of faith.

Helmut Thielicke aptly says:

> There is nothing more cheering than transformed Christian people and there is nothing more disintegrating than people who have been merely "brushed" by Christianity, people who have been sown with a thousand seeds but in whose lives there is no depth and no rootage. Therefore, they fall when the first whirlwind comes along. It is the half-Christians who always flop in the face of the first catastrophe that happens, because their dry intellectuality and their superficial emotionalism do not stand the test. So even that which they think they have is taken away from them.
>
> This is the wood from which the anti-Christians too are cut. They are almost always former half-Christians. A person who lets Jesus only halfway into his heart is far poorer than a one hundred per cent worldling. He does not get the peace that passes all understanding and he also loses the world's peace, because his naivete has been taken from him.[6]

Certainly authentic faith involves great emotion. If there is no emotion, it is a crippled or even bogus faith. But true faith is also a matter of the mind and will. Jesus once cooled a disciple's glib vow to follow him wherever he went by replying, "Foxes have holes, and birds of the air have nests, but the Son of Man has nowhere to lay his head" (Luke 9:58). True belief involves all of the person, who then weathers affliction and even persecution.

The Seed upon the Thorny Soil: The Divided Heart (vv. 18, 19)

Next Jesus explained the image of the sower casting his seed among the thorns: "And others are the ones sown among thorns. They are those who hear the word, but the cares of the world and the deceitfulness of riches and the desires for other things enter in and choke the word, and it proves unfruitful." Here the thornbushes are not visible because they have been burned off the surface, but their roots are intact. When the seed is sown on this soil, then watered and germinated, the entrenched thorns also sprout and grow with a virulent violence, choking out the grain before it can produce any fruit.

The thorns, Jesus explained, represented "the cares of the world and the deceitfulness of riches and the desires for other things." This portrayed a divided heart, a heart divided by irreconcilable loyalties. This heart makes some gestures toward Christ, but "the cares of the world" (literally, "the distractions of this age") draw it back. It is pulled in other directions, leaving no room for spiritual concerns. "The deceitfulness of riches" ("keeping up with the Joneses") draws them with the promise of great good. This involves buying things you do not need to impress people you do not like with money you do not have.

This is a divided heart—like the heart of the girl to which a young man once proposed. He said, "Darling, I want you to know that I love you more than anything else in the world. I want you to marry me. I'm not rich. I don't have a yacht or a Rolls Royce like Johnny Brown, but I do love you with all my heart." She thought for a minute and then replied, "I love you with all my heart, too, but tell me more about Johnny Brown."[7]

A heart that is overcome with a love for riches and the things of this world is *not* a believing heart. "No one can serve two masters, for either he will hate the one and love the other, or he will be devoted to the one and despise the other. You cannot serve God and money" (Matthew 6:24). Many began well, and it looked like they were believers, but the love of the world has strangled all vestiges of Christianity from their lives.

The Seed in the Good Soil: The Fruitful Heart (v. 20)

Finally there is the good soil in which the seed brings forth fruit. Jesus said, "But those that were sown on the good soil are the ones who hear the word and accept it and bear fruit, thirtyfold and sixtyfold and a hundredfold" (v. 20).

The seed of God's Word does not bounce off the surface of this heart. It does not momentarily flourish only to shrivel under adversity. It is not divided by its competing desires and strangled. It is a heart that allows God's

Word to take deep root in it. It produces first a harvest of character: "But the fruit of the Spirit is love, joy, peace, patience, kindness, goodness, faithfulness, gentleness, self-control; against such things there is no law" (Galatians 5:22, 23). Then it produces a harvest of good works (Ephesians 2:10).

The hearing and reception of God's Word is a mystery, and in this great parable Jesus has given us insight into what is going on in the world. He has given us this truth to straighten out the confusion about what true hearing really is and to stress its importance. He himself is the Word, and as such he is the ultimate communication from God. "And the Word became flesh and dwelt among us" (John 1:14).

Jesus conveys to us the love of the Godhead. He, by his death, tells us that we are not only loved, but in need of his atoning blood because we are sinners. We are loved. He died for our sins, that we might live. Is he communicating with you?

Right now, the most important thing is that we *listen* to him and receive the Word, not with *hard* hearts—that is busy hearts, impenetrable hearts that need to be broken up. And not with *shallow* hearts—only the emotions are touched. These are strangled by love for this world: "I love you with all my heart, God, but tell me what the world can do for me."

We should listen to God with a heart that is good soil, where the Word of God grows a rich harvest.

15

Jesus Calming the Storm

MARK 4:35-41

MOODY MONTHLY reprinted an article first published in 1926, a story that has become for me one of the most beautiful examples of God's power to protect his children. Ira Sankey was the co-evangelist, soloist, and song leader for D. L. Moody. Their partnership began in 1870 when Moody heard him sing at a Sunday school convention, and went on to span a quarter of a century. It really took off in 1873 when for two years they held amazingly successful crusades in Edinburgh, Glasgow, and London. When they returned to the States in 1875, they were international figures.

It was Christmas Eve, 1875, and Sankey was traveling by steamboat up the Delaware River. It was a beautiful, starlit evening and many passengers were on deck who encouraged the famous evangelist to sing. Sankey, who was leaning against one of the steamship's great funnels gazing at the stars in silent prayer, consented, intending to sing a Christmas song, but felt compelled to sing William Bradbury's "Savior, Like a Shepherd Lead Us."

There was a deep stillness as his baritone floated across the quiet river that Christmas Eve. When he had finished, a man stepped from the shadows and said: "Did you ever serve in the Union Army?"

"Yes," Mr. Sankey answered, "in the spring of 1860."

"Can you remember if you were doing picket duty on a bright, moonlit night in 1862?"

"Yes," Mr. Sankey answered, very much surprised.

"So did I, but I was serving in the Confederate Army. When I saw you standing at your post, I raised my musket and took aim. I was standing in the shadow, completely concealed, while the full light of the moon was falling upon you. At that instant, just as a moment ago, you raised your eyes to heaven and began to sing. 'Let him sing his song to the end,' I said to myself. 'I can shoot him afterwards. . . .'

"But the song you sang then was the song you sang just now. I heard the words perfectly: 'We are Thine, do Thou befriend us. Be the Guardian of our way.'

"Those words stirred up many memories. I began to think of my childhood and my God-fearing mother. She had many times sung that song to me. . . .

"When you had finished your song, it was impossible for me to take aim again. I thought, 'The Lord who is able to save that man from certain death must surely be great and mighty.' And my arm of its own accord dropped limp at my side."[1]

Oblivious to any danger, Ira Sankey was spared certain death. A coincidence? Hardly! It was God's sovereign power that arranged for him to sing that particular song on that night, the exact familiar strain to evoke tender memories in his would-be slayer and stay his hand. God protects his own, and none of us will go before our time.

What a comfort this story has been to me as I raise a family and minister to the flock God has put under my care. The keeping power of Christ over his people is a truth that we all need to understand and believe, for it is life-changing.

As we take up our story, this is what Jesus' disciples needed to understand and make part of their lives, and that is what his calming of the Galilean storm teaches. For us, this is a peek at the process of understanding the power of Christ, a peek that has been life-changing for thousands upon thousands through the Church's ages. It is one of the Church's favorite stories.

It had been a strenuous day in Jesus' taxing life. It had begun with blasphemous accusations by the Pharisees that he was controlled by Beelzebul; it was a fierce, adrenalin-pumping confrontation. Then his mother and brothers had attempted to kidnap him and take him back to Nazareth, for they thought he was out of his mind. Next, leaving the crowded house he went down by the sea, where amidst a great press he began teaching in parables. So vast and bumptious was the throng that he got into a boat and taught the rest of the day from it in the hot sun. Finally, with the approach of evening, Jesus, exhausted, gave the order to pull out, which verses 35, 36 describe: "On that day, when evening had come, he said to them, 'Let us go across to the other side.' And leaving the crowd, they took him with them in the boat, just as he was. And other boats were with him."

The Greek tense reveals a note of urgency in Jesus' decision to depart.[2] Perhaps he was so tired that he had "hit the wall" and knew he could not go on. At any rate, in the darkening shadows of dusk Jesus moved to the stern of the boat where he wearily reclined on a coxswain's pillow. The boat hoisted sail and began the five-mile trip across the lake, followed by a flotilla of admirers in their tiny boats. It must have been a beautiful scene as they moved slowly across the calm sea with their patched fishing sails below the rising stars—when suddenly without warning they were blasted with a terrific storm!

Learning through the Storm (vv. 37, 38a)

The Sea of Galilee rests at 628 feet below sea level and is surrounded by mountains gouged with deep ravines. These ravines serve as gigantic funnels to focus whirling winds down onto the lake without notice. The way is often "greased" by a thermal build-up in the extremely low valley that, while it rises, invites the cold air to come falling violently from above. Our text says, "And a great windstorm arose, and the waves were breaking into the boat, so that the boat was already filling" (v. 37). The imperfect tense pictures the waves as repeatedly crashing into the boat. Matthew uses the word *seismos* (literally, "earthquake") to describe the storm. It was as though the lake was being shaken. On port and starboard great dark mountains of water rose and washed over the boat. At any moment they would be swamped to a watery grave. Anyone who has been in a storm and has felt the stern plunge like an elevator in the trough of a mountain of green and then rise to the sky like a carnival ride can imagine something of their watery misery.

They had no way at that terrible moment of knowing it, but that miserable storm was a vehicle for teaching them about God and his power in their lives. The storm was essential to their spiritual development. Here we see a principle of universal and spiritual application. Without difficulties, trials, stresses, and even failures, we would never grow to be what we should become. Storms are part of the process of spiritual growth.

Some mature believers believe that every spiritual truth, everything that has enhanced their existence, has come through affliction. They are probably right.

> I asked the Lord that I might grow
> In faith and love and every grace,
> Might more of His salvation know,
> And seek more earnestly His face.
> 'Twas He who taught me thus to pray,
> And He I trust has answered prayer;
> But it has been in such a way
> As almost drove me to despair.[3]

The fact is, we would be spiritual Lilliputians, insufferably self-centered, proud, and empty people, without adversity. This is why Ruth Graham can pray for herself:

> Dear God, let me soar in the face of the wind: up, up, like the lark—so poised and so sure, through cold or the storm with wings to endure. Let the silver rain wash all the dust from my wings. Let me soar as He soars; let me sing, as He sings; let it lift me. . . . Let it buffet and drive me, but, God, let it lift.[4]

Lord, Let Me Ride the Storm to You!

The storm was a step up for the disciples, though they did not know it. Perhaps you have such a storm in your life right now. Why not ask God to help you make the most of it?

The storm continued with all its violence. The sails were in rags; everything was awash. And where was Jesus? "He was in the stern, asleep on the cushion" (v. 38a). This was at least as remarkable as the storm! The Lord was fast asleep on the hard boards and pillow, which only great weariness could make comfortable. And he remained asleep (he wasn't pretending) despite the howling wind and the wet spray. He was utterly, totally exhausted!

We see here a remarkable insight into the Incarnation. Though in a moment Jesus would calm the storm with an extraordinary display of power, he first slept in a weary body. In this grand display the opposites of weakness and omnipotence do not clash but coalesce in a beautiful harmony too magnificent to be the product of human imagination.

The main point here is that to the disciples, Christ seemed to be unaware of their plight. Of course, we know that in the Incarnation Christ chose to always live in conscious dependence upon the Father. Therefore, he could sleep a real sleep knowing that the Father would awaken him to do his will. Nevertheless, their perception of Christ's apparent obliviousness to their misery is a picture of how we often feel in life's storms. So often we mistakenly conclude that we are alone; that no one, not even God, knows what is happening and how we are feeling. How wrong we are! God knows every wave that falls on us. He knows the rate of our hearts, our respiration, the innermost thoughts in our minds, our emotions, even our dreams. That tiny boat bearing Christ and his own was the object of the most minute heavenly attention. And so it is in our difficulties, even in death!

The storm was necessary for the disciples' spiritual development, just as necessary as the ensuing calm that was now to come.

Learning through the Calm (vv. 38b, 39)

Evidently frantic, "they woke him and said to him, 'Teacher, do you not care that we are perishing?'" (v. 38b). Their rebuke of the Lord was unfounded in light of the care he had manifested to all, especially his disciples. Certainly he cared! But we must not expect measured rationality from men who think they are about to die.

Perhaps they shook the Master by his shoulder. Whatever they did, they with their plea did what the storm could not do—Jesus was awake! "And he awoke," says Mark, "and rebuked the wind and said to the sea, 'Peace! Be still!' [literally, "Be muzzled!"] And the wind ceased, and there was a great calm" (v. 39). The tense indicates that the wind immediately stopped, and all three Gospels speak of a sudden calm.[5] There was an eerie silence, as if a great hand had brushed away the wind and pressed down the sea. What a way to get their attention! There were undoubtedly some deep gulps. Maybe some of them sat down round-eyed with a "Twilight Zone" expression.

The truth was there to see, though it would take some time, and more miracles, for them to process it: All power belongs to him! Paul would later explain this in his Colossian hymn—he is the *Creator*: "For by him all things were created, in heaven and on earth, visible and invisible, whether thrones or dominions or rulers or authorities" (Colossians 1:16a). All things were created by him. Every speck of cosmic dust in the universe is his creation—everything! He is the *Sustainer*: "And he is before all things, and in him all things hold together" (Colossians 1:17). Scientists spend thousands of hours every year plumbing this mystery. He is the atomic glue of the universe. He is the *Goal*: "[A]ll things were created through him and for him" (Colossians 1:16b). He is Creator, Sustainer, Goal, and Savior of the soul!

If you believe this, you will weather the storms of life. The disciples came to learn it well. In fact, Peter, who was the principal source for John Mark's information in writing this account, would one day encourage Christians to welcome trials as friends because they were sent for the development of one's soul. Peter had learned this "storm theology" firsthand. It was not theory. He had experienced hurricanes of affliction, and he had seen Christ come and say, "Peace! Be still!" He knew where the power was. The storm and the calm were wonderfully instructive, but Jesus' instructions put on the finishing touches.

Learning through Instruction (vv. 40, 41)

Observing their fear, Jesus addressed his disciples in the silence: "'Why are you so afraid? Have you still no faith?' And they were filled with great fear and said to one another, 'Who then is this, that even the wind and the sea obey him?'"

This was food for much subsequent thought and discussion. What kind of faith casts out fear? A faith that believes the Scriptural revelation about the power and love of Christ. Do you believe in his power? Do you believe in his love? This kind of faith, a conquering faith, sees that he is in the boat with us.

The Early Church picked up on Mark's intended symbolism: Christ in a boat with his followers on a stormy lake is a picture of the Church in the midst of the world. Early Christian art often depicted the Church this way in paintings and mosaics. *Christ shares the boat with us.* Because of that, the boat will never sink!

Fear is endemic to the human situation. Perhaps today you are fearful. Perhaps you fear life in general, that you will not be adequate for the challenges that are coming. It is a sort of amorphous fear, but it is real and continual. Maybe you fear some unspoken problem that has no apparent solution. The winds are howling, and no hope is on the horizon.

What should you do? Understand and believe that it is through storms, afflictions, hardships, and challenges that you grow. Without them you would be captive to the terrible tyranny of self. Understand that Christ wants to develop you through the storms ahead. Know that he is completely capable of delivering you with a word. He is the same Christ who calmed the storm, the same Christ who eased the trigger finger of Ira Sankey's executioner. Know that he is in the boat with you. He is in you. Exercise this faith and lay down your fear. For when this faith is active, fear vanishes!

16

Jesus: Lord of the Spirits

MARK 5:1–20

TWO EXTREMES give Satan great satisfaction. Some fall into the trap of disbelief in his reality. Kenneth Woodward, for example, regards the devil as merely a "trivial personification . . . hardly adequate to symbolize the mystery of evil."[1] Some, on the other hand, have an inordinate interest in the devil and his dark world. In the preface to his famous *Screwtape Letters*, C. S. Lewis wrote:

> There are two equal and opposite errors into which our race can fall about the devils. One is to disbelieve in their existence. The other is to believe, and to feel an excessive and unhealthy interest in them. They themselves are equally pleased by both errors and hail a materialist and magician with the same delight.[2]

There is no doubt that people can go overboard in their fascination with the devil and demons. It was not long ago that in the suburbs of one of our major cities a promising renewal took place among a number of professional families—doctors, lawyers, and business executives. It gave birth to a joyous, thriving Bible study. More of their friends came to Christ. Marriages were enriched, families restored, and the church infused with new life. But some of the leadership became overly fascinated with the subject of spiritual warfare and took their eyes off Christ to become self-styled experts in demons and exorcism.

Things were clearly getting out of hand when one night they became convinced there were demons in the dining room chandelier and ended the "Bible study" by dissembling the light fixture so each could take a part of it and bury it in a different part of the city. The crowning embarrassment to the

Christian community came later when one morning some of their children were seen by neighbors running down the street shouting, "The devil is going to get us! The devil is going to get us!" Responding, the neighbors found the group's women in the backyard hacking a rosewood chest to pieces to dispose of supposed demons. The lesson? If Satan cannot pull you down, he will just as happily push you overboard.

As we study 5:1–20, the story of the Gerasene demoniac, we will affirm the Biblical reality of Satan and his host. But in doing so we will refrain from promoting an unhealthy fascination. Our goal is to reveal Satan's purpose and then to demonstrate Jesus' power over evil forces and his ability to heal the harm that they have done.

Verses 1, 2 reveal that Christ's encounter with the demoniac took place the morning following his calming of the great night storm on the Sea of Galilee. "They came to the other side of the sea, to the country of the Gerasenes. And when Jesus had stepped out of the boat, immediately there met him out of the tombs a man with an unclean spirit." Jesus came straight from his confrontation with the storm in nature to confront an equally violent storm in human nature. The region of the Gerasenes, on the other side of the lake from the strictly Jewish area, was a place where Gentiles and Jews comingled, an unsavory place according to Jewish thinking.

Jesus Confronts Demonization (vv. 3–10)

Mark has given us an elaborate and frank picture of the demoniac. The story is pathetic and heart-wrenching, for this was a human being. To begin with, he was "demonized." Our text regularly speaks of him as being "demon-possessed" (vv. 16, 18), but the literal translation is "demonized"—that is, under the influence of one or more evil spirits. Demonization can vary in degree of influence. Here it was extreme.

> And when Jesus had stepped out of the boat, immediately there met him out of the tombs a man with an unclean spirit. He lived among the tombs. And no one could bind him anymore, not even with a chain, for he had often been bound with shackles and chains, but he wrenched the chains apart, and he broke the shackles in pieces. No one had the strength to subdue him. Night and day among the tombs and on the mountains he was always crying out and cutting himself with stones. (vv. 2–5)

Typically, those under the sway of demons descend to filthy living, both physically and morally. It is not incidental that the rise of occultism and Satanism these last few years has been accompanied by increasing drug abuse, pornography, and obscenity.[3] This man lived in "the tombs," rock-hewn caverns furnished with dead men's bones and carpeted with filth and vermin.

The local townspeople had attempted to restrain him, but with terrifying herculean strength he had broken the fetters that bound him. He was uncontrollable and dangerous. Inside, he was totally wretched. At intervals during the night and day he would let out a preternatural howl, then gash himself with jagged rocks in an obvious attempt to drive out the evil spirits. This poor, naked man was a mass of bleeding lacerations, scabs, infections, and scar tissue, living in a delirium of pain and masochistic pleasure.

The man was running wild, naked, unkempt, and ill, and as a result all were against him. Little children fled at his approach. In his lucid moments he surely realized how repulsive and unloved and unwelcome he was. What unutterable misery!

Of course, not all demonization is so blatantly gross. Second Corinthians 11:14, 15 tells us: "And no wonder, for even Satan disguises himself as an angel of light. So it is no surprise if his servants, also, disguise themselves as servants of righteousness." Demonized men and women can appear utterly conventional. They can even be spiritual leaders in the Christian community. I myself have known some whose bondage to evil was uncovered.

However, we must not foolishly think that human beings must be demonized to descend to the degradation of the Gerasene demoniac. Sin is endemic to the human situation: "each person is tempted . . . by his own desire" (James 1:14). As Turgenev said, "I do not know what the heart of a bad man is like, but I know what the heart of a good man is like . . . and it is terrible."

We need the theological wisdom and honesty of the little girl who had a terrific fight with her brother. When her mother came in and pulled her off, she said to her daughter, "Why did you let the devil put it into your heart to pull your brother's hair and kick him in the shins?" The little girl thought for a moment and said, "Well, maybe the devil put it into my head to pull my brother's hair, but kicking his shins was my own idea." We are very capable of being evil all by ourselves!

Nevertheless, demons do drive men and women to the depths of degradation. Why? Because Satan and his minions hate God. They will do anything to attack him. Mankind was created in the image of God (Genesis 1:27) and brings glory to him the more we manifest his image. Satan hates this. Thus, the demonic function is to distort and destroy the image of God in man. As Werner Foerster says:

> . . . in most of the stories of possession, what is at issue is not merely sickness but a destruction and distortion of the divine likeness of man according to creation. The center of personality, the volitional and active ego, is inspired by alien powers which seek to ruin man.[4]

If Tertullian was right that "The glory of God is man fully alive," then it is true that the slaying of man (the distortion of the divine image through sin) is an attack on the glory of God. We must do everything we can, through Jesus Christ and the power of the Holy Spirit, to enhance the image of God in our lives.

Confrontation was inevitable, and "when he saw Jesus from afar, he ran and fell down before him" (v. 6). Jesus and the disciples beached the boat and made it secure, and the next thing they knew they were being charged by a naked, screaming maniac. Surprisingly, he cast himself on his knees in front of Jesus—animalized, filthy, bleeding. Then he "[cried] out with a loud voice." The tense here indicates that he screamed an inarticulate cry before speaking,[5] a preternatural howl. When the scream subsided, the disciples heard this: "What have you to do with me, Jesus, Son of the Most High God? I adjure you by God, do not torment me" (v. 7). In accordance with ancient belief, the reciting of Jesus' title was not a confession of his Deity but a desperate attempt to gain control over him.[6]

Jesus stood firm, addressing the spirit within the man: "'Come out of the man, you unclean spirit!' And Jesus asked him, 'What is your name?' He replied, 'My name is Legion, for we are many.' And he begged him earnestly not to send them out of the country" (vv. 8–10).

It was a chilling admission. A Roman legion consisted of 6,000 foot soldiers, as well as 120 horsemen and technical personnel. To the Jewish mind, "Legion" brought an image of great numbers, efficient organization, and relentless strength. A host of evil spirits leered upon Christ from behind the poor man's wild eyes. It was time for Jesus' power to be seen in a most unforgettable way.

Jesus Conquers Demonization (vv. 11–15)

Mark gave us the details in verses 11–13:

> Now a great herd of pigs was feeding there on the hillside, and they begged him, saying, "Send us to the pigs; let us enter them." So he gave them permission. And the unclean spirits came out and entered the pigs; and the herd, numbering about two thousand, rushed down the steep bank into the sea and drowned in the sea.

The Greek tense graphically pictures the disappearance of pig after pig into the sea. Why did Jesus allow the demons to enter the swine? The presence of two thousand swine indicates big business. It may very well be that the swineherders were compromising Jews who saw a great profit in selling pork (unclean to Jews) to the Gentile market on the eastern side of the lake. If this was so, then Jesus was taking a swipe at their secularization and materialism. In the process, the pigs became vehicles of judgment to the unsuspecting demons who pled to be cast into the swine. The swine stampeded unexpectedly, due to the shock of demonization, blindly charging into the lake to rid themselves of their new guests. Thus the demons were disembodied and, some scholars think, confined to the Abyss to await final judgment.

The dramatic end of the swine was also powerful visual testimony to the ex-demoniac that he had been delivered. For the rest of his life he would tell about this with all the relish of an Eastern storyteller. It would never be forgotten!

The dramatic destruction of the pigs, coupled with what happened to the man, formed a stupendous display of Christ's power, as we see in verses 14, 15: "The herdsmen fled and told it in the city and in the country. And people came to see what it was that had happened. And they came to Jesus and saw the demon-possessed man, the one who had had the legion."

The man was "sitting there" instead of roaming about purposelessly among the tombs as before. Luke says he was "sitting at the feet of Jesus" (Luke 8:35). He was "clothed" instead of naked. (Dr. Luke tells us it had been a long time since he had worn clothing. He was probably dressed in an extra cloak of one of the disciples.) He was "in his right mind." Literally, he was of sound mind, self-controlled. He was smiling at the right times and was alert, laughing, and even devout.

What a testimony to the power of Jesus Christ! He completely blew away evil! Note, first, that his contest with the demons, despite all its seriousness, was almost farcical.[7] With a word, the illegitimate swine were off to hog heaven and the demons were howling their misery in an incorporeal existence.

Second, Jesus displayed incredible healing power. He restored his image in the life of the profoundly disfigured man. The ex-demoniac was now rational, controlled, at peace, and in communion with God. This is utterly amazing when we think of his wretched, loathsome existence. Such transformation is impossible—except for God.

Perhaps this needs to go directly to your heart. You have descended so low in sin and the marks are so profound that you cannot believe you can be made whole. You may have even been or are being "demonized." As you read this message, you are saying, "You are naive. You know nothing of the grip of evil upon me. You cannot feel my hopelessness. If you could, you would not speak so confidently." My answer is that I know my Christ. I have experienced his healing power. And I have *this* testimony in his Word: *He can do it!*

Are you deeply scarred? Do you have filthy habits—perhaps a mouth that is totally out of control, that has said little that is clean in years? Perhaps you are dishonest. It is your way of life. Maybe your scar is sexual, whether heterosexual or homosexual, and you feel you are beyond help. Not so! Jesus who calmed the stormy seas also calms the storm-tossed soul. He can do this with a word.

What was the reaction of the Gerasenes? Did they rejoice? Was there a revival? Hardly!

". . . they were afraid. And those who had seen it described to them what had happened to the demon-possessed man and to the pigs. And they began to beg Jesus to depart from their region" (vv. 15b–17).

There was first the healthy, reflexive fear that came from sensing they were in the presence of the supernatural. What they had seen was an undeniable miracle. The only explanation was God. There were other considerations too—commercial ones. A huge business had been felled in one blow. This Jesus would demand some changes that would cost. The Gerasenes were a practical people and held property very important, as all decent people would. Actually they preferred pigs to people, swine to souls!

> Rabbi, begone! Thy powers
> Bring loss to us and ours.
> Our ways are not as Thine.
> Thou lovest men, we—wine.
> Oh, get you hence, Omnipotence,
> And take this fool of Thine!
> His soul? What care we for his soul?
> What good to us that Thou hast made him whole,
> Since we have lost our swine?[8]

How very modern! What do we value most? The delivered man stood in sharp contrast to his "friends."

> As he was getting into the boat, the man who had been possessed with demons begged him that he might be with him. And he did not permit him but said to him, "Go home to your friends and tell them how much the Lord has done for you, and how he has had mercy on you." And he went away

and began to proclaim in the Decapolis how much Jesus had done for him, and everyone marveled. (vv. 18–20)

Understandably the man pleaded with Jesus to let him go with him. He was conscious of his weaknesses and was filled with grateful love. Who would not want to stay with Jesus? But the Lord turned him down, and this denial became the very avenue for the man's grateful service.

Some years ago an ophthalmologist, just fresh from college, commenced business. Without friends, without money, and without patrons, he became discouraged, until one day he saw a blind man. Looking into his eyes, he said, "Why don't you have your eyesight restored? Come to my office in the morning." The blind man went. When an operation was performed and proved successful, the patient said, "I haven't got a penny in the world. I can't pay you." "Oh, yes," said the doctor, "you can pay me, and I expect you to do so. There is just one thing I want you to do, and it is very easy. Tell everybody you see that you were blind, and tell them who it was that healed you."

That is what the ex-demoniac did. He heralded the news in Decapolis (The Ten Cities), "and everyone marveled."

This story is part of a trilogy of stories about Christ's power. In our last chapter we saw Christ's power over *nature* as he calmed the storm; this time we have seen his power over *evil* in delivering the demonized man; in our next study we will see his power over *death and sickness*. The point is: he can deliver you from anything if you will come to him—not only a miserable past, but present sins—your hatreds, your prejudices, your loathings. He can not only save your soul, but can restore your proper love for your spouse, your parents, your children.

The thing that will stop Jesus is what the Gerasenes did: they sent him away. Tell him to leave you alone and he will—at least for a season. But tell him enough, and there will come a time when it may be too late. Why put it off? Turn to Christ for salvation. Turn to Christ for healing.

17

Jesus' Power over Illness and Death

MARK 5:21–43

THE DISPLAY OF GOD'S POWER in this text involved two contrasting segments of society. On the one hand it focused on an *outcast* woman who had been suffering a disastrous hemorrhage for twelve years. The hemorrhage rendered her ceremonially unclean in Jewish society (Leviticus 15:25–27), which meant that she was a transmitter of uncleanness to all who came in contact with her. If she had been married, she was likely now divorced from her husband. She was ostracized from normal society and debarred from worship in the synagogue and temple. Her desperate situation had driven her to pursue medical help, and she "had suffered much under many physicians" (v. 26).

The Talmud listed no less than eleven cures for this specific illness. Some were potions, but others were mere superstitious folly. For example, in one place it said:

> Take of the gum of Alexandria the weight of a small silver coin; of alum the same; of crocus the same. Let them be bruised together, and given in wine to the Woman that has an issue of blood. If this does not benefit take of Persian onions three pints; boil them in wine, and give her to drink, and say "Arise from thy flux." If this does not cure her, set her in a place where two ways meet, and let her hold a cup of wine in her right hand, and let someone come behind and frighten her, and say, "Arise from thy flux."[1]

In another place, the Talmud recommended that the afflicted woman carry a barley corn that had been taken from the droppings of a white she donkey![2]

Very likely this woman had tried some of these remedies, but to no avail. Mark says she "had spent all that she had, and was no better but rather grew worse" (v. 26). The wretched woman was broke, cut off from home, society, and religion, and in declining health. She was at the bottom!

On the other hand, there was the *prominent* family of Jairus, leader of the synagogue. Many scholars, including William Lane, believe he was the head ruler of the synagogue.[3] If so, he was president of the board of elders and responsible for the conduct of services.[4] He was a man of wealth and prestige. But he was in equally great need: his twelve-year-old daughter lay dying. She had been the joy of his life—his "only daughter," says Luke (8:42)—and now that joy was about to be snuffed out.

Parental love leaves a parent wide open to towering joys and to the deepest sorrow. Some of us have known what it is like to see a convulsing child and wonder if he was going to make it. We would do anything to save our child. Jairus probably thought, "Take my life, not hers." Jairus and his wife were desolate—at the very bottom.

Here we see two desperate representations of society: one rich, the other poor; one accepted, the other outcast; one familial, the other alone—both beyond natural help. For twelve years the girl and the woman had led such different lives, but now adversity had bound their souls unaware together, and they were both to be recipients of God's life-giving power.

These stories tell us how God brings faith into the lives of those he touches and how he causes it to grow. These stories, united around three encounters, can help us complete our faith and know more of God's power.

Christ and Jairus (vv. 21–24)

Mark tells us in verse 21a: "And when Jesus had crossed again in the boat to the other side, a great crowd gathered about him." From what we can tell, Jesus was back at the shores of Capernaum, which he had left a few days before to escape the crowd. In between, he had calmed the stormy sea and delivered the demoniac's stormy soul. Now a vast crowd had swarmed to the shore to greet him and see what else he might do. It was a noisy, jostling, dangerous crowd, just as before. Though enthused, they quieted for a moment when they became aware of someone approaching unexpectedly.

> . . . and he was beside the sea. Then came one of the rulers of the synagogue, Jairus by name, and seeing him, he fell at his feet and implored him earnestly, saying, "My little daughter is at the point of death. Come and lay your hands on her, so that she may be made well and live." (vv. 21b–23)

The crowd stood riveted in silence. Jairus had not been known to be friendly toward Jesus. Jesus was an outsider and had even been accused of heresy by many. His previous use of the synagogue had proved controversial. Moreover, Jairus was *the* leader, not Jesus. Yet now he was coming to Jesus. Even more, he was bowing in humility, pathetically pleading with all he had for his little daughter. This was amazing indeed. But we must not mistakenly think Jairus had become a devotee of Jesus or that he was a man of great faith. The simple fact was, he was desperate. He had heard of Jesus' miracles (maybe had even seen some) and possibly had talked to some who had been healed. He was not sure about Jesus, but Jesus was his only chance.

Jairus was like so many of us in our coming to Christ. It was not his love for Christ that brought him. It was not what he could do for Christ. *It was his need.* It was his desperation and a glimmer of hope. Despair is commonly the prelude to grace.

Jairus' infant faith was going to bring great rewards, especially as we see Christ develop it in the next events. Mark records that Jesus immediately set out with Jairus—no hesitation. Jesus responded to the need. As they went, "a great crowd followed him and thronged about him" (v. 24). It must have been excruciating for Jairus as he and Jesus were slowed down like an ambulance in heavy traffic. There was no ill meant. It was just that no one wanted to miss a thing. Then, to Jairus' dismay, everything came to a sudden halt.

Christ and the Woman (vv. 25–34)

There was another needy person there that day, an unknown woman with a hemorrhage:

> She had heard the reports about Jesus and came up behind him in the crowd and touched his garment. For she said, "If I touch even his garments, I will be made well." And immediately the flow of blood dried up, and she felt in her body that she was healed of her disease. (vv. 27–29)

The poor woman did her best to escape attention. But she, like so many in her day, believed that sometimes the garments or even the shadow of the godly could bring healing. So as Jesus passed by, she momentarily closed her frail hand about the edge of his cloak, or perhaps one of its four tassels (Numbers 15:37–40). In a vivid, technicolor moment that lives in her eternal memory, she felt healing course through her body, and she was whole! Without a word Jesus' power completely healed her in the anonymity of the jostling throng. The same power that he used to make the sea instantly lie flat and to restore the raving demoniac healed her long-standing illness.

Then the world stopped. Jesus realized that his healing power had gone forth (in fact, he willed it) and began asking repeatedly, "Who touched my garments?" despite his disciples' remonstrances that he was surrounded by a pressing crowd. With his penetrating gaze "he looked around to see who had done it" (vv. 30–32). How Jairus must have chafed at this interruption. Precious time was being wasted while the seconds of his little daughter's life were ticking away. "Come on, Jesus. My daughter is dying and you're worried about someone touching you in this crowd!"

Imagine the woman, her heart throbbing with joy and fear, her eyes tearing with emotion. Christ was calling her to stand before the throng, but not for his sake. It was for her and for Jairus and for some within the crowd—and for us. The woman's faith was at its core an ignorant faith. She sought a cure that was essentially magic-secured (touching the edge of his robe). She had no idea that Jesus would know anything about what she did. Her faith was uninformed, presumptuous, and superstitious, but it was *real*, and Christ honored her imperfect faith.

God still does the same thing today. Beginning faith is often uninformed and mixed with many errors about, for example, Christ's person, the Incarnation, the Trinity, the Atonement, grace/works, the Scriptures, etc. However, such foggy understandings are often the beginning of a deep, informed trust in God. We can take courage in this. One does not need to have it all figured out to possess a faith that pleases God. This is why a child can come to Christ. This is why God often saves those who know virtually no theology. This does not minimize deep understanding, which is meant to foster a profound faith. The point is that a faith that pleases God does not belong only to the informed elite.

The woman's faith was not only ignorant but selfish. She wanted health, but she did not especially care about the Healer. This is so typical of beginning faith: we come to him because of some problem, we reach out with a stumbling faith, he touches us, and we go on to love him and trust him with our lives. The drama here is beautifully instructive. Christ was jostled by the multitude, people were shoving and pushing him as he attempted to go to Jairus' home, but he felt the touch of faith. As Augustine said, "Flesh presses, faith touches."

In a sea of a million hands, Christ will see the one that is raised in faith, though it be infantile and imperfect. Are you sensing within you the stirrings of faith? By God's grace, exercise it. It will not go unnoticed by the Master.

The other thing we see in this drama is that Christ instructs real faith, even if it is imperfect. Jesus said to her, "Daughter, your faith has made you well; go in peace, and be healed of your disease" (v. 34). He was tender with her (this is the only recorded instance of Jesus addressing a woman as "daughter"). "Daughter, your faith has made you well"—not your touch, not your superstition, not magic, but your *faith*. Her faith may have been as tiny as a mustard seed, but Jesus saw it, honored it, and developed it. That is why Jesus called her before the multitude.

This poor woman represents humanity—all of us. We are ill. We have spent our resources trying remedies that do not work. Christ comes to us from the cross. We need to touch him by faith. Do not fear that he will not respond. Do not fear that you are too ignorant. Do not fear that you are too selfish. Fear only one thing—that you will let him pass without reaching out in faith to him.

Jairus had not forgotten his daughter, but he had been elevated by Christ. His fledgling faith had been informed by what he had seen, though he cannot have processed very much of it. His faith and his hope for his daughter had risen through the witnessing of this miracle. Now he wanted to get going. But then came the shock!

Christ and the Little Girl (vv. 35–43)

"While he was still speaking, there came from the ruler's house some who said, 'Your daughter is dead. Why trouble the Teacher any further?'" (v. 35).

In a terrible instant the growing flame of Jairus' hope was extinguished. But in equal swiftness it was rekindled and elevated: "But overhearing what they said, Jesus said to the ruler of the synagogue, 'Do not fear, only believe'" (v. 36).

We must not miss what is happening here. Jairus came to Jesus with an uninformed, wishful "belief" that Jesus could heal his daughter. That belief elevated through Jesus' exchange with the woman. But now Christ challenged Jairus not to believe him for a healing, but for a *resurrection*! This is a radical call and a radical development of Jairus' faith. It is one thing to pray for your child's healing from a life-threatening disease. It is quite another to stand over her cold body and pray for immediate resurrection. "Do not fear, only believe," said Jesus. "Be believing, keep on believing!" And Jairus, however stumblingly, did, for he and Jesus and three of the disciples, the "Inner Ring," set out for the leader's home.

Jesus had set the stage for the resurrection of the little girl and the ultimate elevation of faith.

> They came to the house of the ruler of the synagogue, and Jesus saw a
> commotion, people weeping and wailing loudly. And when he had entered,
> he said to them, "Why are you making a commotion and weeping? The
> child is not dead but sleeping." And they laughed at him. But he put them
> all outside and took the child's father and mother and those who were with
> him and went in where the child was. (vv. 38–40)

At the home, the professional mourners were wailing their antiphonal song.
Jesus rebuked them, saying that the girl was "not dead but sleeping." Real
death is the separation of the soul from God, not the body from the soul. In
this sense, her dead body was asleep, and Jesus would bring it back to life.
Then, with some degree of force, Jesus put the mourners and mockers out.

Peter, one of the three apostolic eyewitnesses, was Mark's informant
here. So beautiful was the event that years later he could still hear Jesus'
voice, for he preserved for us the Aramaic phrase Jesus used. Taking the
little girl's hand in his (which by the way was defiled by death, just as the
woman's was by illness), Jesus said, "Talitha cumi" ("Little girl [or more
literally, little lamb], I say to you, arise"). Can you hear the word as it falls
on the girl's cold, dull ears? Can you see her eyes flutter and open wide? The
first thing she saw was the face of Jesus, and then the faces of her mother and
father, and then the three enraptured apostles!

This was a proto-resurrection. The tender words and loving face of
Jesus, along with the surrounding Church, are revelatory of what we will all
one day experience.

What is the Christ like who gives this life? He is all-powerful. He made
the raging sea instantly lay flat with a word. He cast out a legion of evil spirits with another word. He healed the outcast woman without a word. He tenderly raised the little girl. He is understanding, lovingly gentle, and inviting.

If God is speaking to you, but you fear that your faith is too ignorant and
selfish, do not be put off. He knows every heart. Ask him to give you faith,
and then reach out to him with your faltering touch. He will make you whole.
He will heal your uncleanness and give you resurrection-life. Will you do it?

18

Ministering Midst Unbelief

MARK 6:1–13

THE GOSPELS TAKEN TOGETHER reveal that there had been repeated personal pain for Jesus in his early ministry. A year earlier than the events we will be considering, at the beginning of his public ministry, he had suffered intense rejection in his hometown of Nazareth. It started out well enough when, alone on the Sabbath, he stood in his family's synagogue and read verses 1, 2 of chapter 61 of the Isaiah scroll and "all spoke well of him" (Luke 4:22). But then he began to preach confrontationally, and the mood so violently changed that "they rose up and drove him out of the town and brought him to the brow of the hill on which their town was built, so that they could throw him down the cliff" (Luke 4:29). The loving municipality of Nazareth tried to kill their homegrown boy just as he began his ministerial career. That is rejection!

Recently Jesus had undergone further personal humiliation when his own family had attempted to lure him into a place where they could privately restrain him and take him back to Nazareth because they believed, "He [was] out of his mind" (3:21, 31–34). Even though he was God Incarnate, such rejection was devastating because it was so intimate. He was rejected by his blood brothers and the very townspeople whom he had loved and been loved by as a child and a man. Jesus so wanted to minister to them.

So now Mark records another attempt on Jesus' part to reach out to them.[1] It appears, humanly speaking, that his recent miracles in calming the storm, liberating the demoniac, healing the woman, and raising Jairus' daughter had given rise to the personal hope that his hometown and family would be softened to his claims and receive his ministry. So Jesus planned another trip north to Nazareth in an attempt to reach his people, and thus we have the story before us.

In it, we witness the Lord reaching out to an unbelieving people, what happened to him in return, and how he and his disciples responded. There is considerable wisdom here for ministering to an unbelieving world.

The Thwarting of Jesus' Ministry by Unbelief (vv. 1–6)

Jesus was careful about his approach to the hometown crowd, for we read that he took his disciples, his devoted entourage, with him. This unmistakably identified him as a rabbi. In addition, he waited until the Sabbath to publicly minister. He did the traditional, conventional thing so as to give as little offense as possible.

Verses 1–3 describe his approach and the hometown reaction:

> He went away from there and came to his hometown, and his disciples followed him. And on the Sabbath he began to teach in the synagogue, and many who heard him were astonished, saying, "Where did this man get these things? What is the wisdom given to him? How are such mighty works done by his hands? Is not this the carpenter, the son of Mary and brother of James and Joses and Judas and Simon? And are not his sisters here with us?" And they took offense at him.

Their initial reaction was amazement. They were amazed at two things: his "wisdom" and his "mighty works." They knew he was not a schooled rabbi, and yet he spoke with a lucidity and authority beyond any they had ever heard. Tales of his stupendous miracles had been told and retold. They were truly amazed. But as they began to talk among themselves, a malignant contempt crept over their souls. "Isn't this the carpenter? This man is a common laborer—the village handyman! He's not so great. He has a Galilean accent just like us."

The contempt grew: "Is not this . . . the son of Mary?" This was a cheap slam. Sons were always identified by their fathers, not their mothers, even when the father was dead.[2] They were in effect calling his mother a whore and him the illegitimate offspring.[3] These were the people Jesus grew up with. How this must have hurt. Jesus was victim of what all too often is a law of human relationships: familiarity breeds contempt.

During a sabbatical in Cambridge, England, my wife and I had occasion to take a taxi the evening before national elections, and our taxi driver volunteered his unsolicited political views. He said that though he did not like Margaret Thatcher, he was going to vote for her because he respected her. Then he added, "Even though I can't stand her middle-class accent!" Our cabbie, who certainly did not speak Oxbridge English, disdained Margaret

Thatcher for her common accent—it betrayed her origin as a greengrocer's daughter.

There are people who find it personally offensive if someone who was one of them yesterday should have become much more today. Montaigne, the famous French philosopher, politician, and writer, said that at home he was considered just a scribbling country proprietor, in the neighboring town a man of recognized business ability, and farther away a noted author. The greater the distance away, the greater he became.[4]

There may be a reason familiarity breeds contempt: when you get close to others, you see their inconsistencies, foibles, and contradictions. But not so with Jesus. His *ethos* was perfect. The better people knew him, the more they experienced a growing respect. This was (and is) always true with Jesus. This jealous, rung-dropping attitude toward Jesus by his hometown was simply "part of humanity's contempt for itself."[5] As a result of their contempt, "they took offense at him." Knowing his claims, they were faced with the great trilemma of C. S. Lewis: he was either the Lord, a lunatic, or a liar. They chose liar and a demonized one at that.

There is no danger to us of a physical familiarity with Christ that obscures his divinity and authority over us. But there is a danger of familiarity dulling us to the deep spiritual demands of our faith. The sacred words that so easily get tossed around in Christians' conversations can render holy mysteries banal. This desensitizes us to the personal demands of God. "Oh, I know that. It's not so great. It's everyday."

It is not! Christ, our life, is an ongoing miracle. *Incarnation, grace,* and *resurrection* are the most beautiful, mysterious words. We must never let our growing familiarity rob us of the dazzling wonder and demands of our faith.

What was the effect of the hometown rejection of Jesus? Verses 4–6 make it clear:

> And Jesus said to them, "A prophet is not without honor, except in his hometown and among his relatives and in his own household." And he could do no mighty work there, except that he laid his hands on a few sick people and healed them. And he marveled because of their unbelief.

The Scriptures reveal that Jesus was amazed both by faith and unbelief. In one case he was amazed at the great faith of the Gentile Roman soldier, the centurion who urged Jesus to just say the word and his servant would be healed. "When Jesus heard this, he marveled and said to those who followed him, 'Truly, I tell you, with no one in Israel have I found such faith'" (Matthew 8:10). How marvelous it is to amaze God with the extent of one's faith!

But here Christ is astounded at his own people's *lack* of faith. How terrifying it is to amaze God with one's unbelief!

I know some people like that. They have seen the power of God in others' lives—they have seen it in their spouses' life and in family members—and they just blow it off! Everything is neatly psychologized and rationalized. Jesus' personal witness through his Body, the Church, is despised. What darkness—to have made such a cavalier rejection of Christ! Why is this so terrifying? Because such disbelief ties Christ's hands, so to speak, so that healing power, miracles, and grace cease to come. "And he could do no mighty work there" (v. 5). Unbelief hinders God's power.

Let me make it clear: Jesus could not do miracles because he *would* not. Omnipotence is not omnipotence if it is bound by anything but its own will. Jesus was *morally* compelled not to show his power. Matthew makes this clear: "And he did not do many mighty works there, because of their unbelief" (Matthew 13:58). Unbelief freezes the exercise of God's power. I have experienced this as a preacher. I have sometimes preached sermons that I sensed were used by God, and at other times the hearers were ice sculptures.

The eminent Scottish preacher A. J. Gossip once had the more famous Scottish divine Alexander Whyte ask him why he wasn't at the evening service as usual. Gossip replied that he was preaching to a certain congregation. "And how did you get on?" asked Whyte. "I found it very cold," answered Gossip. "Cold," cried Whyte, "cold—I preached there two years ago and I have not got the chill out of my bones yet."[6]

Unbelief robs the church of its power. We can add new programs until we do not have enough hours in the day to administrate them or enough bulletin inserts to advertise them. But without a believing expectancy in Christ and his power, nothing will come of it. "And without faith it is impossible to please him, for whoever would draw near to God must believe that he exists and that he rewards those who seek him" (Hebrews 11:6).

If we want to please God, to know his pleasure and power, we must believe that the God revealed in the Old and New Testaments exists and that he acts equitably in behalf of his children. Do you believe this? Christ was amazed by faith as well as the lack of it. What about us amazes him?

The disciples, which now included the Twelve, sat transfixed in Nazareth's synagogue as they watched the tragic exchange between Jesus and the hometown crowd. They learned some important things. They had seen his astounding displays of power, such as calming the sea. But now they saw that there were situations in which "he could do no mighty work"—times when faith was subverted. To serve him they must believe. They also learned that it would not be easy out there.[7] If Christ found it hard to work, how much more would they? With these lessons in place, Jesus sent them out to the unbelieving world.

The Instructions of Jesus about Ministering to Unbelievers (vv. 7–13)

Verse 7 records the sending: "And he called the twelve and began to send them out two by two, and gave them authority over the unclean spirits."

The Greek for "two by two" was "*duo, duo.*" These were the original "dynamic duos"! Jesus personally gave each pair their authority.[8] The wisdom in this lay in the fact that having two witnesses met the legal requirement for authentic testimony (Numbers 35:30; Deuteronomy 17:6; 19:15). Moreover, this provided mutual encouragement and prayer for ministry. John the Baptist employed the same technique (Luke 7:18, 19), and so did the Early Church (Acts 13:2, 3; 15:39–41; 19:22).

Some of these duos may have been more dynamic than others. The first was a compatible brother combo (Peter and Andrew). The last was the unlikely pairing of Simon the Zealot and Judas Iscariot. Each of them (even Judas!) was given power. The commissioning meant that they were extensions of Christ. "The sent one is as the man who commissioned him" was the common belief, and here it was true.[9] This commissioning was for a specific ministry and for a specific length of time, but the principles were and are *abiding*, as we shall see in the instructions given to them.

Verses 8–11 spell out their instructions for ministering to an unbelieving world. First, regarding provisions, "He charged them to take nothing for their journey except a staff—no bread, no bag, no money in their belts—but to wear sandals and not put on two tunics" (vv. 8, 9).

It was rabbinic law that when a man entered the temple courts, he must put off his staff, shoes, and money girdle. That is, all ordinary things were to be set aside. It may well be that Jesus was thinking of this and that he meant his men to see that the humble homes they would enter were every bit as sacred as the temple courts.[10] However, the overlying reason was so they would be dependent upon Christ for strength. The minimum of provisions was meant to call out the maximum of faith.

Today we are more in danger of having too much baggage than too little. Through this text, Christ warns us today about having too much, as the demise of some evangelical TV empires so sadly illustrates. The Apostolic Church could say: "I have no silver and gold, but what I do have I give to you. In the name of Jesus Christ of Nazareth, rise up and walk!" (Acts 3:6).

Much of the modern church can say neither. Dependence is necessary to meet and evangelize an unbelieving world.

Second, regarding comfort, Christ said, "Whenever you enter a house, stay there until you depart from there" (v. 10). They were not to change lodging for self-comfort. If there was no air-conditioned doghouse or hot tub, they were to stay anyway! They were not going on a pleasure tour. The English Church of the eighteenth and nineteenth centuries was scandalized by fat country parsons who were authorities on hunting dogs and the vintages in their cellars. True Christianity, world-changing Christianity, is not comfortable!

Third, Jesus was specific about their disposition: "And if any place will not receive you and they will not listen to you, when you leave, shake off the dust that is on your feet as a testimony against them" (v. 11).

Does this suggest a bumptious, short-fused, hostile approach to spreading the gospel? Not at all! It was customary for pious Jews who had traveled abroad to carefully shake the dust of alien lands from their feet and clothing. This act dissociated them from the pollution of those pagan lands and the judgment that was to come upon them. The same action by the apostles symbolically declared a hostile village pagan. It was a merciful prophetic act designed to make the people think deeply about their spiritual condition.[11] We surmise that this ceremonial act made a strong impression on the countryside and brought some to grace. Today there are times when the church must warn the world of judgment. There are even times to disassociate ourselves from sinful society.

What happened with the Twelve? "So they went out and proclaimed that people should repent" (v. 12). They heralded the gospel, preaching that the kingdom was at hand and that people must turn from their sin in preparation for it (cf. Matthew 10:7). The result was, "they cast out many demons and anointed with oil many who were sick and healed them" (Mark 6:13).

In short, the Twelve experienced great power in bringing the gospel to an unbelieving world. It was repentance, deliverance, and healing, just as if Christ were physically there. There was a foretaste of what the Church would do through the centuries when it operated in the power of the Holy Spirit.

Later, at the end of his earthly ministry, on the eve of his death, Jesus spoke of this same principle in the most dramatic terms: "Truly, truly, I say to you, whoever believes in me will also do the works that I do; and greater works than these will he do" (John 14:12). How could his followers (us!) do greater things than he did? I have not seen or heard of the church doing greater things than Jesus. Have you? Was Jesus a mistaken prophet?

A true-life incident may help us understand.

During the war in the Pacific, a sailor in a United States submarine was stricken with acute appendicitis. The nearest surgeon was thousands of miles away. Pharmacist Mate Wheller Lipes watched the seaman's temperature rise to 106 degrees. His only hope was an operation. Said Lipes: "I have watched doctors do it. I think I could. What do you say?" The sailor consented. In the wardroom, about the size of a pullman drawing room, the patient was stretched out on a table beneath a floodlight. The mate and assisting officers, dressed in reversed pajama tops, masked their faces with gauze. The crew stood by the diving planes to keep the ship steady; the cook boiled water for sterilizing. A tea strainer served as an antiseptic cone. A broken-handled scalpel was the operating instrument. Alcohol drained from the torpedos was the antiseptic. Bent tablespoons served to keep the muscles open. After cutting through the layers of muscle, the mate took twenty minutes to find the appendix. Two and a half hours later, the last catgut stitch was sewed, just as the last drop of ether gave out. Thirteen days later the patient was back at work.[12]

It was a great thing—greater than any surgeon could ever have done. Not because it was better, but because of Wheller Lipes, the human instrument. A humble pharmacist's mate operated in less than ideal conditions.

In this way the apostles, the church, and we Christians today can do "greater works"—not because they are greater than Jesus' works, but because we are frail human instruments. Knowing who we are, it is amazing he uses us at all!

What are the abiding principles for those who would minister midst unbelief? We must expect difficulties in ministry. "A servant is not greater than his master" (John 15:20). Nevertheless, Christ fights unbelief through those who truly believe. The faithful follower lives in *dependence*. He travels light. He does not seek *comfort* first, but God's pleasure. He is *straightforward* about the condition of the world and the danger facing lost men and women.

19

Death of a Conscience

MARK 6:14–29

WE HAVE IT STRAIGHT from the lips of Christ that "among those born of women there has arisen no one greater than John the Baptist" (Matthew 11:11). That alone ought to cause us to take note of this extraordinary person.

John was a miracle child—not in the sense of a virgin birth, but because he was born to the aged priest Zechariah and his wife, Elizabeth, long after the time it was biologically feasible for them to have children. Their son was also a Nazirite from birth, due to the explicit orders of the angel, Gabriel. As such, his hair was never cut, and he never touched a dead body or drank fermented drink (Numbers 6). John was from childhood uniquely alive to God. As he grew in his knowledge of the Scriptures and God's call upon his life, he took up the garb of an ancient prophet, wearing a rough coat of camel's hair and a leather belt and subsisting in the wilderness on a diet of grasshoppers and wild honey (Matthew 3:4).

Alone in communion with God in the wilderness, John developed an intense morality and sense of righteousness. He was a man of conscience and moral courage. One day he would lose his head, but not his conscience.

When John burst from the wilderness and onto the national scene, he boldly denounced sin and called the people to radical repentance in preparation for the coming Messiah. John quailed before no one, shouting to the insincere Pharisees and Sadducees, "You brood of vipers! Who warned you to flee from the wrath to come?" (Matthew 3:7). It was inevitable that he would collide with the corrupt Herodian dynasty, its present degenerate leader Herod, and that ruler's wife Herodias.

Herodias was the daughter of Herod's half-brother Aristobulus and was thus Herod's *niece*. Further, when he met her in Rome she was the wife of another of his half-brothers, Herod Philip, and therefore his *sister-in-law*. But he nevertheless seduced her and persuaded her to leave Philip to become his wife. This was totally unallowable under Jewish law (Leviticus 18:16; 20:21).

Straight-shooting John the Baptist let them both have it, proclaiming, as verse 18 records, "It is not lawful for you to have your brother's wife." *How could he be so narrow-minded?* the "liberated" royal couple probably thought. So for very *personal* reasons, "Herodias had a grudge against [John]." For obvious *political*[1] reasons Herod arrested John and threw him in the dungeon of the desert fortress-palace of Machaerus on a high ridge down by the Dead Sea.[2] Machaerus was built as the boundary-fortress for southeast Palestine and was surrounded by thick walls and flanked by towers 160 cubits high.[3] Within, Herod had constructed a magnificent palace, and below were dungeons that can still be seen today with their iron hooks, to which John must have been bound.[4] A more desolate, formidable place is difficult to imagine.

Here John the Baptist and Herod Antipas met in perfect antithesis. John was austere and simple; Herod was flamboyant and ornate. John was righteous; Herod was a debauchee. John was a man of immense moral courage; Herod was a man who lived in spineless relativity. John was a man who kept his conscience and lost his head. Herod was a man who took John's head and lost his own conscience. It was the story of the life and death of a conscience—of the death of a soul. This paradigm has been lived out thousands of times in this century as well as in preceding ages. It bears gracious instruction for those who will learn.

Herod: A Stirred Conscience (vv. 19, 20)

As John languished in the dungeons of Machaerus, a totally unexpected and fascinating relationship developed between Herod and him. Verses 19, 20 describe it:

> And Herodias had a grudge against him and wanted to put him to death. But she could not, for Herod feared John, knowing that he was a righteous and holy man, and he kept him safe. When he heard him, he was greatly perplexed, and yet he heard him gladly.

When the gorgeously robed tetrarch met the hair-coated prophet, there was a confrontation. John held nothing back. As a result, though the king held every advantage, he "feared John." Why? Because *goodness is awful*. Or put another way, goodness is terrifying to evil. Someone has said, "The truth will make you free, but first it will make you miserable." King Herod stood at the outside fringes of this reality in uncomfortable fear.

This has been the initial experience of many who have come to Christ. Confronted with righteousness, perhaps through the witness of the Word or a friend, they saw something of their sin and glimpsed the righteousness offered by Christ. At once they were repelled. Then, drawn by that righteousness, they entered a gracious discomfort that eventually brought them to Christ.

While Herod feared, he was also being drawn to Christ. "He was greatly perplexed," says verse 20b, "and yet he heard him gladly." What pleasure could there be for Herod in this? Why would bologna like the meat grinder? Perhaps John was a breath of fresh air amidst the social climbing and scheming intrigues of the palace court. John cared not at all about court etiquette or whether Herod or anyone else liked him. He was an original, his own (and God's) man. Herod could not say that about himself.

This is the way God's saints are. Think of our modern-day equivalents and you will see the same. There is an originality to saintly lives that comes from their unique openness to God's grace. But there is something more here: even the most degraded recognize the moral authority of goodness.

Herod may have liked listening to John because he felt that listening would somehow atone for his condition. Similarly, some today think they are good Christians because they listen to the truth and even give assent to it. Very likely John's preaching elevated Herod's aspiration to better living. Perhaps he made some attempts at self-reformation, did a good deed, pardoned someone, played with his kids, or gave to a beggar. But he was "a double-minded man" (grossly evil, but with some good impulses) and thus "unstable in all his ways" (James 1:8). Whatever the case, he returned again and again to "take it on the chin" from John. In fact, even though he often wanted to kill John (Matthew 14:5), he also protected him from the murderous intents of Herodias. Herod's conscience was being stirred by this man of God. We might even say that his conscience was coming alive. Unfortunately, this was not to be for long.

Herod: A Violated Conscience (vv. 21–25)

Herodias saw her chance: "But an opportunity came when Herod on his birthday gave a banquet for his nobles and military commanders and the leading men of Galilee" (v. 21).

Stag birthday parties were common to the Herodians,[5] and Herodias knew what to expect: a drinking crowd that would become increasingly sensual and nasty as the evening progressed, and increasingly demanding of "male entertainments." From what we can tell, the evening was well along and the crowd was sufficiently under the influence when she made her move, using her teenage daughter Salome.[6] "For when Herodias's daughter came in and danced, she pleased Herod and his guests" (v. 22). Normally this dance would have been by the *hetarai*, the professional court dancers and prostitutes, but Herodias put forth her daughter. Her sensuous, voluptuous dance, unheard of among women of rank, was outrageous. Young Salome pleased Herod and his guests. This was a treat indeed.

Pleased, the tipsy tetrarch shouted, "Ask me for whatever you wish, and I will give it to you" (v. 22). Then he promised her with an oath, consciously aping the style of the king to Queen Esther (Esther 5:3): "Whatever you ask me, I will give you, up to half of my kingdom" (Mark 6:23). You can imagine the cheers from the men: "All right, Herod. Yeah!" They began to wager on what she would ask. A pair of matched stallions? A pearled dress from Rome? The trap was perfectly sprung.

> And she went out and said to her mother, "For what should I ask?" And she said, "The head of John the Baptist." And she came in immediately with haste to the king and asked, saying, "I want you to give me at once the head of John the Baptist . . ."

Then Salome added her own gruesome idea: ". . . on a platter" (vv. 24, 25). Like mother, like daughter! Suddenly Herod was sober, and the room was silent. This is what Salome wanted? That scheming Herodias!

"And the king was exceedingly sorry" (v. 26). He was in genuine grief. This word was used only one other time in the New Testament, to describe Jesus' pain in the Garden of Gethsemane (Mark 14:34). For a moment at least *Herod's conscience was mightily torn!* On the one hand, John was a good man and had done Herod much good; Herodias had deceived him. But then again, what would his friends think? These tribunes would carry news of his reneging back to Rome, and the whole Imperial Court would laugh. He could not have that. There was only one choice.

> And immediately the king sent an executioner with orders to bring John's head. He went and beheaded him in the prison and brought his head on a platter and gave it to the girl, and the girl gave it to her mother. (vv. 27, 28)

What a tragedy! Herod's conscience had begun to live, and he stifled it because of what he feared others would think. Realizing what was at stake, this seems incredible. But there are many today who are doing just the same thing. How many people's consciences have been awakened to eternal things and their own sinful plight, and yet they have buried it all because of what they feared their friends or family or fiancé or spouse or fellow-students would think. Some spend their entire lives basing their decisions on what other people think. There are politicians who for twenty years have not made one decision according to conscience, but rather according to what they think the people want. There are business people who spend their entire day reckoning their decisions with a visualized corporate ladder before them. There are students who sell their souls to escape ridicule. More people than we realize have lost eternity because they feared what others think. Is the opinion of others keeping you from following your own best instincts and the witness of the Holy Spirit? If so, do not be fooled.

Herod: A Calling Conscience (vv. 14–16)

Meanwhile, Jesus' ministry was flourishing. His dramatic miracles had galvanized the attention of the countryside. His disciples had gone out in his power, and they too were healing many and casting out demons. Eventually word about Jesus crept into the palace. Often those in high places are the last to hear of spiritual news. Verses 14–16 tell us what happened:

> King Herod heard of it, for Jesus' name had become known. Some said, "John the Baptist has been raised from the dead. That is why these miraculous powers are at work in him." But others said, "He is Elijah." And others said, "He is a prophet, like one of the prophets of old." But when Herod heard of it, he said, "John, whom I beheaded, has been raised."

The language here is graphic. The "I" is emphatic in the Greek: "I am the one—I did it!" The sense is that he said it again and again. Herod prefigured Lady Macbeth repeatedly washing her hands, crying for the bloody spot to leave.[7]

We all do evil that we naturally put away from our conscience as if it never happened. We refuse to confess it to God or man. Then some hook tossed at random into the sea brings up a memory we mistakenly supposed was lost in the ocean of oblivion.[8] Trivial incidents may awaken the suppressed conscience—a chance word, a sound, a scent, an expression on a face.

Such an event is meant to call us to repentance and forgiveness. That is what Herod's conscience was furtively doing. But there was no repentance, no radical turning, just a futile occult speculation that Jesus was somehow

John *redivivus*, renewed and returned from the dead. Herod was frightened into a paganistic spiritism that did not lead him to Christ.

This often happens to a truth-rejecting people. It is no wonder that much of post-Christian, gospel-rejecting Europe and America today is falling to a diseased spiritism that can never deliver the conscience. Only the gospel of Christ the Messiah offers true life and forgiveness. "Therefore, if anyone is in Christ, he is a new creation. The old has passed away; behold, the new has come" (2 Corinthians 5:17). That includes the conscience. In poor Herod we see the death of a conscience and ultimately the death of a soul.

Herod: A Dead Conscience (Luke 23:6–12)

The last recorded mention of this Herod (Herod Antipas) in Holy Scripture presents a chilling reality. At the end of Jesus' life, our Lord was sent from Pilate to Herod, for the case was under his jurisdiction and he was in town. Of this meeting, Dr. Luke says:

> When Herod saw Jesus, he was very glad, for he had long desired to see him, because he had heard about him, and he was hoping to see some sign done by him. So he questioned him at some length, but he made no answer. The chief priests and the scribes stood by, vehemently accusing him. And Herod with his soldiers treated him with contempt and mocked him. Then, arraying him in splendid clothing, he sent him back to Pilate. (Luke 23:8–11)

Herod merely wanted to see Jesus because he thought Jesus might amuse him. There was no conscience here. There was no trace of healthy fear or spiritual conviction. Herod stood face-to-face with Christ who is absolute righteousness and absolute goodness and saw nothing in him. More terribly, Christ now saw nothing in Herod. It was the death of a soul.

It is possible for a human being to be so jaded that he or she can stand face-to-face with Christ and feel nothing. It is possible to so squash the repeated warnings of conscience that it becomes as if dead. The primary message here is for nonbelievers. If Christ has been moving one's conscience, if he or she realizes personal sin and that Christ is perfect righteousness, then one must believe in him and rest in him.

But there is also a message for the believer. A neglected conscience will suffer progressive desensitization to God so that we do not hear him when he speaks. We need to cultivate our conscience by filling our minds with God's Word and then obeying it. This is an educated conscience that is in balance with the Word of God. Let us pray that God will give us a conscience worthy of our position in him.

20

The Feeding of the
Five Thousand

MARK 6:30–44

HAVING PREACHED NOW for a considerable number of years, and having preached on many of Christ's miracles, I have come to see that the miracles themselves were not only divinely directed, but also the surrounding details. Thus, the setting of the miracles, the participants, and the manner in which the miracles were performed consistently pointed to a greater spiritual revelation than is apparent at first sight.

This is certainly true in the case of the feeding of the five thousand. It teaches far more than Jesus' power, for it presents him as a second Moses who brings salvation to his people. We see this for several reasons. The location of the miracles before a great crowd in "a desolate place" (literally, "a desert place") was parallel to the wilderness in which Moses performed his miracles.[1] Jesus' proclaiming himself the Bread of Heaven corresponded to the manna.[2] The orderliness of the people in seated regimentation before receiving the bread was reminiscent of the Mosaic camp in the wilderness.[3] The provision of food by Jesus symbolized what it symbolized with Moses— God's saving grace in rescuing his people from bondage.[4]

This great miracle of the feeding of the five thousand teaches us how the second Moses, being far greater than Moses, meets the needs of his people and indeed the whole world.

As the situation developed, there was nothing unusual to suggest that something so remarkable would take place that it would be talked and sung about in the coming centuries. It began with some harried disciples. Verses 30–32 tell us:

The apostles returned to Jesus and told him all that they had done and taught. And he said to them, "Come away by yourselves to a desolate place and rest a while." For many were coming and going, and they had no leisure even to eat.

The Twelve had just returned from their special preaching and healing missions, which may have been terminated by news of the death of John the Baptist. Whatever the case, they reported to Jesus the remarkable results. It appears the report did not last too long because they were wonderfully "peopled to death" by those who had seen their great ministry. They did not even have time for a snack! This was wonderful, but draining on the tired men. Ministry/church life can be like that!

> Mary had a little lamb,
> 'Twas given her to keep,
> But then it joined the local Church,
> And died for lack of sleep!

They needed a time away. So Jesus suggested that they retreat to the other side of the lake. Luke tells us that they withdrew to Bethsaida (9:10), near where the Jordan empties into the Sea of Galilee—a solitary, deserted place.[5] There they were going to be refreshed, but not as they expected. It was about four miles direct sailing and about eight miles by foot to that site. When the people saw the familiar sail headed toward Bethsaida, the young and strong began to charge north along the edge of the lake. Hundreds more from the lakeshore villages joined them, calling out to one another in excited gestures, so that finally thousands converged on Bethsaida in noisy, shoving expectation. Perhaps the winds were contrary or the sea was becalmed, thus allowing the crowd's arrival before Jesus and his men.

Jesus' Compassionate Care for Seekers (v. 34)

When he went ashore he saw a great crowd [perhaps seven to eight thousand including women and children], and he had compassion on them, because they were like sheep without a shepherd. And he began to teach them many things.

Here we see the first thing about how the second Moses meets the needs of those who come to him: with "compassion." This was an intense word that had at its root in the ancient Greek the meaning of *vicera*, the stomach. The New Testament had this original sense, but added the idea of tender emotions—"*tender mercy*," sympathetic emotion.[6] Jesus felt this in the pit of his stomach, so deep was his tender compassion. He saw the thousands as shepherdless sheep, defenseless, lost, unable even to feed themselves. "And he began to teach them many things." More exactly, he taught them at great length.[7]

> An old man whose son had been convicted of gross crimes in the army and sentenced to be shot came to plead with Lincoln. As the boy was an only son, the case appealed to Lincoln; but he had just received a telegram from Butler which read: "Mr. President, I beg you not to interfere with the court-martials of this army. You will destroy all discipline in the army."
>
> Lincoln handed the old man the telegram, and he watched the shadow of disappointment and sorrow come over the man's face as he read the message.
>
> He suddenly seized his hand and exclaimed, "By jingo! Butler or no Butler, here goes!"
>
> He wrote out an order and handed it to the father. The man read the order, which was as follows: "Job Smith is not to be shot until further orders from me. Abraham Lincoln."
>
> "Why," said the father, "I thought this was going to be a pardon. You may order him to be shot next week."
>
> "My old friend," said Lincoln, "evidently you do not understand my character. If your son is never shot until an order comes from me, he will live to be as old as Methuselah."[8]

Regardless of whether you are a believer or not, if you cannot imagine that Jesus has tender compassion for you, you simply do not know what he is like. Jesus "felt it," and may we reverently understand that though he is glorified he still does (Hebrews 4:15). Nine times in the New Testament we read of Jesus having this deep compassion. Sometimes it was when he saw someone ill, at other times because of the effects of sin. Jesus has merciful compassion toward you and toward the needy world, just as he did toward the 5,000. Jesus' deep-felt compassion propelled him among the people, and he labored long and intensely among them in self-forgetting ministry.

Jesus' Omnipotent Care for Seekers (vv. 35–41)

As Jesus ministered, the shadows drew up and then began to lengthen eastward. The disciples came to him with an idea.

> And when it grew late, his disciples came to him and said, "This is a desolate place, and the hour is now late. Send them away to go into the surrounding countryside and villages and buy themselves something to eat." (vv. 35, 36)

It was spring, probably mid-April, and the sun set at about 6:00 in Palestine at that time of year. So perhaps it was around 4:00 that the Twelve approached him with their suggestion. They were hungry, and so was the multitude. None, in their haste, had bothered to pack a meal. Thus it would certainly be best to disperse immediately. But Jesus had a better idea: "You give them something to eat" (v. 37a). The "You" is emphatic and imperative. What an astonishing command! They said to him, "Shall we go and buy two hundred denarii worth of bread and give it to them to eat?" (v. 37b).

Their tone was disrespectful. This was a little too much, even if he was the Master. Any bean-counter could see the foolishness of what was being propounded. Jesus pressed them further: "And he said to them, 'How many loaves do you have? Go and see.' And when they had found out, they said, 'Five, and two fish'" (v. 38).

They had only five small barley cakes and two salted sardine-like fish! The impossibility of the situation was firmly established, and all in the apostolic band were witnesses. It is good to understand our limitations and weakness, because then there can be no mistake as to where the power comes from.

The second Moses then miraculously provided for his children in the wilderness:

> Then he commanded them all to sit down in groups on the green grass. So they sat down in groups, by hundreds and by fifties. And taking the five loaves and the two fish he looked up to heaven and said a blessing and broke the loaves and gave them to the disciples to set before the people. And he divided the two fish among them all. (vv. 39–41)

The seating. Jesus' direction that they all sit down in groups on the grass recalls the order of Moses' camp in the wilderness. Interestingly, the almost contemporaneous Qumran documents used these subdivisions to describe how it was thought true Israel would assemble in the desert in the Last Days.[9] The word for "groups, by hundreds and by fifties" literally means "garden plot."[10] This is a beautiful picture of clusters of colorfully clad people sitting in orderly groups like flower beds cut in a green lawn.

The blessing. Jesus was in their midst, and around him were the apostles. Jesus lifted his eyes to Heaven and gave the traditional blessing: "Blessed art thou, O Lord our God, King of the world who brings forth bread from the earth."[11] This was followed by a five-thousand-voiced "Amen."

The miracle of distribution. As Jesus "gave" (imperfect tense) to his disciples, the bread kept multiplying. The Twelve and their cohorts saw it all firsthand. Thousands upon thousands of broken cakes and tiny fish were given out as the apostles walked on the green turf among the seated thousands.

A God who can do that can do anything! Think about it: Jesus with a word multiplied the molecular structure of those humble barley cakes and pickled fish! It is this *creation power* that he brings to our lives. "Therefore, if anyone is in Christ, he is a new creation. The old has passed away; behold, the new has come" (2 Corinthians 5:17).

Nothing is impossible physically or spiritually for Jesus Christ. No one is beyond his redemption. Christian, if you are willing, there is no moral flaw in your life that God cannot heal.

Jesus' Cooperative Care for Seekers (vv. 35–41)

John gave us further details regarding the five barley loaves and two fish in his account. Andrew announced, "There is a boy here who has five barley loaves and two fish" (John 6:9). Andrew had been out checking with the "brown-baggers" and discovered a little boy whose mom had packed him a lunch *and was willing to give it to Christ!*

This gives us some grand insights into participating in God's program. First, we understand that God wants to use us to bring the Bread of Life to a needy world. He can do perfectly well without us if he chooses to do so. He did not need the little boy's bread. He did not need to use his disciples to distribute it. He could have done it all *ex nihilo* and had it float down to the group of fifties and hundreds on pink parachutes. But wonder of wonder, he delights in including us in his work! "Therefore, we are ambassadors for Christ, God making his appeal through us" (2 Corinthians 5:20).

Second, we learn from this that he can use a very small thing if it is committed to him. It has been said: "God must delight in using ordinary people with ordinary gifts because he made so many of us!"

Consider Gideon, an unknown young man from the "least" family in his tribe (his own word). But God only used this ordinary man after he taught him not to depend upon human power (Judges 7). In the New Testament Paul gave voice to the truth that God does not need the extraordinary when he said:

> But he said to me, "My grace is sufficient for you, for my power is made perfect in weakness." Therefore I will boast all the more gladly of my weaknesses, so that the power of Christ may rest upon me. . . . For when I am weak, then I am strong. (2 Corinthians 12:9, 10)

Paul also explained why God delights to use us in our ordinariness and weakness: "But we have this treasure in jars of clay, to show that the surpassing power belongs to God and not to us" (2 Corinthians 4:7).

God uses common clay jars like us so that there will be no mistake as to where the power comes from. We so often think he wants and needs our strengths, and he does use them when they are committed to him. But what about our barley loaves, our ordinariness, our weaknesses? The truth is, these are harder to give to God. If you are eloquent, it is easy to say, "God, here is my eloquence. Take and use it." If you are a good business person, it is simple to say, "God, you can have my administrative ability." But it is another thing to give God your weaknesses. Elisabeth Elliot expresses the idea this way:

> If the only thing you have to offer is a broken heart, you offer a broken heart. So in a time of grief, the recognition that this is material for sacrifice has been a very great strength for me. Realizing that nothing I have, nothing I am will be refused on the part of Christ I simply give it to Him as the little boy gave Jesus his five loaves and two fishes—with the same feeling of the disciples when they said, "What is the good of that for such a crowd?" Naturally in almost anything I offer to Christ, my reaction would be, "What is the good of that?" The point is, the use He makes of it is His blessing.[12]

One final point: Jesus only worked when the loaves were put into his hands in willing consecration. We are only required to bring what we have. Will you give? This is the way the Bread of Life goes out to the world.

Jesus' Complete Care of Seekers (vv. 42–44)

Needless to say, when Jesus fed the multitudes they were completely satisfied: "And they all ate and were satisfied. And they took up twelve baskets full of broken pieces and of the fish. And those who ate the loaves were five thousand men."

His provision was complete, total, and satisfying. We are "the church, which is his body, the fullness of him who fills all in all" (Ephesians 1:22, 23). "For in him the whole fullness of deity dwells bodily, and you have been filled in him" (Colossians 2:9, 10). *That is satisfaction!*

> We taste Thee, O Thou living Bread,
> And long to feast upon Thee still;
> We drink of Thee, the Fountainhead,
> And thirst our souls from Thee to Fill.
>
> Bernard of Clairvaux

John's account of this miracle says that "the Passover, the feast of the Jews, was at hand" (John 6:4). In addition, the mention of "green grass" in 6:39 verifies the season. Thus, many among the crowd were Passover pilgrims. It was just after Israel celebrated its first Passover in the promised land with Joshua that the miraculous manna ceased (Joshua 5:10–12). Now, just before Passover, the Lord miraculously supplied bread. These associations were certainly in Jesus' mind.[13]

The vocabulary in this miracle passage had a purposeful resemblance with that used at the Lord's Table in Mark 14, where many virtually identical terms and phrases were used.[14] John's account of the miracle was followed by Jesus walking on water (John 6:16–24), and then Jesus' Bread of Life Discourse in which Jesus identified himself as the "bread of life . . . the bread that comes down from heaven" (6:25–53, especially vv. 48–50).

The feeding of the five thousand was meant to instruct us as to the meaning of Communion. The cup and the bread tell us that Christ's life was given as an atonement for our sins. It is from his death and resurrection that we have life. But the feeding of the five thousand also tells us that he truly feels for us with *compassionate mercy*; that he *omnipotently provides* for us through his creative power; that he *fully satisfies* us with his bread; and finally that he calls us to give what we have to him, that he might share the Bread of Life with the multitudes who are like sheep without a shepherd.

Love so amazing, so divine, demands my life, my all.

21

The Storms of Life

MARK 6:45–52

JESUS HAD CALMED THE STORMY SEA with a word after the disciples woke him, thinking the boat was going to sink. In our present text, Jesus came to them in another storm and walked to them on the water. These separate events led early Christian artists to picture the Church as the Twelve in a tiny boat on a storm-tossed sea. The picture is typically stylized, with the boat looking like a little tub from which only the disciples' bearded, wide-eyed faces are seen as they look at the turbulent sea ahead. The symbol seems so right and beautiful that many scholars believe St. Mark himself saw this and meant his readers to see it.[1] The ancient church certainly saw it, for the English name *nave*, which describes the main part of the church building where the congregation meets, came from the Latin word for "ship." I want us to keep this symbol before us as we consider Christ's Church in the storms of life and especially his ministry to the Church and the Church's response to him. It is a symbol we can all relate to because life is a voyage with many storms and stresses for every soul. It is a symbol that gives wisdom for navigating through life's uncertain seas.

Jesus' Ministry to the Storm-Tossed Church (vv. 45–48)

The story took place right after the great miracle of the feeding of the five thousand: "Immediately he made his disciples get into the boat and go before him to the other side, to Bethsaida, while he dismissed the crowd" (v. 45). On the surface this seemed a very strange thing for him to do. Rather, it would have seemed to make better sense to keep the disciples around, so they could take advantage of the ministry opportunities that the miracles afforded:

When the people saw the sign that he had done, they said, "This is indeed the Prophet who is to come into the world!" Perceiving then that they were about to come and take him by force to make him king, Jesus withdrew again. (John 6:14, 15)

The crowd had been dangerously fueled with messianic fervor after the feeding, and Jesus wanted to get the disciples out of there lest they fuel the fire even more.[2]

Evidently Jesus had some difficulty getting them into the boat, because the phrase "he made his disciples get into the boat" was a strong expression indicating urgency and pressure. The Twelve were reluctant, like children who are having a good time and do not want to get in the car to go home. Jesus corralled them, insisting that they get in the boat. Then he probably gave the boat a shove. Keep in mind that Jesus *forced* his disciples to go out onto the sea.

Having sent his disciples away and having dismissed the crowd, Jesus "went up on the mountain to pray" (v. 46). Jesus, realizing the multitude's intention to forcefully install him as king, knew that a turning point had come in his ministry. So he fled to the hills for solitude and a time of prayer with his Father.

A famous Old Testament scholar of past years, George Adam Smith, once climbed the Weisshorn above the Zermat Valley in Switzerland with his guide on a stormy day. They made the ascent on the sheltered side, and when they reached the top, exhilarated by the thought of the view before him and the triumph of having attained the summit, but forgetting about the gale, Smith sprang to the top of the peak and was almost blown over the edge by the wind. His guide grabbed him and pulled him down. "On your knees!" he shouted. "You are only safe here on your knees!"[3]

Just so! Though Christ was one with the Father, he lived in constant prayer, and in times of crisis he took to the mountain or the garden—and to his knees. We can reverently say it was the only "safe" place for Christ, and indeed for us. For what did Jesus pray? He prayed he would live out his mission. The Passover, the wilderness, the lost sheep, the manna, the bread, the coming Supper, the crowd's call—all of these things brought afresh to him what was coming. So he prayed. In the context we can be assured he also prayed for the Twelve in regard to the storms he knew were coming that very night.

As Jesus prayed, the almost full Passover moon rose high in the starry sky, illuminating his praying form and dancing brightly on the sea below, where the infant Church was beginning its struggle. This is a picture we ought to hold close to our hearts, for it portrays the spiritual truth regarding our situation right now:

"For there is one God, and there is one mediator between God and men, the man Christ Jesus" (1 Timothy 2:5). "Simon, Simon, behold, Satan demanded to have you, that he might sift you like wheat, but I have prayed for you that your faith may not fail" (Luke 22:31, 32).

In the ultimate heights of Heaven, our resurrected Lord is praying for us on the storm-tossed seas of life. This is present reality!

Down on the shining lake, the tiny church was straggling: "And when evening came, the boat was out on the sea, and he was alone on the land. And he saw that they were making headway painfully, for the wind was against them" (vv. 47, 48a).

The disciples had dutifully set out for their destination, but a wind had come howling from the northeast, driving them out to the middle of the lake. John was specific about this: they were about three to three and a half miles out (John 6:19). The wind had blown them away from their northwest destination, though they had been struggling for seven to eight hours to get there. The sails were down, the oars were out, and they were literally driving[4] at the oars. Despite their strenuous rowing they were not getting closer, but farther away. Peter had probably taken charge. I can see him with his soggy beard flying in the wind, bellowing orders, with the others leering up at him from their oars. They were not in danger so much as they were miserable. Think of the disciples' misery in that open cockpit, with their feet soaking in icy bilge water, straining at their oars for seven to eight hours. Ironically, the disciples were in this miserable trouble because they obeyed Jesus. What a lesson for the Church! Imagine what disobedience could have gotten those men that night: perhaps a full stomach, a warm bed in someone's home, an opportunity to regale their hosts with stories about Jesus.

It was obedience that made them so uncomfortable. It was obedience that accounted for Helen Roseveare's amazing story of persecution during the sixties in Africa. It was obedience that landed Corrie Ten Boom in Ravensbruck. It was obedience that put the four young missionaries through the rigors of captivity in Sudan. In all these cases, their misery was their own fault. If you submit your life to Christ in obedient commitment, you will expose yourself to a variety of sorrows. Your caring, your commitment to Biblical living, will make you vulnerable to things that the uncommitted heart will never experience.

Our passage is the *coup de grace* to Prosperity Theology. "Name it and claim it!" just does not go with this experience. Yet we must say that while obedience will bring contrary winds, it also will bring joy. Never climb a mountain and you will never bruise your shins, but you will never stand on its peak exulting in victory in the alpine air. Never play baseball and you will never strike out, but you will never hit a home run either. Never obey Christ and you may miss some of life's contrary winds, but you will also never know the winds of the Holy Spirit in your sails bearing you on in service and power!

The scene in our text is beautiful and spiritually enlightening: the night, Christ praying, the clear moonlight reflecting like burnished silver on the lake, the sailless mast of the tiny rolling boat, the contrary wind, Christ's children struggling in their *obedience* and making no progress. In such a dilemma it would be so easy to second-guess one's obedience: "Why did he give such ridiculous orders? Does he even care?" But Mark says that Jesus "saw that they were making headway painfully" (v. 48). Did Jesus see with his human eyes those three miles out into the sea, or is this a manifestation of his divinity? We do not know. But the point is clear: Jesus' focus was upon those who were undergoing difficulty on account of their obedience to him.

The human tendency during difficulty is to imagine the face of God with blind eyes. But our text teaches just the opposite. Followers of Christ in the storms are special objects of his omniscient, compassionate care. This ought to bring great comfort to those of us who are experiencing difficulty because of our commitment.

While visiting Cambridge, I was walking by the entrance to Christ's College when I saw a student wearing a black warm-up that had printed on its back in fuchsia-red letters, "Jesus Walks on Water." I thought to myself, "There is a bold witness. Here is a student affirming the supernaturalness of Christ in the midst of the university's naturalistic environment." I almost stopped him to encourage him. Later that afternoon I walked over the Cam by the Midsummer Common, and I saw the same saying painted in the same color on the buttress of the footbridge. While I do not approve of graffiti, I smiled admiringly at this bold witness—until I came to Jesus College boathouse and saw that their colors were black and fuchsia-red. How glad I was that I had not caught up with the student to encourage him!

The "witness" was not to Christ, but was rather an irreverent testimony to the excellence of Jesus College's crew team, university champions. "Jesus walks on water" is a handy figure of speech that many people use to describe exceptional ability. But the eternal fact is: *Jesus really did walk on water.*

Mark tells us that "about the fourth watch of the night he came to them, walking on the sea" and that "he meant to pass by them" (v. 48b).

It was an eerie scene. Alfred Edersheim, author of *The Life and Times of*

Jesus the Messiah, believes that the present tense pictured Christ as steadily moving across the waves. He says: "As it passed onwards over the water, seemingly upborne by the waves as they rose, not disappearing as they fell, but carried on as they rolled, the silver moon laid upon the trembling waters the shadows of the form as it moved long and dark, on their track."[5] It was a chilling sight. Moreover, it was the "fourth watch," about 3:00 a.m. Apparently he came walking after them and then, catching up, turned parallel as if to pass them, so they would recognize him.

Jesus' approach seemed to be a conscious appropriation of the description of God in the Book of Job:

> . . . who alone stretched out the heavens and trampled the waves of the sea; who made the Bear and Orion, the Pleiades and the chambers of the south; who does great things beyond searching out, and marvelous things beyond number. Behold, he passes by me, and I see him not; he moves on, but I do not perceive him. (Job 9:8–11)

The Twelve would understand the spiritual significance of this only later. Jesus came in the darkest part of the night when they had exhausted their energies and were in deepest despair. This is how he often comes to us, that we might learn the futility of our own strength and depend upon him. The very waves that distressed them became a path for his feet—so transcending was his power. His feet upon the waves bespoke his familiarity with their plight. He not only sees, but enters the human struggle.

The Storm-Tossed Church's Response to Jesus (vv. 49–52)

What was the response of the storm-tossed boat, the incipient Church? "[B]ut when they saw him walking on the sea they thought it was a ghost, and cried out, for they all saw him and were terrified. But immediately he spoke to them and said, 'Take heart; it is I. Do not be afraid'" (vv. 49, 50).

The disciples were in abject terror. Exhausted, they literally "cried up"— they screamed. Some perhaps fought the impulse to go over the side. The Greek says they thought he was a *phantasma*, a phantom, a specter.

Why did they not recognize Jesus? Because they were not expecting to see him! Though they had seen the feeding of the five thousand, they had not yet truly come to see the secret of Jesus' person.[6] As our text says in conclusion, "they did not understand about the loaves, but their hearts were hardened" (v. 52).

So it is with us. So often when Christ comes to us in our misery, we reject him because we do not believe he will really come to our aid. We think he can help others, but that he is unaware of *our* situation and powerless. Or in the perverse pathology of our hearts we may even reject his help when it comes because it does not come in the way we expected. Thus we push away the very hand that would heal us.

But our heads clear when we hear him cry out, "Take heart; it is I. Do not be afraid." Then often comes a response of faith. Though Mark does not record it, "probably because Peter didn't want John Mark to record it in this account—remember, Peter is Mark's informant,"[7] St. Matthew tells us about Peter's venture on the water:

> And Peter answered him, "Lord, if it is you, command me to come to you on the water." He said, "Come." So Peter got out of the boat and walked on the water and came to Jesus. But when he saw the wind, he was afraid, and beginning to sink he cried out, "Lord, save me." Jesus immediately reached out his hand and took hold of him, saying to him, "O you of little faith, why did you doubt?" (Matthew 14:28–31)

Peter-bashing is tempting for all of us. He was always opening his mouth to change feet! And besides, he is not around to defend himself. But though we may chuckle at Peter, how many of us have hung a leg over the side and stepped out on the water? Sure, he fell, but he walked first. In fact, he was the only man in history besides Christ who ever did it!

When we see Christ come and meet us in our troubles, we grow stronger—and sometimes we even take a step or two on the water. "I had heard of you by the hearing of the ear, but now my eye sees you" (Job 42:5).

How did the scene end? Mark, John, and Matthew give us the pieces of the puzzle. Mark said: "And he got into the boat with them, and the wind ceased. And they were utterly astounded, for they did not understand about the loaves, but their hearts were hardened" (vv. 51, 52).

John concludes: "Then they were glad to take him into the boat, and immediately the boat was at the land to which they were going" (John 6:21). Did they get there supernaturally? Did they hydroplane across Galilee? No one knows.

Most importantly, Matthew tells us that they worshiped: "And when they got into the boat, the wind ceased. And those in the boat worshiped him, saying, 'Truly you are the Son of God'" (Matthew 14:32, 33). They ascribed to him his proper title. Their lives moved toward deeper commitment.

If we are obedient to Christ, there will be plenty of storms. There will be danger and difficulty and weariness and exposure and anxiety and dread and sadness.[8] We will be open to an index of sorrows and stresses that are unknown to the uncommitted heart. But take cheer: Christ *sees* all and knows when we feel we are alone and fear that no one knows or cares. He *prays* for us, even while we are in the storm. He *comes* to us in the midst of the gale, treading across the problems that afflict us.

This brings great blessing to us. We learn more about Christ as we venture out onto the troubled waters. And we worship as never before.

Jesus calls all of us who are in the boat to follow his course. Today, with eyes wide open, will you commit yourself to sailing where he directs? Will you commit yourself to following him when the inevitable storms come? Those who keep their lives pointed in the direction that Christ dictates will encounter contrary winds. But they will also experience the wind of the Holy Spirit in their sails, bearing them on in power, healing, and blessing to a needy world.

22

Truly Clean

MARK 7:1–23

THE *MISHNAH*, a compilation of Jewish oral laws made at the end of the second century AD, says, "Tradition is a fence around the law."[1] Tradition, as the Jews saw it, protected God's Holy Word and assisted his people in keeping it.

This fencing of the Law probably began well enough, but as the years passed it produced some famous absurdities. For example, in an effort to protect the Sabbath from being broken through inadvertent labor, the devout were given an amazing list of prohibitions—fences. For example, looking in the mirror was forbidden, because if you looked into the mirror on the Sabbath day and saw a gray hair, you might be tempted to pull it out and thus perform work on the Sabbath. You also could not wear your false teeth; if they fell out, you would have to pick them up and you would be working. In regard to carrying a burden, you could not *carry* a handkerchief on the Sabbath, but you could *wear* a handkerchief. That meant if you were upstairs and wanted to take the handkerchief downstairs, you would have to tie it around your neck, walk downstairs, and untie it. Then you could blow your nose downstairs!

The rabbis debated about a man with a wooden leg: if his home caught on fire, could he carry his wooden leg out of the house on the Sabbath? One could spit on the Sabbath, but you had to be careful where. If it landed on the dirt and you scuffed it with your sandal, you would be cultivating the soil and thus performing work.

The Sabbath, of course, was just one concern of those who would fence the Law. The biggest concern of the *Mishnah* (some 186 pages) was "cleannesses," and much of the concern here was with ritual washing.[2] This

159

originally rose from the Biblical command that all priests must wash their hands (Exodus 30:19; 40:12). Though this was only a priestly requirement, all pious Jews began to do it about two hundred years before Christ. By Jesus' day, it was firmly entrenched as a requirement for those who wanted to be "clean."

According to what Mark said in verses 3, 4:

> (For the Pharisees and all the Jews do not eat unless they wash their hands properly, holding to the tradition of the elders, and when they come from the marketplace, they do not eat unless they wash. And there are many other traditions that they observe, such as the washing of cups and pots and copper vessels and dining couches.)

They were washing all the time! Before meals they would pour a little water over their hands, elevating them slightly so the water would run down to the wrist, and then would rub their hands together. Next they would lower their hands and rinse them, allowing the water to run off their fingertips.[3] This was just for meals. If they were returning from a place where they could be defiled, such as the marketplace, they went to greater extremes. Some commentators think the language of our text means they took a bath![4] When it came to washing the dishes, they really got carried away. The later *Mishnah* indicated something of the extremeness of their bent during Jesus' time, for it devoted thirty-five pages to washing "vessels" and other daily implements.[5]

We can see that a huge legal complex developed over this matter of ritual purity. A rabbi who once omitted washing his hands before eating bread was excommunicated. It is also reported that another rabbi who suffered imprisonment under the Romans nearly died because he used his ration of drinking water to ritually wash up![6] During Jesus' day the Scriptural rituals of purity were so fenced and re-fenced that the concept of true inner purity had been trivialized to a system of external washings. Thus, an inevitable earth-shaking collision was set with Jesus, the preacher of true righteousness. In the text considered in this chapter, Jesus set the scribes and Pharisees straight about the nature of real purity and its source. He taught the need for radical purity that could only be supplied by his life.

Jesus' Encounter with the Legalists (vv. 1–13)

The Pharisees' commitment to ritual purity made them extremely pious, self-righteous, and goody-goody—obnoxious. When they saw some of Jesus' disciples eating with "hands that were defiled, that is, unwashed" (v. 2), they could not contain themselves and went on the attack: "And the Pharisees and the scribes asked him, 'Why do your disciples not walk according to the tradition of the elders, but eat with defiled hands?'" (v. 5).

This was an official question from an official delegation from Jerusalem. They were theological "hitmen" sent to nail Jesus. I can see the contempt on their faces and hear the mock politeness of their question. In their questioning they naturally assumed for themselves a superior position and were not ready for what they got in return as Jesus counterattacked.

The first element of Jesus' rejoinder was a devastating quotation from Isaiah 29:13.

> And he said to them, "Well did Isaiah prophesy [literally, beautifully prophesied] of you hypocrites, as it is written,
>
> > 'This people honors me with their lips,
> >   but their heart is far from me;
> > in vain do they worship me,
> >   teaching as doctrines the commandments of men.'
>
> You leave the commandment of God and hold to the tradition of men."
> (vv. 6–8)

The questioners' blood began to rise. Jesus said their legalism was simply "the commandments of men." This was enough to make them choke, because for the Pharisees the oral law was equally binding with the Scriptures.[7] There were some who even believed it was *more* precious and authoritative than Scripture. They were horrified.

Jesus had also called them "hypocrites," playactors, phonies. Worse, he said that while they outwardly honored God, their hearts (the core of their lives) were not even close. This was particularly galling because they were the acknowledged spiritual athletes of the day.

As they recoiled from this, Jesus pressed the attack with an example of their Scripture-bashing:

> And he said to them, "You have a fine way of rejecting the commandment of God in order to establish your tradition! For Moses said, 'Honor your father and your mother'; and, 'Whoever reviles father or mother must surely die.' But you say, 'If a man tells his father or his mother, "Whatever you would have gained from me is Corban"' (that is, given to God)—then you no longer permit him to do anything for his father or mother, thus making void the word of God by your tradition that you have handed down. And many such things you do." (vv. 9–13)

Every Jew understood that the Fifth Commandment (to "honor" one's father and mother) included taking care of them as they aged. But scribal tradition offered a way to get around it, which was simply to say that one's possessions were "Corban" ("given to God"). Even more, tradition made a man keep his Corban vow even if it was spoken rashly in a fit of anger, for tradition said that one's vow to God was more important than keeping the Fifth Commandment.[8]

This amazing twisting of God's Word by people who esteemed it as holy is especially revealing. Those who try to justify themselves by the Law end up modifying it in order to escape its authority. In the same way, those who handle God's Word without submitting to it are in the constant process of conforming it to their self-complacency.

Jesus had the Pharisees reeling, and he was not going to stop. In fact, he made his closing remarks as public as possible. The crowd was probably standing back at a respectful distance as these religious heavyweights engaged Jesus. Now Jesus motioned them closer.

Jesus' Teaching for the Legalists (vv. 14–23)

What Jesus said was revolutionary:

> And he called the people to him again and said to them, "Hear me, all of you, and understand: There is nothing outside a person that by going into him can defile him, but the things that come out of a person are what defile him." (vv. 14, 15)

Dr. Vincent Taylor, author of the esteemed book *The Gospel According to St. Mark*, says: "In laying down the principle that uncleanness comes from within, and not from without, [Jesus' pronouncement] stated a truth, uncommon in contemporary Judaism, which was destined to free Christianity from the bondage of legalism."[9] William Barclay calls this "well-nigh the most revolutionary passage in the New Testament."[10] The radicalness is difficult for us to grasp because we have the full-blown New Testament revelation and are mostly unfamiliar with fastidious legalism.

For the Jews of that day, this was incredible. The Apostle Peter heard Jesus say this with his own ears. Yet, sometime later, after Pentecost, when Peter was well-experienced with preaching the gospel, he still had trouble with thinking he could be defiled by what went in. So acute was his problem that while he was praying on a rooftop in Joppa,

> . . . he became hungry and wanted something to eat, but while they were preparing it, he fell into a trance and saw the heavens opened and some-

thing like a great sheet descending, being let down by its four corners upon the earth. In it were all kinds of animals and reptiles and birds of the air. And there came a voice to him: "Rise, Peter; kill and eat." But Peter said, "By no means, Lord; for I have never eaten anything that is common or unclean." And the voice came to him again a second time, "What God has made clean, do not call common." This happened three times, and the thing was taken up at once to heaven. (Acts 10:10–16)

The vision prompted Peter's ministry to the "unclean" Gentiles. But it was also revelatory of his Hebrew psyche.

This teaching was tough for the Hebrew mind. Verses 14, 15 seem clear enough, but notice in verse 17 that Jesus' disciples just did not get it: "And when he had entered the house and left the people, his disciples asked him about the parable" (v. 17). It wasn't a "parable"—it was straightforward as can be, but their mind-set couldn't receive it. So Jesus spelled it out again, in more depth. First, regarding what goes in:

And he said to them, "Then are you also without understanding? Do you not see that whatever goes into a person from outside cannot defile him, since it enters not his heart but his stomach, and is expelled?" (Thus he declared all foods clean.) (vv. 18, 19)

Second, regarding what comes out:

And he said, "What comes out of a person is what defiles him. For from within, out of the heart of man, come evil thoughts, sexual immorality, theft, murder, adultery, coveting, wickedness, deceit, sensuality, envy, slander, pride, foolishness. All these evil things come from within, and they defile a person." (vv. 20–23)

One summer our air conditioner stopped, and the repairman and I were doing some probing when we inadvertently stirred up a wasps' nest. Have you ever seen angry black wasps rise from their nest like dark helicopters from the hold of a carrier and swarm toward their target? These verses depict an ugly swarm of death and evil rising from within the soul of man.

These are hideous words. They even sound ugly in the Greek. "Evil thoughts" (*dialogismoi hoi kakoi*) are evil reasonings within oneself. "Sexual immorality" (*porneiai*), "theft" (*klepai*—kleptomania), and "murder" (*moikeiai*) are also condemned. "Coveting" (*pleonexai*) is an appetite for what belongs to others. "Wickedness" (*poneriai*) is a heart that is "completely equipped to inflict evil on any man" (Bengel). "Deceit" (*dolos*) means to bait, to deceive people. "Sensuality" (*aselgeia*) involves plunging into moral debauchery in open defiance of public opinion. "Envy" (*opthalmos poneiros*) refers to an evil eye that watches another's possessions. "Slander" (*blasphemia*) can take the form of blasphemy against God or slander against men. "Pride" (*hupereiphania*) is the sin of a self-praising person who has contempt for everyone but himself. "Foolishness" (*aphrosune*) describes a person who is desensitized morally and spiritually.

What a dark, negative litany! It is so grim that some say it is Pauline and was read back into the Gospel by the early Paul-influenced church. But that does not hold water. Twelve of these thirteen words are found in the Septuagint, the Greek Old Testament. They are not Pauline; they are from Jesus' lips.[11] This is how Jesus viewed the heart of man apart from his grace. Jesus himself taught the doctrine of depravity—that every area of life is tainted with sin, which originates in man's heart.

Now for the application. This is radical stuff if you think that humankind is intrinsically good. This is radical news if you think, like Shirley McLaine, that you are good within and like to repeat, or even shout, "I am God, I am God, I am God!"

The inner life, the heart of man, is the problem. Jeremiah 17:9, 10 tells us: "The heart is deceitful above all things, and desperately sick; who can understand it? 'I the LORD search the heart and test the mind.'"

As it is written:

> "None is righteous, no, not one;
>   no one understands;
>   no one seeks for God.
> All have turned aside; together they have become worthless;
>   no one does good,
>   not even one."
> "Their throat is an open grave;
>   they use their tongues to deceive.
> The venom of asps is under their lips."
>   "Their mouth is full of curses and bitterness."
> "Their feet are swift to shed blood;
>   in their paths are ruin and misery,
> and the way of peace they have not known."
>   "There is no fear of God before their eyes." (Romans 3:10–18)

Romans 3:23 adds, "for all have sinned and fall short of the glory of God." In Romans 7:24 Paul said of himself (and we can say the same), "Wretched man that I am! Who will deliver me from this body of death?"

C. S. Lewis refers rightly to our "permanent, and permanently horrified perception of one's natural . . . corruption."

The Pharisees' problem was that though they had the Scriptures, they had a defective theology of man and sin. Because of this, they treated symptoms with their legalism rather than dealing with the root cause. They made the outside of the cup clean but neglected the uncleanness within. Even today some focus on outward conduct to the neglect of the heart.

When my watch broke, for a while I wore a phony Rolex that a friend gave me. It looked like a $3,000 watch on the outside, but inside it was another story. The truth was revealed by the way it ran, for it lost about five minutes a week and kept confusing the calendar date. That watch needed a radical operation!

Some think education and culture can redeem the heart and society. Not so! I once spent six months in a highly cultured environment in Cambridge, England. I listened, with many others, to an evening of Latin Requiems in Kings College Chapel (the most beautiful aesthetic experience I have ever had), Vivaldi in Great St. Mary's, and Shakespeare at the Arts Theatre. But culture apart from Christ is not redemptive. Many of the same people who were transported by the Requiems watched transvestites perform lewd dances the next night at the theatre. Knowing Latin and Greek and listening to chamber music is good (better than most pursuits), but one can do these good things and be a moral Philistine.

A radical change in the human heart is what is needed. Resetting the hands on the clock will not do it. Education and culture will not do it. Social reform (as needed as it may be!) will not do it. Even revolution and a new world order will not make it. *There is only one answer: regeneration.* There is no power in the world that can make a bad heart good. Only the gospel can do that. Jesus said, "Truly, truly, I say to you, unless one is born again he cannot see the kingdom of God" (John 3:3).

There must be a radical new birth. There must be a new heart. "And I will give you a new heart, and a new spirit I will put within you. And I will remove the heart of stone from your flesh and give you a heart of flesh" (Ezekiel 36:26).

There must be a resurrection!

Do you not know that all of us who have been baptized into Christ Jesus were baptized into his death? We were buried therefore with him by baptism into death, in order that, just as Christ was raised from the dead by the glory of the Father, we too might walk in newness of life. (Romans 6:3, 4)

There must be a new creation! "Therefore, if anyone is in Christ, he is a new creation. The old has passed away; behold, the new has come" (2 Corinthians 5:17). "Behold," says Christ, "I am making all things new" (Revelation 21:5).

The gospel is consummately radical: a new birth, a new heart, a new creation, a resurrection! Apart from Christ, the world is desperately lost. It can only be redeemed by the shed blood of Jesus. There is no other way. We can polish the outside. We can educate ourselves. We can do "good" things. But none of these things will really change us. We need Christ's life.

23

A Pleasing Faith

MARK 7:24-30 AND MATTHEW 15:21-28

THE SCRIPTURES RECORD THIS delighted exclamation from the lips of Jesus: "O woman, great is your faith!" (Matthew 15:28), and that compliment warrants our closest attention. Thousands of named and unnamed people appear in Scripture. Only a few are commended for their faith. We find here in our text the faith of a woman whose name is unknown. Spurgeon has remarked that "Our Lord had a very quick eye for spying faith." He added:

> The Lord Jesus was charmed with the fair jewel of this woman's faith, and watching it and delighting in it he resolved to turn it round and set it in other lights, that the various facets of this priceless diamond might each one flash its brilliance and delight his soul.[1]

In our passage, Jesus held the woman's faith up first to the light of his strange silence and then to his apparent rebuff, so the Church down through the ages could see how beautiful her faith was.

This is the story of a *faith that delighted Jesus.* As such, it can be of great help for any person who has not yet come to faith in Christ. It can be of equally great help to the believer who is struggling with his or her faith in difficult circumstances.

When this beautiful encounter is viewed from beginning to end in its context, it is evident it was divinely arranged. Jesus had just come off a huge clash with the scribal establishment over the concept of ritual defilement, arguing that externals do not defile a person, but what is within makes a person unclean (7:1–23, especially v. 15). The encounter over, Jesus withdrew to get some needed rest, but in doing so he purposely journeyed into Gentile territory, which according to the scribal mind was ritually unclean. There he met an "unclean" Syrophoenician woman. Her faith dramatically contrasted with the hardened unbelief of the Pharisees and scribes, and even outshined the understanding of the disciples (cf. 7:17).[2] As such, her faith became a beautiful prophecy of the gospel of Christ that would be proclaimed with power to the Gentile world. Jesus held it up like a jewel in the light for all to see. Mark tells us:

> And from there he arose and went away to the region of Tyre and Sidon. And he entered a house and did not want anyone to know, yet he could not be hidden. But immediately a woman whose little daughter had an unclean spirit heard of him and came and fell down at his feet. Now the woman was a Gentile, a Syrophoenician by birth. And she begged him to cast the demon out of her daughter. (7:24–26)

This was only a short trip of no more than twenty miles into Gentile territory, as the coastal district of Phoenicia was contiguous to Galilee. As was so often the case, Jesus' fame preceded him, even here in Gentile territory. He was sought out by a Syrophoenician woman. Matthew, in his parallel account, adds that she was "a Canaanite woman" (Matthew 15:22). Thus she was a descendant of the ancient race that Israel had attempted to exterminate. But she was also Greek in the sense that she had been Hellenized by the Greek culture and spoke the Greek language. She was a Greek-speaking, pagan Gentile from Tyre. Accordingly, she was despised by the religious establishment and was considered unclean—a "dog," and a female one at that!

The establishment was scandalized by any rabbi having conversation with such a person. In fact, there was at this time a strict sect called "The Bruised and Bleeding Pharisees" because every time they saw a woman they covered their eyes and thus bumped into whatever happened to be about.[3] Their bruises were the pious marks of their exalted sexual ethics, they thought. Jesus' dealings with this woman would get notorious press from the establishment.

The barrier here was great, and it went both ways. Greek women were socially savaged by their own pagan culture, which made this woman's approach to Jesus even more remarkable. But she had great need: her daughter was afflicted with a demon. Perhaps the affliction was like that of the boy mentioned later by Mark in 9:17ff. If so, it had wrought terrible havoc to the girl's young body. She was being progressively scarred and even maimed. Think how you would feel if she were your daughter. What would you do? The mother was desperate and at the end of herself. She had heard of Jesus, perhaps through the testimony of a merchant who had seen him work miracles. She now *believed* that Jesus was her only hope—and that he *could* and *would* heal her daughter. She came in faith, and Jesus knew it. As Jesus drew her remarkable faith out, the first thing we see is that it was a *persistent* faith.

The Woman's Persistent Faith (Mark 7:27, 28; Matthew 15:23–25)

Mark tells us that she "came and fell down at his feet" (v. 25) and that "she begged him to cast the demon out of her daughter" (v. 26). The tense here means that she did not beg just once, but kept on begging. She would not be denied. Matthew dramatized her persistence: "[A] Canaanite woman from that region came out and was crying, 'Have mercy on me, O Lord, Son of David; my daughter is severely oppressed by a demon'" (Matthew 15:22). She was not only persistent but noisy. Jesus' messianic title had come her way, so she kept repeating, "Have mercy on me, O Lord, Son of David." She did not have a Jew's knowledge of Christ, but the term sounded good to her, and she repeated it over and over.

Knowing the heart of Jesus as we do, his response was amazing, for it was *absolute indifferent silence* (Matthew 15:23a). We rightly say that the opposite of love is not hatred but indifference. Indifference says, "I care nothing about what happens to you." That is what Jesus appeared to be communicating to the woman. Luther said, "Now he is as silent as a stone,"[4] and he was! Can any of us imagine treating someone who is pleading at our feet with cold silence?

Actually Jesus was not being indifferent. Earlier on the stormy Sea of Galilee, "When Jesus lay silent and asleep in the ship, He was more kind and His arm more near to help and more certain than the anxious cry of the doubting disciples suggests."[5] Jesus' silence was the silence of love. By it he would elevate the woman's awareness of her own faith, holding it up for the Church forever to see.

Remarkably, the woman was not silenced by Jesus' silence, nor by the disciples' compassionless annoyance: "Send her away, for she is crying out after us" (Matthew 15:23). Peter probably scowled, quick-tempered John got impatient, and Andrew and Philip and the rest thought her rude and presumptuous. What rejection. But the woman thought about her daughter, and remembered what she knew about the Lord, and persisted.

She even persisted when Jesus himself seemed to speak words of rejection: "I was sent only to the lost sheep of the house of Israel" (Matthew 15:24). First his silence, then this. But not even his suggestion of Jewish exclusiveness could defer her. "Lord, help me!" (Matthew 15:25). She dropped his messianic title and simply cried for help.

The poor woman did not know it, but Jesus Christ, the Creator, Sustainer, and Goal of the universe, was completely taken with her great faith. And here, for reasons we shall see, I believe his tone radically changed. There is no way we can hear the tone and cadence of his voice or see the sparkle of his eye or his playful smile, but I believe it was all there. "And he said to her, 'Let the children be fed first, for it is not right to take the children's bread and throw it to the dogs'" (7:27). The softening in Jesus' tone is seen in the word he used for "dogs": *kunaria*, which referred to household dogs rather than the despised scavenger dogs of the streets.[6] These house pets would find a nice place under the table and wait for what fell or was surreptitiously slipped to them under the table.

The dear woman sensed where Christ was going: "But she answered him, 'Yes, Lord; yet even the dogs under the table eat the children's crumbs'" (7:28). She made Jesus' response her *ad hominem* argument: "Yes, I am a little dog, so I get some of the children of Israel's crumbs." Luther said, "She catches Christ with His own words."[7] She did so because he wanted her to trap him. What a bright persistence of faith!

This is something of what Jesus commended when he said, "From the days of John the Baptist until now the kingdom of heaven has suffered violence, and the violent take it by force" (Matthew 11:12). The kingdom of heaven is for those, like this woman, who are willing to spend untiring energy in pursuit of spiritual things. They are persistent. It is for those like the paralytic's friends who, when they could not get him through the crowd, climbed onto the roof and tore through eighteen inches of sod and branches, lowering him to Christ's feet (Mark 2:1–12). Jesus exults in persistent faith like that of the woman who kept returning to the judge pleading her case, until the judge gave in, saying, "Though I neither fear God nor respect man, yet because this widow keeps bothering me, I will give her justice, so that she will not beat me down by her continual coming" (Luke 18:4, 5). Jesus desires such faith.

The Virgin Mary put it perfectly in her *Magnificat*: "He has filled the hungry with good things, and the rich he has sent away empty" (Luke 1:53). The Lord celebrates a hungry faith, a desperate faith, a violent faith—one that persists.

Do we, do I, do you persistently and passionately pray for anything? We must understand that this is what the Lord wants from every follower. "The prayer of a righteous person has great power as it is working" (James 5:16). The woman's faith was great because it was persistent; it was also great because of its humility.

The Woman's Humble Faith (Mark 7:25, 27, 28)

We would be irresponsible if we left anyone with the impression that the woman's persistence *earned* Christ's ear and then *earned* his healing power. Nothing could be further from the truth! Her persistence was only a demonstration that she had faith. Our Lord wanted us to see the works that resulted from that authentic faith.

The woman was light-years away from supposing that she merited any help from God. May I say seriously, from the context of the passage, that she knew she was a "dog." She knew there was no merit in her that would win Christ's help. She was a Gentile, not a child of the household. The bottom line is: she depended upon Christ's goodness and not her own. It was all of grace. "These with a hungry heart and a broken spirit are the favorites of God."[8] David understood this: "The sacrifices of God are a broken spirit; a broken and contrite heart, O God, you will not despise" (Psalm 51:17). Christ promoted the same when he said, "Blessed are the poor in spirit, for theirs is the kingdom of heaven" (Matthew 5:3), and "Blessed are those who hunger and thirst for righteousness, for they shall be satisfied" (Matthew 5:6).

The Woman's Trusting Faith (Mark 7:27, 28)

One final thing: the woman's faith was great because she took Christ at his word. "Lord, if you say I am a little dog, I am. But that means I have a Master, and that is you. It means I am a humble part of the Household and that I can claim the crumbs." For this, she became part of the fulfillment of Christ's prophetic word recorded in Matthew 8:11—"I tell you, many will come from east and west and recline at table with Abraham, Isaac, and Jacob in the kingdom of heaven."

The writer of Hebrews tell us: "And without faith it is impossible to please him, for whoever would draw near to God must believe that he exists and that he rewards those who seek him" (Hebrews 11:6). She believed that God is, and thus she earnestly sought him, and thus she pleased him.

Her faith was humble: "Nothing in my hand I bring, solely to the cross I cling." It was a faith that believed his word. It was a faith that persisted.

What was the result? Christ's healing power. As Mark says: "He said to her, 'For this statement you may go your way; the demon has left your daughter'" (7:29). Her dear little daughter was completely restored. What a celebration there was in heathen Tyre that evening when she returned to her calm and resting child. In addition there was Christ's eternal commendation, the bounding expression of his delight: "O woman, great is your faith!" (Matthew 15:28).

The Syrophoenician woman came to Jesus on the other side of the cross. She did not have the ultimate revelation of God's love and power toward us. But we do: "For God so loved the world, that he gave his only Son, that whoever believes in him should not perish but have eternal life" (John 3:16). Like the woman, you may not have had all the advantages of being raised in the household of faith. Then again maybe you have. But like her, the word has come to you that Christ can meet your needs. He can heal your heart.

What is required? First, that you believe. Second, that you approach humbly. "Blessed are the meek, for they shall inherit the earth" (Matthew 5:5). Third, that you come to him, just as the woman did. Jesus said, "Come to me, all who labor and are heavy laden, and I will give you rest" (Matthew 11:28).

24

Modeling Ministry

MARK 7:31–37

WHEN JESUS RETURNED to the region of Decapolis, he was faced with a man in bondage to a terrible physical handicap. The man was deaf and almost completely mute. Since he could hardly talk, we surmise that his condition was not due to a birth defect. Sometime in early childhood he had probably lost his hearing from illness or trauma.

The handicap was indeed terrible, especially in ancient times. If we were given the choice between blindness and deafness, the idea of losing our hearing does not seem nearly as debilitating as losing our vision. But medical authorities, and the deaf themselves, tell us otherwise. Terrible as blindness is, the blind do not suffer the social pain and stigma experienced by the deaf—the gawking, impatient stares of those who are not aware of one's condition. There is also the humiliation of being thought stupid because one cannot understand or speak.

In this case the poor man could not ask questions, could not hear explanations, and undoubtedly could not read. Even the truth of the Scriptures was hidden from him. Moreover, there were probably many who attributed his condition to demonization. His situation, to say the least, was miserable and hopeless. He did, however, have some who loved him, and these, having heard about Jesus previously healing the Gadarene maniac, brought him to Jesus when the Savior returned. The poor man and his friends were not to be disappointed.

Mark was remarkably detailed in describing the unique process of the man's healing. Though the account is brief (just verses 33, 34), it vividly describes an elaborate procedure. Jesus took "him aside from the crowd privately" to avoid the embarrassment that had been the man's lot in life.

Only the disciples would be witnesses. "He put [or better, *thrust*] his fingers into his ears,[1] and after spitting touched his tongue." Next, he "[looked] up to heaven." Following this, he exhaled a deep sigh. Finally, he "said to him, 'Ephphatha,' that is, 'Be opened.'"

Why did Jesus follow these steps, and why did Mark record them? First, and most obvious, because of the nature of the man's handicap. Jesus thrust his fingers into the man's ears as a sign language that he was going to heal him. His action of spitting (probably on the tips of his fingers) and then wetting the man's tongue was to indicate that he would soon be articulate. Jesus looked upward to tell him from where the power was to come. His sigh, though inaudible to the man, visibly communicated to him that Jesus was moved by the man's condition, that he cared. "Ephphatha" was the first sound to penetrate the man's ears in years!

Obviously, Jesus accommodated his procedure to the deaf man's condition. In doing so, he also focused attention upon himself as the instrument and source of healing. There was no magic here. The healing was divine. There is another far-reaching reason for the Lord's elaborate procedure: *to give us an example of what is necessary to reach a lost world.*

Since the healing of the Syrophoenician woman, Jesus had been ministering in Gentile territory. Many believe this was for as long as eight months.[2] Almost one-third of his total three years of ministry was devoted to Gentiles! Alfred Edersheim, the great scholar on the life of Christ, notes that this and a similar elaborate healing (8:22–26) took place at the end of this Gentile emphasis, and that this elaborateness was due to the fact that the subjects were Gentiles living in the degradation of paganism.[3]

If Edersheim is right, and I think he is, Jesus' procedure in ministering here provides a beautiful model for how we ought to reach out to our lost, pagan world. His *look*, his *sigh*, his *touch*, and his *word* are helpful symbols for the Church's attempts to rescue needy humanity. My hope is that we will take Jesus' model to heart as we examine our text, so that his power will flow similarly through us.[4]

Christ's Look (v. 34)

When Mark tells us that he "[looked] up to heaven," we understand that the look was a visible indication of Jesus' life of prayerful communion and dependence upon the Father. (The only time in all eternity in which it was broken was when the Son became our sin-bearer and cried out, "My God, my God, why have you forsaken me?") Jesus was in constant communion with the Father, whether he was speaking to him or not. To be sure, he got away for special periods of unencumbered prayer, but he was also *always* in prayer. This was and is our Jesus!

Jesus' look up to Heaven in the midst of busy hands-on ministry is a powerful message to those of us who lead active Christian lives. We can be so given to meeting the needs of our children that we do not take time to pray for them, and thus deny them our greatest service. We can be so intent on glorifying God at work by doing a good job that we do not glorify him in our hearts. We can be so busy doing good things for our neighbors, community, and church that the upward look is little more than a nervous nod, with no real prayer at all. As we minister, we can come to imagine that our service for him is more important than our communion with and love of him. So when there are "not enough hours in a day," we give ourselves to prayerless counseling and preaching, thinking "God will understand."

If I have any sense of where the Christian culture is today, I would say our Number One sin is not sensuality or materialism (though they are close behind) but *prayerlessness*. So often when busy, caring Christians get together and "let their hair down," they talk about the trouble with their prayer lives. Each of us needs to seriously consider the following applications of this matter:

No matter how busy, we should regularly be exposing our souls to God in adoring worship, that he might be glorified and his life burned into ours. If we are not doing this, we are sinning.

We should be praying for our inner life: that our character will have grace to match our profession; that we will walk our talk.

We should be praying *in detail* for every member of our family.

We should regularly pray for our neighbors.

We should have a list of missionaries and systematically pray for them.

We should be praying daily for our churches—going beyond generalization—naming names, programs, and needs.

Prayerlessness is the fundamental sin of the busy Christian. Because of it, much of today's Christian work accomplishes little for the kingdom. "If we would give sight to the blind, we must ourselves be gazing into heaven."[5] All of us are busy. If we pause for even a tenth of a second at a traffic light turned green, the whole world honks at us. But we always manage time for the things we really want to do.

Christ's Sigh (v. 34)

Hugh Rudd, former CBS newsman, came home late one night after putting on the CBS late news and was let off by a taxi at his home on the East Side of New York. As he stepped away from the cab, four scruffy-looking youths surrounded him and said, "Give us your money." He did. Then one of them took a pistol and beat him over the head. Rudd fell into the gutter, just a few steps from home. For seven hours on the fashionable East Side of New York, he lay on that street. He was semi-conscious. A whole parade of people went by: milkmen, people coming home from parties, people going out to work on an early shift. As they passed by him, he kept saying, "Help me, help me." They would shrug and look the other way. His wife, worried sick, finally called the police. They came and found him at seven the next morning.[6]

Compassion and caring were not in vogue in Bible times, and they are not today. But here Mark's record of Jesus' sigh brings a healing balm, for it is the breath of compassion. Jesus' sigh comes from his deep feeling for the poor man, even though he knew exactly what he was going to do for him in the next few seconds.

This is the way Jesus always was. At Lazarus' tomb, "When Jesus saw her weeping, and the Jews who had come with her also weeping, he was deeply moved in his spirit and greatly troubled" (John 11:33). The word for "deeply moved in his spirit" came from the ancient Greek word that described a horse snorting. Here it described our Lord's involuntary gasp. E. V. Rieu translates it: "He gave way to such distress of spirit as made His body tremble." And then, as we know, he went on to weep for them. Such compassion! Perhaps here, when he got the poor deaf and mute man alone, when he saw closely the devastation, his shyness, his crumpled ego, hurt upon hurt upon hurt, it was then that he sighed in compassion. Perhaps the sigh was also for what lay behind it: man's sin, the fallen creation, the devil's world. "There is no place where earth's sorrows are more felt than in heaven" (Faber).

What our text is teaching is that Christ's compassion was part of his healing process for the world. Those of us who desire to minister Christ's healing must share his compassion for hurting humanity. There is a hurting world out there, with thousands who are hurting every bit as much, or more, than the deaf man. We need to come to them with a deep sigh.

George Eliot wrote: "If we had a keen vision and feeling of all ordinary human life, it would be like hearing the grass grow and the squirrel's heart beat, and we should die of that roar which lies on the other side of silence."[7] None of us, as believers, are meant to go through life with dry eyes. We need to be like Jeremiah and Jesus: "Oh that my head were waters, and my eyes a fountain of tears" (Jeremiah 9:1).

Hugh Rudd's world is the real world. But Christ's sigh is just as real. When the Church sighs like him, in genuine compassion, power comes to the hurt. Jesus said, "Blessed are those who mourn"—"Approved are those who mourn over their sins and the sins of the world." And, "Blessed are the merciful."—"Approved are those with a merciful compassionate spirit" (Matthew 5:4, 7).

Are we compassionate people? Have we ever wept over the deformed? Have we ever sorrowed over a life distorted by sin? Have we done anything about it? Does the six o'clock news sometimes make us cry? Do we sigh over divorce? Poverty? Abortion? Broken relationships? Are we tender and caring? If we are deficient here, we need to pray for help.

It is significant, I believe, that Jesus looked to Heaven and then sighed. When we look to Heaven, we see the world through the Father's eyes.

Christ's Touch (v. 33)

Our Lord never recoiled from laying his hand on sinful humanity. On one occasion, a man "full of leprosy" (Luke 5:12)—loathsome, lion-like, grotesque—came and lay prostrate at Jesus' feet. Jesus looked on him as he had never before been viewed. According to Mark's Gospel, Christ was "moved with pity" (1:41), indicating that Jesus was so touched by what he saw that he touched him (cf. Matthew 8:3). Perhaps it had been twenty or even thirty years since the leper had been touched by a non-leprous hand or had received a gentle touch. Now he received the touch of Christ. As Bishop Westcott says, the word "expresses more than superficial contact."[8] It is often translated "to take hold of." Jesus, at the very least, placed his hand firmly on the leper.

How beautiful Christ is. He could have just spoken a word or simply willed it. But he chose to lay his hand on the poor man in front of the multitude. The onlookers and the disciples were shocked. Jesus was now ceremonially unclean! To their way of thinking, he might catch the disease. Why did Jesus do it? There are perhaps several reasons. Reaching out, of course, was the instinct of his loving heart. But he also wanted to clear away any fears the man had. He wanted the leper to feel his willingness and sympathy. The touch said, "I'm with you. I understand."

Those were the human reasons, but there was an overshadowing theological reason. The touch of his pure hand on the rotting leper is a parable of the Incarnation. Jesus in the Incarnation took on flesh, became sin for us, and thus gave us his purity. "For our sake he [God] made him to be sin who knew no sin, so that in him we might become the righteousness of God" (2 Corinthians 5:21). Jesus lay hold of our flesh. He touched us and healed us.[9] Here Jesus' handling of the deaf man, his fingers thrust in his ears, his spittle anointing the man's flopping tongue, was instinctive and natural. *True compassion doesn't just feel. It reaches out.*

If we are to minister, there must be touch. Historically, this is where the established Church in England blew it. John Wesley came with a heart for the poor, those outside the Church whose needs were not being met. The Church was so repulsed by Wesley and his methods that he had to take to the fields. Almost two hundred years later, General Booth found a similar rejection by the Church and society in general as he ministered to the urban poor in places like Spittalfields and Shoreditch in London. As a result, he was forced to found the Salvation Army.

There is very little effect from Christian practice or evangelism that shies away from contact with sin and pain. The surest way to calcify the heart is to fail to do something when we feel compassion. Coldness and hypocrisy are the result. The ring of truth is noticeably absent from such lives.[10]

The hands-on touch is absolutely necessary to healthy, authentic Christianity. While we must send missionaries, and we must give money to the Church and to missions, we cannot touch by proxy. When faced with a need right before him, Jesus did not ask Peter to be his surrogate hands. Neither did he throw money at the need, thinking that that would fix things. The question for us is, have we been reaching out to others, touching them in their misery? Are we giving time to listen to the needs of others? Have we been willing to be uncomfortable to help others? Do we ever run the danger of getting dirty in the process? This is what made Francis Schaeffer what he was. He was brilliant as we all know. He wrote about theology, and he wrote about compassion. But the genius of his life lay in his touch.

In the summer of 1988 Barbara and I visited a friend who spoke of his friendship with Dr. Schaeffer and the man's touch. Once, my friend remembers, Schaeffer had in tow a successful architect who had "dropped out" during the disillusionment of the sixties. He had not yet come to Christ, and he told my friend, "I don't know if what Francis Schaeffer is telling me about Christianity is true or not. But I do know this: *that man loves me.*" This was Christ's touch through Francis Schaeffer. Later the architect became a believer.

Let us bring it all together: the *look*, the *sigh*, the *touch*, and the *word*. God's Word is enough. It can do it alone. But he has chosen to minister through people who pray, who are compassionate, and who are willing to get their hands dirty. This is Jesus' lesson to us who would reach our pagan world. Jesus was in profound communion with God. He had exhaled a sigh of deep compassion over the man. His hands, his very saliva, had anointed the man, and then he spoke: "'Ephphatha,' that is, 'Be opened.'" Those words sailed through the ears of the man and into his brain. His tongue was loosened, and he began to speak and keep on speaking (as the Greek tense indicates).

This was an explosive, spectacular healing, and Jesus could not get them to contain themselves:

> And Jesus charged them to tell no one. But the more he charged them, the more zealously they proclaimed it. And they were astonished beyond measure, saying, "He has done all things well. He even makes the deaf hear and the mute speak." (vv. 36, 37)

Great glory went up to God again and again in Decapolis. It was a day to be remembered.

This is what we need if we are to reach our pagan, secular world for Christ: an upward look of prayer, a heartfelt sigh of compassion, a loving touch upon the hurting, and a bold pronouncement of the good news. Then healing will come to our homes, our neighborhoods, our churches, and our world!

25

Nurturing Spiritual Understanding

MARK 8:1–21

YOU MAY RECALL that just five chapters back we studied the feeding of the five thousand (6:30–44). Now we come to the feeding of the four thousand, an almost identical miracle. Because of the obvious similarities between the two, critics have outdone themselves in attempting to prove that Mark is really explaining the same event twice. The main argument is that the disciples' dialogue regarding where they were going to get enough food to feed the four thousand (v. 4) does not make any sense if they have already seen Jesus previously feed five thousand. In the words of one critic: "the stupid repetition of the question is psychologically impossible!"[1]

In this, the negative critics are absolutely wrong. In the feeding of the five thousand the disciples expressed their skepticism at the possibility of providing food for the multitude (6:37, 38; John 6:5–8). With the four thousand they simply confessed their powerlessness to do anything, and left the solution to Jesus. William Lane rightly says: "It would have been presumptuous for the disciples to have assumed that Jesus would, as a matter of course, multiply a few loaves as he had done on an earlier occasion."[2] *The disciples' answer was psychologically reasonable.*

The feedings of the five thousand and the four thousand are separate accounts that vary greatly in detail. The five thousand were with Jesus for only one day, but the four thouand were with him three days. When Jesus fed the five thousand, he ordered them to sit down in ordered groups on the green grass. With the four thousand, there was no green grass. Jesus offered one prayer of "thanks" for the food for the five thousand, but with the four thousand there were two prayers. In the first miracle Jesus utilized five loaves and two fish. Here he used seven loaves and a few small fish. In cleaning up after the first miracle, they picked up twelve small baskets of bread. After the second, there were seven large hamper-like baskets of remnants. Even more telling, in verse 19 of our text Jesus referred to the previous miracle as distinct.

Finally, and conclusively in my mind, the miracles were done for two opposite groups of people. The five thousand were exclusively Jews, but the four thousand were fed in the Decapolis, a predominantly Gentile area. This was a whole new audience that needed to be exposed to this miracle and its implications. What is more, this repetition of such an instructive miracle for them would help the disciples learn. In other words, this was good teaching technique on Jesus' part. "Repetition is the mother of learning," we say. The disciples had learned something from the first miracle, but there was so much more for them to learn from Jesus' multiplication of the loaves.

This is really what our text is all about. Mark wants us to see how Jesus longed for his disciples to grow in spiritual understanding, and to nurture and maintain it. Study of this passage enhances our own spiritual perception.

Jesus' Self-Revelation (vv. 1–10)

There are at least three things Christ wanted his disciples (and us) to see in these miracles. First, he wanted them to understand that he is the Bread of Life. As the second Moses, Christ consciously paralleled himself with their ancient father. It was through Moses that God announced he was going to rain down "bread from heaven" (Exodus 16:4). In fulfillment of his promise the dawn illuminated "a fine, flake-like thing, fine as frost on the ground. When the people of Israel saw it, they said to one another, 'What is it? [Manna?]' For they did not know what it was" (Exodus 16:14, 15). This "What is it?," which tasted like "wafers made with honey" (Exodus 16:31), became their staple for almost forty years and enabled them to survive in the wilderness. So purposefully premeditated was Christ's personal identification with this manna, this Bread of Heaven, that he gave this explanation after the first feeding:

> I am the bread of life. Your fathers ate the manna in the wilderness, and they died. This is the bread that comes down from heaven, so that one may eat of it and not die. I am the living bread that came down from heaven. If anyone eats of this bread, he will live forever. And the bread that I will give for the life of the world is my flesh. (John 6:48–51)

So startling was his identification that some of the Jews thought he was suggesting cannibalism (John 6:52)! Actually, the fact that Jesus was the Bread of Heaven went all the way back to his birth in Bethlehem, which is literally the "city of bread." And on the final evening of his life he took bread and broke it and said, "This is my body which is for you" (1 Corinthians 11:24). Thus at the beginning and end of his earthly incarnation Christ powerfully underscored the great fact that he is the Bread of Life.

Jesus dearly wanted his disciples to understand this, for reflecting upon it would open them to understanding his ministry. Thought through, the implications of Jesus being the Bread of Life explained virtually everything about his person and his mission in life. They revealed his power, for the miraculous multiplication shouted of omnipotence, and the metaphor of bread pictured his suffering.

Second, Christ wanted his disciples to understand that he was not just Bread for the Jews, but also for the Gentiles. That the four thousand were predominantly Gentiles is substantiated not only because they were in the Gentile-dominated Decapolis, but also because Jesus said "grace" twice at the end. Pronouncing blessing over the bread was a normal Jewish custom, but not the second prayer over the fish. Evidently Jesus was teaching Gentiles to thank God for their daily food.[3] Moreover, the leftover bread was not picked up in the traditional smaller bottle-shaped baskets of the Jews as in the feeding of the five thousand, but in large wicker hampers, the kind used to lower Paul over the city wall of Damascus in escape (Acts 9:25).

The bread miracle among Gentiles meant that Jesus was *spiritual* bread for the pagan world—for you and me. Jesus was saying that the *material* is not enough for humanity. Once, when he was tempted to meet his own physical needs at the expense of the spiritual, he responded, "Man shall not live by bread alone" (Matthew 4:4).

If you are focused on the material, you will shrivel. You may be twenty-five to thirty-five and feel that you and your physical environment are where it is. You eat pasta and yogurt—no fats, no junk. You may lavish yourself in designer labels. You work out regularly and transport your body regularly in a $60,000 sports car. But your reductionist way of thinking, which has shrunk you to a body and little more, will betray you. As the years go by, you will become more aware of your hollowness. When the skin begins to sag, and the clothes no longer look "right," you may learn that "Man shall not live by bread alone." The disciples needed to understand that Jesus is the universal Bread. There is no life for anyone apart from him!

Third, the supply always meets and exceeds the demand. Verse 6 tells us: "And he took the seven loaves, and having given thanks, he broke them and gave them to his disciples to set before the people; and they set them before the crowd." Christ did not break the bread, so that suddenly there were huge piles of bread and fish. Rather, he kept breaking it and handing out what was needed bit by bit.[4] We need to be constantly bringing our needs to Jesus, and he will constantly break the bread and give us what we need.

Mark says of Christ's provision for the multitude: "And they ate and were satisfied. And they took up the broken pieces left over, seven baskets full" (v. 8). These were large baskets, big enough to hold a man! While we must be careful not to go overboard in spiritualizing numbers, the numbers in the two miracles are obviously symbolic. When the five thousand Jews were fed, there were twelve baskets left, emblematic of God's full provision for the twelve tribes of Israel. Here there were seven great baskets, the number of fullness and completion, as Christ is more than sufficient for the whole world!

The people came to Christ famished. They were so hungry that Jesus feared they might collapse on the way home. But when their power to get food was exhausted, Christ's power to feed was not! Whatever the Lord has given us, there is still far more for him to give us. Our souls, so to speak, are elastic. The more we eat, the more they expand. The more they expand, the more we are able to eat. None of us have ever eaten as much as he wants to give us. We are meant to hunger, and to eat and eat and eat. "Listen, disciples," he says by this grand miracle, "I am sufficient for the whole world and all its needs. Learn it well."

With the completion of this event, the disciples had seen two stupendous miracles in which *thousands* of people were fed. Yet had they really seen the miracles? Or had they satisfied themselves with simply looking at the bread and fish and the feasting thousands and that is all? That will be answered shortly. But first we see that Jesus' opponents were blind, and remained blind, to everything.

The Blindness of Jesus' Enemies (vv. 11–13)

Mark tells us that when Jesus finished feeding the four thousand he sailed back across the lake to Dalmanutha, somewhere on the west side of the sea, probably close to Capernaum. There he was accosted by the Pharisees. "The Pharisees came and began to argue with him, seeking from him a sign from heaven to test him" (v. 11). They had already seen great signs that they could not deny, and yet credited them to Beelzebul (3:22). Yet they wanted a "sign from heaven," something spectacular from the skies. This was a diabolical repeat of Satan's temptation of Christ in the wilderness when he tried to get Jesus to do something stupendous, saying if he would do so he would give Christ the kingdoms of the world (Matthew 4:8, 9). It was a temptation to take the easy way, apart from the Father's will. Jesus would have no part of it.

> And he sighed deeply in his spirit [grieved at their moral perversity] and said, "Why does this generation seek a sign? Truly, I say to you, no sign will be given to this generation." And he left them, got into the boat again, and went to the other side. (vv. 12, 13)

Christ was angry! It is difficult to translate the sense of "no sign will be given to this generation." The phrase is literally, "If shall be given to this generation a sign—!" thus leaving the conclusion unstated, which might be "may God punish me" or "may I die." The construction is characteristic of Hebrew oaths—suggesting intense emotion.[5] Jesus knew the hardness of their hearts. Matthew says in his parallel account, "'An evil and adulterous generation seeks for a sign, but no sign will be given to it except the sign of Jonah.' So he left them and departed" (Matthew 16:4). The only sign they would get was that signified by Jonah—the Resurrection!

What a terrible thing it is to have Christ turn his back on you and sail away. But that is ultimately what he does to those who continually refuse his revelation. There comes a time when he gives no more signs, no more help in understanding. But what about those who do follow him?

The Dullness of Jesus' Disciples (vv. 14–21)

The disciples were dull, that is for sure! Physically, Jesus and his disciples were together in the boat, but in their minds they were a universe apart. He gave them a *spiritual* warning, which they misinterpreted because of their material mind-set. The miracle of the four thousand had had little effect in bringing spiritual reflection.

> Now they had forgotten to bring bread, and they had only one loaf with them in the boat. And he cautioned them, saying, "Watch out; beware of the leaven of the Pharisees and the leaven of Herod." And they began discussing with one another the fact that they had no bread. (vv. 14–16).

Apart from Christ's agitation with his disciples in Gethsemane, and with Peter when he objected to the cross, there was nothing like our Lord's frustration with the Twelve here. Humanly speaking, he counted on being misunderstood by the Pharisees, but not by his intimates. How could they misunderstand? Yeast or "leaven" is a common Scriptural symbol for evil.[6] He was warning them about the evil teaching of the Pharisees on the one hand and the power-crazy Herod on the other.

Some people need some extra help, like the man who went into a bank and said he wanted some money. The teller asked him to make out a check. But the man would not do it. So the teller said, "If you won't sign the check, I can't give you any money." The man went across the street to another bank, where the same conversation took place. But after this exchange the teller reached across the counter, took him by the ears, and banged his head three times on the counter. After which the man took out a pen and calmly signed a check. The man then returned to the first bank and said, "They gave me money across the street." "How did that happen?" asked the teller. "They explained it to me!" answered the man.

Jesus now explained it to his disciples by banging their dense noggins against a hail of questions in verses 17–20. "Why are you discussing the fact that you have no bread?" Bang! "Do you not yet perceive or understand?" Bang! "Are your hearts hardened?" Bang! "Having eyes do you not see, and having ears do you not hear?" Bang! "And do you not remember?" Bang! "When I broke the five loaves for the five thousand, how many baskets full of broken pieces did you take up?" "Twelve," they replied. "And the seven for the four thousand, how many baskets full of broken pieces did you take up?" They answered, "Seven." Bang! Bang! Bang!

In those questions Jesus told them that their lack of understanding was due to a hardness of heart. Of course, they were not hardened to him. They were his followers. Their problem here came from familiarity. The repeated exposure to his teaching, when not reflected upon and acted upon, worked a progressive insensitivity and dullness in their lives. We experience this as well when we fail to think and act upon what God has revealed to us. It was a case of "use it or lose it." They were not appropriating what they were seeing and hearing.

> For to the one who has, more will be given, and he will have an abundance, but from the one who has not, even what he has will be taken away. (Matthew 13:12)

If the disciples had truly reflected on the spiritual significance of the miracle feasts, they would have advanced far beyond where they were in their spiritual growth. They would have seen Jesus as the wielder of omnipotence. The multiplication of bread was a creation miracle! Christ could do anything.

The twelve baskets and the seven hampers of bread taught that he was Bread for the whole world—Jews and Gentiles. The bread taught there was no life apart from him. If they would only have pursued the gluttony recommended in Scripture—feasting on Christ!

There is no better shield against spiritual declension and weakness than Christian remembering. That is the way it was for Joshua. During the crossing of the Jordan, the priests of Israel took twelve stones from the riverbed and placed them in a crude mound in Gilgal as a memorial. The celebration in Gilgal (which means, "the reproach has been rolled away") must have been something to behold. Forty years of wandering were over. We surmise that most of them danced and sang around their fires far into the night. Perhaps Joshua himself joined the dancing, or perhaps he was too tired. But we can be sure he returned to observe in the flickering light that mound of unworked stones from the bottom of the Jordan. God had done it! Again and again he reran the mental "tapes" of that day. God was with him! God's power could do anything! Joshua had much to think about as he viewed those stones, and he thought a lot about them over the years. Gilgal became the command headquarters for conquering the promised land. It was the place to which he frequently returned after victories, in the midst of battles, and after his defeats, such as that of Ai. Here he gathered wisdom and strength to go on, for here lay the stones of remembrance.

I have my own Gilgals and my own piles of stones. It is energizing to recall memories of God's deliverance. Our memories can become fountains of power for others as well.

We should also draw upon the remembrances contained in God's Word. We should remember Israel's crossing of the Red Sea. Have you ever purposely imagined what the event was like? You should. We should do this with the miracle of the sun standing still for embattled Joshua, the raising of Lazarus, and Peter's miraculous deliverance from jail, to name a few.

Christ ended with one final question. It is best to see it not as a continuation of the rebuke, but as a searching appeal to the disciples. He said to them in verse 21, "Do you not yet understand?" That is, "Now that I have reminded you that there were twelve bushels left from the Jewish feeding and seven from the Gentile feeding, do you still not understand that I am the Bread of Life for the whole world?"

This is a question for our own hearts. Is he our Bread? Do we understand what this means for the way we live? Do we understand what it means for the world?

Remember, meditate, live!

26

Christ and Human Expectations

MARK 8:22–26

WHEN YOUR LIFE has been touched by Christ, you want to share that touch. That was the way it was for me as a twelve-year-old when I met Christ. I almost drove my poor mother to distraction, for that was all I wanted to talk about and indeed did talk about in those early weeks of faith. I shared Christ's touch with my buddies on the block and received a mixed reception. I testified at church. I spoke up, sometimes unwisely, in the classroom at school. That is what an authentic touch from Jesus can do!

This chapter's text was occasioned by a group of people who had had a touch by Christ and wanted to share it. Whether it was yet a saving touch, we do not know. Perhaps they had been touched by his teaching. Perhaps they or one of their circle had actually been the recipient of Christ's healing touch. Whatever the touch, they thought of a friend, a blind man who was in desperate need of a touch from the Master's hand.

Blindness was endemic to ancient culture. The lack of understanding regarding hygiene, the unavailability of effective medicine, and exposure to the elements and domestic trauma left many blind. Clouded, staring, fly-swarmed eyes were common wherever one went.

The pathetic plight of the sightless man in our text is easy for us to imagine. However, this poor man had at least one thing going for him: friends who believed Christ could heal him. Their belief was not simply theoretical, but practical. "And they [Jesus and his disciples] came to Bethsaida. And some people brought to him a blind man and begged him to touch him" (8:22). They were earnest and forceful in their appeal as they exhorted Jesus to heal their poor friend. They had laudable expectations, and those expectations were specific.

The Expectations of the Blind Man's Friends (v. 22)

They had figured out just how Jesus was going to work. They had heard, and very probably seen, Jesus do it before. When the blind were brought to him, he simply touched them, sometimes without a word, and they were healed.

Since the blind man's friends were likely Gentiles, as this was Gentile territory, it was quite possible they had come to put more trust in Jesus' touch than in Jesus. That had been precisely the case with the woman with the hemorrhage who thought, "If I touch even his garments, I will be made well" (5:28). In that case Jesus honored her uninformed faith, but immediately made it clear that it was her faith that brought healing and not the touch, saying, "Daughter, your faith has made you well" (5:34).

There was probably similar superstition with the blind man's friends. But what we must see if we are to understand this passage is that they not only believed Jesus could heal him—they were sure they knew how Jesus would and should heal their friend!

It is common among followers of Christ to think we know just how Jesus should minister his grace. Recently I shared the details of my call to the ministry with a group of pastors, and I related how as a boy I knew that I was called. My call was so definite and so memorialized in my mind that I can still see the dirt under my fingernails as that night I tremulously turned the pages of my tiny India-paper Bible, rejoicing in God's Word.

After I finished, a pastor came and said he was not sure of his call because he had had no such experience—nothing even close to it. Unwittingly, I had given the impression that real calls were always like mine! I had to backtrack as we discussed the fact that some who are called never have an emotional call, but simply grow into it as the reasonable course of their lives. Their call is just as authentic. God is not limited to a dramatic touch!

Nowhere does the Church at large err more in this way than in its thinking regarding salvation. We came to Christ as we read the Gospel of John, or perhaps as we read Revelation 3:20, or perhaps as we "walked the aisle," or read a certain Christian biography, or after reaching the end of ourselves after some plunge into sin. We sometimes make our experience normative for others. In fact, it is not our *experience* that is normative, but our *belief*, in that we rest our faith in Christ alone, trusting him for salvation. We must realize that the experience of the "touch" varies, but God's grace is the same.

We must be careful never to box God in, because that results in limiting our usefulness. If we think he can work only along one of our experiential or cultural tracks, we will unconsciously resist him when he chooses to work in one of his mysterious ways. The blind man's friends correctly expected Jesus to heal their friend, but they wrongly expected him to do it with a touch. What did the blind man expect?

The Expectations of the Blind Man

Frankly, not very much! We understand this from two things: (1) his initial less-than-enthusiastic demeanor, and (2) the way Christ dealt with him. The initiative for his coming to Jesus came from his friends, and they did the "begging," not him. His passiveness was particularly pronounced compared to the blind Bartimaeus, whom Jesus healed later. Sitting by the roadside, and hearing that Jesus was approaching, Bartimaeus began to shout, "Jesus, Son of David, have mercy on me!" (10:47). Ignoring rebukes from the crowd he cried again, "Son of David, have mercy on me!" When he realized that Jesus beckoned him, he threw his cloak aside, jumped to his feet, and came to Jesus, saying, "Rabbi, let me recover my sight." Jesus responded, "Go . . . your faith has made you well" (10:52). Bartimaeus' faith was grandly aggressive! There was apparently little, if any, of this faith in the present blind man.

His faith was not the kind that Jesus most often chose to honor. Jesus' principle was generally, "According to your faith be it done to you" (Matthew 9:29), as for example in the case of Bartimaeus and the woman with the issue of blood. That is why Jesus took this man through a progressively staged healing. He wanted the man to have a faith that matched the miracle to take place in his life. At present the man, a blind Gentile, was willing but wary. It was the faith of his friends that brought him forward, not his. What did Jesus do?

The Blind Man's Expectations Transcended (vv. 23–25)

First, Jesus "took the blind man by the hand" (v. 23). This was the awaited touch. Yet, nothing happened. This was not what his friends had expected. The Master's touch, they thought, was all that was needed. But what about the man's expectations, his faith? Jesus had taken him by the hand. And it was not a simple handshake! Jesus held on to the man's hand. Holding another's hand is a very personal thing, especially if it is held for any length of time. A profound communication can take place through that contact alone, even if no words are spoken.

The hand of the Master and the blind man remained clasped. The minimum significance has to have been that here was a man who was interested in him. A hope that Jesus was going to do something rose in the blind man. His expectations began to ascend.

Second, Jesus isolated the man: "he took the blind man by the hand and led him out of the village" (v. 23). This is a singularly beautiful picture. Jesus clasped the man's hand and gently guided him around obstacles, verbally directing him where to step and where not to step, steadying him when he stumbled. Can you see the Master guiding the hollow-eyed man along, with the disciples following close behind? Perhaps again the man's friends experienced a letdown. There was yet no great miracle before the "oohing" and "ahhing" crowd. But the man's expectation and faith were being heightened. He could not know it, but he was one of the most honored men who ever lived. Jesus, God Incarnate, was leading him by the hand!

Third, alone with the man, Jesus used tactile, sense-stimulating means to heighten the mans' faith: "when he had spit on his eyes and laid his hands on him . . ." (v. 23). Like me, you are probably repulsed at this description of glazed, diseased-encrusted eyeballs sprayed with spittle and then a carpenter's callused hands pressing in on them. But these things were sublimely beautiful, for they were a *ladder* on which the blind man's nascent faith would cling. Jesus was communicating with the poor man! Spittle and the laying on of hands were perfectly understood in the ancient world. By this means "Jesus entered the thought-world of the man and established significant contact with him."[1] Jesus had his attention! As our Lord held his fingers firmly upon the blind man's eyeballs, the man's heart was surely pounding uncontrollably. Hope and faith were surging.

Next, Jesus, removed his hands and asked the man, "'Do you see anything?' And he looked up and said, 'I see people, but they look like trees, walking'" (vv. 23, 24). Jesus had purposefully performed a partial healing. He did not suffer an energy shortage. The act was premeditated.

Nevertheless, the effect was electrifying. For the first time in years, the man saw light and color. And dimly, as if through water, he saw the form of Jesus' disciples and his friends, like walking trees! If his expectations were surging before, they were now soaring! As he strained to focus, he could hardly contain himself. He believed! Oh, did he believe! In Christ's eyes, the man's faith was far more important than his physical healing.

Now for the final touch. Mark described the scene in verse 25: "Then Jesus laid his hands on his eyes again; and he opened his eyes, his sight was restored, and he saw everything clearly" (v. 25). Some Greek scholars say this is tautological; that is, it contains needless repetition. But that is undoubtedly the way Peter, Mark's informant, enthusiastically described it to him. The last phrase, "and he saw everything clearly," uses a rare word that means literally *to see clearly from afar*.[2] In other words, he had 20/20 vision!

His Friend's Expectations Exceeded

The blind man's friends' expectations had been exceeded. Not only was their friend healed, but he had a dancing, exuberant faith in Christ.

We must understand that our Lord's miracles were more than events of healing. They were parables of spiritual reality. The progressive healing of the blind man reveals to us that God sometimes heals or saves us in inscrutable stages. "For as the heavens are higher than the earth, so are my ways higher than your ways and my thoughts than your thoughts" (Isaiah 55:9). "Thy way was in the sea, and Thy paths in the mighty waters, and Thy footprints may not be known" (Psalm 77:19 NASB). Often God's ways are hidden, but he knows exactly what he is doing!

We ought to come to God for his gracious healing power, but we must not attempt to tell him how to do it. We may and must ask for spiritual growth. But we must not lay down guidelines as to how God ought to produce this. We must not, for example, ask God to develop our spiritual lives, and then when he pulls out the shears and begins to prune say, "No, Lord, you can't do it that way!" Do not ask the Lord to make you sensitive to others, and then resent the difficult person who crosses your life at work or in the church. God often circumvents a proud, presumptuous spirit, whereas spiritual grace may be mediated by a friendship, a discipline, or a hardship.

Regarding the salvation of souls, there no doubt is a millisecond when one crosses from unbelief to belief and into the kingdom of Heaven. But God does not always do things in a perceptible moment we can observe. At times we can see it, as with Paul on the Damascus Road, in a flash of light. But others receive a little light and then more and then more until they see everything clearly.

The bottom line is, we must submit to God to do his work and will in his own way. Tennyson wrote:

Our little systems have their day;
They have their day and cease to be;
They are but broken lights of Thee,
And thou, O Lord, art more than they.[3]

We cannot put God into a box. Anyone who tries to tame him does so at great spiritual risk.

Paul says, "we are [God's] workmanship"—literally, "his *poems*, his masterpieces" (Ephesians 2:10). But we are individual works of art, and the process is unique to each one. We must submit to his touch.

27

What Confessing Christ Means

MARK 8:27–38

WITH THIS STUDY we now come to the middle of the book of Mark, which is also the intersection toward which the theology of the first half of the Gospel converges and from which the dynamic of the second half of the Gospel comes.[1] It is the turning point of the Gospel, and from it all events move toward Jerusalem, the betrayal, the whipping post, and the bloody cross.

The text centers around Peter's famous confession of Christ and explains what it meant for Jesus to be the Messiah and what it requires to be identified with him. As such, it is of the greatest practical importance because it tells us what we must confess and embrace about Christ, and what we must understand and embrace for ourselves if we are to be his disciples.

The Disciple's Confession (vv. 27–33)

The initiative for this immortal confession belonged all to Jesus. He and his disciples were on the road somewhere among the tiny villages surrounding the city of Caesarea Philippi when he asked two questions.

First: "'Who do people say that I am?' And they told him, 'John the Baptist; and others say, Elijah; and others, one of the prophets'" (vv. 27, 28). The average people "on the street" thought he was great. They were impressed with his prophetic character, but did not have the slightest idea that he was the Messiah.

Jesus had their interest, so he asked the second question: "But who do you [the emphasis is on *you*] say that I am?" (v. 29a). Perhaps there was a pause, for they did not answer in chorus as previously, even though they all knew the answer. Predictably, Peter answered for them all: "You are the Christ" (v. 29b). That was what Jesus wanted to hear. Matthew's Gospel records his joyous response:

> Blessed are you, Simon Bar-Jonah! For flesh and blood has not revealed this to you, but my Father who is in heaven. And I tell you, you are Peter, and on this rock I will build my church, and the gates of hell shall not prevail against it. I will give you the keys of the kingdom of heaven, and whatever you bind on earth shall be bound in heaven, and whatever you loose on earth shall be loosed in heaven. (Matthew 16:17–19)

This was a tremendous affirmation! Why Mark did not include it, we can only guess. Perhaps it was because Peter was Mark's source in writing his Gospel and Peter humbly made no mention of it.

What did Peter do in calling Jesus the Christ? To begin with, he did not give Jesus another name (that is, Jesus is not a first name and Christ a second name). "Jesus" is the name of God's Son, and "Christ" is his title. "Christ" is the Greek rendering of the Hebrew title "Messiah" and means *"Anointed One."* Peter's identifying Jesus as the Christ, the Messiah, the Anointed One meant the disciples believed that Jesus was the One Israel had been waiting for since the time of David—a superhuman leader who would overthrow Israel's enemies, regather God's earthly people from the four corners of the world, and make Jerusalem and Palestine the center of the world, establishing the perfect reign of God. Peter said it, but they all believed it, and had believed it for some time.[2] They all nodded and murmured assent. Some, such as Simon the Zealot and Judas, hung everything on the political hopes this Messiah-belief inspired.

Seeing his disciples' eager assent, Jesus "strictly charged them to tell no one about him" (v. 30). The warning was strong, almost a rebuke,[3] because Jesus knew of the powerful forces that were aligning against him, and he did not want to force a confrontation—not yet.

Having warned the disciples, Jesus set about instructing them, and in doing so taught them something that in their wildest imaginations they had never dreamed: namely, *he was to be a suffering Messiah.*

> And he began to teach them that the Son of Man must suffer many things and be rejected by the elders and the chief priests and the scribes and be killed, and after three days rise again. And he said this plainly. (vv. 31, 32a)

In speaking "plainly," he concealed nothing. He laid it all out.[4] This was a detailed outline of the end. He intimately described his coming sufferings. His mention of "the elders and the chief priests and the scribes" was an explicit reference to the three groups in the Sanhedrin who would later officially examine him and would reject him like a counterfeit coin. Even his resurrection was mentioned, though it would remain incomprehensible to the disciples until after the glorious fact. What a nonsensical revelation it was to them at the time!

They were appalled, but they all kept their silence—all except one: "And Peter took him aside and began to rebuke him" (v. 32b). The language here suggests that Peter did this with an air of protective superiority,[5] as if he may have put his arm around Jesus and with a stage whisper said, "Come here, Jesus. Of course I believe you are the Messiah, but you have your information wrong! You have to stop this or you'll lose all your credibility."

Now it was the Savior who was revulsed! As he spun to face Peter, he saw that the other disciples were approving of what Peter was saying. His explosive rebuke was for them as well. "Get behind me, Satan! For you are not setting your mind on the things of God, but on the things of man" (v. 33). These were the harshest words Jesus ever spoke to a devoted, well-meaning heart!

Peter had become the unwitting carrier of demonic doctrine, parallel to that which Christ faced in the wilderness when Satan tempted him to abandon the Father's will and seek an easy Saviorhood. To that he responded, "Be gone, Satan!" (Matthew 4:10). That had been a terrible temptation for Jesus because he knew what horrors awaited him. Satan was in Peter's voice!

It is true that soul-saving salvation could only come through a suffering Messiah. There was no other way. Why were the disciples rejecting Jesus as a suffering Messiah? Because the idea was completely out of sync with human reasoning. Who would ever design a method of saving the world that would include disaster, despair, and death? No one! That is why Israel misinterpreted its own Scriptures that told of the coming *suffering Messiah*. Natural reason says a Savior must come with position and power! But Jesus said if you think that way, "You are not setting your mind on the things of God, but on the things of man" (v. 33b).

If we are to confess Christ, we must embrace a suffering Messiah, a God no one would ever have thought of. Taking our suffering Savior into our heart and loving him may come far easier now, this side of the cross, after his death and resurrection, but there is something more that is required. We must embrace his example as a model for living, and this is not so easy.

The Disciple's Lifestyle (vv. 34–38)

Confessing Christ means we must follow him to crucifixion. "And calling the crowd to him with his disciples, he said to them, 'If anyone would come after me, let him deny himself and take up his cross and follow me'" (v. 34).

The cross is for all who follow Christ. Christ leads the procession carrying his cross, and we, his followers, tread in his steps, bearing our own crosses. We march to death.

What are our crosses? They are not simply trials or hardships. It is typical to think of a nutty boss or an unfair teacher or a bossy mother-in-law as our "cross." But they are not. Neither can we properly call an illness or a handicap a cross. A cross comes from specifically walking in Christ's steps, embracing his life. It comes from bearing disdain because we are embracing the narrow way of the Cross—that Jesus is "the way, and the truth, and the life" (John 14:6). It comes from living out the business and sexual ethics of Christ in the marketplace and world. It comes from embracing weakness instead of power. It comes from extending oneself in difficult circumstances for the sake of the gospel.

Our crosses come from and are proportionate to our dedication to Christ. Difficulties are not an indication of cross-bearing; difficulties *for Christ's sake* are. We need to ask ourselves if we have any difficulties because we are following close after Christ.

There is a second personal effect of confessing Christ: embracing the paradox of the cross. Jesus said further: "For whoever would save his life will lose it, but whoever loses his life for my sake and the gospel's will save it" (v. 35).

Jesus said, "Losers are keepers." This is a fundamental law of life. No one is excepted, in time or eternity.

Nothing could be more opposed to the spirit of our age. The world today says, "Look out for *Numero Uno*. Save yourself. Love yourself. Pamper yourself. Live for yourself." Look at the ad campaigns: "I believe in my car, my friends, my team, Joanne, and beer!" Whereas primitive men used to drink the blood of their victims to capture their soul, our society thinks it can ingest virtue by what we wear, eat, and drink. Narcissism is the order of the day as multitudes ease their souls into a living death by the respectable vice of selfishness. A society of keepers inevitably becomes a society of losers. Ours is a society of losers!

The most famous living author of the 1930s was William Somerset Maugham, "Willie." He was an accomplished novelist, playwright, and short story writer. His novel *Of Human Bondage* is a classic. His play *The Constant Wife* has gone through thousands of stagings. He was a man who lived for his own refined tastes, his comfort, and his sexual perversions. In 1965, at the age of ninety-one, he was still a fabulously rich man, although he had not written a word in years. He still received over three hundred fan letters a week.

What had life brought W. Somerset Maugham? The *London Times* carried this excerpt by his nephew, Robin Maugham:

> I looked round the drawing room at the immensely valuable furniture and pictures and objects that Willie's success had enabled him to acquire. I remembered that the villa itself, and the wonderful garden I could see through the windows—a fabulous setting on the edge of the Mediterranean—were worth £600,000.
>
> Willie had 11 servants, including his cook, Annette, who was the envy of all the other millionaires on the Riviera. He dined off silver plates, waited on by Marius, his butler, and Henri, his footman. But it no longer meant anything to him.
>
> The following afternoon I found Willie reclining on a sofa, peering through his spectacles at a Bible which had very large print. He looked horribly wizened and his face was grim.
>
> "I've been reading the Bible you gave me . . . And I've come across the quotation, 'What shall it profit a man if he gain the whole world and lose his own soul?' I must tell you, my dear Robin, that the text used to hang opposite my bed when I was a child . . . Of course, it's all a lot of bunk. But the thought is quite interesting all the same."

Robin Maugham goes on to describe an empty, bitter old man who repeatedly fell into shrieking terrors, crying, "Go away! I'm not ready . . . I'm not dead yet . . . I'm not dead yet, I tell you . . ."[6]

He was a man who had gained the whole world and lost his own soul, a "keeper" who lost. On the other hand, there are "losers" who are the ultimate keepers.

My wife, Barbara, and I visited John and Lorraine Winston who have been missionaries in France for more than thirty-eight years. The last twenty-two of those years have been given to founding the French Evangelical Seminary in Vaux-sur-Seine. As we sat in their rooftop apartment overlooking the seminary grounds, John reminisced. He said, as we well knew, that life had not been easy. There had been times when they had been pushed to their limits. And Lorraine nodded her assent. "But," he continued, "I have had the best life. It has been challenging, exciting, and fulfilling. I wouldn't change a thing. I have no regrets." Losers are keepers!

Do we believe this? If we do, we are swimming against the stream of our culture. But we will not be sorry!

One hundred and eighty years after the death of Charlemagne, in about the year 1000, officials of the Emperor Otho opened the great king's tomb, where they found an amazing sight apart from the treasures. What they saw was this: the skeletal remains of the king seated on a throne, the crown still upon his skull, a copy of the Gospels lying in his lap with his bony finger resting on this text: "What good is it for a man to gain the whole world, yet forfeit his soul?"[7]

Confessing Christ means taking up one's cross and following him. It means embracing the paradox that losers are keepers. It brings eternal reward to one's soul! We are called to confess Christ. Our chapter ends with Jesus saying:

> For whoever is ashamed of me and of my words in this adulterous and sinful generation, of him will the Son of Man also be ashamed when he comes in the glory of his Father with the holy angels. (v. 38)

We must confess Christ as the suffering Messiah and Savior. We must embrace the life he exemplified and calls us to. We must bear crosses because we are living like him. We must lose our lives for him, for losers are keepers. If we confess him, the Son of Man will rejoice in us.

28

The Midnight Son

MARK 9:2–13

IT WAS LATE AFTERNOON as Jesus led his inner circle of disciples (Peter, James, and John) up the higher elevations of Mt. Hermon "to pray" (Luke 9:28), for the climb took the better part of a day.[1] Mt. Hermon is *the* mountain in Palestine, as its peaks rise some 9,000 feet above sea level and 11,000 feet above the Jordan Valley. On a clear day its snow-clad slopes can be seen from all parts of the land—from Jerusalem to Tyre. And if it was a clear day (as it probably was), the scene was unforgettable.

Years ago Henry Tristram, an authority on Holy Land geography, gave this description of his experience of nightfall on Mt. Hermon:

> [As the sun descended] a deep ruby flush came over all the scene, and warm purple shadows crept slowly on. The Sea of Galilee was lit up with a delicate greenish-yellow hue. The flush died out in a few minutes, and a pale, steel-colored shade succeeded, a long pyramidal shadow slid down to the eastern foot of Hermon, and crept across the great plain; Damascus was swallowed up by it; it was the shadow of the mountain itself, stretching away for seventy miles across the plain—the most marvelous shadow perhaps to be seen anywhere. The sun underwent strange changes of the shape . . . now almost square, now like a domed Temple—until at length it slid into the sea, and went out like a blue spark.[2]

Overhead came the summer sky with its moon and stars illuminating the long patches of snow still left on the mountain. There could hardly have been a more spectacular scene and setting!

Why this long climb with his most intimate disciples to this dramatic setting? The answer is, they needed to be encouraged. Just six days before, Jesus had jolted them with the reality of the coming cross and the necessity of suffering.

Jesus had asked who they believed he was, and Peter had answered with his great confession: "You are the Christ" (8:29). Then Jesus began to teach them that he must suffer many things, and be rejected and killed, and after three days rise again. Predictably, Peter objected, and received a stinging rebuke from Jesus. This precipitated Jesus' calling the crowd to him and telling them that when they embraced him as Messiah, they embraced a suffering Messiah and a life that included taking up their own crosses (8:34–38).

It was a radical, revolutionary revelation—totally out of sync with their messianic expectations. It was naturally confusing and depressing. And with what was coming, the Lord realized that it needed to be balanced with some positive realities. So now he had them in the crisp atmosphere of the alpine heights of Mt. Hermon, away from everything, alone with him under the spinning summer constellations. They were on top of the world with Jesus. Here they were going to be bombarded with the most stupendous blast of encouragement mortals have ever known.

They would not understand it all, but it would provide grist for theological reflection for the rest of their lives. As we know, they apparently let these realities slip during the darkness of the cross, but with the Resurrection and in the ensuing years they grasped them ever more closely. The encouragement remains for us today who are called to embrace the cross. The disciples' experience on Mt. Hermon is something we are all called to put our arms around and hold close to our hearts. We need to stand on top of the world with Jesus.

Encouragement on the Mountain (vv. 2–8)

The first thing we should take hold of is the Transfiguration. Mark tells us, "And after six days Jesus took with him Peter and James and John, and led them up a high mountain by themselves" (v. 2).

Luke supplies further details, telling us that they "went up . . . to pray" (Luke 9:28). So we understand that the evening began with prayer and continued that way. We can only surmise for what Jesus prayed. Perhaps it was along the lines of his High-Priestly prayer in John 17 when he prayed for himself, his disciples, and the lost world. It is very likely that they joined in with his petitions and offered their own praise and requests.

We do know that they became weary, as Luke mentions they were "heavy with sleep" (Luke 9:32) and evidently dozed off. The long climb, the heady atmosphere, and the quiet made sleep irresistible! The Gospels do not indicate who awakened first, whether it was Peter or one of the "Sons of Thunder." But whoever he was, when he got his eyes open, he was wide awake in an instant and then shook the others awake. As verses 2, 3 tell us, "And he was transfigured before them, and his clothes became radiant, intensely white, as no one on earth could bleach them."

What a spectacle! Jesus is framed by a thousand summer stars, and his clothing has begun to glow white. It is "radiant" or glittering, as the word is sometimes translated—"dazzling white," says Luke (9:29). Not only that, Matthew records that "His face shone like the sun" (Matthew 17:2). Overhead are the Bear and Pleiades, and Jesus is shining like a star himself—the Midnight Son!

When as a young father I used to light the fireworks on the Fourth of July for my family, there were two views I enjoyed. There were the fireworks themselves pouring forth a fountain of sparks, and there were the faces of my children, eyes wide with delight and expectancy, their skin reflecting the changing hues of the fireworks. I liked that even better! I can see it today!

This is what Jesus saw: his glory illuminating the faces of his awestruck inner ring of disciples—his very image dancing in their wide eyes. Jesus was "transfigured," more literally "metamorphosed." For a brief moment the veil of his humanity was lifted, and his true essence was allowed to shine through. The glory that was always in the depths of his being rose to the surface for that one time in his earthly life. Or put another way, he slipped back into eternity, to his pre-human glory. It was a glance back and a look forward into his future glory!

Peter, James, and John were to hold on to this in what was to come. It was to be their solace and cause for hope in the darkness that would come with the cross. Note: they did this imperfectly. The cross eclipsed their vision momentarily. However, John would later describe it saying, "We have seen his glory, glory as of the only Son from the Father" (John 1:14).

As they were watching spellbound, they were given something else to embrace: "And there appeared to them Elijah with Moses, and they were talking with Jesus" (v. 4). How they knew who these two were, we do not know. Maybe they addressed each other by name in their conversation.

Why Elijah and Moses? Why not Isaiah and Jeremiah? There are several reasons. Both these men had previously conversed with God on mountaintops—Moses on Mt. Sinai (Exodus 31:18) and Elijah on Mt. Horeb (1 Kings 19:9ff.). These both had been shown God's glory. Both also had famous departures from this earth. Moses died on Mt. Nebo, and God had buried him in a grave known only to himself. Elijah was taken up in a chariot of fire. Moses was the great lawgiver, and Elijah was the great prophet. Moses was the *founder* of Israel's religious economy, and Elijah was the *restorer* of it. Together they were an ultimate summary of the Old Testament economy.

What were they and Jesus talking about? Dr. Luke tells us in his parallel account: "[Moses and Elijah] appeared in glory and spoke of his departure, which he was about to accomplish at Jerusalem" (Luke 9:31).

They were talking about the cross and Jesus' death! The tense indicates that this was an extended conversation. They, the chief representatives of the Law and the Prophets, were carrying on a conversation with Jesus, who himself said, "Do not think that I have come to abolish the Law or the Prophets; I have not come to abolish them but to fulfill them" (Matthew 5:17).

What a theological conversation it must have been! It probably "blew by" the three, as they still had so much to learn. The bottom line was this: Peter's confession that Jesus was the Messiah (8:29) was graphically confirmed by these grand representatives of the old covenant. There was no doubt! The disciples were to take this to their pounding hearts.

Jesus was the fulfillment of everything toward which the Law pointed. He fulfilled what the sacrificial system was teaching. He fulfilled every messianic prophecy—everything toward which their religion and history had been moving.

What an amazing sight! Luminous, dazzling Jesus is talking to Moses who had been dead over fourteen hundred years and to Elijah who had been gone about nine hundred. If there ever was a time for silence, this was it. But enter Peter—a man who always had something to say when there was nothing to be said: "And Peter said to Jesus, 'Rabbi, it is good that we are here. Let us make three tents, one for you and one for Moses and one for Elijah.' For he did not know what to say, for they were terrified" (vv. 5, 6).

What in the world was Peter up to? Perhaps it was just a courteous reflex. He wanted to make thatched booths for his heavenly visitors, so they could wait on them. Some think that Peter's motive was to bring about the promised glory now—and thus avoid the sufferings Jesus had spoken of.[3] We do not know. But we do see that the Lord's only answer was silence as they stood on the peak of Hermon.

A study of the Old Testament reveals that a luminous cloud, the *shekinah* glory, was a sign and manifestation of the presence of God, the form in which God revealed himself to Israel. The pillar of cloud by day and the pillar of fire by night went before Israel in the wilderness (Exodus 13:21). This was the cloud that passed by Moses as God covered him in the cleft of the rock with his hand—so that Moses only saw the afterglow (Exodus 33:18–23). This was the cloud that covered the nearly finished Tent of the Meeting and so filled the new tabernacle with God's glory that Moses could not enter it (Exodus 40:35). It was the same cloud that filled Solomon's temple on dedication day so that the priests could not enter the temple (1 Kings 8:10, 11; 2 Chronicles 7:1). It was the same glory that Ezekiel saw rise from between the cherubim and move to the threshold of the temple because of Israel's apostasy (Ezekiel 8:4; 9:3), and then slowly, hesitatingly moved over the east gate of the temple where it hovered (Ezekiel 10:4, 18, 19), finally rising to be seen no more from the Mount of Olives (Ezekiel 11:22–25).

It had been six hundred years since anyone in Israel had seen the *shekinah* glory. But as Jesus and his inner circle stood in silence in the night air, "a [luminous] cloud overshadowed them" (v. 7a). It was the *shekinah*! It is fair to imagine that from below any who happened to look up at Hermon saw it—the mountain was capped with the divine incandescence. Peter, James, and John were in the cloud that Moses was not even permitted to directly behold. Jesus was with them, and thus they could stand radiant in the *shekinah* glory!

As they stood shimmering with Christ in the cloud, this was not only a declaration about Christ, but a prophecy of what was to come. In the future, in death, they would meet the risen Christ in the incandescent clouds to be with him forever (1 Thessalonians 4:17, 18). They were to put their arms around this blessed experience and pull it into themselves. So must we! It is our hope. The end of verse 17 of 1 Thessalonians 4 says that the same Lord is going to return in a cloud of glory, and that those who die before are going to rise to meet him in the air, and that the living are going to meet him in the air too—in that cloud of glory. Someday *we* are going to be in that cloud! The *shekinah* glory is going to surround us!

Then in the silence, "a voice came out of the cloud, 'This is my beloved Son; listen to him'" (v. 7b). This was the voice of the Father, who said almost the same thing at Jesus' baptism. This was not the disciples' imagination. Years later Peter would write:

> For we did not follow cleverly devised myths when we made known to you the power and coming of our Lord Jesus Christ, but we were eyewitnesses of his majesty. For when he received honor and glory from God the Father, and the voice was borne to him by the Majestic Glory, "This is my beloved Son, with whom I am well pleased," we ourselves heard this very voice borne from heaven, for we were with him on the holy mountain. (2 Peter 1:16–18)

"Listen to him," was the command! The Law and Prophets were only partial expressions, but here is the final statement. "Listen to *him*."

The writer of Hebrews begins his letter by saying, "Long ago, at many times and in many ways, God spoke to our fathers by the prophets, but in these last days he has spoken to us by his Son" (Hebrews 1:1, 2).

Jesus is the ultimate expression of truth! Peter, James, and John were to listen to what Jesus said about the necessity of his death and of their embracing the paradox of the cross. "For whoever would save his life will lose it, but whoever loses his life for my sake and the gospel's will save it" (8:35).

We need to listen to Jesus' words about all of life. "Lord, to whom shall we go? You have the words of eternal life" (John 6:68). May we listen to no other voice. Listen when he says: "If anyone thirsts, let him come to me and drink. Whoever believes in me, as the Scripture has said, 'Out of his heart will flow rivers of living water'" (John 7:37, 38). Listen when he says: "Come to me, all who labor and are heavy laden, and I will give you rest. Take my yoke upon you, and learn from me, for I am gentle and lowly in heart, and you will find rest for your souls. For my yoke is easy, and my burden is light" (Matthew 11:28–30). Listen when he says: "If anyone would come after me, let him deny himself and take up his cross and follow me" (Mark 8:34).

Matthew says that when the three heard the voice from Heaven, "they fell on their faces and were terrified. But Jesus came and touched them, saying, 'Rise, and have no fear'" (Matthew 17:6, 7).

Verse 8 concludes: "And suddenly, looking around, they no longer saw anyone with them but Jesus only." The *shekinah* was gone. Jesus' skin and clothing no longer glowed. Moses and Elijah had disappeared, the voice of the Father was still, and the three disciples saw only Jesus, backlit by the galaxies he had created!

This is what all our experience, all our theology, all our work should come to—seeing only Jesus! When this happens, our hearts honor him in worship. We love all mankind as we ought. We give our lives in his service, and we embrace the paradox of the cross.

Our risen Christ wants to encourage us. He has called us to confess him as Christ, and that involves confessing him as a suffering Messiah. It involves also embracing the suffering that comes from the cross, the suffering that comes from being like him, from living his ethics in a fallen world, from speaking his name when it brings reproach. We must make this our own if we are to follow him.

But along with this, we are to appropriate for ourselves the encouragement that comes from putting our arms around the Christ of the Transfiguration and drawing him to ourselves. Put yourself on the Mount of

Transfiguration, and embrace your majestic Christ. This is the glorious Savior you will know and love throughout eternity!

Jesus Christ was completely man and yet completely divine, so that in a split second he could let his glory shine like the sun. He is the fulfillment of everything Moses and Elijah, the Law and the Prophets, ever intended or suggested, and he brings that fulfillment to us. He brings the presence of the Triune God to our lives and illuminates them, and one day we will bathe in the *shekinah* glory in his presence. We must hold him and this truth close.

Some months later, toward the very end of Jesus' life, as the cross loomed even larger, he was in Jerusalem for the Feast of Tabernacles. It was the end of the festival, and the previous night an unforgettable ceremony, the illumination of the temple, had taken place before the four massive golden candelabra topped with huge torches. It is said that the candelabra were as tall as the highest walls of the temple. At the top of these candelabra were mounted great bowls that held sixty-five liters of oil. There was a ladder for each candelabrum, and when evening came, healthy young priests would carry oil up to the great bowls and light the protruding wicks. Eyewitnesses said that the huge flames that leapt from these torches illuminated not only the temple but all of Jerusalem. The *Mishnah* tells us: "Men of piety and good works used to dance before [the candelabra] with burning torches in their hands singing songs and praises and countless Levites played on harps, lyres, cymbals, and trumpets and instruments of music."[4] The exotic rite celebrated the great pillar of fire (the glorious cloud of God's presence) that led the Israelites during their sojourn in the wilderness, spread its fiery billows over the tabernacle, and later engulfed the temple.

In the temple treasury the following morning, with the charred torches still in place, Jesus lifted his voice above the crowd and proclaimed, "I am the light of the world." There could scarcely be a more emphatic way to announce one of the supreme truths of his existence. Christ was saying in effect, "The pillar of fire that came between you and the Egyptians, the cloud that guided you by day in the wilderness and illumined the night and enveloped the tabernacle, the glorious cloud that filled Solomon's temple, was me!" "I am the light of the world. Whoever follows me will not walk in darkness, but will have the light of life" (John 8:12).

He is the *shekinah* glory! We are to put our arms around the Midnight Son and draw him close. We "have the light of life."

Open your hearts—embrace the light.

29

Unbelieving Faith

MARK 9:14–32

IN THE VATICAN GALLERY hangs Raphael's last painting, which some think to be his greatest. It is entitled, *The Transfiguration*. The uppermost part pictures the transfigured form of Jesus, with Moses on the left and Elijah on his right. On the next level down are the three disciples, Peter, James, and John, recently awakened and shielding their eyes from Jesus' blinding brilliance. Then, on the ground level, is a poor demon-possessed boy, his mouth hideously gaping with wild ravings. At his side is his desperate father. Surrounding them are the rest of the disciples, some of whom are pointing upward to the glowing figure of Christ—who will be the boy's only answer.[1] Raphael has brilliantly captured something of the overwhelming contrast between the glorious Mount of Transfiguration and the troubled world waiting below.

It is now the next day. Peter, James, and John could scarcely keep their feet on the ground as they descended the mountain. High on the slopes of Hermon, under the Milky Way, they had seen Jesus' divine essence gloriously shine through. They had seen the Midnight Son! They had seen Moses and Elijah, the preeminent lawgiver and foremost prophet of Israel, gone for over a millennium, speaking with Jesus. The luminous cloud of the *shekinah* glory had enveloped them. To top it off, they had heard the very voice of God the Father roll from the cloud: "This is my beloved Son; listen to him" (9:7).

What a conversation they must have had as they bounced down the slopes the next day. It was all theology—questions about the relationship of Elijah and Messiah, the timing of it all, the Resurrection (9:9–13). They did not understand it all, but Peter and the "Sons of Thunder" were exhilarated.

But suddenly they were at ground level and facing a world convulsed by demonic powers. Verses 14, 15 describe the encounter: "And when they came to the disciples, they saw a great crowd around them, and scribes arguing with them. And immediately all the crowd, when they saw him, were greatly amazed and ran up to him and greeted him."

The other nine disciples were being heckled and taunted by a group of leering, self-satisfied scribes. The disciples had attempted an exorcism and failed, and the scribes were deriding them for their powerlessness, and were blaspheming Jesus as well. "The messenger is as the man himself. You're phonies and so is your master!" they shouted.[2] The scribes no doubt were recommending *their* formulas for exorcism, and the disciples were giving it back in kind. It was one noisy hassle!

They were all so engrossed, they did not even see Jesus approach and, overcome with surprise, ran to greet him. "Jesus, we were just talking about you!" So he engaged them in conversation:

> And he asked them, "What are you arguing about with them?" And some-
> one from the crowd answered him, "Teacher, I brought my son to you, for
> he has a spirit that makes him mute. And whenever it seizes him, it throws
> him down, and he foams and grinds his teeth and becomes rigid. So I asked
> your disciples to cast it out, and they were not able." (vv. 16–18)

The scribes had remained discreetly silent, but a distraught father had an-swered Jesus. Matthew adds in his account that the father got on *his knees* before Jesus (17:14). Dr. Luke records him saying, "Teacher, I beg you to look at my son, for he is my only child" (Luke 9:38).

What a pathetic picture we get from the Gospels together! The demon seizes the boy (9:18)—the child screams (Luke 9:39)—the spirit throws him to the ground, and he foams at the mouth. He grinds his teeth and becomes stiff as a board (Mark 9:18). Many times he has been cast into a fire or water by the spirit (Matthew 17:15), so that he is covered with burn scars. But even worse, the spirit has made him deaf and mute (Mark 9:17, 25). He lived an aquarium-like existence. He could see what was going on around his pathetic body, but he could not hear or speak.

As such, he was a perfect example of Satan's motivation, which is to destroy the image of God in mankind—as we see also in the pathetic condi-tion of the Gadarene maniac (who was even compelled to engage in self-mutilation, 5:1–5). Satan is at war with the image of God, the *Imago Dei*. Anything he can do to destroy this in man is for him, in his twisted thinking, a triumph over God.

Often this takes place in the mental and moral disfigurement of humanity, as in the case of fourteen-year-old Thomas Sullivan, described in a *Chicago Tribune* article. This studious boy within a matter of weeks became involved in the occult and Satan worship. He stabbed his own mother, set fire to the house (hoping to kill his father and brother), and then cut his own throat and wrists with his Boy Scout knife and died outside in the bloody snow.[3]

However, Satan most often perpetrates more subtle, respectable, civil seduction. Whatever method he uses, he finds ultimate satisfaction in the obscene twisting of lives. As a pastor, I have seen such spiritual distortions. We daily rub shoulders with people who privately indulge in gross, even macabre, spiritual and sensual practices. Satan loves to take people to the lowest common denominator. Believe it!

The attacks upon this boy serve to show how radical and real the struggle is between Satan (the destroyer of life) and Jesus (the Life-giver).

What a sickening shock to see this immediately after the Mount of Transfiguration—moving from light to darkness, from worship to blasphemy. And most tragic of all, it was a descent from power to helplessness. Jesus' disciples were at this point impotent in their opposition to Satan and in their ministry to a broken world.

The rest of the story describes Christ's diagnosis of the problem, and his answer in both word and action. The answer is one that the Church today needs as much or more than the disciples then.

Diagnosis: Powerlessness through Unbelief (v. 19a)

Jesus' initial response was both a diagnosis and an emotional cry from the heart. We know this because the initial word ("O") was rarely used in addressing others directly, as he did here. It was the result of his deep emotion: "O faithless generation, how long am I to be with you?" (v. 19a).

Jesus was in lonely pain and exasperation. Why? Because his twelve disciples, whom he had earlier commissioned "that they might be with him and he might send them out to preach and have authority to cast out demons" (3:14, 15), had failed! They had been successful earlier, but now after a week of his absence they were powerless.

Their failure was not because they did not try. On the contrary, they did their best. Their problem was *unbelief.* They believed in the process, they believed in themselves because they had done it previously,[4] but they were not resting their faith in him. Jesus, fresh from the glorious Transfiguration, was heartbroken! "O faithless generation [i.e., you disciples are just like the rest of this generation], how long am I to be with you? [i.e., will you ever learn?]" (v. 19a).

These are fitting words for the church today, which is so well-equipped, rich, and instructed and yet so often powerless. We cannot, and dare not, duck the Master's diagnosis. For if we accept it, we must carefully listen, with his disciples, to what Jesus now said and did—for in a few moments he would raise the boy's father's faith to a level requisite with the miracles to take place.

Answer: Power through Faith/Belief (vv. 19b–27)

First, Jesus commanded that the demonized boy be brought to him: "'Bring him to me.' And they brought the boy to him. And when the spirit saw him, immediately it convulsed the boy, and he fell on the ground and rolled about, foaming at the mouth" (vv. 19b, 20). The tenses here are terribly graphic. He continued rolling around on the ground and foaming at the mouth. This was a further demonstration of the raging hatred the demonic realm had for Jesus.

Second, Jesus drew the father out: "And Jesus asked his father, 'How long has this been happening to him?' And he said, 'From childhood. And it has often cast him into fire and into water, to destroy him. But if you can do anything, have compassion on us and help us'" (vv. 21, 22). In drawing the man out, Jesus allowed him to unburden himself, and to again recognize the desperate extremity of his boy's plight. Think how the father felt seeing his maimed, burnt son wallowing in the dirt, staring up with an unearthly look through terror-filled eyes. Because of his convulsions, he could not even talk or hear.

Parents can imagine the pain of this father. When my children were growing up, I rose and fell with their rejections and successes. There were times I would rather take a beating than see them endure what they had to experience.

How that father hurt! But also think of how Jesus felt! He cared as no one else ever had, and the father could see it in his eyes. There never has been compassion like that of Jesus! This divine compassion is what drew out the father's desperate cry: "But if you can do anything, have compassion on us and help us." His plea was the annex to faith. He wasn't sure what would happen. He knew Christ could do it, but his own faith had been badly shaken by the disciples' failure to help his son.

Now Jesus took a third elevating step in the process: "And Jesus said to him, '"If you can"! All things are possible for one who believes'" (v. 23). Notice carefully the words, "If you can," for they are the key to understanding Jesus. The boy's father had just said, "if you can do anything," and Jesus is saying back in essence, "You say 'if you can' to me, but that isn't the issue. Of course I can. No, my friend, the burden is on you because 'All things are possible for one who believes.'"[5] Jesus is standing nose to nose with the man and challenging him to believe. The world is standing still. Eternity is passing between them.

This is one of the most abused verses in the Bible today. People have ripped it from its context and made it the rationale for saying that their wishes will come true if they can just mount enough faith! There are some who even teach that faith can control God, that if you believe enough, God has to do it! That is man-made, man-centered religion. The fact is, faith must never go farther than God's clear promises, for "whatever goes beyond God's Word is not faith, but something else assuming its appearance."[6]

For example, say a parent is greatly concerned over a sick child's health and longs for the child's recovery. So he says to himself, "I believe that Christ can heal him. I also believe that he will if I pray in faith, and I know that I will certainly be answered." Wrong! Such a prayer goes beyond God's Word. Certainly Christ can heal his child, but Christ has not told him that his child will indeed be healed. Our faith can be misplaced. This is where so many believers fall short.

Yet there are times when we do not believe God can do anything! There are souls we consider impossible. There are healings we think are beyond his power. In this we also sin!

We fail to believe the promises of his Word, or to pray in faith for their fulfillment. Great things would take place if we would pray for them: salvation of whole peoples, revivals, power in the church, miracles—both physical and spiritual. There *are* times when God reveals through his Spirit that he is going to do a specific healing, and in that case the believer can and must pray in faith.

I have experienced this in my own ministry. The Holy Spirit has given me the subjective assurance that he was going to heal one who was ill, I have prayed in faith, and the person was healed. James 5:14, 15 refers to this phenomena when it says, "Is anyone among you sick? Let him call for the elders of the church . . ." (implicitly, as the Holy Spirit prompts him or her to do so). Then the elders can offer a prayer in faith (that the Spirit will fulfill his prompting and bring healing), "[a]nd the prayer of faith will save the one who is sick, and the Lord will raise him up."

In the story before us, the father was called to believe because Christ told him that his faith was the condition to his son's being healed! The poor father is facing Jesus, and Jesus is saying, "It's not a question of whether I *can* do it, but *will* you believe, for *all things are possible for one who believes.*" If the man doesn't believe, his son is going to remain as he is.

Now comes one of the great responses in all of Scripture: "I believe; help my unbelief!" (v. 24). Here is an honest man, one of the most transparent characters in the Bible. His faith was trembling, imperfect, but real! A faith that declares itself publicly and at the same time recognizes its weaknesses and pleads for help is a real faith.

What an encouragement to us all! You and I need not think we are hypocrites because our faith is not perfect. There are two questions we must answer:

1) Do we believe God can do anything? Or, put another way, do we believe in the God the Scriptures describe?
2) Do we believe that he will do what he has promised to do? The father believed in Jesus and his promise—and it happened.

> And when Jesus saw that a crowd came running together, he rebuked the unclean spirit, saying to it, "You mute and deaf spirit, I command you, come out of him and never enter him again." And after crying out and convulsing him terribly, it came out, and the boy was like a corpse, so that most of them said, "He is dead." (vv. 25, 26)

The boy lay prostrate, stiff, the foam still on his open mouth, his eyes staring. "He cured him all right. He's dead!"

"But Jesus took him by the hand and lifted him up, and he arose" (v. 27). The *Imago Dei* was restored. Satan was defeated.

Luke adds that Jesus "gave him back to his father." "And all were astonished at the majesty of God" (Luke 9:42, 43).

Can you hear the cheers from the disciples? The Lord gave the boy back his mind, his hearing, his speech, his boyhood, his hope, his visions—and he gave him a faith. Could it have been otherwise?

Power comes to the Church when there is faith. But there is something more to be said, and that is why Mark includes a brief epilogue in verses 28, 29.

Power Comes through Prayer (vv. 28, 29)

Mark tells us: "And when [Jesus] had entered the house, his disciples asked him privately, 'Why could we not cast it out?' And he said to them, 'This kind cannot be driven out by anything but prayer'" (vv. 28, 29).

During those six days that Jesus was gone, the disciples had gone about their work, preaching and casting out evil spirits as usual. When they came to the particularly stubborn demon in the boy, they tried and failed. Then another tried. Then several tried, and they tried again, but nothing worked. Why? The answer is, they were self-deceived in somehow thinking that the gift they had received for exorcism was under their own control and could be exercised at will. Thus, they did not think to pray! They forgot that there had to be radical dependence if God's power was to course through their lives. *Jesus was teaching them that the faith that brings power is a faith that prays.* The demon would have long been history if the disciples had given themselves to believing prayer!

Raphael's three-tiered *Transfiguration* sets before us a brilliant pictorial exposition of this text. The disciples stand below with their hands extended up toward the transfigured Christ, in expression of the truth that Christ alone can help the poor father and his gaping son. This says it all. Power on earth comes through a praying faith in our great Christ.

Do you believe in the Christ of the Transfiguration, the Midnight Son? Do you believe that Moses and Elijah came from the realms of the dead to affirm that Christ is the fulfillment of everything to which the Law and Prophets pointed? Do you believe the *shekinah* glory, the pillar of fire, engulfed them all in dazzling glory and that it was the Father's voice that rang out over Hermon? If so, then you believe in a Christ who *can* fulfill his word to you and *will* do so. And if you believe this, then your life will be given more and more to dependent prayer, and there will be power in your life and in the Church. Demons will flee. Souls will be made whole.

A true test of our spiritual walk is our prayer life. We must be people of profound prayer if we believe in the Christ of this chapter. And that will mean power.

30

Attitudes for Ministry

MARK 9:33–41

THE APOSTLES had recently seen the unforgettable Transfiguration, followed by a marvelous healing episode at the foot of the mount, and now, while on the road, they heard Jesus' ominous words regarding his death (9:30–32). This was hardly the time for an argument. Nevertheless, they were engaged in heated debate about—of all things—who was "the greatest"! Unbelievable!

The Gospels do not record their exact words, but undoubtedly some, such as Peter, James, and John, argued that they were "the greatest" because of their privileged relationship with Christ. *They* were the inner circle. *They* had been the only witnesses to the Transfiguration and had seen the Midnight Son. *They* had heard teaching that the others had not. Peter may very well have told the other two, "Listen, men, it has to be one of three, and it's probably me. I am the leader!" To this, James and John, the "Sons of Thunder," perhaps loudly objected. The rest would have none of this. Their deeds were just as notable, and some of them were out *doing* it while these three were talking. This was a tawdry, miserable affair, and Jesus knew what was going on, even though they thought he was beyond earshot.

What a chill this must have brought to his already burdened soul. They had been with him almost three years, and now that he was facing the ultimate humiliation of all time, they were arguing about who was the greatest. They were no different from the petty politicians of Capernaum or the sycophants in Herod's court! Something had to be done! "And they came to Capernaum. And when he was in the house he asked them, 'What were you discussing on the way?' But they kept silent, for on the way they had argued with one another about who was the greatest" (vv. 33, 34).

After all that brouhaha on the road, now, face-to-face with Jesus, no one would utter a word. It was an embarrassing, shameful silence. It was time for some teaching. So, "he sat down and called the twelve" (v. 35a). He postured himself in the official rabbinical position as teacher and superior, with the twelve silent disciples around him as needy learners. If they were going to continue to be his disciples and succeed in their apostolic ministry, they would have to learn this lesson and learn it well. The Church that they were to found would never survive unless there was an attitude change. Thankfully there was, though it did not come until after Jesus' death and resurrection.

Today we live on the other side of these great events, but the Church is in great need of deliverance from these very attitudes. There is a mind-set that defines ministry as a kind of lordship: sitting in the honored seat, being the feted guest at luncheons, speaking to vast throngs, building monuments and collecting honorary titles. This type of attitude values being served. For those caught up in such thinking, Christianity exists to give *me* eternal life, to increase *my* physical health, to coddle *my* body, to enlarge *my* power, to elevate *my* prestige.

Some of us in the ministry have attended ministerial conventions that were given wholly to personality promotion and ended with a well-defined (though unspoken) pecking order. The "important people" were easy to identify; busy, busy, busy, going from one "important" meeting to another, playing up to the media. True, there were no Popes in sedan chairs, but there were executive limos with smoked glass and fawning, patronizing followers.

The Church has been assaulted with a cultural perspective that sanctifies "winning." Being Number One is "American," and it is even thought to be "Christian." Don't misunderstand: the Scriptures do call God's people to do their very best. Paul strove to do so (Philippians 3:12–14), and he encouraged Timothy to do the same in his ministry (1 Timothy 3:1). But to be *"Numero Uno"*—to want always to be served—is sub-Christian. The disciples were blowing it, as are many today.

Ministry with a Servant's Attitude (vv. 35–37)

Christ was now authoritatively seated in the uneasy quiet. He broke the silence with this: "If anyone would be first, he must be last of all and servant of all" (v. 35b).

Now that was (and is) a radical statement! It was *countercultural*. Contemporary Jewish culture was constantly immersed in questions of procedure and rank. The German New Testament scholar A. Schlatter says: "At all points in worship, in administration of justice, at meals, in all dealings, there constantly arose the question of who was greater, and estimating the honor due to each was a task which had constantly to be fulfilled and was felt to be very important."[1]

Precedence was a cultural preoccupation, but the radical Jesus attacked it and tossed it away. His teaching was, and is, *counter-natural*. The natural human instinct is to dominate. Thus, if any of us will live Jesus' words out, not seeking preeminence, but seeking to serve all, he or she will be a *cultural radical*! Your life will be a gift to many, while it will equally be a threat to many others. Such a lifestyle is not easy.

Initially the disciples were not able to do this. The night before Jesus died, when they came to the upper room, they were again so busy arguing as to who was "the greatest" that no one would condescend to be a servant and wash the others' feet. That is when Jesus removed his outer garment and then his tunic. Next he took a towel and wrapped it about his body and then poured water into a basin and began slowly to move around the circle, washing each of the disciples' outstretched feet, wiping them with the towel with which he was wrapped. The Incarnate Son, God himself, *washed the feet* of his prideful, arrogant creatures. Then he said, "If I then, your Lord and Teacher, have washed your feet, you also ought to wash one another's feet. For I have given you an example, that you also should do just as I have done to you. Truly, truly, I say to you, a servant is not greater than his master, nor is a messenger greater than the one who sent him" (John 13:14–16). Coming from his lips, such an idea was infinitely compelling, but they would only find the power to do it when they were filled with the Spirit at Pentecost. And they did! The Early Church lived this way, just as St. Polycarp admonished: "Likewise must the deacons be blameless . . . walking according to the truth of the Lord, who is the servant of all."[2]

We are all called to this radicalness—there are no exceptions! Christian business executives who spend their day telling others what to do and being waited on are to be servants. This does not mean an abdication of authority—it requires a disposition of heart. Are you serving your "superiors" *and* your "inferiors"? Do you have places of humble (even hidden) service for your church and your fellow man? If not, you are failing God! As Christians, we are captive to God's Word, and we must embrace our captivity to him through obedience.

The same goes for homemakers, and teachers, and educational executives, and craftsmen, and bankers, and lawyers, and, perhaps in a double portion, to ministers, by virtue of what we claim to be! We are all called to radical servanthood! This is the way to true "firstness" in God's eyes.

As Jesus' words were sinking in (with various degrees of success!), he decided to dramatize the truth by enacting a parable of how they were to treat one another. It was all so very beautiful. The house they were in was in Capernaum and may well have been Simon Peter's, and the child Jesus enfolded may even have been one of Peter's.

"And he took a child and put him in the midst of them, and taking him in his arms, he said to them, 'Whoever receives one such child in my name receives me, and whoever receives me, receives not me but him who sent me'" (vv. 36, 37). The power of this enacted parable to the disciples lies in this: in the Aramaic language, which Jesus spoke, *child* and *servant* were the same word.[3] Thus, Jesus was saying that the disciples must receive his children (other servants and disciples) with the open arms and love with which he was holding that child. There was to be no thought of precedence (who was better than whom), but simple, open-armed affection. Jesus said that when they did this in his name, they welcomed not only Jesus himself, "but him who sent me"—God the Father.

Why? Because Jesus (along with the Father and the Spirit) resides in the children of God—in the wondrous mystery of Christ's Body, the Church. So practically speaking, when we welcome other children of God in Christ's name, there is a sense in which we receive and open ourselves further to Christ, because he indwells them and is identified with them. What a marvelous truth!

Jesus' dramatization is a call to a wonderful, liberating spiritual egalitarianism. We are to receive all of God's people as we do children, with no thought of their accomplishments, their influence, their fame, or their gifts, but simply because they are his children. This rules out seeking the powerful or influential for what they can do for us. This is a warning about neglecting the simple, the humble, the ordinary. James extended this same warning when he said,

> My brothers, show no partiality as you hold the faith in our Lord Jesus Christ, the Lord of glory. For if a man wearing a gold ring and fine clothing comes into your assembly, and a poor man in shabby clothing also comes in, and if you pay attention to the one who wears the fine clothing and say, "You sit here in a good place," while you say to the poor man, "You stand over there," or, "Sit down at my feet," have you not then made distinctions among yourselves and become judges with evil thoughts? (James 2:1–4)

An open, accepting, status-consciousless reception of others opens us to Christ. If we want to be Spirit-filled, we have a divine mandate to be lovers of everyone, and especially those in Christ's Body. It is possible to reach a stone wall in spiritual growth because the world has infused us with a status-conscious heart—a desire to dominate and be served. Christ's living parable gently calls each of us to repent.

Ministry with a Tolerant Attitude (vv. 38–41)

Apparently as the Apostle John heard Jesus' words and saw them acted out, his conscience was stirred. He responded, half confessing and half asking, "Teacher, we saw someone casting out demons in your name, and we tried to stop him, because he was not following us" (v. 38). What volumes of human experience were contained in John's words, for here we have an apostolic example of ministerial intolerance and jealousy. It reveals the origin of so much of the exclusivism and narrowness we experience.

This man was apparently a believer in Jesus, but certainly not as informed as the disciples—and when they told him repeatedly to desist, he would not. But what was particularly galling was his success. He really was experiencing power through Jesus' name—a supreme irony in the light of their recent powerlessness![4]

Joshua had been likewise adamant when he found Eldad and Medad "prophesying" (preaching) in the camp and called Moses to stop them (Numbers 11:26–28). John the Baptist's disciples had done almost the same thing when they saw Jesus' star rising as John's was setting. "And they came to John and said to him, 'Rabbi, he who was with you across the Jordan, to whom you bore witness—look, he is baptizing, and all are going to him'" (John 3:26). It is no different today. Chuck Swindoll has observed:

> It is a curious fact that jealousy is a tension often found among professionals, the gifted, and the highly competent. You know, doctors, singers, artists, lawyers, business men and women, authors, entertainers, preachers, educators, politicians, and all public figures. Strange, isn't it, that such capable folk find it nearly impossible to applaud others in their own field who excel a shade or two more than they? Jealousy's fangs may be hidden, but take care when the creature coils . . . no matter how cultured and dignified it may appear.

In religious circles we hear such things as: "He's not in our denomination." "Never heard of his seminary." "What a strange style."

> Believe as I believe, no more no less,
> That I am right, and no one else confess.
> Feel as I feel, think as I think,

Eat what I eat, and drink what I drink,
Look as I look, do always as I do,
Then and only then, I'll fellowship with you.

What a sad way to go! But there has always been a proper response. Hear Moses' reply to Joshua: "Are you jealous for my sake? Would that all the LORD's people were prophets, that the LORD would put his Spirit on them!" (Numbers 11:29).

Listen to John's answer to his disciples: "A person cannot receive even one thing unless it is given him from heaven. You yourselves bear me witness, that I said, 'I am not the Christ, but I have been sent before him.' The one who has the bride is the bridegroom. The friend of the bridegroom, who stands and hears him, rejoices greatly at the bridegroom's voice. Therefore this joy of mine is now complete. He must increase, but I must decrease" (John 3:27–30).

John said, regarding Jesus' expanding ministry, that he was like the friend of the bridegroom—the *Shoshben,* who on the wedding day stood guard over the bridal chamber, waiting to rejoice over the voice of the bridegroom and open the chamber door.[5] John found joy in Jesus' ascendance!

Here in Mark 9 Jesus' response gives guidance for all time. "But Jesus said, 'Do not stop him, for no one who does a mighty work in my name will be able soon afterward to speak evil of me. For the one who is not against us is for us. For truly, I say to you, whoever gives you a cup of water to drink because you belong to Christ will by no means lose his reward'" (vv. 39–41). The criterion for ministry is not style or tradition or denomination, but Jesus' name being lifted up and glorified. We are to rejoice in *this.*

The proper attitude for those in ministry and for all who desire to minister is a spirit that is tolerant and free from jealousy and is supportive of others.

As one pastor has said, "We're all branch offices of the same business; when one branch prospers, we all prosper!" No Christian should want another's job. There should be no climbing. Rather, when one does well, the others should pat him on the back. If a brother or sister has difficulty, there should be concerned counsel and prayer.

In Christian ministry and walk, it is no exaggeration to say that *attitude is everything!* As Jesus observed the ambitious, jealous, grasping attitude of his disciples, he knew this to be true. There is no place in the Church for seeking dominance and first place. Imagine Jesus saying to you, "If anyone would be first, he must be last of all and servant of all" (v. 35).

Are you seeking to be served and be first? Or have you embraced the radicalness of servanthood? Imagine Christ as "he took a child and put him in the midst of them, and taking him in his arms, he said to them, 'Whoever receives one such child in my name receives me, and whoever receives me, receives not me but him who sent me'" (vv. 36, 37).

Is your attitude grudging, suspicious? Or are your arms open to others among God's people, just as you open them to your children?

Finally, hear Jesus call John to loving tolerance to others in ministry. "But Jesus said, 'Do not stop him, for no one who does a mighty work in my name will be able soon afterward to speak evil of me. For the one who is not against us is for us'" (vv. 39, 40).

Is your attitude exclusive, narrow, clubbish? Or do you have the informed tolerance of Christ, which rejoices when his name is glorified?

31

The Demanding Requirements of Discipleship

MARK 9:42-50

Ministering with Integrity (v. 42)

As Jesus continued instructing the Twelve, he further galvanized their attention with a terrifying statement of *ministerial responsibility*: "Whoever causes one of these little ones who believe in me to sin, it would be better for him if a great millstone were hung around his neck and he were thrown into the sea" (v. 42).

This had in fact been the fate of the leaders of an insurrection under the early Zealot leader Judas the Galilean, whom the Romans drowned in a lake.[1] Suetonius, the Roman historian, also mentioned a graphic case having a similar punishment.[2] The apostles knew what Jesus was talking about and in their imaginations could see the drowned bodies of the victims tethered to great millstones as they swayed to and fro with the currents. There is something particularly horrifying about this image—being dropped down, down into the darkness, struggling, and then hanging motionless in the darkness, hidden from life and the world. Jesus used the most graphic terms to make the point that it would be better to be drowned than to cause humble believers ("little ones") who served him to fall into sin!

Woe to those engaged in spiritual seduction—the Joseph Smiths and Jim Joneses and David Bergs and Judge Rutherfords and Shirley MacLaines! Have you ever listened to such as these and sensed the sickening horror that awaits them . . . and mourned? Double woe to preachers who claim to be preaching Biblical Christianity and even use the sacred vocabulary, but redefine the words, emptying them of meaning—and thus lead untaught believers astray. It would be better for them if they had been drowned years before in the sea! Because this comes directly from the lips of Jesus, it bears terrifying authority.

What a sobering revelation—even to those of us who love Christ and attempt to follow him. Few things disturb Christ more than causing new or weak or uninformed believers to sin. And those who do so, stand in the way of stern discipline from Christ. Jesus' words are a warning to make sure there is nothing in our lives that would make one of his "little ones" stumble. In view of the context, the warning is specifically against causing them to sin because of our elitist, superior attitudes: the attitude that projects a kind of superior toleration for the bumbling enthusiasm of a new believer; that condemns his spiritual efforts with faint praise; that belittles his accomplishments and douses them with cold skepticism. Christ loathes this in his Church!

Donald Hubbard, one-time pastor of Calvary Baptist Church of New York City, tells of seeing a high school girl excluded while he was leading a week-long camp. She was severely handicapped and literally had to drag herself from cabin to chapel. When she ate, she had to have a spoon strapped onto her wrist to eat. In the process some of the food would fall on the table and on her lap. No one had time for her, so she went around by herself and ate alone. Dr. Hubbard says that this particular group of high schoolers, though they were from good churches, were an unusually sophisticated and hardened bunch. They could quote the Scriptures, but little spiritual reality was evident in their lives.

On the final night, in keeping with a camp tradition, a great bonfire was struck, and all gathered around to give a testimony and cast a stick in the fire. But no one responded except this handicapped girl. As Dr. Hubbard tells it, she picked up a stick and then stumbled around the fire, looking each camper in the face. And when she had finished she said to all in her slurred speech, "I don't know why God made me like this, but he can have all of me there is!" And she wrenched her body around and threw her stick into the fire. She refused to be a casualty of their sinful, superficial hearts! Bless her forever!

But sadly, many "little ones" who began well have been sunk by the temper of an older believer. George Fox, the Quaker, tells how when seeking God he asked advice from a clergyman of the established church. The minister began to advise Fox, but when young Fox accidentally stepped back on a flower in the garden, the clergyman fell into a rage. Fox concluded that he would find no help there and went on to seek help elsewhere. Others would not weather such treatment so well. How many have been turned off by an unforgiving spirit, or by a dishonest business transaction of a church member, or by the worthless, crude street language that sometimes falls from a believer's mouth, or by the sarcasm of a malignant gossip. Thousands! And some have never recovered!

If we wish to minister, we must "walk our talk!" Christians, lay this to heart. Someone is watching you, and if you disappoint him or her, that person will stumble. And the great personal tragedy is, it may be someone you love deeply—a child, a grandchild, a boyfriend, a teacher, a student.

But the fact that we are watched also has its upside, for our lives have the potential of causing others to reach up to Christ.

After discussing the responsibility to not cause others to stumble, Jesus naturally moved on to the responsibility to keep one's own life free from sin.

Living in Holiness (vv. 43–48)

Jesus couched the necessity for personal holiness in the most drastic of terms, actually suggesting the removing of a hand or foot or eye from the body:

> And if your hand causes you to sin, cut it off. It is better for you to enter life crippled than with two hands to go to hell, to the unquenchable fire. And if your foot causes you to sin, cut it off. It is better for you to enter life lame than with two feet to be thrown into hell. And if your eye causes you to sin, tear it out. It is better for you to enter the kingdom of God with one eye than with two eyes to be thrown into hell, "where their worm does not die and the fire is not quenched." (vv. 43–48)

Tragically, there have been some who have taken this literally. A. J. Gossip, the renowned Scottish preacher, told of a brilliant theological student who suddenly went crazy one night and cut off his hand with a razor. And when Gossip found him, he was laughing exultantly, saying, "I did right . . . I can look Jesus in the face."[3]

The most famous case of crass literalism was Origen of Alexandria, who had himself emasculated in an attempt to overcome sensual desires. It is significant that not long after that, the Council of Nicea outlawed this practice. Such mutilation is not only contrary to the Scripture, but it is possible to be minus hands, feet, and eyes and to be neutered and still be the most libidinous, materialistic, proud person in town!

What Jesus is calling for is not physical mutilation, but spiritual mortification—the cutting off of harmful practices from one's life. The hand, foot, and eye encompass the totality of life. The hand symbolizes what we *do*, the foot where we *go*, and the eye what we *see*. His logic is impeccable and compelling. It is better to clean up your fleeting life here through some healthy self-denial than go bearing your sins to an unending Gehenna, an eternal, smoking rubbish heap where the worms eternally gorge themselves on the refuse of your life.[4] Any sacrifice, any discipline, any self-denial is worth it!

These gory metaphors tell us that halfway measures just will not do it. There must be a severing, a gouging out of sin if there is to be victory. This must be decisive and complete—as serious and final as a hand or foot or eye cast upon the floor.

The metaphorical language here further suggests that you alone must do it. It is "*your* hand," "*your* foot," "*your* eye" that you must cast away. It is a delusion to think that anyone else can or should do it for you.

Christ's compelling logic demands some answers. Are there places where your feet carry you that you have no business being—perhaps a social establishment that you visit after-hours? Are there events that you attend that involve temptations you cannot handle? Regarding the hand, are there hidden activities or habits that occupy you, things perhaps that if someone else knew about, you would be most embarrassed?

Let me paraphrase some questions from a sermon by Joe Bayly titled "Is Holiness Possible Today?": What are we reading? Do we have books or magazines that we want no one else to see? What are we renting at the local video stores? How many hours do we spend watching TV—how many murders? How many chapters of the Bible did we read last week? Where do our minds go when we have no duties to perform? If our answers leave us guilty, Jesus says we must go to extremes to rid ourselves of the offending member—and that only we ourselves can do it!

Finally, and importantly, Jesus' metaphors recommend that we be willing to endure pain to conquer our sinful habits. It hurts to sever your foot or to tear out an eye, and it hurts to give up wrong things in our lives. Better your blood on the ground than your life on the rubbish heap for eternity. If God is speaking to you to do it—*do it now!*

Are these words appropriate for our sophisticated modern age? Most certainly, for nice clothing and proper manners can mask immensely destructive evil. As always, the ball is in our courts. It is up to us to say no to sin and yes to God.

We are responsible to make sure we do not cause others to stumble, and not to cause ourselves to stumble. Then Jesus mentioned a third responsibility.

Living with Suffering (v. 49)

Note Jesus' enigmatic statement, "For everyone will be salted with fire" (v. 49). The key to understanding this is to realize that in Old Testament times, the temple sacrifices had to be accompanied by salt (Leviticus 2:13; Ezekiel 13:24; cf. Exodus 30:35). Salt speaks of *sacrifice*.[5] So the thought here is that everyone who follows Christ, every disciple, is to be a willing sacrifice.

Paul puts this memorably in Romans 12:1—"I appeal to you therefore, brothers, by the mercies of God, to present your bodies as a living sacrifice, holy and acceptable to God." Everyone who would minister for Christ is called to be a willing, free sacrifice. Along with the salt comes the fire, which symbolizes persecution. Every disciple is to willingly accept suffering.

If the wind was in Jesus' face, it will also be in ours, and we must embrace it. Hear Paul's advice to Timothy: "Indeed, all who desire to live a godly life in Christ Jesus will be persecuted" (2 Timothy 3:12). Paul warned the Thessalonians, "For you yourselves know that we are destined for [trials]. For when we were with you, we kept telling you beforehand that we were to suffer affliction" (1 Thessalonians 3:3, 4). He told the Christians in Antioch the same thing: ". . . through many tribulations we must enter the kingdom of God" (Acts 14:22). "Beloved," said Peter, "do not be surprised at the fiery trial when it comes upon you to test you, as though something strange were happening to you. But rejoice insofar as you share Christ's sufferings, that you may also rejoice and be glad when his glory is revealed" (1 Peter 4:12, 13).

Bonhoeffer put it perfectly:

> Suffering, then, is the badge of true discipleship. The disciple is not above his master. . . . That is why Luther reckoned suffering among the marks of the true church. . . . Discipleship means allegiance to the suffering Christ, and it is therefore not at all surprising that Christians should be called upon to suffer. In fact, it is a joy and a token of His grace.[6]

If we wish to be disciples—to minister—we must willingly be "salted with fire."

Living as Salt (v. 50)

The Jews' maxim, "The world cannot survive without salt"[7] is a vivid reminder that salt was used in the ancient world because it preserved food from rotting. Jesus' call to be "salt" is a challenge for his disciples to be a preserving influence in a decaying world. William Wilberforce, the man who almost single-handedly brought about the Slavery Emancipation Bill in England, is living proof that a little salt goes a long way. He did not appear to be much. However, James Boswell wrote of him, after listening to one of his speeches,

"I saw a shrimp become a whale." Tiny, elfish, misshapen, he was salt to British society, not only bringing preservation but enticement to Christ by his beautiful life. If we are salty, those around will know it.[8]

Whatever or wherever we are, whether in the military, in business, in education, on a campus—Christ calls us to have a preserving influence. Our presence ought to quicken the conscience, elevate conversation, restrain ethical corruption, promote honesty, and raise the moral atmosphere of society. What happens when we get to know people who are without Christ? Does our presence make a difference?

Christ's use of this metaphor is boldly positive. In the Sermon on the Mount he said, "You [you alone] are the salt of the earth" (Matthew 5:13). Jesus believes that despite Christendom's frequent failures we can have a healing, preserving influence on our society and the world. He believes that we can bring flavor to life—that we can make the world thirsty for him. And the Church has done that again and again!

Christ wants us to cultivate our saltiness, and in the context of Mark 9 this comes through in three ways.

First: we are to live in such a way that not one of his "little ones" is caused to stumble. We are to be open, loving, accepting, and tolerant of all.

Second: he does not want us to stumble. If our hand offends us, we are to cut off the sinful activity. If our foot offends us, we are to stop going to the place of disobedience. If our eye offends us, we may need to throw away the television set or certain magazines.

Lastly, we must willingly embrace the "salt" of a sacrificial life and the "fire" of persecution that comes with it. And in doing so, we will be the salt of Christ to a thirsty world, for only he who indwells us can slake that thirst!

32

What Jesus Says about Divorce

MARK 10:1–12

THERE IS NO QUESTION THAT the pursuit of self-fulfillment is very high on today's American cultural agenda. "Self-fulfillment"—"self-realization"—"self-actualization"—these are clichés that we regularly hear in places as diverse as the athletic field and the pulpit. In fact, they are the buzzwords of the new mysticism that is currently sweeping America.

So pervasive is our culture's preoccupation with these matters that commitment to life's most sacred institutions is often made conditional to the question, "Am I getting fulfillment from this?" For instance, in regard to marriage, John Adam and Nancy Williamson write in their book *Divorce: How and When To Let Go*:

> Your marriage can wear out. People change their values and lifestyles. People want to experience new things. Change is a part of life. Change and personal growth are traits for you to be proud of, indicative of a vital searching mind. You must accept the reality that in today's multifaceted world it is especially easy for two persons to grow apart. Letting go of your marriage—if it is no longer fulfilling—can be the most successful thing you have ever done. Getting a divorce can be a positive, problem-solving, growth-oriented step. It can be a personal triumph.[1]

What an amazing thing! By making self-fulfillment the guiding principle of life, one can call *failure* "success," *disintegration* "growth," and *disaster* "triumph." The human mind is capable of immense perversity.

Tragically, such thinking has even come to dominate minds that are ostensibly Christian. A few years ago, when I learned an old college friend of mine was leaving his wife, I caught a Sunday night red-eye special and stood unannounced at 7 A.M. Monday morning on his doorstep. There was no way he could refuse to talk to me. I spent the day convincing him, I thought, that he should and could make a go of it. But several weeks later he left his lovely wife and children, saying that he knew that the Bible did not condone what he was doing, but that he was "under grace" and knew God would forgive him.

A year later I received an invitation to his wedding aboard the yacht *Mia Vita* in Huntington Harbor, California. *Mia Vita*, ironically, means "My Life." I imagined for a moment the fitting background music: Frank Sinatra singing, ". . . but best of all, I did it my way." My friend was saying so long to twenty-two years of marriage, so long to the call of Christ, so long to comfortable intimacy with his children and grandchildren, so long to a life of meaning. I could not bring myself to RSVP.

I do not know how things have gone with my friend. Not too well, I suspect. As Milton's Lucifer said:

> Which way I fly is Hell;
> myself am Hell!

However, I do know that my friend's decision has been devastating on his wife and his now-adult children. The primrose path of "self-fulfillment" is strewn with the bones of innocent victims, many of whom are the offspring of professing Christians.

Regarding this growing unhealthy emphasis on self-fulfillment becoming the bottom-line among Christians, Lawrence Crabb writes:

> In the last decade or so, we have dignified the shallow appeal of "be happy, feel good" by substituting the more Christian-sounding invitation to find "a fulfilling life" and to become "self-actualized." The joy and peace available to the Christian have become confused with the similar sounding, but very different, idea of fulfillment. This has been seized upon by our sinful natures and translated into a priority on subjectively experiencing this deep joy and a secondary concern with whether the route to fulfillment conforms to God's holy character as revealed in Scripture. In some circles, people warmly speak of fulfillment in relationships to the point where adultery and divorce are acceptable if they enhance one's own sense of meaning. "I must be happy, I must express who I am. Don't condemn me to a life of limited fulfillment. Don't box me in with your legalistic morality. Let me be Me. I must do what is best for Me. God wants me to become a whole person, and I cannot be whole within the boundaries of traditional morality."
>
> We have become so conditioned to measuring the rightness of what we do by the quality of emotion it generates that a new version of relativistic ethics has developed that might be called the Morality of Fulfillment. "Fulfillment" has taken on a greater urgency and value than "obedience."[2]

My pastoral experience has confirmed this over and over—as with a professing Christian woman who wrote me saying that though she had *no Biblical grounds* for divorce, she knew it was God's will because now that she was out of the relationship she was growing. She had never been happier in her life—and this would be best for her brokenhearted husband too—and she was praying that God would give him a wife who would love him and help him grow. Her divorce, according to her, was a healthy act of love.

What a tragedy! The elevation of one's own self-fulfillment as the ultimate good functionally reduces God's Word to an optional guidebook to meet one's emotional needs. The inerrant Bible is replaced with a humanistic value system in Christians' lives.[3] This error is deadly.

More important than self-fulfillment, or even our own happiness, is obedience to God's Word. God is not sitting in Heaven biting his celestial fingernails over our happiness, but he is looking for obedience among his people. Samuel said God desires obedience more than actual worship (1 Samuel 15:22). If we are believers, God's truth must direct our every decision.

To be sure, God cares about our well-being. There is nothing wrong with desiring an increasing sense of self-fulfillment. But the path to fulfillment, well-being, *shalom*, is not marked by the signs that say "my happiness first" or "self-realization." The Bible says there is a way that seems right to man, but the end of the path is destruction (Proverbs 14:12; 16:25). Rather, the path to fulfillment is obedience: finding one's life by losing it, being crucified with Christ—surrender.

I know that many Christian brothers and sisters are experiencing or have experienced the misery of divorce. Some are caught between warring parents. Some may have been the offending party in divorces that took place before becoming Christians or while untaught believers. I know there are situations in some lives that are so convoluted it is difficult to know how to apply Biblical principles. At the same time, the Church must be prophetic, speaking God's Word in and to a hostile culture—regardless of what the culture thinks. The bottom line is, what does Jesus say about marriage and divorce? In light of his words, how should we live?

To understand our Lord's statements on divorce, we must know something about the heated social and theological context in which he made them. The controversy centered on the interpretation of a phrase in Deuteronomy 24:1. It is the *only* passage in the Old Testament stating the grounds or procedures for divorce. The verse begins: "When a man takes a wife and marries her, if then she finds no favor in his eyes because he has found some indecency in her, and he writes her a certificate of divorce . . ." It is in these opening words that the controversy lay. It taught that a man could divorce his wife if he found "some indecency" in her.

The burning question in Jesus' day was, what does "some indecency" mean? The very liberal rabbinical school of Hillel interpreted "indecency" in the widest manner possible. They said that a man could divorce his wife if she spoiled his dinner! They also extended "indecency" to mean walking about with her hair down, speaking to men on the street, or speaking disrespectfully of her husband's parents in his presence. Think of it! A wrong word about a mother-in-law and a woman could be out on the street. Rabbi Akiba, who was of this school of thought, went even farther, saying that the phrase "finds no favor in his eyes" meant that a man could divorce his wife if he found another woman who was more beautiful.[4]

Fortunately, these rabbis were opposed by the school of Shammai, which limited "some indecency" to offenses of marital impropriety short of adultery. Adultery was punished by execution, and so "some indecency" *could not mean adultery*, but rather actions that suggested the possibility of sexual misconduct (for example, shameful exposure).[5]

So it was in the context of this conservative-liberal controversy over the meaning of "some indecency" as a grounds for divorce that some "Pharisees came up and in order to test [Jesus] asked, 'Is it lawful for a man to divorce his wife?'" (10:2). Matthew records more completely what they said: "Is it lawful to divorce one's wife for any cause?" (Matthew 19:3). They were obviously trying to draw Jesus into the longstanding debate and then exploit his response to their own ends. Some even think they were hoping to use Jesus' answer to get him in trouble with the house of Herod, because a negative answer would publicly announce Jesus' alignment with the point of view that brought about John the Baptist's beheading.

Significantly, Jesus did not begin by directly answering their loaded question, but took the conversation back to God's creational design, giving us the most extensive teaching on divorce in the New Testament. And here we need to turn to the parallel account in Matthew 19:1–12, which gives a more detailed record than does Mark. Matthew contains virtually everything in Mark, but presents it in a slightly different order. It provides more details, including the famous "exception clause."

Jesus' Teaching on Divorce (Matthew 19:4–12)

Jesus begins his answer by stating the ideal from the Creation Ordinance of Genesis 2:23, 24—"He answered, 'Have you not read that he who created them from the beginning made them male and female, and said, "Therefore a man shall leave his father and his mother and hold fast to his wife, and the two shall become one flesh"? So they are no longer two but one flesh. What therefore God has joined together, let not man separate'" (vv. 4–6). In the beginning divorce was inconceivable and impossible.

Jesus quoted from Genesis to emphasize two things. First, the *intimacy* of the marriage relationship: "the two shall become one flesh." Marriage affords the deepest intimacy possible in earthly relationships, deeper than with the children that issue from our bodies. An amazing bonding took place the moment I saw my newborn children and held them in my arms. In the ensuing months and years the bonding has increased. I am close to my children, interwoven with them. Yet, I am *not* one flesh with them! I am one flesh only with my wife.

Next, Jesus' emphasis was on *permanence.* You will note in verse 6 that Jesus added his own comment to the Genesis statement: "So they are no longer two but one flesh. What therefore God has joined together, let not man separate." There was no thought of divorce—ever! God's ideal was, and is, a monogamous, intimate, enduring marriage. Anything less is a departure from the divine model.

Moreover, the fall did not change the ideal. We all know that some things that were possible before the fall were not possible afterwards. But in regard to marriage, God's standard did not change. Malachi 2:14–16a (TLB) tells us:

> "Why has God abandoned us?" you cry. I'll tell you why; it is because the Lord has seen your treachery in divorcing your wives who have been faithful to you through the years, the companions you promised to care for and keep. You were united to your wife by the Lord. In God's wise plan, when you married, the two of you became one person in his sight. And what does he want? Godly children from your union. Therefore guard your passions! Keep faith with the wife of your youth. For the Lord, the God of Israel, says he hates divorce. . . .

Divorce is always a tragedy, always a departure from the divine ideal. All the modern talk about "creative divorce" and "positive, growth-oriented" steps is a lot of pseudo-scientific and pseudo-liberated bunk. Christians who go ahead with an un-Biblical divorce "sin with a high hand," as the Old Testament puts it. They place themselves in harm's way. The outcome will not be *shalom.*

Now follow the reasoning of the conversation. The Pharisees had alluded to the controversy in Deuteronomy 24 by asking if a man may divorce his wife for any reason at all. Jesus responded by saying divorce is not God's standard. Now the Pharisees counter with another reference to Deuteronomy 24, as we read in verse 7: "They said to him, 'Why then did Moses command one to give a certificate of divorce and to send her away?'" The argument is, "Moses made provision for divorce in Deuteronomy 24:1. How, then, can you say it is not part of the ideal?"

Note Jesus' answer in verse 8: "Because of your hardness of heart Moses allowed you to divorce your wives, but from the beginning it was not so." His answer corrects the Pharisees, for Moses only *permitted* divorce. He didn't command it, as the Pharisees asserted.[6] What Moses did command was the granting of a divorce certificate for the woman's protection. Without a certificate she would be subject to exploitation and even recrimination. The certificate also prevented the man from marrying her again. Thus she could not be treated like chattel. Marriage was not something one could walk in and out of.

The reason God allowed divorce was that the hearts of the men of Israel were hard. This was a divine concession to human weakness, a concession to man's sinfulness, but it cannot be taken as approval. It was reluctant permission at best.

The So-Called Exception Clause (Matthew 19:9)

Understanding this, we come to the very center of Christ's teaching: why divorce is permitted! "And I say to you: whoever divorces his wife, *except for sexual immorality*, and marries another, commits adultery" (Matthew 19:9). Here everything rests upon the correct interpretation of the phrase "except for sexual immorality," and especially the simple word "immorality."

The Greek word here is *porneia*, from which we derive the English word *pornography*. Greek dictionaries tell us that *porneia* means unchastity, fornication, prostitution, or other kinds of unlawful intercourse. When *porneia* is applied to married persons, it means, as our text says, "sexual immorality," illicit intercourse, which may involve adultery, homosexuality, bestiality, and the like.

We should note (and this is very important) that all these offenses were originally punished by death under Mosaic Law. These sins terminated marriage not by divorce but by death! However, by Jesus' time the Roman occupation and its legal system had made the death sentence for such offenses difficult to obtain. Jewish practice had therefore *substituted divorce for death*. Thus, the rabbinical schools of Hillel and Shammai were not discussing whether divorce is permissible for adultery. It was rightly taken for granted by all.

The point is, Jesus was far stricter than Hillel or Shammai because he superseded the teaching of Deuteronomy 24 and said that the *only* grounds by which one could divorce his or her spouse was sexual immorality, an offense that was originally punished by death.[7]

The simple, plain meaning of Jesus' words in verse 9 ("And I say to you: whoever divorces his wife, except for sexual immorality, and marries another, commits adultery") is that divorce is allowed if your mate is guilty of sexual immorality. If you divorce for any other reason and remarry, it is you who commits adultery. This is likewise the meaning of Jesus' similar statement in the Sermon on the Mount in Matthew 5:32—"But I say to you that everyone who divorces his wife, except on the ground of sexual immorality, makes her commit adultery [if she marries], and whoever marries a divorced woman [a woman who had been divorced for something short of unchastity] commits adultery."

Jesus' teaching is plain to see. I have read everything I could get my hands on regarding these passages, and some of the views have been unbelievably convoluted. But this is where I return to the plain, unadorned sense of the text. Jesus means what he says!

Some object that these exception clauses do not fit with Jesus' teaching in two other Gospel passages, Mark 10:11, 12 and Luke 16:18, which contain no exception clauses. For instance, Mark records, "And he said to them, 'Whoever divorces his wife and marries another commits adultery against her, and if she divorces her husband and marries another, she commits adultery'" (Mark 10:11, 12).

Because of this, some have argued that Mark represents the earlier and the most pure teaching of Jesus, but Matthew contains a scribal addition (the exception clause) and is unauthentic. However, we must hold that it *is* authentic because none of the ancient manuscripts for Matthew omit it—all of them have it. Why the difference between the Gospels then? John Stott gives the answer:

> It seems far more likely that its absence from Mark and Luke is due not to their ignorance of it but to their acceptance of it as something taken for granted. After all, under the Mosaic law adultery was punishable by death . . . so nobody would have questioned that marital unfaithfulness was a just ground for divorce.[8]

The Lord Jesus Christ permitted divorce and remarriage on one ground, and one ground only: sexual immorality.

Notice that he permitted it—he did not command it. Divorce is never mandatory. Too often men and women eagerly pounce on the infidelity of their mate as the opportunity to get out of a relationship they haven't liked anyway. It's so easy to look for a way out instead of working through the problems.

We must never minimize the sin of adultery—like the man who said to his wife, "I don't understand why you're so disturbed. All I did was have an affair." At the same time, I believe (this is my personal opinion) that we should not regard a one-time affair as an easy excuse for divorce. Rather, we should think about this issue in terms of an unfaithful lifestyle—a mate who refuses to turn from his or her adulterous ways.

Jesus' exception clause should be viewed like this: No matter how rough things are, regardless of the stress and strain or whatever is said about compatibility and temperament, nothing allows for divorce except one thing, *sexual immorality*. And then it is not to be used as an excuse to get out of the marriage.

The Radicalness of Jesus' Teaching (vv. 10–12)

Jesus' had done away completely with the loopholes of the Mosaic divorce provision (Deuteronomy 24:1). This was revolutionary. The disciples' response indicates just how radical Jesus' teaching was (Mark 10:10): "The disciples said to him, 'If such is the case of a man with his wife, it is better not to marry.'" If the only ground for divorce was sexual immorality, if none of the exceptions suggested by Hillel and Shammai were valid, it was better to stay single!

The radicalness of what Jesus taught is further underlined in Matthew 5 where it is used as one of the six statements that begin with variations of "You have heard that it was said, but I say to you . . ." They demonstrate the superior righteousness of Christ. A righteous person must view his or her marital relationship as supremely sacred. Nothing can sever it but unrepentant unfaithfulness. Even then, it is not an excuse, but the sorrowful ground of divorce.

Such teaching is out of sync with our culture. If you are into the soaps, what I have been saying sounds primitive. Today some Christian counselors are recommending divorce and remarriage on grounds that are in opposition to the clear teaching of Christ. Marriage has been trivialized into a provisional sexual union that dissolves when our little love gives out or we do not find fulfillment! According to Christ, marriage demands total commitment that only death or the most flagrant, ongoing sexual infidelity can bring to an end.

Having seen Christ's teaching, does the Bible say anything else about divorce? The answer is yes.

Paul's Teaching on Divorce (1 Corinthians 7:8–16)

In 1 Corinthians 7, the Apostle Paul gives advice first to the *unmarried* (vv. 8, 9), then to *married believers* (vv. 10, 11), and finally to those who have *mixed marriages*—those in which one's spouse is not a believer (vv. 12–16). It is on this last category that we must focus.

Paul begins his teaching by saying in verse 12: "To the rest I say (I, not the Lord) . . ." This has been misunderstood by some as meaning that Paul is saying that his teaching is not as authoritative as Christ's. Really he is saying in effect, "I am now going to deal with cases on which the Lord himself did not give a verdict."[9] Paul speaks with full apostolic authority! He says: "To the rest I say (I, not the Lord) that if any brother has a wife who is an unbeliever, and she consents to live with him, he should not divorce her. If any woman has a husband who is an unbeliever, and he consents to live with her, she should not divorce him" (vv. 12, 13).

Paul knew that in Corinth there were many marriages in which either the husband or wife had become a Christian after marriage, thus producing a pagan-Christian marriage. His advice was that the Christian must not leave his or her unbelieving spouse. Then in verse 14 he gives the reason: "For the unbelieving husband is made holy because of his wife, and the unbelieving wife is made holy because of her husband. Otherwise your children would be unclean, but as it is, they are holy."

The reason for staying together is that the unbeliever will be influenced toward Christ, and also the children, by the life of the believer. We often think the believer will be corrupted by the unbeliever. But Paul says it is generally otherwise. If you are in an unequal union, take heart! Your faith can prevail—though, sadly, not always.

Next in verse 15 we have Paul's new teaching: "But if the unbelieving partner separates, let it be so. In such cases the brother or sister is not enslaved. God has called you to peace." The sense is: if the unbeliever deserts and is determined not to come back, then let him or her go. Moreover, the Christian is "not enslaved," which means that the unbeliever has broken the marriage bond. Thus, the believer is free to divorce and remarry. The consistent use of the word "enslaved" in this passage and others argues that "is not enslaved" means is not *bound* in marriage.[10] This is the plain sense of the passage.

Summation of Biblical Teaching

So we see that the Bible allows for divorce for two reasons: sexual immorality and the desertion of a believer by an unbelieving spouse.

The Scriptures allow for remarriage in three instances. First, when one's mate is guilty of sexual immorality and is unwilling to repent and live faithfully with the marriage partner, divorce and remarriage are permissible. Second, when a believer is deserted by an unbelieving spouse, divorce and remarriage are again permitted. And third, as an extension of the allowance for divorce and remarriage when deserted by an unbeliever, I personally believe that remarriage is permissible for those who have been married and divorced before coming to Christ.

Second Corinthians 5:17 says, "Therefore, if anyone is in Christ, he is a new creation. The old has passed away; behold, the new has come." "New" (*kainos*) means new in quality.[11] The same word is used of the "new man" in Ephesians 2:15 and the "new self" in Ephesians 4:24. Not only are believers really new, Paul says that "The old has passed away."

Those who come to Christ are completely forgiven. Among the old things that have passed away are *all* sins, including divorce prior to salvation. If it is otherwise, then divorce is the only sin for which Christ did not atone.

Divorce is not the ideal. It is a divine concession to human sin and weakness. God hates divorce! But we must realize that if someone divorces and remarries within Biblical guidelines, it is not sin, though it is due to sin. We must mourn every divorce!

How foreign to the Biblical mind are phrases like "creative divorce" or "the magic of divorce" or, in an ad that appeared on the back of *TV Guide*, "Order your DIVORCE RING BAND today . . . *Now* is the time to celebrate your new beginning."[12]

We have fully discussed the non-offending party. What advice is there for the offending party? I can do no better than quote Dr. Martyn Lloyd-Jones:

> "Have you nothing to say about others?" asks someone. All I would say about them is this, and I say it carefully and advisedly, and almost in fear lest I give even a semblance of a suggestion that I am saying anything that may encourage anyone to sin. But on the basis of the gospel and in the interest of truth I am compelled to say this: Even adultery is not the unforgivable sin. It is a terrible sin, but God forbid that there should be anyone who feels that he or she has sinned himself or herself outside the love of God or outside His kingdom because of adultery. No; if you truly repent and realize the enormity of your sin and cast yourself upon the boundless love and

mercy and grace of God, you can be forgiven and I assure you of pardon. I hear the words of our blessed Lord: "Go and sin no more."[13]

Finally, what do we say to the Church, to ourselves? Number one: we must resist the climate of our soap-opera culture, which determines its commitments by what it is going to get (self-fulfillment). Rather, obedience to God's rule in our lives is more important than fulfillment. The truth is, obedience to God's Word will likely expose us to pains we could have avoided if we pursued self-fulfillment. Commitment to a godly life in no way guarantees that your marriage will work. But God's way is *right*, and those who obey God's Word have his smile as the Holy Spirit makes them whole.

Next, we must refrain from self-righteous judgmentalism. We must exercise our dealings with those who have fallen realizing that all of us are adulterers in heart. Jesus said, "But I say to you that everyone who looks at a woman with lustful intent has already committed adultery with her in his heart" (Matthew 5:28). We must endeavor to share the suffering of those ravaged by divorce, and we must not call unclean that which God has called clean (Acts 10:15).

Lastly, the Church should make provision for the remarriage of those who have been Biblically divorced.

May God's Holy Word have its rightful place in our hearts and churches.

33

Like a Little Child

MARK 10:13–16

CHILDREN OCCUPIED a precarious position in the Hellenistic society of the first century. Sometimes children were loved and sometimes exploited, depending upon how they were perceived as benefiting the family.

For example, a papyrus letter written by a man named Hilarion (which ironically means "cheerful") to his expectant wife, Alis, dated June 17, 1 BC, instructs her: "if it was a male child let it [live]; if it was female, cast it out."[1]

This practice of infanticide was severely attacked by the Christian Church, which rightly boasted, for example in The Epistle of Diognetus, that it did not expose its children.[2] The practice was not outlawed in Roman law until AD 375. Even then the law was not very effective.[3] Roman law gave the father absolute power (*patria potestas*) over his family—which extended to life and death. As late as AD 60 a son was put to death by the simple order of his father.[4]

Further evidence of the nature of the world to which the gospel came is seen in the family abuses of the house of Herod and his public slaughter of babies at the Advent (Matthew 2:16–20). Children clearly were not presumed to be blessings in the non-Christian culture of Christ's day.

How refreshing then was the Biblical, Hebrew culture where all children were considered to be gifts from the Lord. Rachel spoke as the mother of her people when she cried, "Give me children, or I shall die!" (Genesis 30:1). Hannah prayed in the temple for a child. When God answered, she named him Samuel ("God has heard"). She later gave Samuel to the Lord's service (1 Samuel 1:20, 28). Hebrew culture elevated the family and *children*!

Mark 10 shows a further elevation of children by our Lord. The great nineteenth-century Princeton theologian B. B. Warfield said that "childhood owed as much to the gospel as womanhood,"[5] and he was right. The text elevates children as people and elevates their faith, and as a result elevates ours.

The account opens in verse 13 with Mark telling us that "they were bringing children to [Jesus] that he might touch them, and the disciples rebuked them." As best we can gather, fathers and mothers, and perhaps older children, were bringing young children, many of whom were babies (for that is how Luke describes them in his parallel account, 18:15), to Jesus for his blessing. This was in keeping with a classic Jewish custom that dated all the way back to the time when the patriarch Israel laid his hands upon the heads of Ephraim and Manasseh and blessed them (Genesis 48:14). It was all very proper, traditional, and wonderful. Proud parents held out their precious children to Jesus, who took them in his arms where they snuggled close. He placed his hand on their warm little heads and, lifting his eyes to Heaven, pronounced a blessing.

We can surmise that quite a number of cheerful families stood in line chatting, with babes in arms and children scurrying around. Then it stopped. Outside the house the disciples were sending them away with a rebuke!

Why were they doing this? They were *protecting* Jesus. They knew Jesus was under pressure. Wherever he went, he found conflict—one time demons, another time the religious establishment, etc. And if that was not enough, there were the crashing crowds. The disciples even pressured Jesus themselves, and in their better moments some of them actually realized it. This matter of blessing children was simply one more drain.

Besides, these were just *children*. They were of little importance. They could not enter debate or contribute to the cause, even if they did understand about Jesus. So the disciples stopped the flow. Those parents who were stubborn received a rebuke, perhaps along the lines of "The Master is a busy man. Now, *shalom*—be on your way—and take your stroller!"

Verse 14 indicates that Jesus saw what was happening, and "he was indignant." The Greek word translated "indignant' occurs only here in the New Testament and is a combination of two words: "much" and "to grieve." He was *much grieved*! The things that grieve us or make us indignant reveal much about the kind of people we are, and what Jesus said and did here tells us volumes about him, as well as about our children and ourselves.

Our Lord's Elevation of Children (v. 14)

Jesus was hot, and his words have a clipped, staccato ring to them: "[He] said to them, 'Let the children come to me; do not hinder them, for to such belongs the kingdom of God'" (v. 14).[6] What should we draw from these passionate words?

First, *Jesus loves children*. Jesus, after all, had been a child himself. Jesus never thought to himself, "They think I'm a child, but I'm really not. I'm the Creator of all!" He was a real baby, child, teenager, man (and perhaps father, in that when Joseph died he, as head of the house, undoubtedly raised his brothers and sisters).

In the second century St. Irenaeus said of Christ, "He came to save all by means of Himself . . . who through Him are born again unto God,—infants and children, and boys and youth. . . . He therefore passed through every age becoming an infant for infants . . . a child for children . . . a youth for youths. . . ."[7]

We see Christ's love for children as he celebrates the delight of a mother on giving birth (John 16:21), the gentle love of a father who cuddles his children (Luke 11:7), and parental love that listens to a child's every request (Matthew 7:9; Luke 11:11).

Many of his miracles involved children: the nobleman's little son (John 4:46–54), the demonized son of the man at the Mount of Transfiguration (Mark 9:14–29), Jairus' daughter to whom Christ tenderly said, "*Talitha cumi*," which means, "Little girl, I say to you, arise" (5:41). Jesus truly, as man and God, loved children!

George MacDonald once said that he doubted a man's Christianity if children were never found playing around his door.[8] Since Jesus was a lover of children, and since his Spirit dwells in us, we are very near the heart of Christ when we love children.

So we learn from Jesus' indignation, first, that Jesus loves children, and, secondly, that Jesus affirms and respects the personhood and spirituality of children. In saying, "for to such belongs the kingdom of God," he affirms their full spirituality. They *are* the hearts he takes to himself! We shall see why in verse 15, but we note here that Christ affirms and proclaims the spiritual capacity of children. If there ever was a text relevant to child evangelism, this is it. Children can authentically come to Christ early on!

Some years ago a barefoot kindergartner made her way across the brown, sun-dried lawns of an apartment complex—the kind built after the war to house servicemen and their families. As she hurried along, the breeze parted her too-long bangs, revealing large, bright eyes made even bluer with anticipation. A woman had promised that every child who memorized the special Bible verses would receive a little book that told a story even though it contained no words. If she won the book, she would have a story she could truly read!

Sitting quietly with her friends she was transfixed. Before her were the treasured books, each with a brown leather cover that neatly snapped shut, and inside four colored, felt pages—black, red, white, and gold. She was sure she knew the verses that went with each page because she had demanded that her older sisters read the verses over and over and over. At last her time came . . . and her memory did not fail! Black, Romans 3:23; red, John 3:16; white, Isaiah 1:18; gold, John 14:2, 3. She could hardly believe it as she held her tiny treasure and opened the pages as they sang in unison: "Once my heart was *black* with sin, until the Savior came in. His precious *blood* I know, has washed it *whiter* than snow. And in this world I'm told, I'll walk the streets of *gold*. O wonderful, wonderful day! He washed my sins away."

On that wonderful day my wife, Barbara, became personally acquainted with Jesus. That experience saw her through an uncertain childhood and later blossomed into a deep commitment to Christ when she was a sophomore in high school. Jesus teaches, and experience confirms, that a young child can consciously come to Christ.

The insights of Harvard-trained theologian James Fowler (*Stages of Faith*) and others can be used to advantage in bringing children to true faith. But we must not be reductionist in our view of faith. It is a mystery, and Paul says it is "the gift of God" (Ephesians 2:8) and therefore not rigidly bound to a clinician's developmental ladder. Jesus is optimistic about the spirituality of children, and we should be the same.

Charles Spurgeon, soul-winner *par excellence*, said: "I will say broadly that I have more confidence in the spiritual life of the children that I have received into this church than I have in the spiritual condition of the adults thus received. I will go even further than that, and say that I have usually found a clearer knowledge of the gospel and a warmer love to Christ in the child-converts than in the man-converts. I will even astonish you still more by saying that I have sometimes met with a deeper spiritual experience in children of ten and twelve than I have in certain persons of fifty and sixty."[9]

Dr. Jim Slack, head of demographics for the Southern Baptist Foreign Missionary Society, shared the results of a Gallup Survey: nineteen out of twenty people who became Christians did so before the age of twenty-five. At age twenty-five, one in 10,000 will become believers; at thirty-five, one in 50,000; at forty-five, one in 200,000; at fifty-five, one in 300,000; at seventy-five, one in 700,000.

What a call for parents, young people, Bible school teachers, and club workers to keep at it! While we parents must never resort to extracting bogus conversions from our children, we must cultivate their spiritual awareness and sensitivity—and above all, pray fervently and in detail for them.

D. L. Moody once returned from a meeting and reported two and a half conversions. "Two adults and a child, I suppose?" asked his host. "No," said Moody, "two children and an adult. The children gave their whole lives. The adult had only half of his left to give."

How sobering are Jesus' words, "do not hinder them." The *Talmud* says, "A child tells in the street what its father and mother say at home." What are children learning in our homes and in our churches? We need teachers who will humbly and willingly minister to children under the reality of James 3:1—"Not many of you should become teachers, my brothers, for you know that we who teach will be judged with greater strictness."

Verse 14 elevates the spiritual capacity of children for all the Church to see. Next, in verse 15, the Lord elevates the children's faith.

Our Lord's Elevation of Children's Faith (v. 15)

Hear our Lord's words: "Truly, I say to you, whoever does not receive the kingdom of God like a child shall not enter it." The word translated "not" is very strong. New Testament scholar William Lane comments: "The solemn pronouncement is directed to the disciples, but has pertinence for all men confronted by the gospel because it speaks of the condition for entrance into the Kingdom of God."[10] *No one will get into the Kingdom of God unless he or she receives God's salvation like a child—no one!* How are we to understand and apply this?

For starters, coming as a "child" does not infer innocence. Any two-year-old dispels such a notion! Neither does "like a child" suggest the wondrous *subjective* states we often find in children such as trustfulness, receptivity, simplicity, or wonder, beautiful as these are.

What Jesus has in mind here is an *objective* state that every child who has ever lived, regardless of race, culture, or background, has experienced— *helpless dependence*.

Every single child in the world is absolutely, completely, totally, objectively, subjectively, existentially helpless! And so it is with every child who is born into the kingdom of God. Children of the kingdom enter it helpless, ones for whom everything must be done.

> Nothing in my hand I bring,
> Simply to Thy cross I cling;
> Naked, come to Thee for dress:
> Helpless, look to Thee for grace.

There is no other fundamental meaning for verse 15. Have you come to Christ like this? Is it his grace plus your nothingness?

The realization that one is as helpless as a child naturally fosters humility. Jesus gave reference to this connection when, in a similar but separate statement, he said, "Truly, I say to you, unless you turn and become like children, you will never enter the kingdom of heaven. Whoever humbles himself like this child is the greatest in the kingdom of heaven" (Matthew 18:3, 4).

The world refuses to come to Christ because of its "self-respect"—often a euphemism for pride and independence. Come as a helpless child? How humiliating! But Jesus says, "That is the way you must come—as a baby, in profound obedience."

Now watch what happens to the waiting children: "And he took them in his arms and blessed them, laying his hands on them" (v. 16). Children were always comfortable with Jesus. They could tell he loved them. They lay their heads against his chest, and he "blessed them." Bengel says, "He did more than they asked,"[11] and he is probably right, for the word translated "blessed" means "fervently blessed." Christ did this joyfully, with a fervent heart, for they refreshed his spirit.

Do you desire to be held in Christ's arms, to hear him pronounce blessings over you? Eternity will reveal that is all we ever wanted, and our Spirit-given response is, "Dearest Father"—"Abba! Father!" (cf. Romans 8:15; Galatians 4:6).

Jesus has elevated children. He believes they can know him as truly as anyone else, that they can have a vibrant relationship with him.

Jesus also elevated the faith of children. No one will receive the kingdom of God without this helpless dependence and humility. Jesus said, "Let the children come to me; do not hinder them, for to such belongs the kingdom of God."

34

The Rich Young Man

MARK 10:17–31

JESUS' STARTLING PRONOUNCEMENT to his disciples ("Truly, I say to you, whoever does not receive the kingdom of God like a child shall not enter it," 10:15) set down for the disciples and all subsequent history that helpless dependence is necessary for entering the kingdom—being saved. In contrast, the rich young man in this passage is the very opposite of a helpless, dependent babe. Matthew mentions that "he had great possessions" (Matthew 19:22), and Luke identifies him as "a ruler" (Luke 18:18). He was both affluent and powerful.

Moreover, we discern from the whole of his exchange with Jesus that he was an aggressive, self-assured young man who went after what he wanted. He was what we call today an "achiever." He was also an exemplary "good man" who felt a need. Evidently he had been listening to Jesus and was dazzled with his brilliance and moral excellence. So he decided to "go for it."

Verse 17 records this man's approach: "And as he was setting out on his journey, a man ran up and knelt before him and asked him, 'Good Teacher, what must I do to inherit eternal life?'" He did not walk up to Jesus—he came dashing. When he got to Jesus, he threw himself to the ground in genuine respect. He had the Lord's attention for sure! With his chest still heaving for breath, he asked *the* great question concerning eternal life. The language (aorist tense) indicates that he expected Jesus to prescribe some great deed he could do that would settle things with God once and for all. From his point of view he certainly had the ability and will to do whatever would be required, just as he always did.

Jesus' response was like a douse of cold water, though in fact it was not intended to dampen the young man's enthusiasm, but rather to awaken him to spiritual realities. "Why do you call me good? No one is good except God alone" (v. 18).

Calling a teacher, or anyone else for that matter, "good" was virtually without parallel in the Jewish sources of the day.[1] "Good Teacher" was extravagant language in light of the fact that the man did not know Jesus was God. Jesus was saying in essence, "What are you saying? Don't you know that calling me good is calling me God?" Jesus was attacking the man's shallow use of the word to get him to think about what he was saying, with the purpose of elevating him to understand that *Jesus really is God!*

Then, with the splash of water graciously administered and the young man's mind engaged, Jesus told the young ruler what was necessary for eternal life: "You know the commandments: 'Do not murder, Do not commit adultery, Do not steal, Do not bear false witness, Do not defraud, Honor your father and mother'" (v. 19)—"are you keeping the commandments?" This was the proper answer because the Old Testament taught that those who keep the Law will live (Deuteronomy 30:15ff.; cf. Ezekiel 33:15). The rabbis seriously spoke of people who kept the whole Law from A to Z, or more exactly *Aleph* to *Taw*.[2]

There is an *external* sense in which this can be true. That is why Paul could say about himself that "as to righteousness under the law," he was "blameless" (Philippians 3:6). This was how he regarded himself before he faced the full implication of the Law's command not to covet. Then the apostle realized that he was guilty of gross covetousness and was thus guilty of breaking the entire Law (Romans 7:7–12).

Quite naturally, the rich young ruler reflected on Jesus' answer from the perspective of his own superficial understanding. *He* had not murdered, committed adultery, stolen, lied, or failed to honor his father and mother. Therefore he replied, "Teacher, all these I have kept from my youth" (v. 20), "since my coming of age at my *Bar Mitzvah*." Jesus was asking him to do that which had been a habit with him since childhood. His self-assurance surged.

But Jesus now responded with a memorable *coup de grace*, a stroke of mercy. "And Jesus, looking at him, loved him, and said to him, 'You lack one thing: go, sell all that you have and give to the poor, and you will have treasure in heaven; and come, follow me'" (v. 21).

Does Jesus' demand seem harsh? Is he is asking too much? Peter undoubtedly told Mark about Jesus' loving eye contact with the young man. Jesus *loved* him, was drawn to him. The Savior's words were spoken in the tenderest tone, and yet Jesus meant every syllable of what he said. This was the only way for the rich young man.

Why did Jesus command the young ruler to divest himself of his riches? Jesus knew, despite the man's laudable piety, that materialism occupied the place of God in his life, and that because of this he lived in perpetual transgression of the First Commandment against having other gods before the true God (Exodus 20:3). Not only that, but the man's great wealth prevented the helpless, childlike dependence that Jesus had just said was necessary for kingdom entrance.

This is not general advice for all believers, though it was appropriate in this instance. Jesus always demands that those who come to him put away their gods, whether they be possessions, position, power, a person, or a passion!

The world had stopped for the wealthy young man. The loving eyes of Jesus were steadfastly upon him. What would he do? Mark graphically records that he was "disheartened by the saying" (v. 22a). The word he used was also used by Matthew to describe the sky becoming overcast in anticipation of a storm (Matthew 16:3). There was a progressive darkening of the man's face.[3] Mark concludes, "he went away sorrowful, for he had great possessions" (v. 22b).

A missionary poetess and mystic, Amy Carmichael of Dohnavur, described in her famous book *Things As They Are* sitting with a Hindu queen in her palace as the queen revealed her spiritual hunger. As the conversation developed, she kept pushing Miss Carmichael regarding what was necessary for salvation, and Amy attempted to deflect her, saying she should wait.

> But she was determined to hear it then and, as she insisted, I read her a little of what He says about it Himself. She knew quite enough to understand and take in the force of the forceful words. She would not consent to be led gently on. "No, I must know it now," she said; and as verse by verse we read to her, her face settled sorrowfully. "So far must I follow, so far?" she said, "I cannot follow so far."[4]

That is, in effect, what the rich man said. He was overcome with profound sadness because he had so much money. He could not possibly bring himself to give it up. Dante referred to this as "The Great Refusal." It was, for from there he became a wandering star—lost, haunted by what might have been.

Jesus would build on this powerfully drawn picture of the power of wealth with one of his most famous "hard sayings." But before we look at this, we must note a few points of qualification.

Jesus was not making a case for universal asceticism (giving up all wealth and living a life of conscious denial and negation). The Old Testament holds up some godly rich men (such as Abraham and Boaz and Job) as examples, though it constantly guards and warns against the greed of the rich. Tertullian, the Apostolic Father, was right when he called it irreligious to scorn this wonderful world and refuse to enjoy God's bounty and thank him for it. He says: "It was goodness, goodness, goodness that made it all."[5] We are right to enjoy it.

Neither was Jesus recommending poverty to his people, because poverty does not deliver one from the love of money. As George MacDonald said: "It is not the rich man only who is under the dominion of things; they too are slaves who, having no money, are unhappy for the lack of it. . . . The money the one has, the money the other would have, is in each the cause of an eternal stupidity."[6]

The fact is, wealth can be spiritually beneficial. It can teach us the hollowness of things, and if used for Christ can enhance one's spiritual growth—a benefit that, sadly, too few experience. For the disciples, as they watched the rich young man trudge slowly away, it was one of those "teachable moments"—and here comes the hard saying.

The Disadvantage of Wealth (vv. 23–27)

And Jesus looked around [making sure he had their attention] and said to his disciples, "How difficult it will be for those who have wealth to enter the kingdom of God!" And the disciples were amazed at his words. But Jesus said to them again, "Children, how difficult it is to enter the kingdom of God! It is easier for a camel to go through the eye of a needle than for a rich person to enter the kingdom of God." And they were exceedingly astonished, and said to him, "Then who can be saved?" (vv. 23–26)

We do ourselves a disservice if we water down Jesus' words. The *Babylonian Talmud* contains quotations regarding elephants passing through the eye of a needle, illustrations of impossibility. Jesus' reference to a camel, the largest beast in Palestine, being thrust through, humps and all, was readily understood as a humorous illustration of the impossible. This same proverb is current among the Arabs today.[7] Jesus categorically says it is impossible for a man or woman who *trusts* in riches to get into Heaven.

Mark says the disciples were "exceedingly astonished" at these words—overwhelmed, "struck outside themselves."[8] Why? Because they believed in an ancient rendition of "prosperity theology" taught by the rabbis, who used Old Testament passages to equate God's blessing with material prosperity and taught that the rich could build up future merit and reward for themselves by giving to the poor. To the Jewish mind it was inconceivable that riches could be a barrier to the kingdom.[9]

Protestantism has frequently been afflicted with the same kind of errant thinking. Historically some of our ancestors twisted Reformed theology so as to make economic prosperity evidence that they were the elect.[10] Today we see this in the crass materialism of the "name it and claim it" school and similar embarrassments for the Church.

We need to hear what Jesus was really saying, and to hear it well: *wealth is a handicap!* We think the rich to be overprivileged; Jesus said they were underprivileged.[11] At the end of the Sermon on the Mount he warned:

> Do not lay up for yourselves treasures on earth, where moth and rust destroy and where thieves break in and steal, but lay up for yourselves treasures in heaven, where neither moth nor rust destroys and where thieves do not break in and steal. For where your treasure is, there your heart will be also. (Matthew 6:19–21)

He also said, "No one can serve two masters, for either he will hate the one and love the other, or he will be devoted to the one and despise the other. You cannot serve God and money" (Matthew 6:24; cf. Luke 16:13).

The parable of the rich man and Lazarus is a dramatic warning about this matter (Luke 16:19–30). The same is true of the Parable of the Rich Fool (Luke 12:13–21). There is a proper "Christian fear" of being rich.

What are the disadvantages of wealth? Primarily what it can do to the soul. How easy it is for an earnest man or woman to become so attached to material riches that he or she forgets what is infinitely more important. Wealth naturally works at perverting one's values. We soon know the price of everything and the value of nothing.

Paul tells Timothy, "As for the rich in this present age, charge them not to be haughty" (1 Timothy 6:17). Pride, arrogance, insensitivity, indifference, self-satisfaction, worldliness, and other ungodly mind-sets feed on affluence.

Most tragic, wealth can steel one against the *objective* requirement for entering the kingdom of God: *helpless dependence.* Jesus said to the church, "For you say, I am rich, I have prospered, and I need nothing, not realizing that you are wretched, pitiable, poor, blind, and naked" (Revelation 3:17), and he says it today to thousands.

It would be easy to think that this applies only to the extra-rich among us. But nearly all Americans are wealthy. We have everything we need and more. For most of the world, our problems, our debts, our payments would be welcome luxuries. So this passage has something to say to us. What we do with our wealth will determine the spiritual health of ourselves and our families. With prosperity comes great danger. Militant idealists who were living for Jesus have sometimes become hardened, self-focused materialists. We must beware.

What are we to do? First, we must divest ourselves of dependence on our wealth. We must make this a matter of prayer—not just once or once in a while, but regular, frequent prayer.

Second, we must invest our wealth. That is, as our income rises, we must give to God's work in such a way that it affects our lifestyle, so there are some things we do not buy and some places we do not go because we have given so much to God, as he has directed us.

Divestment and *investment*—that is what God calls us to.

The disciples were so awestruck by Jesus' hard saying that they were flabbergasted—"'Then who can be saved?' Jesus looked at them and said, 'With man it is impossible, but not with God. For all things are possible with God'" (vv. 26, 27). Jesus said salvation was impossible for the rich and for the poor, totally beyond the range of human possibility. For the rich or poor, the materialist or the idealist, there is but one hope. They must drop that possession . . . that position . . . that passion . . . that person . . . and come to Christ.

The rewards for doing this are stupendous. Hearing this, Peter got excited:

> Peter began to say to him, "See, we have left everything and followed you." Jesus said, "Truly, I say to you, there is no one who has left house or brothers or sisters or mother or father or children or lands, for my sake and for the gospel, who will not receive a hundredfold now in this time, houses and brothers and sisters and mothers and children and lands, with persecutions, and in the age to come eternal life. But many who are first will be last, and the last first." (vv. 28–31)

I like Jesus' math. He does not say 100 percent more, but a hundredfold more! "One house gone; but a hundred doors are open! One brother in the flesh lost; but a thousand brothers in the spirit, whose love is deeper and whose kinship is profounder."[12]

This has been the testimony of many missionaries who have joyfully quoted this verse and described their experience with it.

In eternity, all of us who know and serve Jesus Christ will join the Church Triumphant in Heaven, to be loved and lavished by Jesus and to love him in return for eternity.

35

Blind Sight

MARK 10:46-52

IN CHAPTER 1 of this commentary on Mark, we discussed 10:35–45, emphasizing that verse 45, the key to the whole book, encapsulates the theology and structure of Mark's Gospel under two headings: *servanthood* and *sacrifice*. "For even the Son of Man came not to be served but to serve, and to give his life as a ransom for many." This is why we jump now to verse 46 and the story of blind Bartimaeus.

Interestingly, it is after this point that Mark's Gospel becomes dominated by the second half of its great servanthood/sacrifice theme as Jesus moves quickly toward the cross. Before his Triumphal Entry, however, Jesus had to pass through Jericho, some eighteen miles northeast of Jerusalem and five miles west of the Jordan—a beautiful city recently refurbished by the Herodians, who made it the site of their magnificent winter palace, "The City of Roses."

Blind Bartimaeus' Plea (vv. 46–48)

Mark introduces us to the situation: "And they came to Jericho. And as he was leaving Jericho with his disciples and a great crowd, Bartimaeus, a blind beggar, the son of Timaeus, was sitting by the roadside" (v. 46).

As Jesus came into Jericho, he was in the company of a large crowd made up of his disciples as well as numerous pilgrims making their way up to Jerusalem for Passover. It was customary for distinguished rabbis to travel with an entourage and to teach as they walked. So Jesus' passage was not unusual, except for the great size of the crowd. Passing through Jericho compounded the crowding because the city was full of Levitical priests who were waiting their turn to make the day's journey to the temple to serve.

Also, virtually everyone had heard of Jesus and undoubtedly wanted to see him. Vincent Taylor, the venerable New Testament scholar, believed that Jesus' passage through Jericho bore the character of an ovation,[1] with some of the crowd hostile and others giving forth enthusiastic "Hosannas." The City of Roses was alive.

For our Lord Jesus, the end of the earthly road was in sight. Nevertheless, he would perform one final healing miracle (the last of the healing miracles recorded by Mark) before entering Jerusalem. This miracle is of special significance because through it Jesus, in his eleventh hour, teaches us what brings his power to bear on our greatest needs.

The day began like any other day for blind Bartimaeus. Waking up, he shook the straw from his shabby, torn garments, stretched, got to his feet, and began tapping his way along the familiar turns that led to the main gate in Jericho. Perhaps he was able to beg a crust of bread or two at some familiar stops along the way. Arriving at the gate he took his regular place with the other beggars, where he drew his greasy cloak tight around him because, though it was spring, it took the sun to dispel the chill.

As he sat there, just like so many days before, he listened to the city come to life—first a donkey loaded with melons for market, after that several women chatting as they bore pitchers toward the well, then the clomp of camels' hooves and the aroma of fish borne along to market. Soon Jericho was humming, and the blind man was intoning his beggar's cry.

Suddenly Bartimaeus tensed and lifted his head, for his blind-sensitive ears heard the hubbub of a great crowd approaching. First came young boys running before the crowd with shrill cries, then more people hurrying past the gate talking excitedly. Bartimaeus, brushed by a robe, reached out and asked what was happening. The passerby, pulling his robe away, called back, "Jesus of Nazareth—the one who heals the lame and lepers and *blind*—the one some are saying is the Messiah—is passing by!" Everyone had been talking about this man's exploits and words. Bartimaeus had perhaps even heard a first-person testimony from someone who had heard him and had seen his miracles. Bartimaeus had been doing a lot of thinking, and now he made up his mind. *This must be the Messiah, and now he is coming.*[2] His heart began to pound, and he was trembling, though the warm sun was standing high.

The crowd was passing. People called to one another. Intermittent hosannas rang out. Bartimaeus was jostled. Jesus would soon be gone. *He had to do something!*

So, Mark tells us, "when he heard that it was Jesus of Nazareth, he began to cry out and say, 'Jesus, Son of David, have mercy on me!' And many rebuked him, telling him to be silent. But he cried out all the more, 'Son of David, have mercy on me!'" (vv. 47, 48).

Bartimaeus had not yet gotten to his feet. Perhaps it was impossible in the press of the throng. Yet he was making himself heard. He was crying pitifully, chanting at the top of his lungs. He was desperate, frantic.

I remember doing something like this at the 1962 Rose Parade. UCLA was playing in the Rose Bowl, and as their float came by I saw an old high school friend who was now a Bruin cheerleader. I began to shout, "Hey, Patti, it's me! Remember me? Kent Hughes!" and then realized that everybody was looking at me!

Poor Bartimaeus would have made my outburst look like a sedate conversation. The people around him surely tried to shush him—"Bartimaeus, you are making a scene." Others chided him or insulted him—"Shut up, beggar!"

No way was Blind Bart going to be shut up! "Son of David, have mercy on me!" "Quiet, beggar." "Son of David, have mercy on me!" "Will somebody shut him up?" "Son of David, have mercy on me!" "If you don't stop, you will need some mercy!" "Son of David . . ." He was beyond their control.

If we turn down the volume for a moment and reflect on what was implicit in his cries, we will see that his cries were going to get him everything.

First, *he was pitifully aware of his condition.* He knew he was blind and in perpetual darkness. From the darkness of his mother's womb he had passed into the darkness of the world. He had never seen a tree wave its arms in the spring, or the blue of a summer sky, or the face of his mother or anyone else who loved him. Unlike so many who are in spiritual darkness today, he knew what his problem was.

Charles Colson, in his brilliant book of essays, *Who Speaks for God?*, tells about watching a segment of television's *60 Minutes* in which host Mike Wallace interviewed Auschwitz survivor Yehiel Dinur, a principal witness at the Nuremberg war-crime trials. During the interview, a film clip from Adolf Eichmann's 1961 trial was viewed that showed Dinur enter the courtroom and come face-to-face with Eichmann for the first time since being sent to Auschwitz almost twenty years earlier. Stopped cold, Dinur began to sob uncontrollably and then fainted while the presiding judge pounded his gavel for order.

"Was Dinur overcome by hatred? Fear? Horrid memories?" asks Colson, who answers, "No, it was none of these." Rather, as Dinur explained to Wallace, all at once he realized Eichmann was not the godlike army officer who had sent so many to their deaths. This Eichmann was an ordinary man.

"I was afraid about myself," said Dinur. "I saw that I am capable to do this. I am . . . exactly like he."

Wallace's subsequent summation of Dinur's terrible discovery— "Eichmann is in all of us"—is a horrifying statement. But it indeed captures the central truth about man's nature. As a result of the fall, sin is in each of us—not just the susceptibility to sin, but sin itself.

Colson follows his penetrating observation with this question: why is it that today sin is so seldom written or preached about? The answer is in Dinur's dramatic collapse, for to truly confront the sin within us is a devastating experience, and yet an experience that brings grace.[3]

That is why Christ gave us the marvelously paradoxical beatitude, "Blessed are those who mourn, for they shall be comforted" (Matthew 5:4). When people truly understand the darkness of their souls apart from God, they are compelled to turn to him in whom they find healing and ultimate comfort.

This was Charles Colson's own experience the night he came to Christ:

> That night when I . . . sat alone at my car, my own sin—not just dirty politics, but the hatred and evil so deep within me—was thrust before my eyes, forcefully and painfully. For the first time in my life, I felt unclean, and worst of all, I could not escape. In those moments of clarity I found myself driven irresistibly into the arms of the living God.[4]

Blind Bartimaeus' pitiful cry, "have mercy on me," came from a profound clarity of self-understanding, and it brought grace. Christ rejoices to meet such clear self-understanding as this.

Second, *Bartimaeus displayed penetrating insight into the person of Christ.* He kept repeating to everyone's distress, "Jesus, Son of David"— "Jesus, Son of David," a blatantly messianic title. This is significant because though Matthew twice records that Jesus was called "Son of David" during his Galilean ministry (Matthew 9:27; 12:23), this is the only place in Mark that he is called so, outside Jesus' later calling himself the "son of David" (12:35). Though Bartimaeus was certainly no theologian, and probably did not understand much of the implications of what he was saying, he had come to an exalted conclusion about Christ.

Someone once bluntly asked blind and deaf Helen Keller, "Isn't it terrible to be blind?" To which she responded, "Better to be blind and see with your heart, than to have two good eyes and see nothing." So it was with blind Bartimaeus. Perhaps blindness has its benefits. Bartimaeus had a lot of time to think, without visual distractions—to develop the interior life and a contemplative spirit and to see with his heart. He thought about Christ and came to an exalted Biblical view of him, realizing his own darkness and need and who Jesus was, which opened him to the person of God.

This promoted the third aspect of his heart—*his amazing, passionate persistence*. Bartimaeus rejected the crowd's control, shouting again and again, "Jesus, Son of David, have mercy on me!" Understanding something of who Jesus was, and his own personal need, he kept saying it over and over again, like a helpless infant. Not long before, Jesus' had said regarding children, "Truly, I say to you, whoever does not receive the kingdom of God like a child shall not enter it" (10:15). Bartimaeus did just that.

Bartimaeus' extreme sense of urgency is a mirror of what ought to be in our souls. This is the meaning of Jesus' words, "From the days of John the Baptist until now the kingdom of heaven has suffered violence, and the violent take it by force" (Matthew 11:12). Spiritual blessings belong to those who "go for it." Jesus said, "Blessed are those who hunger and thirst for righteousness, for they shall be satisfied" (Matthew 5:6).

Helpless Bartimaeus "went for it." And Bartimaeus was heard above the crowd. Jesus heard him.

Jesus' Call and Bartimaeus' Response (vv. 49, 50)

Mark records, "And Jesus stopped and said, 'Call him'" (v. 49a). We must remember that Jesus is on the way to the terrible cross. The last stop is Jerusalem, just eighteen miles away, and yet Jesus has time for this poor beggar. The Son stood still.

What a window into our risen Savior's heart. He is alive today doing in a far more exalted fashion the things that he did while here on earth. Now in Heaven, he hears constant hosannas from the heavenly host and the Church. Yet he is instantly attentive to all our cries, even when a million of us beggars cry to him at once! The heart's cry of one in need is far sweeter to Christ than the shallow hallelujahs of the crowd. Are you hurting? Do you feel helpless? If so, understand that your plea will be sweetness to his ears.

Jesus said, "'Call him.' And they called the blind man, saying to him, 'Take heart. Get up; he is calling you.' And throwing off his cloak, he sprang up and came to Jesus" (vv. 49, 50). The instant Bartimaeus heard the commands, he stopped his bawling, threw off his moth-eaten cloak (an extreme gesture for a blind man, who would normally keep his cloak where he could touch it), sprang to his feet, and stumbled with the help of others to Jesus. Can you imagine Bartimaeus' thrill? If his heart was pounding before, what was it doing now? What a painting this would make. Face to face! Jesus with the most penetrating eyes ever, and the sightless sockets of Bartimaeus framed by a countenance of ultimate expectation. This is the way to come to Jesus!

Now hear the exchange: "And Jesus said to him, 'What do you want me to do for you?' And the blind man said to him, 'Rabbi, let me recover my sight'" (v. 51). Our Lord made Bartimaeus articulate his desire so he could strengthen the man's faith. Bartimaeus knew *exactly* what he wanted. If we knew our needs as well as he, what blessing would follow. "And Jesus said to him, 'Go your way; your faith has made you well.' And immediately he recovered his sight and followed him on the way" (v. 52).

On February 17, 1982, the *Chicago Sun-Times* carried a story originally printed in the *Los Angeles Times* about Anna Mae Pennica, a sixty-two-year-old woman who had been blind from birth. At age forty-seven, she married a man she met in a Braille class. For the first fifteen years of their marriage, he did the seeing for both of them, until he completely lost his vision to *retinitis pigmentosa*. Mrs. Pennica had never seen the green of spring or the blue of a summer sky. Yet because she had grown up in a loving, supportive family, she never felt resentful about her handicap and always exuded a remarkably cheerful spirit.

Then in October 1981 Dr. Thomas Pettit of the Jules Stein Eye Institute of the University of California at Los Angeles performed surgery to remove the rare congenital cataracts from the lens of Mrs. Pennica's left eye—and she saw for the first time ever!

The newspaper account does not record her initial response, but it does tell us that she found that everything was "so much bigger and brighter" than she had ever imagined. While she immediately recognized her husband and others she had known well, other acquaintances were taller or shorter, heavier or skinnier than she had pictured them. Since that day, Mrs. Pennica has hardly been able to wait to wake up in the morning, splash her eyes with water, put on her glasses, and enjoy the changing morning light. Her vision is almost 20/30—good enough to pass a driver's test!

Think how wonderful it must have been for Anna Mae Pennica when she looked for the first time at faces she had only felt, or when she saw the kaleidoscope of a Pacific sunset, or a tree waving its branches, or a bird in flight. The gift of physical sight is wonderful. And the miracle of seeing for the first time can hardly be described.

Imagine how it was for Bartimaeus. Blind at the beginning of Christ's sentence, he was seeing at the end of it! No surgery! No bandages! No adjustment! Boom—sight! He saw human beings for the first time. He saw the gawking crowd. He saw "The City of Roses" hung with palm trees, and the hills of Moab off in the distance. But the thing he saw first was the face of Jesus.

> And for you and me, too, that will be the greatest of all sights. When we awake from the dream men call life, when we put off the image of the earth and break the bonds of time and mortality, when the scales of time and sense have fallen from our eyes and the garment of corruption has been put off and when this mortality has put on immortality and this corruption has put on incorruption and we awaken in the everlasting morning, that will be the sight that will stir us and hold us.[5]

Said Jesus to gaping, saucer-eyed Bartimaeus, "your faith has made you well." Christ had responded to Bartimaeus' understanding of his own darkness, his penetrating assessment of Christ, and his persistence. But in the final analysis it was all of Christ. Jesus came to him, for blind Bartimaeus could not come to Jesus, and the Savior called forth his faith. Bartimaeus was saved both physically and spiritually, and he followed Jesus. Scholars say the reason Mark preserves Bartimaeus' name was that he became a stalwart in the Jerusalem church. He followed Jesus, witnessing the Triumphal Entry on Palm Sunday, the horror of the Crucifixion, and the joy of the Resurrection. Talk about getting one's eyes full!

What do we learn from this story? For one thing, we are to say what the crowd said at Jesus' request: "Take heart. Get up; he is calling you." We are to reach out to those to whom the Holy Spirit has shown their inner darkness and helplessness.

What are such people to do? First, they are to cry to him: "Jesus, Son of David, have mercy on me!" Second, they are to come stumbling to him and tell him what they want: "Lord, take away my darkness, my sin. Give me life!"

Jesus was passing through Jericho, never to come that way again. If Bartimaeus had not responded, he would never have had another chance. Jesus of Nazareth is passing by some of those around us today.

36

Welcoming the King

MARK 11:1–11

IN MAY 1981 I remember being miserably hot as I sat in a KLM 747 at Manila's International Airport. Because Philippine President Ferdinand Marcos and his wife were giving a state welcome for the visiting Prime Minister of Sri Lanka, our jet, having just arrived, was made to sit for almost an hour with the air conditioning *off!* Since I could do nothing but watch, I took careful note of what I saw.

Alongside the president and his wife stood a platoon of navy-clad honor guards wearing shining gold pith helmets. Next to them was another platoon dressed in forest green and white gloves and hats. Then came a crimson and gold uniformed band. Finally came a group resplendent in white naval uniforms. Add to the scene swaying Philippine dancers in chartreuse and purple, a baby elephant clad in scarlet, a long red carpet, a Philippine jet bearing the epigram "Hurrah for Hollywood," a twenty-one-gun salute, several gleaming black limousines, a temperature of 100 degrees, and you have the picture.

As I sat perspiring and gazing through the mirage-like heat waves rising from the runway, I thought to myself, *This is the best the world has to offer in honor and material pomp, but it is so transitory.* And it was! There were a few words, some ringing volleys, and everyone was gone, except for those rolling up the red carpet and sweeping the blazing asphalt.

In subsequent years, similar thoughts came again to me as I read of the Marcoses' incredibly obsessive materialism: how Mrs. Marcos owned some three thousand pairs of shoes and hundreds upon hundreds of designer dresses. On one occasion she spent one million dollars in one day. All this to festoon her aging body that is, as the Scriptures say, "wasting away" (2 Corinthians 4:16). Of course, now the reign, the palace, the shopping sprees are all gone! The Marcoses tried their very best to make it last forever. But they could not! So it is with the rulers of the earth.

But it was not so with the King of kings. He was a new kind of King. He operated from a different kind of principle. As we examine his example, we will escape the transitoriness that haunts our human pursuits.

Before we take up the actual story, we must get some of the flavor of that first Palm Sunday. To begin with, Jesus was at the end of a journey that had begun some nine months before when he purposefully began to zigzag through Galilee, then Samaria, then Perea, and finally Judea.

During this final journey he had ministered in at least thirty-five localities, timing the journey so he would end up in Jerusalem for Passover. Significantly, since attending the Passover at the beginning of his public ministry, Jesus had absented himself from the intervening three because of the rulers' initial animosity, even though Jewish law required that all males attend the Feast of the Passover (Exodus 23:17).

Now that he was back in Bethany, on the outskirts of Jerusalem, expectations were running high. Earlier he had raised Lazarus from the dead (John 11). The sensational news had spread around Jerusalem many times. The numbers of those observing his entourage had dramatically increased. Most recently, as he journeyed to this Passover he had healed blind Bartimaeus in Jericho, and the pilgrims moving on before him were enthusiastically spreading the news to everyone (10:46–52). Now, as he resided in Bethany, great crowds were coming out from Jerusalem to see him and the resurrected Lazarus. The religious leaders were counseling together as to how they might kill Jesus, because many of the people were believing in him (John 12:9–11).

There was unparalleled tension in Jerusalem. None, not even the oldest, had seen anything like it. Wherever one could go—in the marketplace, in the doorways, on the corner, in the temple—everyone was talking about it. The Passover was only a few days away. Would Jesus make a move? If so, when? What would the authorities do? As the pressure mounted, the Lord indeed took definite, calculated, and premeditated action.

The King's Deliberate Preparation (vv. 1–6)

Now when they drew near to Jerusalem, to Bethphage and Bethany, at the Mount of Olives, Jesus sent two of his disciples and said to them, "Go into the village in front of you, and immediately as you enter it you will find a colt tied, on which no one has ever sat. Untie it and bring it. If anyone says to you, 'Why are you doing this?' say, 'The Lord has need of it and will send it back here immediately.'" And they went away and found a colt tied at a door outside in the street, and they untied it. And some of those standing there said to them, "What are you doing, untying the colt?" And they told them what Jesus had said, and they let them go.

Bethphage was a little hamlet or district between Jerusalem and Bethany. A traveler approaching Jerusalem from the east, coming from Jericho, would come to Bethany about two miles from Jerusalem on the slopes of the Mount of Olives. As he rounded the south side of the Mount of Olives, he would pass by Bethphage before entering Jerusalem.

On that blessed day, the first Palm Sunday, Jesus was walking in front of his disciples (10:32) when they came to Bethphage. Here Jesus sent two of his disciples into the hamlet to obtain a donkey's unridden colt. As to how Jesus knew it was there, the Scriptures are silent. Perhaps one of his disciples told him, or maybe it was revealed by the Father. Whatever the case, we may surmise that the owners gave it to him because they had heard of Jesus and reasoned they could trust him with the colt. They very likely were honored that he would ask.

In all of this we observe Jesus' painstaking premeditation. He had carefully ordered everything. The day and hour were selected from eternity with countdown perfection. This Triumphal Entry on the first day of the week would precipitate his terrible death on Good Friday, his "rest" in the grave on the Sabbath, and his triumphant resurrection on the following first day of the Church, his Body! Not only the time of his entry, but the mode as well, a previously unridden donkey, was carefully chosen. He was purposely going public. Never before had he done anything to promote a public demonstration. In fact, he had repeatedly withdrawn from the crowds if there was any hint of this. But now he invited it. He courted danger and did it with calculated purpose.

Why the choice of a young donkey? Because over five hundred years before, Zechariah had prophesied that the Messiah would come riding on the foal of a donkey: "Rejoice greatly, O daughter of Zion! Shout aloud, O daughter of Jerusalem! Behold, your king is coming to you; righteous and having salvation is he, humble and mounted on a donkey, on a colt, the foal of a donkey" (Zechariah 9:9). Jesus consciously fulfilled this prophecy to the letter, and in fact exceeded it, for he chose a colt upon which no one had ever ridden. This was because in Biblical culture (and ancient culture in general) an animal devoted to a sacred task must be one that had not been put to ordinary use (Numbers 19:2; Deuteronomy 21:3; 1 Samuel 6:7).

In addition to this, Jesus told his disciples they would find the colt "tied" (tethered) in Bethphage. This points to the messianic oracle pronounced by Jacob upon Judah in Genesis 49:10, 11: "The scepter shall not depart from Judah, nor the ruler's staff from between his feet, until tribute comes to him; and to him shall be the obedience of the peoples. Binding his foal to the vine and his donkey's colt to the choice vine, he has washed his garments in wine and his vesture in the blood of grapes."

Christ, the Lion of the Tribe of Judah, wants us to see the connections here. By riding a donkey, he fulfilled not only Zechariah 9:9, but (in Genesis) Jacob's prophecy to Judah.[1] What is more, riding a donkey (contrary to what we think today) was a kingly act that identified him with the royal line of David. (The donkey was a royal animal during King David's reign. After him, the Hebrew kings switched to horses, and the donkey was considered unsuited to the dignity of kings.)[2]

King Jesus knew exactly what he was doing when he rode a donkey into Jerusalem to fulfill the great Old Testament messianic prophecies and identify himself with the royal line of Judah!

What an honored beast that animal was:

When fishes flew and forests walked
And figs grew upon thorn,
Some moment when the moon was blood
Then surely I was born.

With monstrous head and sickening cry
And ears like errant wings
The devil's walking parody
On all four-footed things.

The tattered outlaw of the earth,
Of ancient crooked will;
Starve, scourge, deride me: I am dumb,
I keep my secret still.

Fools! For I also had my hour;
One far fierce hour and sweet:
There was a shout about my ears,
And palms before my feet.[3]

Jesus' choice of the donkey told the whole world who he was, but it also proclaimed what he was like. Zechariah's prophecy described Jesus as "humble and mounted on a donkey." Jesus came peacefully, bringing peace (*shalom*) to our war-torn world. Seven hundred and fifty years earlier, Isaiah had prophesied that the Messiah would come as the "Prince of Peace"

(Isaiah 9:6). When he was born, the angels announced "on earth peace among those with whom he is pleased" (Luke 2:14). Now he rode into Jerusalem upon an animal of peace.

Jesus told his disciples, "Peace I leave with you; my peace I give to you. Not as the world gives do I give to you. Let not your hearts be troubled, neither let them be afraid" (John 14:27). "Peace be with you" (the *Pax Vobiscum*) is still a supreme Christian greeting and a gospel offer today. Our gentle/humble Jesus also said, "Take my yoke upon you, and learn from me, for I am gentle and lowly in heart, and you will find rest for your souls" (Matthew 11:29); "Blessed are the poor in spirit, for theirs is the kingdom of heaven" (Matthew 5:3); "Blessed are the meek, for they shall inherit the earth" (Matthew 5:5).

Jesus is unlike any other king who ever lived. How unlike he is to the Alexanders, Napoleons, and Marcoses of this world. What a contrast to the triumphal entry of ancient kings on their warhorses, riding proudly through the gates, cruel-lipped, swords aloft, trailed by captive kings and princes in chains. Jesus slowly, purposefully came riding the colt of a donkey.

In the past, critics have portrayed Jesus as attempting to turn the wheel of history, only to be crushed himself.[4] But in truth Jesus was in control of every detail that day as he rode past the Roman pomp and power and toward the Jewish temple. His riding of the donkey perfectly portrayed his *position* as Messiah and his person, the Prince of Peace, humble and gentle. "Behold, your king is coming to you; righteous and having salvation is he, humble and mounted on a donkey" (Zechariah 9:9).

Have you received this King into your life? Have you let him give you his love, joy, peace, gentleness, self-control?

The King's Triumphal Entry (vv. 7–10)

Having obtained the donkey, the triumphal march began as verse 8 describes it: "And many spread their cloaks on the road, and others spread leafy branches that they had cut from the fields." All eyes were focused on Jesus, and all homage was poured forth. Not only did exuberant followers place their clothing on the donkey as a saddle, some flung their robes to the ground as a gesture of reverence, indicating their willingness for him to have everything—even to trample their property if he so desired. They did this repeatedly as the procession moved forward.[5] It was a magnificent gesture. Theirs was a swelling, mounting joy!

As Jesus rode up toward the ridge where "the way [goes] down the Mount of Olives" (Luke 19:37), fresh pilgrims from Bethany and Bethphage joined him, and the procession enlarged its exuberance. When they reached the spot where they caught a glimpse of the southeastern corner of the city with its magnificent terraces and imposing towers, they broke into loud Eastern praise.[6] These were Hebrews on holiday!

Mark says in verse 9 that "those who went before and those who followed were [repeatedly] shouting." This was an antiphonal chant between those in front of Jesus and those behind. Some scholars suggest that it went like this:

> *First group:* "Hosanna!"
> *Second group:* "Blessed is he who comes in the name of the Lord! Blessed is the coming kingdom of our father David!"
> *First group:* "Hosanna in the highest!"[7]

One of the lines repeated regularly and mentioned in all four Gospels is from Psalm 118:26—"Blessed is he who comes in the name of the Lord!" (v. 9b). This was often used as a greeting for pilgrims, but here it perfectly fits Jesus. Luke has them also saying, "Blessed is the King who comes in the name of the Lord" (Luke 19:38).[8] The growing throng was caught in something of a mass prophetic ecstasy as the long procession moved along the slope of the Mount of Olives.

The other Gospel accounts add to Mark's picture of joy. John tells us, "So they took branches of palm trees and went out to meet him, crying out, 'Hosanna!'" (John 12:13). The palm branches represented their nationalistic desire to be delivered, for when Simon Maccabaeus delivered Jerusalem one hundred fifty years earlier, it was celebrated with praise, palm branches, and musical instruments (1 Maccabees 13:51). The palm frond was the symbol of the Second Maccabean Revolt.

"Hosanna!" was a customary religious greeting at Passover, but on the lips of the fervent crowd it was an anticipatory cry that literally meant, "Save!" or "Save us!" The people were prophetically repeating over and over and over that Jesus was their deliverer: "Save us! . . . Save us! . . . Save us!" Not even the disciples themselves understood the full import of what they were saying. It was only after Jesus was glorified that his followers pieced it all together (John 12:16).

Our Lord was in control, and he was making a statement, for their words *were* his statement. The donkey he straddled prophesied of his *position* and his *person*. The Hallel Psalm, "Blessed is he who comes in the name of the Lord," repeated his messianic character. The "Hosannas!" described his work. This was his moment, the moment set before the foundations of the world.

The King's Tears (Luke 19:41–44)

The road down to Jerusalem descended into a hollow, and the sight of the city was again withdrawn from the multitudes because of the intervening ridge. But after a few moments of walking, the path mounted again, and in an instant the *whole city*, not just part of it, burst into view! With the Kedron Valley falling below, Jesus saw the Holy City as if gloriously rising out of a deep abyss. Before him spread the Temple courts with its great Temple tower, all framed by the gardens and suburbs of the western plateau behind.[9]

And with the whole city before his eyes (Luke 19:41), the Savior began to weep. We must never forget this. It was not with quiet tears that he wept, as he had done at the grave of Lazarus, whom he was going to resurrect, but with loud and deep sorrow.[10] There in the middle of the road, with the great city in dramatic panorama, the stunned multitude ceased their hosannas and heard the Lord of the universe wail over Jerusalem! This was a new kind of king!

Jesus' wailing turned to lamentation, and verses 42–44 preserve his words:

> Would that you, even you, had known on this day the things that make for peace! But now they are hidden from your eyes. For the days will come upon you, when your enemies will set up a barricade around you and surround you and hem you in on every side and tear you down to the ground, you and your children within you. And they will not leave one stone upon another in you, because you did not know the time of your visitation.

By prophetic vision, the Lord saw the proud, unrepentant Holy City reduced to a pile of rubble wet with the blood of his people. Forty years later this all came true under Titus' Roman legions. The Jews' resistance was so fierce that Titus finally ordered his besieging legions to encircle the walls of Jerusalem with a barricade and starve them out. The resulting famine made Jerusalem a graveyard, and finally when the Jews lacked the strength to bury their dead they cast them over the walls into the surrounding ravines. So great was the destruction that toward the end, as Josephus records: "When Titus, going his rounds, beheld these valleys choked with dead, . . . he groaned and raising his hands to heaven, called God to witness that this was not his doing. Such was the situation of the city."[11]

Of the final destruction, Josephus says:

> Caesar ordered the whole city and the temple to be razed to the ground, leaving only the loftiest of the towers, Phase 1, Hippicus, and Mariamme,

and the portion of the wall enclosing the city on the west; the latter as an encampment for the garrison that was to remain, and the towers to indicate to posterity the nature of the city and of the strong defenses which had not yet yielded to Roman prowess. All the rest of the wall encompassing the city was so completely leveled to the ground as to leave future visitors to the spot no ground for believing that it had ever been inhabited. Such was the end to which the frenzy of revolutionaries brought Jerusalem, that splendid city of world-wide renown.[12]

Jesus saw all this in prospect and wailed in grief. This was the heart of a new kind of King. Jesus' sorrow indicated his humanity, but it was also a revelation of the heart of God.

Fix this in your thoughts. This is how Jesus Christ and God the Father and the blessed Holy Spirit sorrow over hearts that miss their "day" and "the things that make for peace"—namely, repentance toward God and faith in the Lord Jesus Christ.

As your life stands right now, what does Jesus Christ see in your future? Judgment? Your towers pulled down? Desolation?

> The Son of God in tears,
> The wondering angels see.
> Be thou astonished, O my soul,
> He shed those tears for thee.[13]

The tears of Christ measure the infinite value of your soul. Christ wept and lamented over Jerusalem, as he always weeps over the souls of the unrepentant.

This is our King. Let us worship him with all that we have!

37

The Wrath of Jesus

MARK 11:12–26

THROUGH THE YEARS, overly critical minds have found reasons to reject the account of Jesus' cursing of the fig tree in 11:12–14 as spurious. In recent history the celebrated New Testament scholar T. W. Manson wrote: "It is a tale of miraculous power wasted in the service of ill-temper (for the supernatural energy employed to blast the unfortunate tree might have been more usefully expressed in forcing a crop of figs out of season); and as it stands, it is simply incredible."[1] William Barclay agrees, adding, "The story does not seem worthy of Jesus. There seems to be a petulance in it."[2]

So these minds reject the story because it seems to them that Jesus is acting like a spoiled child who did not get his way. Still others have rejected Jesus' cursing the tree because it is unthinkable to them that Jesus would blast a poor, innocent tree simply because it was fruitless.

What do we say to these objections? To the last we answer that such an objection comes from an unhealthy eagerness to find fault. If we assume that lower creation has no soul and is there for our use (as we do every day), then where is Jesus' sin?

The same thinking applies to an earlier description of a herd of swine (Mark 5). Turn them into pork sausage and we think how nicely they have fulfilled their destiny. But sacrifice them for the salvation of a poor lunatic's soul—use them up in order to restore him to health, and the whole thing is shocking![3] Here in Mark 11, if the fig tree continued to be barren and useless, it would be cut down for firewood and no one would object. But when Jesus withers the tree with a word to teach an eternal spiritual lesson, the critics cry out.

This is where the essential answer lies: Jesus did not spitefully curse the tree because he was hungry and it didn't provide what it promised. He could do without food, as for example when he refused to satisfy his hunger by turning stones into bread even though he had been fasting forty days in the wilderness (Matthew 4:1–4). Jesus was a man who would forego food and rest to minister to a soul, as he did at Jacob's well (John 4:1–9).

The reason Jesus cursed the barren fig tree was because he wanted it to become a visual parable of what was happening to Israel. In actuality he honored that tree, making it the most useful tree that ever grew! It was, and is, a tree from which thousands have learned about themselves and turned back to God. If one soul has been made to consider its life through that tree, it did not wither in vain.

Three years earlier, at the beginning of Jesus' ministry, he had made a whip out of cords and cleansed the temple. Yesterday he had made his Triumphal Entry into Jerusalem. He had received the hallelujahs of the people, wept over the city, and then, as 11:11 says, "went into the temple . . . looked around at everything," and "went out to Bethany with the twelve." The temple was doing business as usual. Jesus was deeply grieved by this.

Now, early in the morning, as he returns from Bethany to Jerusalem (perhaps after a night alone in prayer), he is hungry and sees a fig tree in full leaf. At first he is drawn to it, but then realizes that though the tree is in full leaf, it is not yet time for figs, as fig season is five weeks away. Nevertheless, he continues to approach the tree because he sees that it perfectly portrays what he wishes to prophesy. He knew that the unexpected action in looking for figs at a time when no fruit would be found would stimulate his disciples' curiosity and point to a deeper significance.[4]

The fig tree was a standard symbol for Israel, as numerous Old Testament passages attest (Jeremiah 8:13; 29:17; Hosea 9:10, 16; Joel 1:7; and Micah 7:1–6, for example). The fact that this particular fig tree had luxuriant foliage but bore no fruit portrayed exactly what Jesus had seen in Jerusalem.

Israel was a barren fig tree, and the leaves only covered its nakedness. The magnificence of the temple and its ceremonies hid the fact that Israel had not brought forth the fruit of righteousness demanded by God. When Jesus cursed the luxuriant but fruitless tree, he may well have had Jeremiah's words in view: "When I would gather them, declares the Lord, there are no grapes on the vine, nor figs on the fig tree; even the leaves are withered, and what I gave them has passed away from them" (Jeremiah 8:13).

The fig tree was meant to be a visual parable to Israel, and later to the Church (us). Just because we look good, because our leaves are large and shiny, does not mean that we are bearing fruit pleasing to God. This is a valuable image for us and our large western churches. But whatever the application to us, it was a perfect frame for Jesus' visit that day to the temple, because he would return the next day to see his prophecy fulfilled.

Jesus' Cleansing of the Temple (vv. 15–19)

Having pronounced the curse, Jesus walked on toward Jerusalem, and this is what he saw: As he approached the temple, he saw the cream of her marble walls and the gleaming gold of her pillars' capitals illuminated by the morning sun. Huge Passover crowds were already flowing up the steps to the great Court of the Gentiles—a walled, marble-paved area adjacent to the south side of the temple, the length of three football fields and some two hundred fifty yards wide.[5]

Great throngs surged against the tables of the money-changers. Exodus 30:13–16 commanded that a half-shekel be given for every male worshiper over twenty years of age. For this, and all other offerings in the temple, foreign money (with its idolatrous images) could not be used. So everyone had to exchange their money for Tyrian coins. They had to pay a charge for this service. This arrangement was a great boon to the establishment—the chief priests and scribes.

Jesus also observed huge crowds lined around the stalls selling livestock, fowl, wine, and salt for the sacrifices. Josephus, the Hellenic Jewish historian, says that during Passover, AD 65, 255,600 lambs were offered. If there were ten offerers to a Passover lamb, that would mean there were close to 2,700,000 celebrants in Jerusalem.[6]

The noise in this Court of the Gentiles was terrific. Merchants shouted from their stalls to the customers, and noisy, haggling, pushy pilgrims jostled one another for position. The incredible din was heightened by the constant bawling of livestock. The aroma of the livestock, accentuated by the enclosure, made it like a county fair and the Stock Exchange all rolled into one!

To top it off, the Court of the Gentiles was used as a regular Jerusalem thoroughfare because it afforded a convenient cross-town route to the Mount of Olives. Even though the *Mishnah* contained an ordinance aimed at curbing traffic by forbidding anyone to enter the Temple Mount carrying his staff or sandal or wallet, or to use it as a shortcut,[7] people still did so. The Court of the Gentiles was a huge religious circus!

The Lord saw this for what it was: a monstrous desecration of holy ground. The Royal Porch, which sat on the site of Solomon's original temple, bordered the Court of the Gentiles on the south side. This had been holy ground for a thousand years, ever since King Solomon finished his great dedicatory prayer and the glory of the Lord so filled the temple that the priests could not enter, and all Israel knelt on the pavement outside as they saw the fire of glory descend on the temple (2 Chronicles 7:1–3).

It was there seven hundred fifty years before that Isaiah, mourning the death of Uzziah, was caught up in a vision of the sovereign Lord majestically enthroned above him with the train of his robe carpeting the temple floor. Above the Lord, burning seraphim hovered, beating the air with one set of wings while covering their faces and feet with the remaining pinions in humble recognition that they were in the presence of perfect holiness. As Isaiah watched, he heard them chant to one another, "Holy, holy, holy is the LORD of hosts; the whole earth is full of his glory!" (Isaiah 6:3). This is also where the foundations of the temple began to sway and the smoke of God's presence filled the sanctuary as the glowing seraphim continued their chant. Isaiah was smitten with the trauma of God's holiness and cried, "Woe is me! For I am lost; for I am a man of unclean lips, and I dwell in the midst of a people of unclean lips; for my eyes have seen the King, the LORD of hosts!" (Isaiah 6:5).

This was the place where all this had happened, and which was still officially called holy. Now all this sacrilege was taking place before Jesus' eyes! Jesus agonized as he surveyed the vast court! In his earlier cleansing of the temple, the disciples remembered that it was written: "Zeal for your house will consume me" (John 2:17). Literally, the Greek idea is, *eat me up*, and the Hebrew means, *burn up in a flame*. Any way we take it, Jesus was being burned up with zeal for the Lord's House.

Mark is very clear about what Jesus did: "And they came to Jerusalem. And he entered the temple and began to drive out those who sold and those who bought in the temple, and he overturned the tables of the money-changers and the seats of those who sold pigeons. And he would not allow anyone to carry anything through the temple" (vv. 15, 16).

None of the Gospels indicate that he used a whip as he had in the original cleansing. But it is obvious that he used force in driving out those who were misusing the House of God. There was shouting and resistance, but Jesus prevailed.

Have you ever seen a table flipped over? This is a violent act. And to top it off, we see Jesus halting the traffic of those who were using the Court of Gentiles as a shortcut—he "would not allow anyone to carry anything through the temple." So much for the one-sided "gentle Jesus, meek and mild."

There is a memorable passage in C. S. Lewis's *Voyage of the Dawn Treader* that touches on these matters. Lucy and Edmund are off on their adventure when they come to a large grassy area. The green of the grass spreads into the blue horizon, except for a white spot in the middle of the green expanse. As Edmund and Lucy look at this spot intently, they have difficulty making out what it is. With their adventurous spirits, they travel forward until the white spot comes into closer view. It is a lamb! The lamb, white and pure, is cooking a breakfast of fish. The lamb gives Lucy and Edmund the most delicious meal they have ever eaten. Then ensues conversation as they talk about how to get to the land of Aslan (or Heaven). As the lamb begins to explain the way, a marvelous thing happens: "His snowy white flushed into tawny gold and his size changed and he was Aslan himself towering above them and scattering light from his mane."[8] Lewis was illustrating the great truth of our faith: the Lamb is the Lion. Or in Biblical terms, the Lamb of God who takes away the sin of the world is the Lion of the tribe of Judah! Qualities we consider to be lamb-like—gentleness and meekness—are indeed in Christ, but so are the regalness and the ferocity of a lion. Our Savior is also Judge. The Scriptures speak of the "wrath of the Lamb" (Revelation 6:16).

To be sure, Jesus is the meekest, gentlest person who ever lived. He said, "I am gentle and lowly in heart" (Matthew 11:29), and "Blessed are the meek, for they shall inherit the earth" (Matthew 5:5). But meekness is not weakness. It is, rather, strength under control. Meekness has the strength to not defend oneself (Jesus when he went to the cross, for example). But meekness will boldly defend others. And here Jesus struck out in defense of the holiness of God the Father.

It must be said with proper reverence that holiness is a divine obsession! When Jehovah said, "You shall be holy, for I the LORD your God am holy" (Leviticus 19:2), there was a divine intensity, which was here echoed by the Son. As individual temples of his Spirit we are called to holiness. To this end, we are commanded to honor God with our bodies (1 Corinthians 6:19, 20). Covetousness is at odds with his holiness. Impure thoughts are incompatible with his holiness. Jesus stood (and stands) with his "sleeves rolled up" to rid his people of all unholiness, and the floor quickly cleared. He meant business.

Notice too what Jesus said: "And he was teaching them and saying to them, 'Is it not written, "My house shall be called a house of prayer for all the nations"? But you have made it a den of robbers'" (v. 17). The call for the temple to be "a house of prayer for all the nations" was a direct quotation from Isaiah 56:7 and stated a main purpose for the Court of the Gentiles— to be a place where the Gentiles could come for prayer and meditation in seeking God. But as it was, it was impossible to concentrate on anything, much less to pray and worship. This desecration of the Court of the Gentiles was a massive national sin against God and the lost people of the world! It was doubly serious at this Passover time when the heart of Jewish religion was especially revealed.

Instead of the temple being a house of prayer, they had made it "a den of robbers." The high priest's family had perverted temple worship into a means of extortion well-known to all. But the real shame of this spiritual robbery was that Gentiles, and indeed all seeking Israel, were being perverted from true worship!

Jesus' words tell us, first, how important our corporate worship is. Our worship must be authentic and from the heart. When we hear the Holy Word read, our hearts should stand at attention and we should attempt to absorb every syllable. When we pray, we should piggy-back the prayers of the one praying with our silent and verbal "amens" and "yes, Lord's" and "hallelujahs." There must be in all of this a willingness to devote our will to God's service.

Here we can do no better than quote Archbishop William Temple's definition of worship: "to quicken the conscience by the holiness of God, to feed the mind with the truth of God, to purge the imagination by the beauty of God, to open the heart to the love of God, to devote the will to the purpose of God."[9]

When a seeking heart enters our churches, our homes, our lives, our Court of the Gentiles, may our actions say that God is alive—that God is holy—that God is loving. May our worship and service say to others that we love him with all our hearts.

It is so easy for us to seem so worshipful, so ecclesiastical, and yet to be as disrupted and distracted as the Court of the Gentiles then. Proverbs 5:14 says, "I am at the brink of utter ruin in the assembled congregation," and we continually face that danger. These are not matters to be taken lightly. They involve God's holiness and the spiritual health of our loved ones and the Church.

What Jesus did and said that day came with power, and it did two things: it sealed his rejection by the religious leaders, and it momentarily captured the people's hearts: "And the chief priests and the scribes heard it and were seeking a way to destroy him, for they feared him, because all the crowd was astonished at his teaching" (v. 18). This shows the desperate ways people so often respond to the radical demands of our holy Lord Jesus.

Confirming Jesus' Prophecy (vv. 20, 21)

Tragically, the religious establishment and the people came to reject Jesus, nailing him to the cross at the end of that very week, and thus sealing their fate as a nation. Jesus returned to Bethany that night, having cleansed the temple. Then came the morning. "As they passed by in the morning," says Mark, "they saw the fig tree withered away to its roots. And Peter remembered and said to him, 'Rabbi, look! The fig tree that you cursed has withered'" (vv. 20, 21). Mark is careful to tell us that it was withered from the roots, emphasizing the totality of its destruction. Such a graphic warning—a fig tree with full foliage, yet dead and sagging. The disciples never forgot it!

What a lesson to us as we appear to be sprouting new branches and turning green leaves. The question is, is there internal fruit? "But the fruit of the Spirit is love, joy, peace, patience, kindness, goodness, faithfulness, gentleness, self-control; against such things there is no law" (Galatians 5:22, 23).

Are our lives an invitation to meet a holy God?

38

A Warning to the Unreceptive

MARK 11:27—12:12

JESUS STOOD ON Solomon's Porch on the east side of the Court of the Gentiles, amidst a forest of huge Corinthian columns, each rising almost forty feet to a richly ornamented roof, forming a colossal veranda extending several hundred feet to the north and south. Below the immense porch the breath-taking Kidron Valley dropped to a depth of 450 feet. What a view this afforded for one who had the leisure to stand in its cool stone shade and look out through the brightness of the day into the Kidron or across to the Mount of Olives and the sun-drenched Judean hills.

But Jesus had no time for such leisure. He was engaged in terminal conflict. He had entered Jerusalem and was openly proclaimed Messiah. He had cursed the fig tree (symbolic of spiritually barren Israel), and it was found withered the next day. With righteous anger he had cleansed the temple. And now on Solomon's Porch, surrounded by "the chief priests and the scribes and the elders"—in effect, the Sanhedrin, he refused to tell them where his authority came from, because of their malevolent unbelief. With effortless brilliance he asked them a counter-question that they dared not answer, thus freeing him from any obligation to answer their evil-intentioned query. Jesus had them, and there was nothing they could do about it!

He further used the occasion to give them what is called one of his Judgment Parables: the Parable of the Wicked Vineyard Keepers. This would devastate them, but at the same time it was gracious, for this convicting summary of God's dealings with his people was meant to reach their hearts. In it Jesus described: 1) the *hope* of God for his people, 2) the *kindness* of God for his own, 3) the *severity* of God, and 4) the ultimate *triumph* of God in history. For us, this parable is not meant to be a slice of ancient history, but a grid through which we can evaluate our own lives. May the Spirit of God help us to minister these truths to receptive ears, and even more to those who have been unresponsive to Christ.

Jesus began by picturing God's hope for Israel as being like the hope of a man who built a vineyard and waited expectantly for it to produce. "And he began to speak to them in parables. 'A man planted a vineyard and put a fence around it and dug a pit for the winepress and built a tower, and leased it to tenants and went into another country'" (12:1). As Jesus spoke these words everyone understood them, whether they liked them or not, because the vineyard was a national symbol for Israel. In fact, the very temple in which Jesus was standing sported a richly carved grapevine, seventy cubits high, sculpted around the door that led from the porch to the Holy Place. The branches, tendrils, and leaves were of finest gold. The bunches hanging upon them were costly jewels. Herod first placed it there, and rich and patriotic Jews from time to time added to its embellishment. One contributed a new grape, another a leaf, and still another a cluster of the same precious materials. This vine had an uncommon importance and a sacred meaning in the eyes of the Jews.[1]

In addition, the old Maccabbean coins bore the same symbols (sometimes a bunch of grapes, and at other times a grape leaf).[2] Moreover, Jesus used phrases directly from the beautiful Song of the Vineyard in Isaiah 5:1–7, a song about Israel. Jesus' hearers knew that the vineyard in his parable was Israel!

They also understood that the owner (the Lord) had taken great pains to make the vineyard healthy and productive. He "put a fence" up to keep wild animals such as "the boar from the forest" from ravaging it (cf. Psalm 80:12, 13), as well as intruders. He "dug a pit for the winepress." That is, he dug it out of solid rock, forming two vats—an upper shallow place where the grapes were trod, and a lower vat into which the juice ran through a channel in the rock. He "built a tower" some fifteen to twenty feet high.[3] This was a place for shelter and storage. But most of all, it was a vantage point from which all the vineyard could be observed and protected with a sling. He "planted a vineyard"—"He dug it and cleared it of stones, and planted it with choice vines" (Isaiah 5:2). He created a beautiful garden from which it appeared great things would come.

This God had done with the vineyard of the nation of Israel. Under God's leadership, Abraham had left Ur because it was evil, and he became the father of a chosen people that was to be a blessing to the world. Moses came to deliver the people from Egypt and bring them to a land flowing with milk and honey. God delivered them and gave them the Law. Finally, under Joshua and again with God's help, they were planted in Canaan. As the Psalmist says, "You with your own hand drove out the nations, but them you planted" (Psalm 44:2; cf. Exodus 15:17).

God expected great things to come from his spiritual vineyard. Then, says Jesus, "[he] leased it to tenants and went into another country." Such lease agreements were common in the Jordan Valley, with the owner usually getting one third to one half the produce.[4] But here, of course, our Lord means by "tenants" the spiritual leadership of Israel. God's expectations were understandably high, for with all their advantages, he expected the development of a people who so radiated him that they would be a light to the Gentiles. In the divine plan, so much rested with the farmers, the spiritual leadership.

We must take great care that we do not leave the spiritual relevance of this back in the dusty passages of time. We farm a far richer vineyard than that of ancient Israel. We have no living prophets like Isaiah or Daniel, but we do have the complete Word of God and the testimonies of his messengers. We have so much more in our risen Christ and the indwelling Holy Spirit, along with the full revelation of both the Old and New Testament Scriptures. Added to this is the testimony of the saints for the last two thousand years.

I think about this frequently. I am sure my preoccupation is heightened by my pastoral calling. We are so rich spiritually, intellectually, and materially. Jesus said, "Everyone to whom much was given, of him much will be required, and from him to whom they entrusted much, they will demand the more" (Luke 12:48).

Every Christian is in view. If we have been Christians for any length of time, it is inexcusable to lack any of the fruits of the Spirit (Galatians 5:22). There is no excuse (heredity, environment, whatever) for being dominated by temper, jealousy, lasciviousness, covetousness, or whatever—none!

So there on Solomon's Porch, the very pinnacle of the temple, at the top of the world with the bright panorama of Israel as a backdrop, Jesus told the hardhearted leaders in no uncertain terms about God's expectations. They must understand this.

The Kindness of God (vv. 2–8)

God's patient love is seen in how he allows himself to be treated in his servants: "When the season came, he sent a servant to the tenants to get from them some of the fruit of the vineyard. And they took him and beat him and sent him away empty-handed. Again he sent to them another servant, and they struck him on the head [the Wycliffe version quaintly says, "brake his head"] and treated him shamefully. And he sent another, and him they killed. And so with many others: some they beat, and some they killed" (vv. 2–5).

What an outrage! The flagrant, ascending violence described here—first beating, then wounding, and finally murdering—agreed with what historians tell us was going on in Judea and Galilee at that time. Papyrus records tell of disputes between hostile farmers and absentee landlords.[5] Moreover, if the Biblical restrictions given in Leviticus 19:23–25 were followed, five years had to pass before fruit could be harvested. This would mean that the farmers had ample time to come to regard the owners' property as their own.

So such outrages were actually being committed in Israel even as Jesus spoke, and they all knew what he was talking about. But even more, they knew he was referring to the way the leadership of Israel had treated God's prophets and that Jesus' parable was no exaggeration. Elijah was driven into the wilderness by the monarchy (1 Kings 19:1–5). Isaiah, according to tradition, was sawn asunder. Zechariah was stoned to death near the altar (2 Chronicles 24:21). John the Baptist was beheaded. The writer of Hebrews summarizes: "They were stoned, they were sawn in two, they were killed with the sword. They went about in skins of sheep and goats, destitute, afflicted, mistreated—of whom the world was not worthy—wandering about in deserts and mountains, and in dens and caves of the earth" (Hebrews 11:37, 38).

All of this was done, said Jesus' parable, because Israel's leaders wanted the vineyards' fruits for themselves! God's servants, his prophets, through announcing his Word, threatened the leadership's position and their monetary profits.

This has a contemporary ring to it. We read about it in our newspapers. Men who have disqualified themselves from ministry are hanging on to *"their* ministries" as if the vineyard was their own! They, by their rejection of God's Word and the spiritual advice of their peers, are stoning the prophets who are sent to them. Spiritually there is no difference between them and the violent leaders of old.

As Jesus continued the parable, the leaders were visibly stung. Some undoubtedly drew their robes closer as he told of the ultimate indignity, moving from history to prophecy, and so unmasked their ultimate intention, which was to put him to death: "He had still one other, a beloved son. Finally he sent him to them, saying, 'They will respect my son.' But those tenants said to one another, 'This is the heir. Come, let us kill him, and the inheritance will be ours.' And they took him and killed him and threw him out of the vineyard" (vv. 6–8).

From earth level, Palestinian level, the motivation for these men's action was easily discernible. They supposed in seeing the master's son come alone that the master was dead. Therefore, if they killed the son, they would command the property. They wanted the proceeds of the vineyard all for themselves. They wanted to be God!

In three days Jesus' malevolent listeners would haul him before their own authorities and condemn him. They would then arrange for his death outside the city (symbolically, outside the vineyard). This was their final indignity, the desire of their hearts—that the vineyard be theirs alone.

In the face of humanity's refusal to receive God's love, he persisted and persisted and persisted. One representative after another of God was abused and slain. "If I were God," cried Martin Luther, "and the world had treated me as it treated Him, I would kick the wretched thing to pieces." No doubt Luther would have!

But instead of turning his back on the world, God continued sending servant after servant. Rebuffs, insults, beatings did not stop him, and finally he sent his Son. Spurgeon said, "If you reject him, he answers you with tears; if you wound him, he bleeds out cleansing; if you kill him, he dies to redeem; if you bury him, he rises again to bring resurrection. Jesus is love made manifest."[6]

Here we are reminded that the Incarnation and the death of Christ were acts of love of the Father, Son, and Holy Spirit. The Son dwelt with the Father and Holy Spirit in inconceivable glory—so inconceivable that I tremble at trying to describe it. They were co-equal, co-eternal, possessing all the fullness of Deity. They were always proceeding toward one another in fellowship. In sending the Son, there was nothing more God could do! Jesus was God's ultimatum! In consequence, nothing remains when Christ is refused!

God's love is still coming even to those who have cast his messenger aside. In fact, the Son is coming to them right now, persistent in his love for them.

To deny that Christ is, in a sense God, is to kill him. Some have been killing him this way all their lives. They may find some twisted pleasure in hearing about Jesus and in consciously rejecting him. If they continue to do so in this life, they will succeed in killing themselves forever. This is a great tragedy.

There can even be a strain of this in the believer who does not consider Christ worthy of his or her attention. "You put your finger in the eye of God, when you slight His Son."[7]

Jesus persists in reaching out to a person until death. We must urge others to not toy with his love, for there does come a day when it is too late, and then there is only the severity of God.

The Severity of God (v. 9)

"What will the owner of the vineyard do?" asked Jesus. He gave the answer: "He will come and destroy the tenants and give the vineyard to others." As we all know, a great national judgment came upon Israel under Titus only a few years later. In the vineyard of the Church the leadership eventually became mostly Gentile.

There is tremendous peril in remaining in opposition to Christ. The thought of this is probably not half as horrible to anyone who is without Christ as it is to me, because *I believe it!* The penalty is damnation, the wrath of the Lamb! Paul believed this, and he said in the context of teaching about the coming judgment, "Therefore, knowing the fear of the Lord, we persuade others" (2 Corinthians 5:11). Are you persuaded?

The Coming Triumph of God (vv. 10, 11)

Jesus concluded his parabolic teaching with a description of the triumph that would accompany his judgment: "Have you not read this Scripture: 'The stone that the builders rejected has become the cornerstone; this was the Lord's doing, and it is marvelous in our eyes'?" This was a quotation from the Hallel Psalms they had been singing that Passover Week—Psalm 118:22, 23, to be exact. It was understood by all to be a messianic Psalm.

The picture it gives is so beautiful, for it depicts one of the building stones gathered for Solomon's Temple that was rejected in the construction of the Sanctuary, but then became the keystone of the entrance.[8] Christ is the keystone in the eternal, spiritual temple of God. He went from rejection to the highest exaltation. Keep in mind that Jesus was saying these words as he stood by the remains of Solomon's temple.

Dr. Luke adds in his parallel account a further comment by Christ: "Everyone who falls on that stone will be broken to pieces, and when it falls on anyone, it will crush him" (Luke 20:18). Those who reject Christ will be smashed by the divine stone spoken of by Daniel, the stone hewn without hands, which is coming with "the momentum of holy wrath,"[9] and they will become like chaff on a summer threshing floor. The wind will carry them away without leaving a trace (Daniel 2:35).

As Jesus' final words echoed through Solomon's Porch and then died away, the Sanhedrin had heard an outline of sacred history past and present.

They had heard an eloquent description of the *hope* of God, the *kindness* of God, the *severity* of God, and the *triumph* of God. They had heard all this from the most authentic voice that ever spoke.

And what was the result? Mark tells us: "And they were seeking to arrest him but feared the people, for they perceived that he had told the parable against them. So they left him and went away" (v. 12). How unutterably sad.

The leaders of Israel stood at the pinnacle of the temple, and if not upon the very foundation of Solomon's temple, next to it. Close by, the great golden vine symbolizing Israel gleamed in the sun. Before them stood the Lord of the temple, the keystone to the entire structure. Behind him spread the vineyard-clad slopes of Israel, pleading reinforcement for his words. And they rejected him! Spiritually, they stepped into the abyss gaping below.

The choice is just as dramatic today—as are the consequences. His plea is just as eloquent and poignant. Let us, by prayer and example, encourage others to choose Christ and life indeed.

39

Christians' Allegiances

MARK 12:13-17

THERE ARE TWO DISPARATE POWERS that can bind people together. One is love, and the other is hatred. Of course, love is to be preferred by far. It is the glue of the Holy Trinity. It is God's gift to the Church. In fact, it is his command for her (John 13:34, 35). Nevertheless, hatred, though ultimately destructive and fragmenting, can serve as a devilish cement among otherwise diverse people.

Such was the case with the Pharisees and the Herodians. There could hardly be two groups with such opposing outlooks. The Pharisees were nationalistic, the B'Nai B'Rith (so to speak) of Israel, whereas the Herodians had sold themselves out to the Romans and served as their stooges. The Pharisees represented narrow, conservative Judaism, and the Herodians were liberal and syncretistic in their convictions. The Pharisees were right-wingers; the Herodians were left-wingers. The Pharisees represented resistance to Rome, the Herodians accommodation. But they were cemented together by their mutual hatred for Jesus. The Pharisees hated him because he was disrupting their *religious* agenda, the Herodians because he threatened their *political* arrangement. They both wanted him dead.

So, as in the past, these natural enemies allowed their common hatred to flow back and forth in grim solidarity as they got together for a powwow (cf. 3:6). Jesus was a formidable opponent, they agreed—look how he had just turned their questioning of his authority back on them (11:27–33). Yet, there had to be a way. Approach after approach was suggested, tossed around, and dismissed. Then a great idea came: they would ask a question that, no matter how Jesus answered, would put him in mortal trouble with either the Jews or the Romans.

So they selected representatives who they thought could best carry out their evil purpose and sent them to accost Jesus, probably again in one of the temple's great colonnaded porches. Verses 13–15 describe their approach:

And they sent to him some of the Pharisees and some of the Herodians, to trap him in his talk. And they came and said to him, "Teacher, we know that you are true and do not care about anyone's opinion. For you are not swayed by appearances, but truly teach the way of God. Is it lawful to pay taxes to Caesar, or not? Should we pay them, or should we not?"

Their lips dripped with insincere flattery as they attempted to appear as innocent inquirers. They hoped to disarm Jesus, throw him off guard, so he would unwittingly give a self-condemning answer. Ironically, their flattery contained a modicum of truth: Jesus was not (and is not) influenced by man. And certainly he was not about to be intimidated now. Jesus walked into their trap with his eyes wide open. As always, he would answer with *truth*.

Jesus' enemies were confident they had him this time! Silence, a refusal to answer, would have been disastrous. Evasion would have been equally so. If he answered that it was right to pay taxes to Caesar, his people would brand him a collaborationist and a traitor and abandon him in disgust. If he answered that no taxes should be paid to Caesar, the Romans would see him as an insurrectionist. Rome tolerated diversity in religion, but she used steel to deal with political problems. With an answer like that, Jesus would be a dead man.

His antagonists waited with bated breath—the Pharisees hoping for a "yes" that they could herald to the nation, and the Herodians equally eager for a "no" that could be taken to the Romans, bringing about Jesus' *terminus ad quem*. There was no way Jesus could escape. How delicious the prospect! How joyous their hatred!

Jesus, fully aware of their treachery and hypocrisy, responded, "Why put me to the test? Bring me a denarius and let me look at it" (v. 15). The denarius was a small silver coin weighing about 3.8 grams. One side bore the head of Caesar and the abbreviated inscription TI. CAESAR DIVI AVG. F. AVGVSTVS (Tiberius Caesar, son of the divine Augustus, Augustus).[1] On the reverse side was the inscription PONTIFEX MAXIMVS—"Chief Priest."[2] It was the amount paid into the Roman *fiscus* (treasury) by all adult men and women just for the privilege of existing. It could only be paid with this coin.

As our Lord held up the coin, a hush fell upon the entire throng. His question broke the silence: "Whose likeness and inscription is this?" (v. 16).

"Caesar's," came the grudging reply. They had hoped to avoid using that name. Then rang forth from Jesus' lips, "Render to Caesar the things that are Caesar's, and to God the things that are God's" (v. 17).

This was an astonishing answer to them, just as it was for a brilliant young American lawyer who saw it for the first time. Someone had given him a New Testament, and as he was reading it through he came to this account, which he read with great interest because he was involved in a similar type of legal dilemma. He said that he could not read it fast enough and that when he saw Jesus' answer he was so astonished, he actually dropped his Bible, exclaiming, "That's the most amazing wisdom!"[3]

Jesus' enemies thought they had caught him in an inescapable *dilemma*, but his incredibly dexterous mind saw that it was really a *trilemma*—and that his answer, "Render to Caesar the things that are Caesar's," could not be gainsaid. The reason for this was that ancient coins were actually understood to be the property of the person whose picture and inscription were on them. Jesus' use of the coin left them speechless. Who could object to giving "to Caesar the things that are Caesar's"?

The statement by our Lord was not only astounding the instant it was uttered, but is even today universally acclaimed to be the single most influential political statement ever made in the history of the world! It was decisive and determinative in shaping western civilization. Paul's exposition of it in Romans 13:1–7 gave shape to the political world as we know it today. It orders and prioritizes the believers' allegiances in this life.

The Christian's Earthly/Temporal Allegiance (v. 17a)

Christ's words first set out the shape of the Christian's earthly or temporal allegiance: "Render to Caesar the things that are Caesar's." Essential and implicit in Christ's teaching is that the state is a valid institution. Richard Halverson, former chaplain of the United States Senate, said:

> To be sure, men will abuse and misuse the institution of the State just as men because of sin have abused and misused every other institution in history including the Church of Jesus Christ; but this does not mean that the institution is bad or that it should be forsaken. It simply means that men are sinners and rebels in God's world, and this is the way they behave with good institutions. As a matter of fact, it is because of this very sin that there must be human government to maintain order in history until the final and ultimate rule of Jesus Christ is established. Human government is better than anarchy, and the Christian must recognize the "divine right" of the State.[4]

Jesus assumes the validity of the secular state and its demands, even when it is controlled by a man who thinks he is god. A poorly run state is better than no state at all.

Not only is the state valid, but it also makes legitimate claims on our behavior. In Romans 13, Paul expands on Jesus' words, saying, "Let every person be subject to the governing authorities. For there is no authority except from God, and those that exist have been instituted by God" (v. 1). There are, of course, limits upon the authority of the state.

There are also at least three areas in which a Christian must resist authority:

First, *when he or she is asked to violate a command of God*. The perfect example of this is found in Acts 4, 5, when the authorities arrested the disciples for preaching, summoned them before the Sanhedrin, and ordered them not to teach in the name of Jesus (Acts 4:17–20). Of course, the disciples went right back to it and were arrested again. "'We strictly charged you not to teach in this name, yet here you have filled Jerusalem with your teaching, and you intend to bring this man's blood upon us.' But Peter and the apostles answered, 'We must obey God rather than men'" (Acts 5:28, 29). The disciples went out and took up preaching where they had left off. Christians must never violate a command of God, regardless of what the state says.

Second, *Christians must resist when asked to do an immoral act*. The sexual application for this is obvious and easiest to understand. But it also extends to ethical areas in which many are constantly asked to compromise—whether in the context of government service, business, home, community, or even church. Christians must never think it is okay to commit immoral or unethical acts.

Third, *believers must never go against their Christian conscience to obey government*. This may involve such diverse things as participation in licentious entertainment, to working in institutions that perform wholesale abortions, to participating or not participating in war, as one's conscience dictates. Here it is imperative that Christians immerse themselves in God's Word so that their ethics are radically Biblical.

The overall point here in Mark, however, is that, noting the exceptions just stated, Christians are called to a profound obedience to their government. Christians are to be markedly law-abiding, even down to the traffic laws and the speed limits.

Believers must never cheat on their taxes. One conscience-stricken taxpayer wrote the IRS, "Dear Sir, My conscience bothered me. Here is the $175 which I owe in back taxes." Then came a P.S.: "If my conscience still bothers me, I'll send the rest." We may feel like it's the *Infernal* Revenue Service or perhaps the *Eternal* Revenue Service, but we must pay every penny we owe!

There also ought to be respect. The conduct of many officials defies our respect, but even then we must always respect their position.

Also, if we are to give to Caesar what is his, we must participate in the process. In the last national election, only 42 percent of the registered voters voted. People between the ages of eighteen and twenty-four were the worst offenders, with only 16 percent voting. It is our God-given duty to take our share of responsibility in civic, state, and national politics. Not to do so is sin!

Last, we are to pray for those who rule over us. As Paul said to Timothy, "First of all, then, I urge that supplications, prayers, intercessions, and thanksgivings be made for all people, for kings and all who are in high positions, that we may lead a peaceful and quiet life, godly and dignified in every way" (1 Timothy 2:1, 2). Our Lord says we must give to Caesar what is Caesar's. Are we doing so? Even more importantly, are we giving to God the things that are God's?

The Christian's Heavenly/Eternal Allegiance (v. 17b)

In considering this second half of Jesus' answer, we see its amazing brilliance. By saying that we are to give "to God the things that are God's," Jesus recognized only one God, thus obviating Caesar's claim to divinity. Moreover, because Jesus named God in the second half of the statement, the demands of the ultimate, eternal King subsumed the petty reign of Caesar.[5] Jesus put Caesar in his place, and again there was nothing his critics could do about it!

Next, Jesus' call to give "to God the things that are God's" subtly stated God's claim to total ownership of us all. Here is why: the coin was Caesar's because it bore his image; we are God's because we bear his image! Moses wrote: "So God created man in his own image, in the image of God he created him; male and female he created them" (Genesis 1:27). Jesus' Jewish listeners, with their oriental listening habits, automatically made this connection. We are from God's mint and are totally his!

How do we bear God's image? In many beautiful ways, including *our awareness of being.* God has said of himself, "I AM WHO I AM" (Exodus 3:14). This was a statement of eternal existence. We are the only creatures in the universe who can say, "I am," and that is because he has created us and made us to be. Also, no other thing that is created has a *moral* sense of right and wrong. We are moral beings due to his impress, no matter how much we attempt to efface it. These are awesome resemblances, and they denote an equally awesome ownership of us! We are God's coin. We bear his image.

This whole beautiful thing calls us to the greatest *optimism*. Because we are made in his image, wonderful things can happen to us. Through his grace God restores our moral sense. He revitalizes our sense of eternity. He re-sculpts his character in our hearts.

This is, of course, part of the work of the Holy Spirit, which begins with his sealing us to redemption. The Scriptures speak of it with phrases like this: "you also . . . were sealed with the promised Holy Spirit" (Ephesians 1:13)— "the Holy Spirit of God, by whom you were sealed" (Ephesians 4:30)—"[God] has also put his seal on us and given us his Spirit in our hearts as a guarantee" (2 Corinthians 1:22). Just as when an ancient wax seal was placed on a container or letter, and the owner took his ring and pressed it into the hot wax, so does the Holy Spirit do with us as he warms us, makes us malleable, and then presses his image, his character, into us. As we grow in the Spirit, the mark of his divine impress burns deeper and deeper into us as we conform more and more to his image. What a positive outlook is ours as we submit to the work of the Holy Spirit!

Finally, this is a call for profound commitment to God. To us who bear the image of God by virtue of our humanity, and then have had the character of God further pressed upon our souls by the sealing and progressive work of the Holy Spirit, Jesus stands before us and says, "Render to Caesar the things that are Caesar's, and to God the things that are God's."

Have we given to God what is his? He says, "I AM WHO I AM." Have we said, "I am yours"?

40

Resurrection? Yes!

MARK 12:18–27

I WILL NEVER FORGET my first visit to the chapel of Trinity College, Cambridge, for when I stepped through the entrance I was surrounded by bigger-than-life statues of Isaac Newton, discoverer of the law of gravity and author of the monumental *Principia*; Samuel Taylor Coleridge; Thomas Babington Macaulay; Francis Bacon; and Alfred Lord Tennyson. They all attended Trinity College Cambridge! I was astounded, for even today Trinity has little more than a thousand students. Such a concentration of intelligence! However, the Son of God, born on earth as a Jew, was the possessor of the finest human intelligence ever to grace this earth. We see it not only in his parables and teaching (for example, the Sermon on the Mount), but in his brilliant exchanges with his detractors. Here in Mark's Gospel we have seen it when the representatives of the Sanhedrin attempted to corner him with a deadly question regarding authority.

It was not wise to cross swords with Jesus intellectually. He had the greatest knowledge of Scripture of anyone who ever lived. He was the greatest rabbi, the greatest interpreter, ever! Those who challenged Jesus had about as much chance as Truman Capote against Michael Jordan in a slam dunk contest!

But Jesus' enemies, being slow learners, sent yet another platoon after Jesus (this time the Sadducees). The Sadducees came from families of the highest standing.[1] They were wealthy and worldly, though few in number compared with the Pharisees.[2] They were also ill-mannered and bumptious. Josephus wrote: "The Sadducees . . . are, even among themselves, rather boorish in their behavior, and in their intercourse with their peers are as rude as aliens."[3]

They evidently did not like anybody very much! But their main distinction, and the one that is important to our text, is that they rejected the supernatural, apart from God himself. Acts 23:8 informs us that they denied the existence of angels and spirits. Josephus says they did not believe there was any life after death, and therefore there was no judgment, no rewards, no penalties.[4] And, of course, according to them there was no resurrection. They said it was not taught in the Torah, and therefore it was a false doctrine.[5]

Now they came to Jesus. Being mean-spirited, superior, and self-righteous, they would take care of this country bumpkin. "Teacher, Moses wrote for us that if a man's brother dies and leaves a wife, but leaves no child, the man must take the widow and raise up offspring for his brother" (v. 19). At the heart of their trick question was the custom of Levirate marriage: if a man's married brother died, he must marry the widow (cf. Deuteronomy 25:5, 6). This was an ancient custom that existed long before the Law, and its neglect brought the scandal of Judah and Tamar (Genesis 38:6–10). Its purpose was to keep a family from dying out, and to keep family wealth intact.

Having stated the Levirate promise they put forth the puzzle:

> There were seven brothers; the first took a wife, and when he died left no offspring. And the second took her, and died, leaving no offspring. And the third likewise. And the seven left no offspring. Last of all the woman also died. In the resurrection, when they rise again, whose wife will she be? For the seven had her as wife. (vv. 20–23)

We can surmise that this was a stock conundrum they had used with success in their debates with the resurrection-believing Pharisees. They may have borrowed the idea from the apocryphal book of Tobit, which tells the bizarre story of a woman who married seven times only to have each husband strangled by a demon in the bed chamber on the wedding night (a kind of intertestamental Stephen King tale—Tobit 3:8, esp. 15; 6:13; 7:11). However they had come up with the question, they now waited on Jesus in smug self-satisfied confidence. Little did they know that they had met with the supreme mind of the centuries, and they were going to be kindly "slam-dunked."

Jesus stated the foundation for his answer in verse 24: "Is this not the reason you are wrong, because you know neither the Scriptures nor the power of God?" Their problem had two sources: 1) ignorance of God's Word, and, 2) ignorance of his power. Almost all theological error can be traced to one or the other. Our Lord would deal with both errors, and it is a marvel to see.

The Old Testament on the Resurrection (vv. 26, 27)

Jesus addressed the problem of ignorance of the Scriptures by diving right into the heart of the Torah, where the Sadducees claimed the resurrection could not be found. He quoted from Exodus 3:6 as proof: "And as for the dead being raised, have you not read in the book of Moses, in the passage about the bush, how God spoke to him, saying, 'I am the God of Abraham, and the God of Isaac, and the God of Jacob'? He is not God of the dead, but of the living. You are quite wrong."

Jesus' logic is obvious, as Origen in the second century pointed out.[6] It is this: it is ridiculous for God to say that he is the God of men who have no existence. Therefore, because God says, "I am the God of Abraham, and the God of Isaac, and the God of Jacob," they must be living, and thus the resurrection is a reality. Or put another way: if Abraham, Isaac, and Jacob are nothing more than dust, God cannot now, at this moment, be their God. God is not the God of that which has ceased to be. "Take that, Sadducees! It is right out of Book Two of the five books you claim to accept."

It was a powerful argument, and it is easy for us to appreciate with our western approach to logic. But actually Jesus' words convey something that is even more compelling to the ancient Hebrew mind. It is this: these three patriarchs—Abraham, Isaac, and Jacob—enjoyed a special covenant relationship with God that was so dynamic, so profound, that it demanded a continued living relationship with God after death.[7] God does not make an everlasting covenant (promise) with insects that last an hour.[8]

The writer of Hebrews tells us that the patriarchs knew that the covenant promises transcended earthly life and were eternal. Hebrews 11:10 says Abraham "was looking forward to the city that has foundations, whose designer and builder is God." "These all died in faith, not having received the things promised, but having seen them and greeted them from afar, and having acknowledged that they were strangers and exiles on the earth" (Hebrews 11:13). Verse 16 adds, "But as it is, they desire a better country, that is, a heavenly one." The eternal God does not covenant with creatures that live only three score and ten years, and then go out like a candle.[9]

Jesus' words were powerfully compelling to the Hebrew mind, and his concluding thrust, "He is not God of the dead, but of the living. You are quite wrong" (v. 27), must have caused a murmur in the crowd. If God is the God of the living, and since God said, long after the death of the patriarchs, that he is their God, then they must be alive and *resurrection is coming!*

The Powerful God on the Resurrection

If they had understood the nature of the miracle-working God of the Old Testament, they would not have doubted his power to raise the dead. There are numerous Old Testament passages outside the Torah from which the resurrection can be understood.[10] But the Torah bears evidence itself as well.

1) There is, of course, the Creation, in which God created everything *ex nihilo* and then specifically breathed life into the lifeless body of Adam (Genesis 2:7)—a *proto-resurrection*.

2) Genesis 5:24 concludes, "Enoch walked with God, and he was not, for God took him." This is the language of rapture and not death. The implication is that God took him from life to life.

3) When Abraham took Isaac up the mount to sacrifice him, he ordered his servant to "Stay here with the donkey; I and the boy will go over there and worship and come again to you" (Genesis 22:5). This implies belief in the resuscitating, if not resurrection, power of God.

4) Israel's deliverance from Egypt was a national resurrection brought by miracle after miracle after miracle—not the least of which were the crossing of the Red Sea and then the manna, quail, and water. These all involved life-giving power.

The Sadducees truly did not know Scripture or the power of God. What about us? Do we know the reality and relationship that the patriarchs experienced? If so, we expect resurrection! Knowing Christ, having an exchange of soul with him, is a powerful personal argument for the life hereafter, and eventually resurrection. Something so real, so dynamic, so pervasive, so right, so energizing, so holy cannot end! Resurrection is the signature of my soul.

Furthermore, the nature of God demands resurrection. The grave could not hold Jesus, and those in him will certainly burst from the grave.

There is a final thrust in Jesus' argument, which has to do with correcting the Sadducees' false assertions about the Heaven in which they did not believe.

The Resurrected State (v. 25)

In verse 25 Jesus described the exalted state of the resurrected, a state that transcends marriage and questions of multiple marriages: "For when they rise from the dead, they neither marry nor are given in marriage, but are like angels in heaven." The current Jewish belief was that families simply took up their living where they left off on earth. Jesus said that was far too earthbound a vision.

As we shall see, the implications of Jesus' answer are wonderful. But I must say that we earthlings have also found a lot in Jesus' words to trouble us. I have heard questions like: "If there is no marriage in Heaven, and we are like angels, will we have wings? Will we recognize each other? Will we be neutered, sexless?" We have probably all heard happily married people say, "If there is no marriage, I don't want to go!"

Those of us who have indulged in such questions need to recognize the implications of our whole text, which teaches that *our bodies will be resurrected*. Hebrew thought regarded each person as a unity with corporal and incorporal parts which are perfectly fused together so that one is incomplete without the other. In other words, our bodies are part of who we are. When God said he was "the God of Abraham, and the God of Isaac, and the God of Jacob," he was saying he was the God of their whole person—body and soul. The whole person will be resurrected. Our bodies, to use Paul's word, will be raised "imperishable" (1 Corinthians 15:42). Eternal life will be experienced by the whole person. *You*, not just your soul, will be resurrected!

This means that your individuality will be preserved for eternity. Abraham has everything about him that was Abrahamic. Isaac has everything that properly belongs to him. Jacob has everything that makes him God's Israel. These great men have lost nothing. Rather, they have grown and developed gloriously. They are Abraham, Isaac, and Jacob at their very best—or at least, they will be at their ultimate when the trumpet sounds.[11]

George MacDonald, commenting on this grand truth, said: "The new body must be like the old. Not only that, it must be the same body . . . with all that was distinctive of each from his fellows more visible than ever before. The accidental, the nonessential, the unrevealing, the incomplete will have vanished. That which made the body what it was in the eyes of those who loved us will be tenfold there. Will not this be the resurrection of the body?"[12]

The point of all of this is that we will be more recognizable and more lovable in Heaven than we ever were before. When someone asks you, "Will you know me in Heaven?" answer, "I have known you well here, and I will not be a bigger fool in Heaven than I am here now. I will know you, and you will know me."

To be sure, there will be no marriage in Heaven and no concern about past husbands or wives, but that does not suggest in the slightest a reduction in love. We will be ourselves at our ultimate best, and we will be more lovable and more capable of loving than ever before.

The new shall then be dear as the old, and for the same reason, that it reveals the old love. And in the changes which . . . must take place when the
mortal puts on immortality, shall we not feel that the nobler our friends are,
the more they are themselves; that the more the idea of each is carried out
in the perfection of beauty, the more like they are to what we thought them
in our most exalted moods, to that which we saw in them in the rarest moments of profoundest communion.[13]

*The final implication we wish to note is that in Heaven there will be
no death.* People who are like angels do not die. Susan Wegner, a friend of
mine, was diagnosed as having rheumatoid arthritis when she was two years
old. Stunted by massive doses of cortisone, she grew to only 4'3" in height.
Susan's condition meant that normal childhood diseases were a trauma. The
slightest bumps and bruises left disproportionate hurts and scars. The last of
her thirty-five years was a physical nightmare—immobilized in bed, not even
able to turn over. But what a heart! She had—*has*—more spunk than anyone
I have known.

And when I see Susan again or you see friends who have gone ahead of
you into Heaven, it will be the same body in which they died. We will recognize them at once. Everything that was theirs will be perfected. Their bodies
will be glorious, grown to their eternal potential. Their personalities will be
at their fullest—their wit, their charm, their tenacity, their love. They will be
noble, beautiful, regal—they will be like Jesus!

Jesus said of the Father, "He is not God of the dead, but of the living"
(v. 27). He has an eternal relationship with the living. Is he your God? Are
you alive? Is he going to make you all he ever intended you to be?

How our hearts should burn at this truth! I have not told the half of it, but
what I have said is so stupendous, so shaking, I hope it grabs your soul. We
should be distinguished from all others by our hope and zeal.

41

Not Far from the Kingdom

MARK 12:28–34

FEW PEOPLE HAVE SO AFFECTED HISTORY that its very epochs were marked by their births—let alone their spiritual rebirths! John Wesley was one of the few. Had it not been for Wesley's conversion and the ensuing revival with its social impact, England would probably have undergone something similar to the French Revolution. John Wesley's coming to faith was one of the important historical events of the western world.

John Wesley was born in 1703, the fifteenth child of Samuel Wesley, the rector of Epworth, and his wife, Susanna. He enjoyed a good upbringing under his unusually talented and dedicated mother and went on to a brilliant career at Charterhouse and Oxford, where he was elected fellow of Lincoln College in 1726. There he served as a double professor of Greek and logic. After serving on his father's curate on two occasions, he was ordained a priest in the Church of England in 1728.

Returning to Oxford, he joined a group of undergraduates led by his brother, Charles, and the later-to-be-great evangelist George Whitefield, a group dedicated to building a holy life. It was derisively nicknamed by fellow Oxonians the "Holy Club." Though Wesley was not yet truly converted, he met with these men for prayer, the study of the Greek New Testament, and devotional exercises.

He set aside an hour each day for private prayer and reflection. He took the sacrament of Holy Communion each week and set himself to conquer every sin. He fasted twice a week, visited the prisons, and assisted the poor and the sick. Doing all this helped him imagine he was a Christian.

In 1735, still unconverted, he accepted an invitation from the Society for the Propagation of the Gospel to become a missionary to the American

Indians in Georgia. It was a great fiasco. He utterly failed as a missionary—undergoing miserable conflicts with his colleagues and almost dying of disease. When he returned to England, he wrote: "I went to America to convert the Indians; but, oh, who shall convert me?" His mission experience taught him the wickedness and waywardness of his own heart.

However, not all was lost, because in his travels aboard ship he met some German Moravian Christians whose simple faith made a great impression on him. When he returned to London, he sought out one of their leaders. Through a series of conversations, to quote Wesley's own words, he was "clearly convinced of unbelief, of the want of that faith whereby alone we are saved."

Then, on the morning of May 24, 1738, something happened that Wesley would never forget. He opened his Bible haphazardly, and his eyes fell on the text in Mark 12:34—"You are not far from the kingdom of God." Wesley said that the words reassured him. And well they should, because before he went to bed that night, he crossed that invisible line into the kingdom of God. This text was to become Wesley's life verse, a reminder of the shape of his life for the first thirty-five years of his existence—"You are not far from the kingdom of God." It is also part of the final verse of the passage under consideration in this chapter.

Beautifully, not only the verse but its setting (the Lord conversing with a scribe, a *lost* clergyman of the house of Israel) bears remarkable parallels to Wesley's own lostness. Both were clergymen. Both were highly educated. Both were Bible scholars who knew the Scriptures inside and out. Both were confronted with Christ, who said to both, "You are not far from the kingdom of God." We will consider this verse in its context, and then Wesley's experience, and then this matter of getting into the kingdom of God.

Being Near the Kingdom of God

The exchange began with a question from the scribe: "And one of the scribes came up and heard them disputing with one another, and seeing that he answered them well, asked him, 'Which commandment is the most important of all?'" (v. 28). The scribe had initially come to witness the confrontation between Jesus and the Sadducees. Though he disliked the Sadducees' doctrine, he came rooting for them because they, like he, had a religion of human achievement. Jesus was a threat to his belief system. However, as he witnessed the breath-taking intelligence of Jesus in answering the resurrection question, refuting the Sadducees with a quotation from Exodus 3:6 (from the very heart of the Torah), he found himself inwardly applauding Jesus and subconsciously drawn to him. Before he knew it, he was impulsively asking a question, and it was *his own* question. It came from the scribal mind game of trying to reduce their religion to a single axiom, as for example when Rabbi Hillel was promised by a Gentile that he would convert if Hillel could give him the whole Law while he stood on one foot. Hillel answered with a version of the Golden Rule: "What you yourself hate, do not do to your neighbor; this is the whole Law—the rest is commentary. Go and learn it!"[1] This is the kind of answer the scribe was looking for from this brilliant Jesus. The scribe was standing heart to heart with eternity.

He was not to be disappointed, for Jesus' reply was consummately brilliant:

> Jesus answered, "The most important is, 'Hear, O Israel: The Lord our God, the Lord is one. And you shall love the Lord your God with all your heart and with all your soul and with all your mind and with all your strength.' The second is this: 'You shall love your neighbor as yourself.' There is no other commandment greater than these." (vv. 29–31)

The first part of Jesus' answer was known to everyone, for it was from the *Shema Israel*,[2] "Hear, O Israel," the opening sentence of every synagogue worship service, taken from Deuteronomy 6:4. It was also repeated by every pious Jew morning and evening every day. In fact, it was worn by the devout in a tiny leather box, called a *phylactery*, on the forehead and on the wrist while in prayer. Godly households also hung the *Shema* on their doors in a small round box called a *Muzuzah*.[3] Everyone knew this part of Jesus' answer. It was the creed of Israel. Heart, soul, mind, and strength were not intended as a breakdown or a psychological analysis of human personality—they simply meant that everything was to be devoted to loving God. It does not take much of a man to be a believer, but it takes all there is of him!

The second part of Jesus' answer was taken from Leviticus 19:18—"love your neighbor as yourself." This also was familiar to all Jews. So where was the genius in Jesus' answer? It was in this: the thoughts of loving God and loving humankind had been voiced by other rabbis and scribes,[4] but *this was the first time any rabbi had fused these two specific Scripture references together.*[5]

The brilliance of this lay not only in its formulation, but in its implications. First, it summarized the entire Ten Commandments. The first part of Jesus' answer summarized the first four commandments, which have to do with our love for God (Exodus 20:2–11). The second part of Jesus' answer summarized the final six, which have to do with our love for humankind (Exodus 20:12–17). Jesus' answer is comprehensive to the nth degree.

Second, Jesus' double answer showed that love for God and love for humankind cannot be divided. This teaching had a powerful impact on the subsequent teaching of the Apostolic Church. The Apostle John later would write: "whoever loves God must also love his brother" (1 John 4:21; cf. Romans 13:8, 9; Galatians 5:14; James 2:8).

Third, Jesus' command to love your neighbor "as yourself" radicalized the call to human love. None of the earlier formulations included this qualifying clause. Including "as yourself" provides us with a conscious and conscience-convicting standard, because we sinners all love ourselves, despite our psychological demurrals.[6] Just how radical Jesus' demand was is seen in his similar teaching in the story of the Good Samaritan, where he portrayed a neighbor not as a fellow Jew, as the Jews held it, but as an enemy, a Gentile, the world next door (Luke 10:25–37).

What powerful teaching this was! This marvelous symmetry of devotion—loving God *and* loving man—could not be gainsaid. The way Jesus said it had never been put so well, or so Scripturally, as now! It was brilliant! It was perfect! It truly encompassed the whole Law. And the obvious *ethos* of Christ's person (he was living it!) made it all so compelling.

How would the scribe answer? Remember, his cronies were standing by, watching. C. E. B. Cranfield, in his Cambridge commentary, says that the opening words in verse 32, which our text renders "You are right," should really be an exclamation[7]—perhaps, "Beautifully said, teacher!" or "What a beautiful answer." The scribe told Jesus, "You are right, Teacher. You have truly said that he is one, and there is no other besides him. And to love him with all the heart and with all the understanding and with all the strength, and to love one's neighbor as oneself, is much more than all whole burnt offerings and sacrifices" (vv. 32, 33). Our Lord was clearly pleased with his response: "And when Jesus saw that he answered wisely, he said to him, 'You are not far from the kingdom of God'" (v. 34). Jesus' answer was tantalizingly ambiguous. He was after the scribe's soul.

This was a *compliment*. From the scribe's response, Jesus saw that the man was capable of thinking for himself. He saw that the scribe understood that the Law was more than a system, that it was essentially spiritual. So he complimented him: "The way you're thinking, you're not very far from the kingdom of God." Some people are far from the kingdom of God, some at the threshold. The scribe was *very close*.

This was also a *warning*. Though he was close, he was decisively separated. It is possible to be within an inch of Heaven, yet go to Hell!

Here Jesus' point was positive: the man was near! How so? He realized that loving God and humankind "is much more than all whole burnt offerings and sacrifices." This tells us much about his heart, for he speaks of the entire ceremonial system as not being as important as loving God. What he was saying was light-years beyond where many people are today who imagine that their good works will suffice. The scribe was near!

The scribe was also a thinking man. Jesus complimented this by telling him that he had "answered wisely." He was intellectually convinced that Christ was right. Samuel Johnson said: "If a man thinks deeply he thinks religiously." In a world that is about as shallow as a birdbath, those who enter the kingdom are those who are willing to pause and truly think about eternal things.

He was also near because he faced head-on the implications that the love of God is the highest priority of all. Squarely faced, this is a sobering reality, because the natural man does not love God with all his heart, no matter how hard he tries. There has to be a radical change inside a person in order to do this. This is a work of the Spirit of God. The scribe's embracing the necessity of love placed him near Heaven's door.

He was also near because he was honest. He was a scribe and naturally sided with his fellow scribes and Pharisees. But he did not let his natural allegiance keep him from acknowledging the truth. There is always hope for a person who will break ranks to keep his conscience. The scribe was nearer than most men.

He was also near because he was not a coward. He was willing to risk mocking to step up to the door of the kingdom of God. Lack of courage and a love of approval has been fatal to many souls. This man was so near to the kingdom—so near!

John Wesley was like that. Sitting at the feet of one of England's most famous mothers, he was taught that the love of God was the highest priority of all. Susannah Wesley's own testimony was that she spent regular time with each of her nineteen children, instructing them in the things of God.[8]

Wesley was a thinking man if there ever was one! He was famous for his unadorned clarity in a day of ornamental obfuscation. He brought all his intelligence to bear on eternal things. Wesley was honest—honest in personal matters and honest in spiritual matters. After his experience in America, he bared his soul without guile to those he thought could help him. Wesley was also brave and was not a man-pleaser.

With all of this he was so near, but still not in the kingdom. His biggest problem was understanding the inward nature of Christ's requirements.

Wesley was a master of external discipline (fastings, prayers, and good deeds). Yet, as he later explained, after he stood in the face of death his religious exercise gave him little comfort and no assurance of his acceptance by God.[9]

Being Far from the Kingdom

If we are to believe God's Word first, and secondly the testimony of John Wesley, we must take to heart this truth: *while the scribe and his clerical counterpart John Wesley were not far from the kingdom, they were still on the outside.* Being almost there is not being there!

Perhaps you recall some years ago that stuntman Evil Knievel was going to jump the Snake River in his jet-motorcycle—and how he went up with a burst of power, then fizzled out across the canyon, ignominiously pulling the ripcord of his parachute. Making it halfway (or even one inch short) is not making it.

Today in some circles it is fashionable to talk about "spiritual pilgrimages," and that is okay in the context of a regenerated life. We are certainly part of a growing experience. However, if the word *pilgrimage* is used to sanctify or baptize the state of not arriving as something good, it is a deception. Being on a pilgrimage can sound so humble. It implies that you are *not* an "absolutist," something akin to a Fascist or racist in the mind of a relativist-thinking world. But being a pilgrim must not be an end in itself. You must make it into the kingdom or it is no use at all.

Did the scribe ever make it into the kingdom? We do not know. The Scriptures are silent.

Getting into the Kindom

If the scribe finally did enter the kingdom of Heaven, it was because he submitted to the logic of his own words. Loving God is more important than the entire ceremonial system. Perhaps he attempted to love God with all his heart and failed, thus realizing he could never achieve the moral excellency of the Law and that he was a lost sinner. Finally seeing himself for what he was, he cast himself on the mercy of God, only to find salvation.

When a religious man sees and acknowledges the profundity of his sin, it is a great day. Sir James Simpson, the discoverer of chloroform, used to say that the greatest find he ever made was learning that he was a sinner and that Jesus Christ was just the Savior he needed. Such a discovery will lead to a casting of one's self on the mercy of God and thus receiving the gift of faith, repentance, and salvation.

This is what happened to Wesley. His experience in America had brought him to the end of himself. Wesley's honest interchange with the Moravians who witnessed to him brought further conviction of his inner failure. On one occasion as he talked with them, he heard them speak of their personal faith as a gift from God. When he asked how this could be, "They replied with one mouth that this faith was a gift, the free gift of God, and that He would surely bestow it upon every soul who earnestly and perseveringly sought it." Wesley wrote after the meeting: "I resolved to seek it to the end."[10]

Finally it was May 24, 1738, and as Wesley randomly opened his Bible he read that beautiful statement that in nine words condensed the progress of his spiritual pilgrimage: "You are not far from the kingdom of God." Then came evening, and the famous statement in his journal tells the story: "In the evening I went very unwillingly to a society in Aldersgate Street where one was reading Luther's preface to the Epistle to the Romans. About a quarter before nine, while he was describing the change which God works in the heart through faith in Christ, I felt my heart strangely warmed. I felt I did trust in Christ, *Christ alone*, for salvation; and an assurance was given me, that He had taken away my sins, *even mine*, and saved me from the law of sin and death."[11]

The rest of the story is well-known history. *Wesley became a dynamo.* He preached in Saint Mary's in Oxford. He preached in the churches. He preached in the mines. He preached in the fields and on the streets. He preached on horseback. He even preached on his father's tombstone. *John Wesley didn't tire!* John Wesley preached forty-two thousand sermons. He averaged forty-five hundred miles a year. He rode sixty to seventy miles a day and preached three sermons a day on an average. When he was eighty-three, he wrote in his diary, "I am a wonder to myself, I am never tired, either with preaching, writing, or travelling!"[12]

As we all know, the Church has never been the same. Wesley's disciples, including Francis Asbury, were mighty powers in evangelizing England and frontier America. Read his life and the lives of his circuit riders and you will find chronicled the most amazing love for Christ and a tenacious love for lost souls. Their lives are among the great glories of the Church Universal.

During his search, Wesley had sought the advice of famous Christians. Perhaps the most prominent had been the great William Law, the author of the still famous and still read *A Serious Call to a Devout and Holy Life*. It is one of the most influential devotional books ever written, one that has helped thousands of believers. But Law did not make clear the way of grace. Wesley wrote: "How will you answer to our common Lord, . . . that you, sir, never led me into the light? Why did I scarcely ever hear you name the name of Christ? Why did you never urge me to faith in his blood? Is not Christ the First and the Last? If you say that you thought I had faith already, verily, you know nothing of me."[13] Wesley softened on Law later in life. But the fact remains, Law failed to show Wesley the way. Let us not fail to make clear the grace of God.

What are the lessons for us? First, it is entirely possible to have grown up in the Church, to have consistent, godly parents, and never have come to a saving knowledge of Christ.

Second, it is also completely possible to have studied theology and have never become a true Christian. One can know the Scriptures in the original, as Wesley did, and know more than the preacher and be unregenerate.

Third, it is possible to have heard the grace of Christ preached all your life and still be resting on your own goodness.

Fourth, it is possible to become gospel-hardened, and so seal your damnation even within the Church. It is possible to fool everyone and have the preacher preach your funeral and assure everyone that your soul is resting in Heaven when it really is in Hell.

Fifth, it is possible to be within an inch of the kingdom of God.

The abiding truth is: convictions not acted on, die; truths not followed, fade; lingering can become a habit; and we can either go in or go further away.[14]

Are you near to the kingdom of God, but not in? There are times when a single step makes all the difference. When a man or woman stands at the entrance to an airplane, one step and they are on the way to a new destination. But if they stay inactive, they will never go anywhere.

42

Whose Son Is the Christ?

MARK 12:35–40

THE EYES OF JESUS' ENEMIES had become preternaturally sharp through the intense malice they bore against him. Their evil intelligence had spawned wicked angles of attack as they came at Jesus with political, theological, and religious questions. Jesus had brilliantly escaped the *political* trap by holding up a tiny denarius, bearing the image of Caesar, and saying, "Render to Caesar the things that are Caesar's, and to God the things that are God's" (12:13–17). The *theological* conundrum put to him by the Sadducees regarding the resurrection he easily dismissed with a brilliant answer from Exodus 3:6, the heart of the Torah. The *religious* question regarding the greatest commandment, an honest question by an interested scribe, occasioned Jesus' immortal fusion of the commandments to love God and love humankind, thus laying down for all time the priorities of the Church.

With this we come to the end of the religious establishment's questions. Mark concludes: "And after that no one dared to ask him any more questions" (12:34). They felt like the fourth platoon of Philistines who were asked to wake up Samson after they had seen him wipe out earlier detachments sent to take him!

Seeing they were pulling back, Jesus decided to go on the attack. The specific recipients of Jesus' counterattack were the scribes, those who were Biblical scholars and teachers of the Law. It is important that we catch something of what they were like if we are to appreciate what Jesus said. To begin with, one could always recognize a scribe because he wore a long white linen robe that reached to his feet and was hemmed by a long white fringe. Their resplendent white attire made them stand out wherever they went, especially among the common people who customarily wore bright colors.[1] They were

power dressers *par excellence*! They were ecclesiastical swans regally gliding amongst the common mudhens of humanity.

Jeremias, a great New Testament authority, says in his book *Jerusalem in
the Time of Jesus* that all the people rose respectfully when a scribe passed by
and that only tradesmen busy at their work were exempt. These scribes were
greeted respectfully as "rabbi" ("my great one") or "Master" or "Father."
When the wealthy gave feasts, scribes were considered necessary ornaments
to adorn the meal. They were given a place of honor, reclining to the right
or left of the host. The scribes were honored above the aged, even above
their own parents. When they came to the synagogue, they sat in the place
of ultimate honor: facing the congregation with their backs against the chest
holding the Torah, so all could see their pious visages.[2] It was to these proud
birds that Jesus turned. His aggression and the subsequent exchange will tell
us wonderful things about him and sobering things about his enemies. As a
result, they will tell us much about ourselves.

Jesus' Teaching about Himself (vv. 35–37)

Very likely the scribes were nervous when Jesus began to question them. He
began with a warm-up question: "How can the scribes [that is you!] say that
the Christ is the son of David?" (v. 35). The question was meant to get them
thinking about the Old Testament Scriptures, for there were many that taught
that the Christ (the Messiah) had to be a physical descendant of David.[3] For
example, God told David, "When your days are fulfilled and you lie down
with your fathers, I will raise up your offspring after you, who shall come
from your body, and I will establish his kingdom" (2 Samuel 7:12).

Isaiah, speaking of the Messiah, said that he would reign on David's
throne (Isaiah 9:7), and Jeremiah quoted the Lord as saying, "I will raise up
for David a righteous Branch" (Jeremiah 23:5ff.). The Messiah, the Christ,
had to be a descendant of David. The scribes were looking, rightly, for a
national warrior-deliverer who was of David's bloodline. Jesus had warmed
them up. They were reflecting on the relationship of Messiah and the bloodline of David. There was no thought of the supernatural.

Then Jesus tossed in a Scriptural surprise that blew their thinking (v. 36).
It was a quotation from Psalm 110:1, which the scribes correctly recognized
as a messianic prophecy.[4] Jesus emphasized the authority of this passage
by saying, "David himself, in the Holy Spirit, declared . . ." In other words,
"This is an inspired text, my friends. Now listen to Psalm 110 when David
says, 'The Lord [Jehovah] said to my Lord [prophetically, the Messiah], "Sit
at my right hand, until I put your enemies under your feet."'"

Then came the punch line: "David himself calls him Lord. So how is he his son?" (v. 37). There was no mental sleight-of-hand here. It was a good question! *How can the Messiah be both David's son and his Lord if he is merely human?* Given their Davidic understanding of Messiah, and their admission that this is a messianic prophecy, they could think of no answer. Jesus was using the Scriptures, in which they were supposedly such experts, to explode their limited idea of the Messiah! It would take a divine/human being to fulfill the Scriptural requirements for Messiah. This was a point the Apostolic Church made again and again.[5]

At Pentecost, Peter said in his great sermon, "For David did not ascend into the heavens, but he himself says, 'The Lord said to my Lord, "Sit at my right hand, until I make your enemies your footstool."' Let all the house of Israel therefore know for certain that God has made him both Lord and Christ, this Jesus whom you crucified" (Acts 2:34–36).

The writer of Hebrews affirmed Jesus' supernatural superiority by using Psalm 110, saying, "And to which of the angels has he ever said, 'Sit at my right hand until I make your enemies a footstool for your feet'?" (Hebrews 1:13). The supernatural Jesus fulfills Psalm 110.

Jesus' exchange with the scribes was a veiled self-annunciation that he himself was Messiah, the divine/human fulfillment of this prophecy. He spoke as a divine/human being, with human lips animated and controlled by his divine nature. Before the week was over, he, the Son of David, would die in fulfillment of prophecy (see Psalm 22). Then his mighty resurrection would make everything clear concerning his humanity and divinity. As Paul said in the prologue of his Epistle to the Romans, ". . . concerning his Son, who was descended from David according to the flesh and was declared to be the Son of God in power according to the Spirit of holiness by his resurrection from the dead, Jesus Christ our Lord" (Romans 1:3, 4; cf. 2 Timothy 2:8).

Finally came the ascension to the Father and the fulfillment of Psalm 110:1, for then "The Lord said to my Lord, 'Sit at my right hand, until I put your enemies under your feet.'" We must lay this to our hearts.

> If Christ is not divine,
> Then lay the Book away
> And every blessed faith resign
> That has so long been yours and mine
> Through many a trying day;
> Forget the place of bended knee
> And dream no more of worlds to be.
> If Christ is not divine,

Go seal again the tomb;
Take down the cross, Redemption's sign,
Quench all the stars of hope that shine,
And let us turn and travel on
Across the night that knows no dawn.[6]

Mark reports regarding Jesus' question to the scribes, "And the great throng heard him gladly" (v. 37b). Though the crowd probably understood little of Jesus' argument, they could see the pompous scribes squirm with discomfort, and this gave them great pleasure. Again Jesus had them. And there was not a thing they could do.

Jesus' Teaching about His Antagonists (vv. 35–40)

Jesus implicitly assaulted the scribes where it hurt most—their self-proclaimed superiority on the Scriptures. Obviously they had never faced the messianic implications of Psalm 110. Why? They were dominated with political, nationalistic dreams of a human deliverance, an earthly kingdom. Their earthly dreams made them gloss right over the obvious spiritual meaning of the Scriptures they vainly expounded.

What does this have to do with us? Quite a bit, I think. Historically, the account of Christianity has shown that the church easily falls captive to culture. Sir Arthur Bryant in his famous *English Saga* in a chapter entitled "Dark Satanic Mills" describes the unbelievable abuse that came to children in the early part of the nineteenth century in England. "Children of seven or eight years old in coal mines was almost universal. In some pits they began work at a still earlier age: a case was even recorded of a child of three. Some were employed as 'trappers,' others for pushing or drawing coal trucks along the pit tunnels. A trapper, who operated the ventilation doors on which the safety of the mines depended, would often spend as many as sixteen hours a day crouching in solitude in a small dark hole."[7] "The Factories' Inquiry Commission of 1833 showed that many manufacturers were still employing children of six and seven and that the hours of labour were sometimes as high as sixteen hours a day. Flogging was regarded as a necessary part of the process of production. Harassed parents, with their eye on the family budget, accepted all this as inevitable and even desirable: many fathers acted as subcontractors for the employment of their own children. . . . In 1833 the cotton mills employed about 60,000 adult males, 65,000 adult females, and 84,000 young persons of whom half were boys and girls of under fourteen."[8] All the while upstanding employers, good churchmen, expanded their businesses and their abuses—and the Church did little. It was the established order of things.

We thank God that some Christians, such as Shaftesbury, broke ranks with popular order and allowed the Bible to triumph over culture. Lest we point our fingers at the British, all we have to do is think back one hundred years to slavery in our own country and the unbelievable Biblical gerrymandering of born-again Christians. Thank God for the early witness of John Woolman and the later voices of such people as Henry Ward Beecher.

Is the Bible made captive to culture today? I think so. For example, millions of Christians are obsessed with materialism to the point that they are no different than the society around them. The Bible's warnings are downplayed or simply not heard.

> "Name it and claim it," that's what faith's about!
> You can have what you want if you just have no doubt.
> So make out your "wish-list" and keep on believin'
> and you'll find yourself perpetually receivin'.
>
> Now, some Christians say we should live like our Lord
> Who didn't much worry 'bout his room or his board.
> But we know our Bibles say he became poor
> So he could enrich us and give us some more, and more, and more![9]

Someday future believers will look back on our day and shake their heads in disbelief, just as we do with past slavery and industrial abuse. We need to read God's Word with a first-century freshness, escaping the bondage of our culture and allowing it to penetrate our being.

In verses 38–40 Jesus stepped up his attack, moving from implicit criticism of the scribes to straightforward attack as he excoriated their actions and motives.

> And in his teaching he said, "Beware of the scribes, who like to walk around in long robes and like greetings in the marketplaces and have the best seats in the synagogues and the places of honor at feasts, who devour widows' houses and for a pretense make long prayers. They will receive the greater condemnation."

There was divine rage as Jesus described them as gliding about in their power suits receiving the obeisance of the masses in the marketplace, sitting facing the congregation with studied religious expressions on their faces. They were proud lovers of praise and position!

We have our evangelical counterparts—always in a sweaty hurry running from meeting to airport to news conferences to talk shows—now pious, now a good ole boy, and now an intellectual. Pride fuels those who thrive on the adulation of the *hoi polloi*—like the minister Woodrow Wilson described as the only man he knew who could "strut while sitting down."[10] Jesus did not like this at all.

But his most scathing indictment was next: "[They] devour widows' houses and for a pretense make long prayers" (v. 40a). During Jesus' time, most scribes lived off subsidies because they were forbidden to take money for their work. Supporters were relatively easy to come by because supporting a scribe was considered a meritorious work.[11] Very often it was people of limited means who supported those with such dramatic piety. This has a familiar ring, only today it is Social Security checks instead of shekels.

I once received a colored brochure that featured eight separate pictures of an "evangelist" designed to show what a versatile man of God he was. It included pictures of him praying by a waterfall, praying with his hands placed on a pile of letters, holding a baby (he liked children), shaking the hand of a poor man (he knew poor people). But what really got my attention was the offer of a specially blessed handkerchief that had been dipped in the Jordan River and that, if prayerfully applied, would bring healing. The cost was $15.00!

Jesus assails the greed of such religious establishments, even today. "We've had Watergate, Koreagate, Irangate, and now the latest scandal is Pearly gate,"[12] says Warren Wiersbe. "For nineteen centuries the church has been telling the world to admit its sins, repent, and believe the gospel. In the twilight of the twentieth century, the world is telling the church to face up to her sins, repent, *and start being the true church of that gospel.*"[13]

Our Lord's judgment was especially pronounced on those who persisted with their phony, proud, profit-making lifestyle—"They will receive the greater condemnation" (v. 40b). It is possible for a clergyman to sink by such slow degrees that long after his fall he goes on thinking himself a good Christian. This is a terrifying pronouncement. There will be no exceptions! James wisely says, "Not many of you should become teachers, my brothers, for you know that we who teach will be judged with greater strictness" (James 3:1). We must all take this to heart!

Our study of this text should encourage us to ask two major questions of ourselves. First, what place does God's Word have in our lives? Do we know it? Do we read it? Or are we being bound by our culture so that the Word is not going to our hearts? Do we want the Bible to really do its work? This calls for a resolve to be carefully, even painfully, Biblical in our Christianity.

The second question is, why do we serve God? Do we like parading around in our pinstriped Brooks Brothers power combos? Do we sit on the platform and look holy for all to see? God help us if that is our motivation—whether we are preachers, youth workers, Sunday school teachers, Bible study leaders, or nursery workers! God have mercy on us if piety is used as an avenue for gain.

Finally, there is the biggest question of all: "What do you think about the Christ? Whose son is he?" (Matthew 22:42). This is the question that the Synoptics indicate Jesus used to get the whole discussion going. If you answer only that he was the Son of David, you have made an eternal error that will separate you from life now and forever. If you answer that he was the Son of David and the Lord in the flesh, you are on the right track. If you believe this, resting your soul upon it, you have eternal life.

The very health of your soul will rest on what you think and understand about Christ. Unworthy thoughts bring soul sickness. Narrow notions narrow our love. If you believe:

That he was with the Father and the Spirit from all eternity—
That, out of love, he came in the flesh, as the Son of David—
That he lived a sinless life—
That he never sought his own prestige, power, or wealth—
That he is your model—
That he died for you—
That he was resurrected from the dead—
That he ascended to the right hand of the Father where

> "The Lord said to [him] . . .
> 'Sit at my right hand,
> Until I put your enemies
> under your feet'"—

That he prays for you now—
That he prays that you will model his character—
That he loves you infinitely—
That he cares about the smallest details in your life—
That he is coming again for you—
That he will judge the world—
That you will be like him—
Then you will be eternally joyful.

If you believe all this, you are thinking rightly about Christ. And the more you believe it, the healthier and more joyful you will be!

43

Money Speaks

MARK 12:41–44

ENTREPRENEURS LEASED THE Los Angeles Convention Center to display the 25,000 to 30,000 objects left from the estate of Wladziu Valentino, better known as Liberace. Thousands of people willingly paid six dollars each for the dubious privilege of viewing the remains of Liberace's grotesque materialism. This was followed by an auction at Christies in Los Angeles, where another admission charge of $10.00 was levied in a desperate attempt to regulate the crowd. In a frenzied sell-off, a king's ransom was paid by the bejeweled crowd for Liberace's belongings.[1]

On that incredible night, money was the only speech acknowledged by the auctioneer. It also spoke in other ways, for as the evening progressed it spoke volumes about the heart of the deceased entertainer and the hearts of the bidders. Jesus said, "For where your treasure is, there your heart will be also" (Matthew 6:21). In 1984 Americans spent $177 billion on gambling, fifteen times more than they gave to their churches. Tragically this declares the heart of our country![2] Money speaks! This is an ancient truth.

Aware of this, the Lord Jesus chose the temple treasury for his departing shot before leaving the temple for good. Money—giving—reveals the state of the heart as few other things can. Thus Jesus chose this place to contrast the phony righteousness of the religious establishment with true devotion to God.

"And [Jesus] sat down opposite the treasury and watched the people putting money into the offering box" (v. 41). The treasury where they placed their offerings consisted of thirteen brass treasure chests called trumpets because they were shaped like inverted horns, narrow at the top and enlarged at the bottom.[3]

According to the *Mishnah*, each of the chests bore inscriptions designating what the offerings were for: "'New Shekel dues,' 'Old Shekel dues,' 'Bird offerings,' 'Young birds for the whole offering,' 'Wood,' 'Frankincense,' 'Gold for the Mercy-seat,' and, on six of them 'Freewill-offerings.'"[4] Because of the Passover, the treasury was a most busy place as both the local inhabitants and pilgrims crowded past the thirteen *shopharoth* (chests) and inserted their offerings into the narrow brass mouths made shiny by the constant friction of worshipers' hands.

Here amidst the noisy din Jesus found a place to observe the givers without drawing attention to himself. Have you ever sat at the airport or the shopping mall and watched the people over your newspaper or coffee? Jesus was a people watcher. He was not only watching their actions but their motives. Here we have a divine revelation: neither the widow (the principal focus of Jesus' attention) nor the rest of the people had any idea they were being watched! We too are being watched in our least conscious moments. As George MacDonald said, "When we feel as if God is nowhere, He is watching over us with an eternal consciousness, above and beyond our every hope and fear."

What a staggering moment it is for a worshiping soul when one first awakes to this reality. Jesus really is watching. As Hannah of old said, the Lord is weighing our actions (1 Samuel 2:3). This means that every action is important.

Jesus' Observations of the Wealthy's Donations (vv. 41b, 42)

What did Jesus see as he sat across from the treasury chests and watched the worshipers make their deposits? Initially he saw that "Many rich people put in large sums" (v. 41b). Here it should not automatically be assumed that he disapproved of all the offerings of the wealthy. Very likely there were a number who had noble motivations. But Jesus also saw much that displeased him.

Public giving such as this setting required promotes self-conscious ostentation. Consider the man who stood up in a meeting where they were taking subscriptions for donations and said, "I want to give $100—anonymously."[5]

Would the stars have turned out to support "Live Aid" if there were no cameras and they could not stand with Stevie Wonder to sing "We Are the World"? What would happen to our great national charities today without celebrity benefits, or published subscribers' lists, or bronze plaques, or pictures taken with crippled children?

The huge Passover crowds and the public display made possible by the thirteen trumpets combined to create some outrageous preening and prancing. We can imagine the hush that came over the crowd when a notable person approached, perhaps with an offering too heavy to carry himself, and the audible gasp as the shekels crashed into the brass trumpets. Can you see their pious countenances, their "see if you can top that" expressions?

The fashionable religious world of Jerusalem and the *Diaspora* paraded before Jesus' eyes. It was in reality a world of souls in peril. Being able to do a good deed on a scale that is impossible for others can inbreed a delusion of superiority and safety.

Jesus also saw something that made his heart applaud. He saw that "a poor widow came and put in two small copper coins, which make a penny" (v. 42). Jesus, and everyone else who happened to see her, knew that she was a poverty-stricken widow because widows wore distinctive clothing, which in her case was worn and tattered (cf. Genesis 38:14). The life of widows in Biblical times was proverbially difficult.[6]

Here we wish we knew more. This woman's beauty of soul makes us wonder where she lived and how, and what had been her suffering. Her offering was two coins, so small they were called *lepta* (literally, "peeled" or "fine," the idea being a tiny thin coin).[7] The miniature *lepton* was worth only one four-hundredth of a shekel, or about one-eighth of a cent.[8] The two *lepta* represented her day's earnings, hardly anything and yet a considerable sum to her.

She undoubtedly approached the trumpets quietly, almost stealthily, head bowed, hoping to draw no attention to herself. Though she did not know Jesus was watching, she knew that God saw her, and that was whom she came to please. Seen in the whole context of chapter 12, this is a withering reproach to the earthbound rationalism of the Sadducees. Her humble motivation could be nothing but love. She was living out the *Shema*, loving God with all she had.

When she slipped the two coins into the mouth of the "trumpet," they fell inaudibly against the shekels of the rich. But she had given all! J. A. Bengel, an eighteenth-century commentator, beautifully noted that she gave "two— one of which the widow might have retained."[9] *She gave everything!* On this Passover she was silently saying to God, "I love you, and all I have is yours. Here's my heart, my life."

The Passover crowd had been "oohing" and "aahing" over the munificence of the rich, and Jesus had remained unmoved. But when the widow passed by, though he sat still, he was inwardly on his feet clapping. She was a rare flower in a desert of official devotion, and her beauty made his heart rejoice.[10]

Jesus' Observations of the Widow's Offering (vv. 43, 44)

And he called his disciples to him and said to them, "Truly, I say to you, this poor widow has put in more than all those who are contributing to the offering box. For they all contributed out of their abundance, but she out of her poverty has put in everything she had, all she had to live on." (vv. 43, 44)

John Calvin correctly saw Jesus' words as double-edged, encouraging to those who have little and a sobering exhortation to those with much. Calvin remarks:

The lesson is useful in two ways. The Lord encourages the poor, who appear to lack the means of doing well, not to doubt that they testify to their enthusiasm for Him even with a slender contribution. If they consecrate themselves, their offering which appears mean and trivial will be no less precious than if they had offered all the treasures of Croesus. On the other hand, those who have a richer supply and stand out for their large giving are told that it is not enough if their generosity far exceeds the commoners and the underprivileged, for with God it rates less for a rich man to give a moderate sum from a large mass, than for a poor man to exhaust himself in paying out something very small.[11]

Realizing that Jesus' commendation cuts both ways calls for some soul-searching observations. First, *when it comes to giving, the posture of our hearts makes all the difference*. When I write a check to the I.R.S., the I.R.S. does not care whether I give willingly or grudgingly. Not so with the Lord. "If I give away all I have, and if I deliver up my body to be burned, but have not love, I gain nothing" (1 Corinthians 13:3). But if I give a penny with the widow's heart, it is great gain to me and to God.

Not what we give, but what we share,
For the gift without the giver is bare;
Who gives himself with his alms feeds three,
Himself, his hungering neighbour, and Me.[12]

God weighs our motivations. This truth is at the same time a terror and a comfort. Which way does it strike you?

The second observation is, *God can do great things with tiny offerings*. Those two pennies (equaling a quarter of a cent), given quietly with the widow's motive, have produced more for the kingdom in the intervening two thousand years than all other gifts presented that Passover week. Down through the ages those two minuscule coins have been multiplied into billions and billions for God's work as humble people have been liberated to give from their little. The Lord has converted those two coins into a perennial wealth of contentment and instruction for his Church.

If there is love and sacrifice with the giver, there will be spiritual power in the gift. In this respect, we can say that what the Church needs is not larger gifts, but gifts given with the positive spiritual quality of the poor widow. Jesus meant to encourage all of us with this.

The third observation is, *at the Judgment Christ will square his accounts*. There is no evidence that the woman ever knew what Jesus thought of her gift or that she ever became a prosperous woman in this life. In fact, since the final judgment and the ultimate bestowing of eternal rewards is still future for the whole Church, there is every possibility that she does not know to this very day what we know about her. The Judgment is going to reveal her work, the architecture of a beautiful soul adorned with gold, silver, and precious stones. She will be *first*, in compliance with the irrefragable Law of God.

Finally, a fourth observation: *God is sublimely egalitarian*. There is no advantage to the poor or the rich, to the unlettered or the educated, to the unknown or known. Billy Graham has no advantage over the humblest believer, and vice versa. All of us, without exception, can do great things for God!

Is there any secret, unobtrusive service born of love for God that the Judgment will reveal in me or you? How do we give? What is our attitude when we are not watched—sharp . . . caustic . . . patient . . . gentle?

Is it possible for the Church to love and give like the widow? Has it ever done so? The history of the Apostolic Church answers with a resounding yes! Paul told the Corinthians:

> We want you to know, brothers, about the grace of God that has been given among the churches of Macedonia, for in a severe test of affliction, their abundance of joy and their extreme poverty have overflowed in a wealth of generosity on their part. For they gave according to their means, as I can testify, and beyond their means, of their own accord, begging us earnestly for the favor of taking part in the relief of the saints—and this, not as we expected, but they gave themselves first to the Lord and then by the will of God to us. (2 Corinthians 8:1–5)

God does not want our money. He wants *us*. Yet, we cannot give ourselves to him apart from our money.

It is true: *money speaks*. It tells us where our hearts are. What does our giving say about us?

There is a disease that is particularly virulent in this modern age. It is called cirrhosis of the giver. It was actually discovered about 34 AD and ran a terminal course in a couple named Ananias and Sapphira (Acts 5). It is an acute condition that renders the patient's hand immobile when it attempts to move from the billfold to the offering plate. The remedy is to remove the afflicted from the House of God, since it is clinically observable that this condition disappears in alternate environments such as golf courses or clubs or restaurants.[13]

Actually, the disease is really not a motor problem, but a heart problem. The best remedy is to fall in love with God with all your heart, for where your heart is, there will your treasure be (Matthew 6:21 reversed).

44

Jesus' Farewell Prophecy

MARK 13:1–37

CHAPTER 13 records what is called Jesus' Olivet Discourse, by far the most difficult passage in the book of Mark and, along with its parallels in the other Gospels, one of the most difficult texts in the New Testament. This is so because of the rich nature of the prophetic language that Jesus used (virtually every verse has multiple allusions to both the Old Testament and to other Jewish apocalyptic literature) and because of the nature of prophecy itself—multiple fulfillments culminating in a final fulfillment.

The fact is, we have yet to find a scholar who can perfectly unravel the knotty problems of the Olivet Discourse. Study of it requires a proper humility and a willingness to admit that we do not know everything. We must mind Chesterton's dictum: "It is only the fool who tries to get the heavens inside his head, and not unnaturally his head bursts. The wise man is content to get his head inside the heavens." In this chapter we will try the latter.

During the preceding days Jesus had made his Triumphal Entry into Jerusalem, prophesied destruction for Israel in cursing the fig tree, cleansed the temple, and entered into debates with the religious establishment that he repeatedly won. Then, in exalting the poor widow and her offering, he passed judgment on the religious leadership of Israel. Now Jesus left the temple for good. The cross awaited him. The Olivet Discourse formed a fitting bridge to Jesus' final days. It was his final address, his farewell prophecy.

As to which disciple called Jesus' attention to the temple, we can only guess. Perhaps impulsive Peter felt Jesus' departing grief and wanted to say something positive. Whatever the case, Mark tells us: "And as he [Jesus] came out of the temple, one of his disciples said to him, 'Look, Teacher, what wonderful stones and what wonderful buildings!'" (v. 1). There was no hyperbole in this! The temple was considered one of the great wonders of the Roman world. It had been under construction forty-six years (John 2:20) and was just nearing completion. Its spectacular location on Mt. Moriah gave it an imposing dominance over ancient Jerusalem. From a distance it looked like a mountain of gold, because its nine massive gates[1] and much of its exterior was plated with gold and silver. The great bronze gate alone was worth more than any of the other gates.

Josephus wrote:

> The exterior of the building wanted nothing that could astound either mind or eye. For, being covered on all sides with massive plates of gold, the sun was no sooner up than it radiated so fiery a flash that persons straining to look at it were compelled to avert their eyes, as from the solar rays. To approaching strangers it appeared from a distance like a snow-clad mountain; for all that was not overlaid with gold was of purest white. Some of the stones in the building were forty-five cubits in length, five in height and six in breadth.[2]

The incredible size of the foundation's stones, almost the size of box-cars,[3] was breath-taking.

The temple was indeed a wonder. But if that disciple hoped to raise Jesus' spirit, he failed. Jesus' unexpected response left him flabbergasted: "Do you see these great buildings? There will not be left here one stone upon another that will not be thrown down" (v. 2). Jesus' words were tragically true. When Titus first conquered Jerusalem, he ordered that the temple be preserved, but it was gutted by a fire set by one of his soldiers. As a result, Titus ". . . ordered the whole city and temple to be razed to the ground,"[4] a task especially carried out in respect to the temple as soldiers driven by avarice pulled the stones apart in an attempt to reclaim the melted gold.

Riveted by this astounding prophecy, the inner circle of the disciples (Peter, James, and John), with the addition of Peter's brother, Andrew, sought a private audience with Jesus that providentially took place on the Mount of Olives.

Rising one hundred fifty feet higher than Jerusalem, the mountain afforded a dramatic view of the temple. So there, with the ivory and gold temple lying below them, the disciples asked Jesus the questions that precipitated the Olivet Discourse: "Tell us, when will these things be, and what will be the sign when all these things are about to be accomplished?" (v. 4). We need to keep this stunning scene and these questions before us as we proceed. What would be the *times* and the *signs* that would precede the destruction of the temple? We should also remember that it was on this very mount that the *shekinah* glory had departed from the temple six hundred years before (Ezekiel 11:22–25), and it would be upon the Mount of Olives that the Lord would return (Zechariah 14).

Jesus would answer their questions, but some of his reply would go far beyond them, instructing his Church about his return. We shall also see that Jesus was not interested in giving date-setting details, but in encouraging his own to be steadfast and faithful until he returns. Jesus spoke pastorally.

Events Prior to the Destruction of the Temple (vv. 5–13)

First, Jesus warned the disciples not to be deceived by the disturbing events that were coming. "And Jesus began to say to them, 'See that no one leads you astray. Many will come in my name, saying, "I am he!" and they will lead many astray'" (vv. 5, 6). We must not be deceived by *false teaching*. "And when you hear of wars and rumors of wars, do not be alarmed. This must take place, but the end is not yet. For nation will rise against nation, and kingdom against kingdom" (vv. 7, 8a). We must not be deceived into thinking it is the end because of such *social convulsions*. "There will be earthquakes in various places; there will be famines. These are but the beginning of the birth pains" (v. 8b). *Natural catastrophes* will continue as they always have.

It is so natural to think the end has arrived when we personally experience any of these things. Wars have always been with us. Will Durant wrote: "War is one of the constants of history, and has not diminished with civilization and democracy. In the last 3,421 years of recorded history only 268 have seen no war."[5] What about the huge volume of unrecorded history? Surely there has never been a minute without wars!

Yet, when you or I are touched by war, it is so easy to think apocalyptically—"surely the end of the world is here!" This is how the Russians felt in the Napoleonic wars, and how many believers felt in Germany in 1945. This is all very natural, but sometimes it becomes absurd, like the man who told me that the return of the Lord must be imminent because our national debt is out of hand. This is narcissistic, self-centered, money-clip eschatology!

It is so easy to regard natural catastrophes the same way. During the years between Christ's death and the destruction of the temple, there was a terrible earthquake in Laodicea, Vesuvius buried Pompeii, and there was a famine in Rome itself. This did not mean the end of all things. Neither would it mean the end if California fell into the sea and you could sail to Hawaii from Las Vegas. The truth is, with the rise of every war and earthquake there comes an increase of false christs who say they have the answer. We are not to be deceived by any of this. These things are a result of man's sin and will continue to the end of time. "See that no one leads you astray," says Jesus.

Next, having warned his disciples about what would be happening in the world, Jesus informed them about what would happen to them personally:

> But be on your guard. For they will deliver you over to councils, and you will be beaten in synagogues, and you will stand before governors and kings for my sake, to bear witness before them. And the gospel must first be proclaimed to all nations. And when they bring you to trial and deliver you over, do not be anxious beforehand what you are to say, but say whatever is given you in that hour, for it is not you who speak, but the Holy Spirit. (vv. 9–11)

His disciples would face religious persecution, ironically at the hands of the local Sanhedrins and synagogues that should have been havens for them. They would suffer under the secular state and bear powerful witness. This persecution would mean their forced dispersion, and thus the gospel would be preached to the Gentiles, fulfilling prophecy. Persecuted disciples would dazzle their interrogators with their wisdom—for example, Paul before Agrippa, Peter and John before the Sanhedrin, Martin Niemoller before Hitler.

They would also experience intense personal hatred. Jesus went on, "And brother will deliver brother over to death, and the father his child, and children will rise against parents and have them put to death. And you will be hated by all for my name's sake" (vv. 12, 13a). The radical commitment that the gospel demands can disrupt even the most natural and sacred human relationships, and still does. Announce your conversion in a Muslim country or in a hard-line Communist country and Jesus' words take on a terrible reality. Jesus said, "Do not think that I have come to bring peace to the earth. I have not come to bring peace, but a sword. For I have come to set a man against his father, and a daughter against her mother, and a daughter-in-law against her mother-in-law. And a person's enemies will be those of his own household" (Matthew 10:34–36).

In saying, "And you will be hated by all," Jesus was making a generic statement. Evangelicals sometimes receive favorable press, but they should never forget that the same media powers can quickly turn the world against Christians. Jesus said, "If the world hates you, know that it has hated me before it hated you. If you were of the world, the world would love you as its own; but because you are not of the world, but I chose you out of the world, therefore the world hates you" (John 15:18, 19). Any follower of Christ who conforms to his image will suffer persecution. But that person will also know how to "share his sufferings" (Philippians 3:10), a state that Jesus said was "blessed" (Matthew 5:10, 11).

Jesus ended this part of his warning by saying, "But the one who endures to the end will be saved" (v. 13b). Rather than being blown away by persecution (religious, secular, or domestic), we are to persevere. The Christian life is not a sprint, but a marathon. What needed words for us all. Over the years I have been repeatedly surprised by acquaintances who have dropped by the way. Jesus' warning is painfully relevant.

Regardless of one's theological construct, a warning given by the Apostle John must be taken to heart: "They went out from us, but they were not of us; for if they had been of us, they would have continued with us. But they went out, that it might become plain that they all are not of us" (1 John 2:19). True believers keep on going on through thick and thin. We should pray that we will finish well.

> That I should end before I finish or
> finish, but not well.
> That I should stain your honor, shame your name,
> grieve your loving heart.
> Few, they tell me, finish well . . .
> Lord, let me get home before dark.[6]

With his solemn warning, Jesus then turned to the specific signs his disciples were asking for that would tell them that the temple's destruction was imminent.

Signs, Trials, and the Destruction of the Temple (vv. 14–23)

Perhaps Jesus motioned toward the temple radiating in the late afternoon sun as he said, "But when you see the abomination of desolation standing where he ought not to be (let the reader understand), then let those who are in Judea flee to the mountains. Let the one who is on the housetop not go down, nor enter his house, to take anything out, and let the one who is in the field not turn back to take his cloak" (vv. 14–16).

The inner circle knew exactly what Jesus meant by "the abomination of desolation." This term originated in the prophetic section of Daniel (in 9:27, and then in 11:31), which described a coming figure who would desecrate the temple and abolish daily sacrifice there. It meant "an abomination so detestable it would cause the Temple to be abandoned by the people of God and provokes desolation."[7] This had happened one hundred fifty years earlier when the Seleucid King Antiochus IV Epiphanes conquered Jerusalem and attempted to Hellenize the people, forbidding them to circumcise their children (1 Maccabees 1:60) or offer Levitical sacrifices (1 Maccabees 1:45), and forcing them to sacrifice swine (1 Maccabees 1:47). In the words of the writer of Maccabees, "on the fifteenth day of Chislev [December we think] in the one hundred and forty-fifth year, they erected a desolating sacrilege upon the altar of burnt offering" (1 Maccabees 1:54). It was a statue of Zeus and probably an image of Antiochus himself! Antiochus also set up a brothel in the temple chambers (2 Maccabees 6:4). This abomination caused the Jews to abandon the temple until their successful revolt.

Obviously, as terrible as Antiochus had been, he did not completely fulfill the prophecies in Daniel, for Jesus said another abomination was coming, and then the temple would be destroyed. This was almost fulfilled in AD 40 when the insane Emperor Caligula, thinking he was a god, almost succeeded in having an image of himself installed in the temple.[8] Ironically, partial fulfillment of this came from among the Jews themselves (Zealots who amidst the turmoil occupied the temple in the winter and spring of AD 67 and 68). They permitted criminals to enter the Holy of Holies and committed murders in the temple themselves. Finally, they crowned their sacrilege with a circus-like investiture of one Phanni, who according to Josephus "was such a clown that he scarcely knew what the priesthood meant."[9]

I personally believe that "the abomination of desolation" will find its ultimate fulfillment in the future and that the destruction of Jerusalem is a paradigm that contains the essential elements of the Great Tribulation at the end of time. The already multiple fulfillment of the term argues for this. Also, "the man of lawlessness" referred to by Paul in 2 Thessalonians 2:3–10 supports the view that "the abomination of desolation" refers to the ultimate Antichrist who will also fulfill Daniel's prophecies. The destruction of Jerusalem and the advent of a God-usurping personage will signify the approach of the end of the age.

When the Zealots' sacrilege took place, history records, great numbers of people fled Jerusalem, many of them Christians. The fourth-century historian Eusebius records:

The people of the church in Jerusalem were commanded by an oracle given by revelation before the war to those in the city . . . to depart and dwell in one of the cities of Perea which they called Pella. To it those who believed on Christ migrated from Jerusalem, that when holy men had altogether deserted the royal capital of the Jews and the whole land of Judea, the judgment of God might at last overtake them for all their crimes against the Christ and his Apostles, and all that generation of the wicked be utterly blotted out from among men.[10]

Josephus records them as leaving the city "as swimmers deserting a sinking ship,"[11] an image that accords very well with Jesus' command to leave everything behind.

The horror that Jesus predicted for Jerusalem, in the powerful prophetic language of verses 17–20, came with the fall of the temple and is a matter of historical fact. "And if the Lord had not cut short the days, no human being would be saved" (v. 20a). The roofs were thronged with famished women with babes in arms, and the alleys with corpses of the elderly. Children and young people swollen from starvation "roamed like phantoms through the market-places and collapsed wherever their doom overtook them." But there was no lamenting or wailing, because famine had strangled their emotions. Jerusalem could not bury all the bodies, so they were flung over the wall. The silence was broken only by the laughter of robbers stripping the bodies.[12]

Jesus finished his warning (v. 23) by saying, "But be on guard; I have told you all things beforehand." What a blessing it was to the Church when Christians who believed God's Word fled destitute but alive to serve God. And many non-believers came to faith. Jesus' words were not wasted on the Apostolic Church. The call is for us to maintain the same vigilance as we watch the flow of history.

Having told the disciples everything about the fall of the temple, Jesus jumped thousands of years into the future to inform them of his second coming. He does not tell them that it is millennia distant, but only that it is on the other side of the destruction. We have the advantage of history to instruct us.

His Second Coming (vv. 24–27)

Perhaps Jesus removed his eyes from the temple and looked beyond as he continued speaking:

> But in those days, after that tribulation, the sun will be darkened, and the moon will not give its light, and the stars will be falling from heaven, and the powers in the heavens will be shaken. And then they will see the Son of Man coming in clouds with great power and glory. And then he will send out the angels and gather his elect from the four winds, from the ends of the earth to the ends of heaven. (vv. 24–27)

Virtually everything Christ said at that time was from Old Testament material too vast to refer to here. We see that the end will feature unnatural disasters. The language suggests a heavenly earthquake as star after star falls and the universe moves toward disorganization.[13] Earth's own star dims, and the moon's reflected light is too little to see by. Terrifying!

In this cosmological confusion Jesus will come in shining clouds of glory. He is the "son of man" of Daniel 7:13, 14—"the Ancient of Days . . . his dominion is an everlasting dominion, which shall not pass away, and his kingdom one that shall not be destroyed" (cf. Mark 2:10; John 1:51).

His angels are dispersed, not as grim reapers, but as joyous reapers to the harvest as he gathers his Church from every nook and cranny of the world.

Lo, He comes with clouds descending
Once for favored sinners slain;
Thousand thousand saints attending
Swell the triumph of His train:
Alleluia! Alleluia!
God appears on earth to reign.

Charles Wesley

This is our dream. And it will be our reality! When will this happen?

The Timing of the End (vv. 28–37)

First, regarding the destruction of the temple, Jesus said:

From the fig tree learn its lesson: as soon as its branch becomes tender and puts out its leaves, you know that summer is near. So also, when you see these things taking place, you know that he is near, at the very gates. Truly, I say to you, this generation will not pass away until all these things take place. Heaven and earth will pass away, but my words will not pass away. (vv. 28–31)

The fig trees on Olivet were tender at that very moment, providing a perfect illustration. Warm weather was coming. All they had to do was watch Jerusalem for the details he described and they would know.

He closed this teaching with the stupendous declaration, "Heaven and earth will pass away, but my words will not pass away" (v. 31). Jesus put his words on equal footing with the Old Testament Scriptures. History has proved him correct to the smallest detail! *We can trust his word!*

What about his second advent? Jesus said, "But concerning that day or that hour, no one knows, not even the angels in heaven, nor the Son, but only the Father" (v. 32). We are not able to figure this one out! Not even one angel in Heaven knows. Jesus knows the time of his return now, as he resides in his glorified body with the Father. But when he was here he did not know, due to the integrity of his Incarnation. Anyone who says that he knows the date of Christ's return borders on blasphemy. Our duty is to stay awake.

> Be on guard, keep awake. For you do not know when the time will come. It is like a man going on a journey, when he leaves home and puts his servants in charge, each with his work, and commands the doorkeeper to stay awake. Therefore stay awake—for you do not know when the master of the house will come, in the evening, or at midnight, or when the rooster crows, or in the morning—lest he come suddenly and find you asleep. And what I say to you I say to all: Stay awake. (vv. 33–37)

The call to vigilance is universal. It is meant for us today. Jesus issued the command from the Mount of Olives, the official site of his return. Will it be in the next decade? Possibly . . .

Don't be fooled by all the earthbound, secular voices that say that life will go on and on. It will not! All of life is moving toward him. "He is the image of the invisible God, the firstborn of all creation. For by him all things were created, in heaven and on earth, visible and invisible, whether thrones or dominions or rulers or authorities—all things were created through him and for him" (Colossians 1:15, 16).

We are to keep looking up. "[The grace of God trains] us to renounce ungodliness and worldly passions, and to live self-controlled, upright, and godly lives in the present age, waiting for our blessed hope, the appearing of the glory of our great God and Savior Jesus Christ" (Titus 2:12, 13).

"Beloved, we are God's children now, and what we will be has not yet appeared; but we know that when he appears we shall be like him, because we shall see him as he is. And everyone who thus hopes in him purifies himself as he is pure" (1 John 3:2, 3).

Keep looking up!

45

Love's Extravagance

MARK 14:1–11

MARK'S GOSPEL TELLS US that the religious establishment had wanted to kill Jesus for some time. Their murderous resolve had unified when he healed the man's withered hand on the Sabbath (3:6). It dramatically intensified when he cleansed the temple. So the scribes and chief priests began actively looking for ways to do away with him. When he told the Parable of the Wicked Vineyard Keepers, they looked for a way to arrest him right then, but they were afraid of the crowd (12:12).

Now, after devastating verbal exchanges with him, they could hardly restrain themselves: "It was now two days before the Passover and the Feast of Unleavened Bread. And the chief priests and the scribes were seeking how to arrest him by stealth and kill him, for they said, 'Not during the feast, lest there be an uproar from the people'" (vv. 1, 2). The tension ran high.

Passover was a time of intense nationalistic feeling among the people because it called to remembrance their deliverance from slavery in Egypt. Moreover, there were a lot of Galileans in town, and they were noted for being excitable people capable of violence. However distressing, the religious leaders would have to bide their time until the right opportunity came.

Meanwhile Jesus, having left the temple for good and having delivered his great Olivet Discourse regarding the judgment of the temple and his final advent, had retired to Bethany on the southern slope of the mount, about two miles out of town. There he accepted an invitation to dinner in the home of a man known as "Simon the leper" (v. 3). Who was Simon? There have been numerous speculations, but the most plausible is that he had been healed by Jesus, and this was an appreciation dinner. Whatever the explanation, he had invited some excellent company. The Apostle John, in his similar account, tells us that the magnificent women Mary and Martha were there and that resurrected Lazarus was reclining at the table along with the rest of the disciples (John 12:2).

Simon had brought together the ingredients for a terrific evening. Jesus would be free from tension amidst people who loved him. No doubt the meal went well. Imagine the conversation about the temple, questions about the Olivet Discourse, and questions to Lazarus—"Lazarus, what did you see on the other side? What is it like to come back to life?"

As they were reclining, they witnessed a remarkable event that they would never forget: "a woman [John's Gospel reveals it was Mary, 12:3] came with an alabaster flask of ointment of pure nard, very costly, and she broke the flask and poured it over his head" (v. 3). John adds, "[she] anointed the feet of Jesus and wiped his feet with her hair. The house was filled with the fragrance of the perfume" (John 12:3).

What an astounding moment! Mary, who loved to sit at the feet of Jesus (Luke 10:39), unexpectedly approached her reclining Lord, bearing a priceless alabaster vial of imported Indian perfume (very likely a family heirloom), snapped the narrow neck of the flask, poured a generous portion on Jesus' head, anointing him, and then poured the rest of the contents on his feet—humbly, worshipfully wiping his feet with her hair. It was an intensely fervent expression of devotion, as fervent as found anywhere in sacred Scripture!

We can assume that due to the intensity of her devotional focus upon Christ, she had given no thought as to what others would think of her action. Thus she was mortified by the unexpected response of the disciples. Here again John gives us further insight, because he tells us that Judas Iscariot, the keeper of the money bag, and soon to be Jesus' betrayer, originated the objection, which the others picked up.

Mark says, "There were some who said to themselves indignantly, 'Why was the ointment wasted like that? For this ointment could have been sold for more than three hundred denarii and given to the poor.' And they scolded her" (vv. 4, 5). Judas, with calculator in hand, a man who knew the price of everything and the value of nothing, instantly calculated the waste (in terms of economy, $25,000 to $30,000).

Besides, there were people in need of food and clothing in Jerusalem at that very instant. As it was customary to give gifts on the evening of Passover to the poor, it would have made a remarkable gift.[1] But now it was gone, sinfully wasted! All that was left was the evaporating aroma, so "they scolded her." The Greek indicates that they snorted their indignation like angry horses. How humiliating this was for poor Mary!

The disciples thought they knew the mind of Jesus, but they were badly mistaken, because Jesus then put himself between Mary and her attackers, defending her with a heart-searching exposition ending with these words: "And truly, I say to you, wherever the gospel is proclaimed in the whole world, what she has done will be told in memory of her" (v. 9). These words will plumb any submissive heart, and I hope they take the measure of mine and yours as we sit under God's Word.

How did Jesus come to Mary's defense?

Jesus' Defense of Mary's Act of Worship (v. 6)

He began by affirming that what Mary had done was beautiful: "Leave her alone. Why do you trouble her? She has done a beautiful thing to me" (v. 6). Why did Jesus call it beautiful?

First, because *he was aware of her loving motive*. Paul tells us that if we have the greatest of gifts, if we sacrifice all, but do not have love, it comes to nothing (1 Corinthians 13:1–3). Love makes our gifts pleasing to God.

Years ago when my son Kent was a little boy, my wife, Barbara, won a beautiful cardboard decorator recipe box. It was very unusual, a conversation piece, and this became the incentive for her to organize a drawer full of loose recipes. As a result she recopied all her recipes on cards and filed them in the box. Our little boy had watched her do this and knew the box was very special to her.

Then came Barbara's birthday, and some friends dropped by to take her out to a surprise lunch. When she returned home she saw that the box was missing and was just about ready to call out, "Where's my box?" when she saw Kent. His eyes were wide, and she could see he was holding something behind his back from which water was dripping. She knew what it was, and though her heart sank she smiled. He said, "Mom, I have a birthday present for you," and he presented her with her wet recipe box, saying, "Mom, I knew you liked the box." Kent had thrown the recipes in the trash (and the garbage had been picked up that day!) and had "washed" the box, scraping off the hand-made decorations and lining the box with tinfoil. When she opened it, this is what she found: a nickel, a black plastic alligator, and a picture of Kent. My wife still has that box, and it is one of her most treasured possessions. If the house burned down, the first things we would save are the family pictures and that box. Why? Because the motive behind that gift was pure, innocent love.

Those things done from simple, real love for Christ become his treasure. Correspondingly, those things done without it are futile. Mary's beautiful gift came from a beautiful heart.

The second reason it was beautiful is that *it came from a spontaneous response to the promptings of the Holy Spirit.* John Calvin insightfully says: "she was guided by the breath of the Spirit that in sure confidence she should do this in duty to Christ."[2] The Holy Spirit led her to do so for reasons she would only know in eternity, not the least of which was to be an example to the Church Universal. Among the tragedies of life are the times we are moved to do something fine or noble, and we do not do it.[3] Instead, we yield to "common sense" or the busyness of life. We ignore the impulse to write a letter of appreciation, or the prompting to tell someone we love them, or the urge to give to a need. Thus the possibility of a thing of beauty is gone forever.

The third reason Mary's work was so beautiful was that *it was not dominated by practicality.* It was simply done to and for Jesus with no thought of whether it was practical or sensible. If you are an artist or a musician, you can find affirmation in knowing that Jesus aligns himself with you by praising Mary's non-productive act of devotion.

Jesus has a lot of strange things in his treasury: widows' pennies, cups of water, broken alabaster vases, ruined recipe boxes. Has he anything of yours? Do you feel the impulse to do something beautiful for God? Then crown it with action.

The Motive of Mary's Act of Worship (v. 7)

Next, Jesus defended Mary's action because it placed him before anything else. He says: "For you always have the poor with you, and whenever you want, you can do good for them. But you will not always have me" (v. 7). Here we have a sublime irony: Mary's gift was really a gift to the poor. She saw Jesus in those ominous days before the crucifixion as the poor man *par excellence*, and thus her act was ultimately an act of kindness toward the poor.[4]

We must understand that Jesus is not arguing against caring for the poor or against social involvement. The Scriptures celebrate the believers' service to the needy: "And whoever gives one of these little ones even a cup of cold water because he is a disciple, truly, I say to you, he will by no means lose his reward" (Matthew 10:42). "Religion that is pure and undefiled before God, the Father, is this: to visit orphans and widows in their affliction, and to keep oneself unstained from the world" (James 1:27).

> Then the righteous will answer him, saying, "Lord, when did we see you hungry and feed you, or thirsty and give you drink? And when did we see you a stranger and welcome you, or naked and clothe you? And when did we see you sick or in prison and visit you?" And the King will answer them, "Truly, I say to you, as you did it to one of the least of these my brothers, you did it to me." (Matthew 25:37–40)

It is impossible to be true disciples without serving others. Jesus is not diminishing our obligation to care for the poor. In saying, "whenever you want, you can do good for them," he is implying ongoing responsibility to help the poor.

Our Lord's commendation to Mary for putting him above all else, properly understood, condemned an either/or approach to spirituality. Christians are to worship God *and* minister to others. The ideal is a lavish, contemplative devotional life in which we love Christ so much that we pour ourselves out for others. One without the other falls far short of the dynamic that Christ wants for us.

The Completeness of Mary's Act of Worship (v. 8a)

Jesus has defended Mary's anointing of him as *beautiful* because it put Christ *first*, and it was also *total*. As Jesus said in verse 8: "She has done what she could."

And indeed she did! She gave *all*! Mary was not a person of means. But she gave Jesus the most she could give. She did it with lavish abandon. Jesus would never have said, "She has done what she could" if she had measured out the perfume in grudging drops—"Here's a drop for your head, and here's two for your feet!"

Complete sacrifice is the only adequate expression for a life that has been redeemed by God. That is what Paul meant when he wrote: "I appeal to you therefore, brothers, by the mercies of God, to present your bodies as a living sacrifice, holy and acceptable to God, which is your spiritual worship" (Romans 12:1). We must ask ourselves: Is my devotion to Christ costing me anything? Is there ever any deprivation to it? Any inconvenience? "She has done what she could." How about us?

There is something else in this phrase: she did what she could being the person she was, according to her personality, her disposition. Mary followed her heart. Snap went the bottle neck, out poured the fortune, down came her hair. We have no trouble dreaming exalted visions. But getting from the heart to the lips, from the heart to the hands, from the heart to the bank account, from the heart to the needy—that is another matter. The fragrance that is so honoring to him and refreshing to others does not come from giving half our heart or half our wallet or half our talents or half our ambition. What a bouquet—"She has done what she could."

God wants us to give everything with all that we are!

Mary's Insightful Act of Worship (v. 8b)

Lastly, Jesus lauded the insightfulness of Mary's worship: "she has anointed my body beforehand for burial" (v. 8b). Though Jesus had repeatedly spoken plainly of his death, the disciples characteristically passed it off. The concept of a suffering Messiah did not meet their predilections or desires. But Mary yielded to his teaching and accepted what was coming. She realized that when tragedy came she would not be able to do anything, so she did it while she could. This explains the passion of her devotion.

Jewish women considered their hair their glory, and Mary's letting it down and drying Jesus' feet with it meant that all her humanity, all her "glory" was devoted to him in worship.

One can never know what the ultimate significance of his or her devotion and service may be! The widow with her two mites never dreamed that anyone saw her offering, let alone that it would be memorialized for two millennia. Those who fed the hungry never knew they were feeding Christ. Mary had not the slightest idea that more would be done for the poor with her "wasted" perfume than ten million times three hundred denarii could ever do. "The fragrance was soon dissipated in the scentless air, but the deed smells sweet and blossoms forever."[5]

Jesus said in closing: "And truly, I say to you, wherever the gospel is proclaimed in the whole world, what she has done will be told in memory of her" (v. 9). We are doing that right now!

Her story is part of the "gospel" (good news) because she was a demonstration of what happens in a life touched by the Savior of love.

What does her magnificent example tell us Jesus wants from us? He wants something beautiful. Beautiful because of its motivation: a ruined recipe box, a couple of tiny copper coins, an empty flask, the artifacts of our heart's love. Beautiful because it comes spontaneously from our hearts at the prompting of the Holy Spirit, done solely for our Savior's glory. He wants us to put him before anything else, even the poor. He wants us to do what we can. He wants every last drop. Everything.

> High Heaven rejects the lore
> of nicely calculated less and more.[6]

He wants us to have the courage to follow our hearts as we do what we can. He wants our devotion to be informed by a deep understanding of who he is.

Such full devotion will be memorialized by him. We must desire nothing else!

46

The Master's Mastery

MARK 14:12–21

AS BEAUTIFUL AS MARY'S anointing of Jesus was, it was funereal—she was anointing Jesus' body for burial (14:8). From the anointing on, a palpable gloom settled over the remaining days of Christ's life. That gloom darkened as Judas secretly made arrangements to deliver Jesus to the priests when there would be no Passover crowd around to interfere (14:10, 11).

Some eminent scholars believe that from here on matters simply escaped Jesus' control, so that Jesus became a helpless victim. Albert Schweitzer, in his famous *The Quest for the Historical Jesus*, a study of the history of attempts to write the life of Christ, gave eloquent voice to this opinion:

> There is silence all around. The Baptist appears, and cries: "Repent, for the Kingdom of heaven is at hand." Soon after that comes Jesus, and in the knowledge that He is the coming Son of Man lays hold of the wheel of the world to set it moving on that last revolution which is to bring all ordinary history to a close. It refuses to turn, and He throws Himself upon it. Then it does turn; *and crushes Him.* Instead of bringing in the eschatological conditions, He has destroyed them. The wheel rolls onward, and the mangled body of the one immeasurably great Man, who was strong enough to think of Himself as the spiritual ruler of mankind and to bend history to His purpose, is hanging upon it still.[1]

According to Schweitzer, Jesus simply overplayed his hand and as a result was mangled like a doll in the merciless gears of history, where he flops helplessly still. This is a powerful image: Jesus wedged in the grinding clogs of history, his best-laid plans gone awry. *But it is utterly false.* In reality, Jesus wielded profound command from the very beginning of the final journey to the cross. The Master's mastery of his dark times gives us great hope during the darknesses that await us as a natural part of living.

The Master's Control over Arrangements for the Passover (vv. 12–16)

We are introduced to Jesus' mastery by his premeditated arrangements for the celebration of the Passover. That he had given the Passover meal much thought is evidenced by his ready, detailed instructions to the disciples when they asked what they were going to do for Passover. Mark records:

> And he sent two of his disciples and said to them, "Go into the city, and a man carrying a jar of water will meet you. Follow him, and wherever he enters, say to the master of the house, 'The Teacher says, Where is my guest room, where I may eat the Passover with my disciples?' And he will show you a large upper room furnished and ready; there prepare for us." (vv. 13–15)

Evidently Jesus had previously made secret arrangements with a home-owner in Jerusalem to use his upper guest chamber for Passover. The man obviously was a follower because he also agreed to use the coded behavior of one of his servants to direct the two disciples (Peter and John, Luke 22:8) to the upper room.

Customarily only women carried waterpots, while men bore only water skins. Thus, a man carrying a waterpot was as unusual as a man carrying a purse! Peter and John easily spotted the servant, followed him, met the owner, and were quietly ushered to the secret chamber. Why all this care?

First, because it hid the location from Judas so it was impossible for him to reveal it. Judas would only learn it when he arrived. The other disciples were oblivious to Judas' intentions, but Jesus knew all too well.

The second reason Jesus took such great care is that he wanted to control the environment of the Passover meal. This upcoming meal was easily the most important meal eaten in the history of the world! Why? It identified Christ as *the* Passover lamb *par excellence* who would deliver Israel (see Exodus 12). It would be the final meal Christ would eat on this earth. The Passover would graphically explain the centrality of Christ to salvation: his blood must be wine to us, and his flesh our bread.

The final reason Jesus took such great care in preparation for the Passover meal was that it was a night when devout Jews were filled with hope of God's intervention once more. Exodus 12:42 says of the Passover, "It was a night of watching by the LORD, to bring them out of the land of Egypt; so this same night is a night of watching kept to the LORD by all the people of Israel throughout their generations." The Jewish commentary on that passage reveals that "in that night they were redeemed and in that night they will be redeemed in the future."[2] Jesus' fulfillment of the Passover was in accord with the dream of Israel, and he wanted them to see it!

Far from being crushed in the gears of history, Jesus was turning its wheels just as he wished. His death was no accident! In fact, the Last Supper and his words ("Take; this is my body" and "This is my blood of the covenant, which is poured out for many," 14:22, 24) make no sense at all if Jesus was not master of his own death. Jesus maintained sovereign, premeditated, and detailed mastery. A God who is in control when the foundations of his own earthly existence are crumbling is a God who can be trusted to sustain us when it appears our life is tumbling in.

Peter and John, having found things exactly as Jesus had told them, "prepared the Passover" (v. 16b). No doubt the owner and his servants helped with the festive details. Then came the ritual search for leaven, and the answer as expected—none to be found anywhere. Peter and John then purchased a lamb that they took to the temple, where it was sacrificed in the huge assembly-line procedure set up by the Levites. Its blood was dashed upon the altar. Tables were brought to the upper room and assembled in a large square, with low-lying couches placed around them. The lamb was set to roasting on a pomegranate spit, just like thousands of others in Jerusalem. The whole city was redolent with the inviting aroma of roasting lamb.

The Master's Control over the Announcement of His Betrayal (vv. 17–21)

In the evening, which in the Jewish reckoning began sometime after 6 PM, Jesus and his men arrived and were placed around the table. From what we can piece together from the other Gospels (especially John 13:23–26), it seems rather certain that the seating (from left to right) was, in part, Judas, Jesus, and John. This, reclining on the left elbow, as was customary, put Jesus' head at Judas' chest, and John's at Jesus'. Jesus, of course, was in charge of the celebration, leading them by pronouncing a blessing on the Passover festival. Then he took the wine, drinking the first cup. He recited the story of their exodus and redemption from Egypt. Jesus led the singing of "a new song" for their redemption, which was the first part of the ancient Hallel from Psalms 113—115. He then directed their drinking of the second cup. After this he blessed and broke the bread, which he handed to the disciples, who ate it by dipping it into the bitter herbs and stewed fruit.[3]

It was at this stage that Jesus, "troubled in his spirit" (John 13:21), unleashed a bombshell: "And as they were reclining at table and eating, Jesus said, 'Truly, I say to you, one of you will betray me, one who is eating with me'" (v. 18). It was a horrifying announcement, especially in its final wording—"one who is eating with me," an allusion to Psalm 41:9, which speaks of the infamous treachery of Ahithophel. "There is an Ahithophel among us, one who is actually eating bread here, who acts as if he is a friend, but is really a traitor!" The disciples were aghast. They suspected no one, and especially not Judas.

We know from the other Scriptures that Judas' motivation was greed. He was the man with the adding-machine mind who instantly knew the price of Mary's spikenard ointment and was pilfering from the apostles' funds.

It seems unbelievable that one could be immersed in such a fellowship and yet living out such great evil. But actually this has a contemporary ring to it. Consider the "evangelical bank robber" William Matix, described in the April 14, 1986 *Chicago Tribune*, who killed two F.B.I. agents before he himself was gunned down. Though involved in numerous robberies, he maintained the image of a born-again Christian family man who gave testimonies in his church and was even featured in *Home Life Magazine* as an upstanding Christian example.[4]

Judas would have understood him perfectly. All one has to do is master a few *shibboleths*—say a few buzzwords with the correct inflections in the right place—and he can fool the elect.

Jesus knew in his dark hour who was going to betray him, and that the traitor would succeed. Our Lord was hardly a doll caught in the crush of history!

John tells us that "[t]he disciples looked at one another, uncertain of whom he spoke" (John 13:22). None suspected Judas, and as our text says, "They began to be sorrowful and to say to him one after another, 'Is it I?'" (v. 19). Judas, ever cool, mouthed the same words, fooling everyone but Jesus.

All Jesus would have had to do was to point at Judas and shout, "Traitor!" and Peter would have had him in a headlock before the word echoed away. Mark records Jesus' public answer: "It is one of the twelve, one who is dipping bread into the dish with me" (v. 20). "Thanks a lot, Lord," they were probably thinking, "that helps a whole bunch."

The Master was in control. In fact, he was so much in control that despite the closing doom he was reaching out to Judas in love. When he had washed the disciples' feet, he had washed Judas' feet. Moreover, while washing their feet he actually said "'And you are clean, but not every one of you.' For he knew who was to betray him; that was why he said, 'Not all of you are clean'" (John 13:10, 11). "Judas, old friend," he was saying, "you're not clean." It was a loving appeal to Judas' conscience.

Then when Jesus alluded to Psalm 41 about Ahithophel, the traitor who hung himself, he was again saying, "Judas, my friend, why not give up?

Think of what happened to Ahithophel." We know, of course, that Judas ultimately did hang himself, as did Ahithophel before him.

Even the seating arrangement demonstrated Jesus' love. He had given Judas an honored seat to his left, so that Jesus' head was just inches away from Judas' heart. Thus, they could converse without anyone hearing, a perfect opportunity to repent.

Lastly, we see that Jesus reached out to Judas to the very end. John, in his account, records some rich details: "One of his disciples, whom Jesus loved, was reclining at table at Jesus' side, so Simon Peter motioned to him to ask Jesus of whom he was speaking. So that disciple, leaning back against Jesus, said to him, 'Lord, who is it?' [the seating arrangement made it so easy. John only had to turn his head and quietly say, "who is it?"]. Jesus answered, 'It is he to whom I will give this morsel of bread when I have dipped it.' So when he had dipped the morsel, he gave it to Judas, the son of Simon Iscariot" (John 13:23–26).

What an act of love! In the culture of the day, to take a morsel from the table, dip it in the common dish, and offer it to another was a gesture of friendship. For example, when Boaz invited Ruth to fellowship with him, he said, "Come here and eat some bread and dip your morsel in the wine" (Ruth 2:14). Jesus was reaching out to Judas. Quietly, intimately, he was saying in effect, "Here is my friendship and forgiveness. All you have to do is take it, my old friend. Will you?"

But Judas took the bread without repentance, but rather in arrogance. John tells us: "Then after he had taken the morsel, Satan entered into him. Jesus said to him, 'What you are going to do, do quickly.' Now no one at the table knew why he said this to him. Some thought that, because Judas had the moneybag, Jesus was telling him, 'Buy what we need for the feast,' or that he should give something to the poor" (John 13:27–30). It was midnight for Judas' soul.

Jesus' offer was genuine. If Judas had repented, he would have remained among the Twelve, though Jesus would have gone to his death nonetheless.

Jesus is the only man who has ever been the captain of his own soul. What testimony to his mastery is his reaching out to his betrayer on the very night he would suffer so much.

With the loss of Judas sealed by his own sinful heart, with Judas exiled from the apostolic fellowship, Jesus proclaimed his sovereign control: "For the Son of Man goes as it is written of him, but woe to that man by whom the Son of Man is betrayed! It would have been better for that man if he had not been born" (v. 21). Jesus was in control, but Judas' sin was solely due to his greedy heart. Jesus' verbal epitaph was a cry of sorrow! "There is a sinning which utterly negates the good of human existence."[5]

The Master's mastery when surrounded by seemingly triumphant sin was a crowning glory. He, "The Son of Man," did "[go] as it is written of him" in such texts as Psalm 22 and Isaiah 53 and in the symbolism of the Old Testament sacrificial system. His mangled body does not dangle impotently from the wheel of the world. Rather, all history is moving toward him (Colossians 1:16). He is a Master who brings his mastery to our dark times when we see only doom around us.

> Many years ago Frederick Nolan was fleeing his enemies during the North African persecution. Hounded by his pursuers over hill and valley with no place to hide, he fell exhausted into a wayside cave expecting to be found. Awaiting his death, he saw a spider weaving a web. Within minutes, the little bug had woven a beautiful web across the mouth of the cave. The pursuers arrived and wondered if Nolan was hiding there; but they thought it impossible for him to have entered the cave without dismantling the web. And so they went on. Having escaped, Nolan emerged from his hiding place and proclaimed, "Where God is, a spider's web is like a wall. Where God is not, a wall is like a spider's web."[6]

Where is God in relation to your life? Is the wheel of your personal history in his hands? Fate will never determine the course of your life. If you follow him, you will never be crushed in the gears of history, though all Hell should assail you.

47

The Institution of the
Lord's Supper

MARK 14:22–26

THERE WERE TIMES in the ministry of the prophets of old when words were not adequate to make their point, so they resorted to dramatically symbolic actions. This was especially true of Ezekiel, who on one occasion drew a picture of Jerusalem on a clay tablet and then erected a miniature enemy camp and siege works against it (Ezekiel 4:1–3). On another occasion he had his head and beard shaved (an outrageous act in Hebrew culture) and then divided the shorn hair in three mounds. The first he burned, the second he struck with a sword, and the third he scattered to the wind to prophesy the future of Israel (Ezekiel 5:1–3). Few agreed with the prophecy, but none ever forgot the bald prophet's message.

Jeremiah made a yoke and wore it to prophesy the Babylonian Captivity (Jeremiah 27:1–7). The prophet Ahijah tore his robe into twelve pieces and gave ten pieces to Jeroboam to indicate to him that God was going to tear ten tribes from Solomon's kingdom and give them to him, thus forming the Northern Kingdom (1 Kings 11:29–33). This was why Jesus, the ultimate prophet of Israel, was in profound continuity with prophetic practice when during the celebration of the Passover feast with his disciples he dramatically reinterpreted the meal and instituted a radically new observance for his followers. Jesus combined word and symbol to maximize the communication of the most important truth for man in the universe.

Just how and when Jesus did this is apparent from the order of the Passover ritual. When the meal had been completely laid out before them, with the roast lamb as the centerpiece, the host (in this case Jesus) interpreted each of the foods on the table as it related to their deliverance from Egypt. The bitter herbs recalled their bitter slavery. The stewed fruit, by its color and consistency, recalled the misery of making bricks for Pharaoh. The roasted lamb brought to their remembrance the lamb's blood applied to the door-posts, their eating of the lamb within the house, and the death angel's passing over them as it destroyed the firstborn of Egypt.

We do not have a record of the words of Jesus' explanation, but we believe that it went beyond any ever given before this time. It prepared them for the coming words of institution. With the explanation complete, Jesus as family head sat erect from his reclining position, took a piece of the unleavened bread, and pronounced this blessing: "Praised be Thou, O Lord, Sovereign of the World, who causes bread to come forth from the earth," to which the apostles responded, "Amen."[1] Jesus then broke the bread, which was then distributed in silence from hand to hand around the table. During this silence Jesus shattered the Passover custom with the radical words recorded in verse 22 of our text: "Take; this is my body."

With this, the disciples began to soberly eat the sacred meal. The earlier prediction of intimate betrayal, and now Jesus' astounding command, left them incapable of levity. The silence was birthing an imperfect but ascending comprehension that would quickly mature in the events to come.

When the meal was complete, Jesus rose again from his reclining position and repeated the traditional charge: "Speak praises to our God, to whom belongs what we have eaten." The disciples responded, "Praise be to God for our food we have eaten." Then with his right hand he took the third cup of red wine and gazing upon the cup gave thanks: "May the all-merciful One make us worthy of the days of the Messiah and of the life of the world to come. He brings salvation of his king. He shows covenant-faithfulness to His anointed, to David and his seed forever. He makes peace in His heavenly places. May He secure peace for us and for all Israel. And you say, 'Amen.'"[2] Then in silence Jesus passed the common cup with the words of verse 24: "This is my blood of the covenant, which is poured out for many."

There was prophetic continuity in Jesus' graphic use of the bread and the cup, and immensely powerful communication. Paul tells us in 1 Corinthians 11:24, 25 that Jesus instituted his graphic observance for all time as a "remembrance" of himself. This remembrance is meant to convey to all an increasing understanding of the mystery of Christ and the atonement he provided.

We ought always to keep in mind that the Lord's Table is an *acted parable* and to consider what we are proclaiming through the parable. First, what do Jesus' solemn words, "Take; this is my body" (v. 22) mean?

The Meaning of the Bread (v. 22)

To begin with, Jesus was not saying that the bread was *literally* his body, and thereby teaching the Roman Catholic Church's doctrine of Transubstantiation. Some medieval theologians met all challenges against Transubstantiation by pounding their fists and quoting the Latin Vulgate (*hoc est corpus meum*—"This is my body") and arguing that this is the plain sense of Christ's words. But the Jews, with their prophetic legacy of parabolic acts and language and their customary symbolic expression, understood that Christ was speaking *figuratively*.

What did the figure mean? In a word, bread referred to the life of Christ. In the Incarnation at Bethlehem ("City of Bread"), Christ, the Bread of Life, took on a human body. He demonstrated his divine life to all the world by living a sinless life in that *body*. He bore our sins on the cross while in that human *body*. He triumphed from the grave by bringing that *body* back to life, and he now lives in that glorified *body* at the right hand of the Father where he prays for us. As members of his *Body* we share that life. This is why Paul says in 1 Corinthians 10:16, "The bread that we break, is it not a participation in the body [i.e., life] of Christ?" Thus, through the bread we see Jesus' incarnation, death, and resurrection life. Our partaking of the bread *symbolizes our real participation in his life!* If we are believers, we all partake of the life (the body) of Christ. This is what the bread means to us.

The bread also means that we participate in each other's lives. Paul goes on to say in 1 Corinthians 10:17, "Because there is one bread [Christ], we who are many are one body, for we all partake of the one bread." So the second earthly benefit of the bread, in addition to underscoring our participation in Christ's life, is sharing in the lives of one another. The Lord's Table promotes the communion of the saints. Celebrating this, Stephen Olford's father used to say as he greeted his friends after the Communion service, "Good morning, brother (or sister), I have already met you in the bread."

So what are we announcing to the world around us as we take the bread? That we are partakers in the life of Christ—that we really have received and are participating in that life. We are also proclaiming that by virtue of being partakers of his body, we participate in the life of one another. There is something organic, life-giving in the bread of the Table. Our partaking is not only an announcement, but an invitation to partake. It is meant to make those around us hungry.

The Meaning of the Cup (vv. 23, 24)

What was the meaning of Jesus' pronouncement in verse 24: "This is my blood of the covenant, which is poured out for many"? The redness of the wine in the cup represented Jesus' atoning blood. Being "poured out for many" is an allusion to Isaiah 53:12, which speaks of Messiah as one who "poured out his soul to death." This described a violent death. "Many" referred to those who would benefit from his atoning death. His blood was the blood of a *new* covenant (1 Corinthians 11:25). The old covenant of the Law at Sinai was solemnized by the shedding of sacrificial blood (Exodus 24:6–8). Jesus' blood sealed the new covenant, whereby men, women, and children would be saved by resting their faith in his atoning blood.

With the bones of the Passover on the table and the aroma of sacrifice in the air, Jesus' words confirmed the prophetic declaration that he was "the Lamb of God, who takes away the sin of the world!" (John 1:29).

The cup is meant to drive home to us who believe the *objective* fact of our redemption as those who partake and share fellowship in the blood of Christ. Jesus shed his blood for our sins!

The benefit of holding the cup before us, in the words of John Calvin, is: "The godly ought by all means to keep this rule: whenever they see the symbols . . . to think and be persuaded that the truth is surely present there. For why should the Lord put in your hand the symbol of His [blood], except to assure you of a true participation in it?"[3] In other words, as we take the cup we will benefit most by saying in our hearts, "Yes, I really am forgiven" and resting in the objective fact.

The Demand of the Bread and the Cup (John 6:53–56)

The reality these symbols so powerfully portray makes exacting demands upon us in regard to the depth of our belief. Earlier in Jesus' ministry, in his Bread of Life Discourse, Jesus gave us one of his "hard sayings," undoubtedly anticipating the Lord's Table:

> So Jesus said to them, "Truly, truly, I say to you, unless you eat the flesh of the Son of Man and drink his blood, you have no life in you. Whoever feeds on my flesh and drinks my blood has eternal life, and I will raise him up on the last day. For my flesh is true food, and my blood is true drink. Whoever feeds on my flesh and drinks my blood abides in me, and I in him." (John 6:53–56)

Jesus, of course, was speaking figuratively about belief. As St. Augustine commented: "*Crede, et manducasti*"—"Believe and you have eaten."[4] The great emphasis of Christ's hard saying was that having eternal life involves a real partaking of him through faith, which can best be understood by the indelicate metaphor of ingesting his body and blood. Christ's choice of words dramatized this idea because in verse 54 the word for feeds in "Whoever feeds on my flesh . . ." was a vulgar word that indicated a somewhat noisy feeding—"munching" or "crunching."[5] It was a startling word that emphasized the need for truly partaking of Christ. "He who crunches my flesh . . ."

We must truly feed on Christ or there is no life, regardless of what we say. To those who have not yet believed on Christ, this hard saying demands that he be as real to them spiritually as something they can eat.

At the risk of sounding impious: he must be as *real* and *useful* to us as a hamburger and french fries. Is he that real to you? For too many people he is far less.

The metaphor also tells us that *Christ is absolutely indispensable.* Bread was the staple of life in those days. Spiritually it is impossible to live without Christ. He is our bread (John 6:51), our all, our everything.

Dr. Charles Malik, one-time Secretary-General of the United Nations, once proclaimed from the steps of the Billy Graham Center, Wheaton College: "I can live without food, without drink, without sleep, without air, but I cannot live without Jesus." That is what the Church proclaims to itself and to those outside.

Through the divinely instituted parable of the Lord's Table we proclaim the following: *Our sin*—that apart from the redemptive blood of Christ we are eternally separated from God and lost. *Our faith*—that we believe in the death, resurrection, exaltation, and bodily return of Christ. *Our dependence*—that without him we cannot live and dare not die. *Our hope*—that Jesus' words in verse 25 of our text are certainly true: "Truly, I say to you, I will not drink again of the fruit of the vine until that day when I drink it new in the kingdom of God." This expresses Jesus' eager anticipation of the messianic banquet when the Passover fellowship with his children will be renewed in the kingdom of God.

48

Steeling the Church

MARK 14:27–40

WHEN I HEAR inexperienced believers confidently assert they will follow Christ come what may, I have feelings of both pleasure and concern. They have experienced new life in Christ, forgiveness, release from guilt, expansive joy. So it is natural to say, "I know where I have come from, and I'm not going back." As a pastor, such talk gives me a thrill. But it also fills me with apprehension because it is naive. A picture comes to my mind of Dorothy and the Tin Man skipping down the road gaily singing, "I have decided to follow Jesus . . . no turning back, no turning back." Naive presumption that one can follow Christ by the simple assertion of the will invites a rude awakening. I am much more comfortable when I hear a neophyte say, "I know I can't do it alone, but by God's grace I'm going to do my best."

Presumption has always been dangerous for anyone who follows Christ, for following him necessarily involves some hardship. Many are those who have fallen along the way. That is why Jesus invited Peter, James, and John to be with him while he prayed in Gethsemane. Not long before that night, James and John, "Sons of Thunder," had confidently answered Jesus that they had it in themselves to drink from the cup he would drink (10:38–40). Then, with the crucifixion only hours away, Peter had loudly proclaimed, "Even though they all fall away, I will not" (14:29). This was perilous talk indeed, as the next couple of days would so tragically demonstrate. What they saw that night in the garden would steel them for the years to come. And prayerfully considered, it will steel us for the years to come.

The Steeling of Jesus (vv. 32–35)

"And they went to a place called Gethsemane. And he said to his disciples, 'Sit here while I pray.' And he took with him Peter and James and John, and began to be greatly distressed and troubled. And he said to them, 'My soul is very sorrowful, even to death. Remain here and watch'" (vv. 32–34).

The name *Gethsemane* means "oil press." Scholars surmise that the garden was probably owned by a wealthy acquaintance of Jesus. It was a walled orchard on the side of the Mount of Olives and contained its own olive press. Here Jesus left the body of disciples near the entrance and took the three farther up on the property, where he underwent a stress of cosmic dimensions, the greatest in the chronicles of the universe.

The words "greatly distressed" bear the element of astonishment.[1] Or as one commentator put it, "terrified surprise."[2] The *King James Version* suggests the same in its rendering, "sore amazed." Jesus, of course, knew the cross was coming and what it entailed. But as he looked into the cup he must drink that night, he was astonished and overcome with horror. No human being, however great his or her anguish, has ever experienced anything like this!

Peter, James, and John saw the Master's horrified astonishment and heard his pathetic self-revelation: "My soul is very sorrowful, even to death." This is difficult for us to fathom, but it was a sorrow that threatened life itself.[3] *Impossible!* we may think. That is because we are not as holy as he, nor can we imagine the terrors he saw in the cup. We are called to believe God's Word: Jesus came close to death as the horror overwhelmed him.

Mark takes us even deeper into this terror-filled mystery: "And going a little farther, he fell on the ground and prayed that, if it were possible, the hour might pass from him. And he said, 'Abba, Father, all things are possible for you. Remove this cup from me. Yet not what I will, but what you will'" (vv. 35, 36).

The inner circle saw Jesus fall prostrate to the ground.[4] From the other Gospels we piece together that he went first to his knees (Luke 22:41) and then on his face (Matthew 26:39). There he prayed repeatedly the substance of his prayer in our text—and it was not in a whisper! Hebrews 5:7 refers to this instance, saying, "In the days of his flesh, Jesus offered up prayers and supplications, with loud cries and tears, to him who was able to save him from death." Jesus was only a stone's throw from the three (Luke 22:41). They could see his prostrate form convulse, and they could see his tears and the sweat falling to the ground like drops of blood (Luke 22:44).

This was an amazing revelation. But even more amazing (in the light of redemptive history) was what he prayed. He was repeatedly asking that if possible, the "hour," the "cup" (metaphors for his death) might be avoided! How could he desire something contrary to the Father's will? Jesus was truly God and man. As a man he had a human will—and voluntarily limited knowledge. His prayer was not to do something other than the Father's will, but he did pray that if there was a possibility of fulfilling his messianic mission without the cross, he would opt for that. As a man Christ cried for escape, but he desired the Father's will even more.

John Calvin quotes Cyril of Alexandria: "You see that death was not voluntary for Christ as far as the flesh was concerned, but it was voluntary, because by it, according to the will of the Father, salvation and life were given to all men."[5]

Christ asked that the cup be taken away because he was truly man as well as God. We must also realize that his request for another way came from the two things he saw in the cup.

First, *it was a cup full of sin*. He saw all the brutality of a thousand "Killing Fields"—all the whoring of earthly civilizations—blasphemy—profanity—a cup brimming with jealousy, hatred, and covetousness—*which he must drink!* And Jesus recoiled!

Second, he saw that *it was a cup full of wrath*. As sin-bearer, he became the object of the Father's holy wrath against sin. "For our sake he made him to be sin who knew no sin, so that in him we might become the righteousness of God" (2 Corinthians 5:21). The drinking also made him a curse. Galatians 3:13 says, "Christ redeemed us from the curse of the law by becoming a curse for us—for it is written, 'Cursed is everyone who is hanged on a tree.'" Gazing into the cup, Jesus saw Hell opened for him, and he staggered (cf. Isaiah 51:17, 22). It is no wonder that we see the bloodlike sweat and the tears, that we hear him crying out for deliverance. It is no wonder, as we read in Luke, that the Father sent an angel to strengthen him (Luke 22:43).

In all of this anguish there was unconditional submission. Doing the Father's will had been his supreme concern in life. Coming of age he said, "Did you not know that I must be in my Father's house?" (Luke 2:49). Early in his ministry he said, "My food is to do the will of him who sent me and to accomplish his work" (John 4:34). We also read: "For I have come down from heaven, not to do my own will but the will of him who sent me" (John 6:38); "No one takes it from me, but I lay it down of my own accord. I have authority to lay it down, and I have authority to take it up again" (John 10:18).

Such supreme concern with doing the Father's will culminated in this amazing act of submission. The writer of Hebrews sums it up with this triumphant passage:

In the days of his flesh, Jesus offered up prayers and supplications, with loud cries and tears, to him who was able to save him from death, and he was heard because of his reverence. Although he was a son, he learned obedience through what he suffered. And being made perfect, he became the source of eternal salvation to all who obey him. (Hebrews 5:7–9)

In the greatest display of obedience that will ever be known, Jesus took the full chalice of man's sin and God's wrath, looked, shuddering, deep into its depth, and in a steel act of his will drank it all!

What was it that steeled Jesus? From earth's level it was his life of dependent prayer! There are three recorded instances of Jesus in prayer in Mark (1:35, 6:46, and here). The similarity of the setting (night, solitude, demonic pressures) and the positioning of the passages at the beginning, in the middle, and at the end tell us that Mark saw these events as fundamental to understanding Jesus.[6] Without the vibrant discipline of prayer, Jesus, the Son of God, would never have made it. If the actual Son of God needed a life of dependent prayer to fulfill God's will, how much more do we adopted sons and daughters need it. It is this reality that brings us to the steeling of the disciples.

The Steeling of the Disciples (vv. 34b, 37–42)

We must understand that Jesus invited the inner circle to be with him in Gethsemane not because he needed company, but because they needed to learn (especially with their presumption) the secret of steeling their lives for service. The scandal of their failure that night could not be suppressed and underlines the necessity of what Jesus was teaching for the Church Universal.

Verse 34b shows that when Jesus was overtaken with the horror, he told them, "Remain here and watch." He wanted them to observe his battle. Luke tells us that he even stated the reason: "Pray that you may not enter into temptation" (Luke 22:40). If they had watched closely and entered into prayer like his, they would have found the steel necessary to make it through what was coming. They did watch for a little while, but then shamefully dozed off despite the mortal, noisy combat and suffering of Christ. Jesus desired so much that they learn from him that in the midst of his unparalleled agony he returned twice more to look after his three weak followers.

When he first returned, he singled out the most vocal of the three, Peter. "And he came and found them sleeping, and he said to Peter, 'Simon, are you asleep? Could you not watch one hour? Watch and pray that you may not enter into temptation. The spirit indeed is willing, but the flesh is weak'" (vv. 37, 38). There was kindness here. Jesus understood human weakness, but they must pray or they would fall. Mark says, "And again he went away and prayed, saying the same words. And again he came and found them sleeping, for their eyes were very heavy, and they did not know what to answer him" (vv. 39, 40). Finally we read: "And he came the third time and said to them, 'Are you still sleeping and taking your rest? It is enough; the hour has come. The Son of Man is betrayed into the hands of sinners. Rise, let us be going; see, my betrayer is at hand'" (vv. 41, 42).

Jesus, who so steeled himself in prayer while asking that "the hour might pass from him," accepted it, saying, "The hour has come" and went out to drink the cup and win the greatest victory ever won. The disciples all failed, and significantly Peter, who fell asleep three times, went on to deny his Lord by that same number—hardly a poetic coincidence! But all was not lost. Their scandal was to become their salvation because in the years to come all came to steel their lives in prayer. Peter and James died martyrs' deaths, and John was a man of steel who endured to the end.

The lessons are here if we wish to see them.

The Steeling of the Church

It begins with this: if we truly follow Christ, we will experience our own personal Gethsemanes. Jesus said:

> If the world hates you, know that it has hated me before it hated you. If you were of the world, the world would love you as its own; but because you are not of the world, but I chose you out of the world, therefore the world hates you. Remember the word that I said to you: "A servant is not greater than his master." If they persecuted me, they will also persecute you. If they kept my word, they will also keep yours. (John 15:18–20)

All paths that are, or shall be,
Pass somewhere through Gethsemane.

Joy and woe are woven fine,
A clothing for the soul divine,
Under every grief and pine
Runs a joy with silken twine.

It is right, it should be so.
Man was made for grief and woe.
And when this we rightly know
Through the world we safely go.[7]

Gethsemanes are the inevitable lot of those who follow Christ. We must embrace this truth.

But there is a steeling available for all who go through the inevitable Gethsemanes. It comes through dependent prayer. Such prayer sometimes delivers us *from* our Gethsemanes, but more often *through* them. The Father heard Jesus' cry and answered his prayer, and he was crucified. Whatever the answer, there is always steel for God's children.

The application is simply this: all of us should give ourselves to regular, daily prayer. If you are not living a life of dependent prayer, you are sinning. You cannot and will not have the steel necessary to follow Christ.

As one example: men, you who are fathers should be praying daily *in detail* for your spouse and each of your children (cf. Job 1:5). If you are not doing so, you are sinning. There is more: if the only time you pray for the ill or the grieving or the needy in your local church body is during the Sunday pastoral prayer, you are sinning (cf. 1 Samuel 12:23). We are all called to daily, dependent prayer—all of us!

The call to prayer is a call to discipline. Unfortunately, many reject this idea. They argue that such thinking promotes legalism. But there is an eternity of difference between legalism and discipline. Legalism has at its core the thought of becoming better and thus gaining merit through religious exercise. Discipline springs from a desire to please God. Paul, an outspoken opponent of legalism, admonishes us to ". . . discipline [literally gymnasticize] yourself for the purpose of godliness" (1 Timothy 4:7 NASB). God's servants must exercise themselves with an athletic-like discipline as they pursue God's purposes for their lives. There will be no prayer life without this.

As we all know, this is not always easy! How can we discipline ourselves to pray? Helpfully, Dr. J. Sidlow Baxter once shared his own pastoral diary with a group of pastors who asked just this question. He began by telling how in 1928 he entered the ministry determined that he would be the "most Methodist-Baptist" of pastors, a real man of prayer. However, it was not long until his increasing pastoral responsibilities, administrative duties, and the subtle subterfuges of pastoral life began to crowd prayer out. He began to get used to it, making excuses for himself.

Then one morning a crisis came as he stood over his work-strewn desk and looked at his watch. The voice of the Spirit was calling him to pray. At the same time another velvety voice told him to be practical and get his letters answered—he ought to face up to the fact that he was not of the spiritual sort, that only a few people could be like that. That did it! "That last remark," said Baxter, "hurt like a dagger blade, I could not bear to think it was true."

He was horrified by his ability to rationalize away the very ground of his ministerial vitality and power. That morning Sidlow Baxter took a good look into his heart, and he found there was a part of him that did not want to pray and a part that did. The part that didn't was his emotions, and the part that did was his intellect and will. This analysis paved the way to victory. In Dr. Baxter's own inimitable words:

As never before, my will and I stood face to face. I asked my will the straight question, "Will, are you ready for an hour of prayer?" Will answered, "Here I am, and I'm quite ready, if you are." So Will and I linked arms, and turned to go for our time of prayer. At once all the emotions began pulling the other way and protesting, "We're not coming." I saw Will stagger just a bit, so I asked, "Can you stick it out, Will?" and Will replied, "Yes, if you can." So Will went, and we got down to prayer, dragging those wriggling, obstreperous emotions with us. It was a struggle all the way through. At one point, when Will and I were in the middle of an earnest intercession, I suddenly found one of those traitorous emotions had snared my imagination and had ran off to the golf course; and it was all I could do to drag the wicked rascal back. A bit later I found another of the emotions had sneaked away with some off-guard thoughts and was in the pulpit, two days ahead of schedule, preaching a sermon that I had not yet finished preparing!

At the end of that hour, if you had asked me, "Have you had a good time?" I would have had to reply, "No, it has been a wearying wrestle with contrary emotions and a truant imagination from beginning to end." What is more, that battle with the emotions continued for between two and three weeks, and if you had asked me at the end of that period, "Have you had a 'good time' in your daily praying?" I would have had to confess, "No, at times it has seemed as though the heavens were brass, and God too distant to hear, and the Lord Jesus strangely aloof, and prayer accomplishing nothing."

Yet something was happening. For one thing, Will and I really taught the emotions that we were completely independent of them. Also, one morning, about two weeks after the contest began, just when Will and I were going for another time of prayer, I overheard one of the emotions whisper to the other, "Come on, you guys, it's no use wasting any more time resisting: they'll go just the same." That morning, for the first time, even though the emotions were still suddenly uncooperative, they were at least quiescent, which allowed Will and me to get on with prayer undistractedly.

Then, another couple of weeks later, what do you think happened? During one of our prayer times, when Will and I were no more thinking of the emotions than of the man in the moon, one of the most vigorous of the emotions unexpectedly sprang up and shouted, "Hallelujah!" at which all the other emotions exclaimed, "Amen!" And for the first time the whole of my being—intellect, will, and emotions—was united in one coordinated prayer-operation. All at once, God was real, heaven was open, the Lord

Jesus was luminously present, the Holy Spirit was indeed moving through my longings, and prayer was surprisingly vital. Moreover, in that instant there came a sudden realization that heaven had been watching and listening all the way through those days of struggle against chilling moods and mutinous emotions; also that I had been undergoing necessary tutoring by my heavenly Teacher.[8]

We know that the Holy Spirit prompts us to pray, even making intercession for us. But we also know there is our part. We are called to be fellow workers with God. "Therefore, my beloved . . . work out your own salvation with fear and trembling, for it is God who works in you, both to will and to work for his good pleasure" (Philippians 2:12, 13). This requires discipline.

We can hear a thousand sermons preached about the secret to the Christian life, but it gets right down to our own discipline. If we do not have that, we are sinning. All of us need to live lives of dependent prayer, that there might be steel in our soul—the steeling of the church.

49

The Betrayal of Jesus

MARK 14:41–52

JESUS STAGGERED IN GETHSEMANE as he gazed into the cup he must drink, for taking it meant he would drink man's *sin* to the full and would drink the *wrath* of God that man's sin deserved. Casting himself to the ground in passionate night-long prayer empowered our Lord Jesus to go in sovereign submission to meet death. The struggle in Gethsemane ended with Jesus admonishing his sleepy disciples, "It is enough; the hour has come. The Son of Man is betrayed into the hands of sinners. Rise, let us be going; see, my betrayer is at hand" (vv. 41, 42). From here on, Jesus' steeled humanity willingly took all that our sin could heap on him.

Jesus' Sovereign Submission in Judas' Betrayal (vv. 43–46)

And immediately, while he was still speaking, Judas came, one of the twelve, and with him a crowd with swords and clubs, from the chief priests and the scribes and the elders. Now the betrayer had given them a sign, saying, "The one I will kiss is the man. Seize him and lead him away under guard." And when he came, he went up to him at once and said, "Rabbi!" And he kissed him. And they laid hands on him and seized him. (vv. 43–46)

This was the consummation of Judas' own diabolical scheming. His motivation, according to Scripture, was naked greed, for he was a thief who had been regularly pilfering from their common purse (John 12:5, 6). When his profit-motivated heart saw that Jesus' kingdom plans would not result in his personal gain, he arranged to sell the Savior to the authorities at a time when he could be taken alone and there would be no chance of riot (Mark 14:1, 10, 11). The identifying kiss was agreed upon as a fail-safe method in the shadowy darkness of the garden.

It was the middle of a spring night. The Passover moon was full. It was probably cloudless, for it was a cold night (John 18:18). The ancient olive trees were casting eerie shadows across the encampment. Beyond the ravine lay the sparse, scattered lights of Jerusalem where Judas had earlier made his rendezvous with a detachment from the Roman cohort (Matthew 26:47). The soldiers were fully armed, each carrying a short sword. With them came the Jewish temple guards with their clubs. Jews and Gentiles were united for once in a common cause. It must have been a chilling sight from Gethsemane as the mob exited Jerusalem and its flickering torches moved down to the Kidron and up the slopes of Olivet. The plan was perfect. There would be no riot on this night, and if there was resistance they were more than ready.

It appears that as Jesus saw the mob approaching Gethsemane, he led Peter, James, and John to the place where the remaining disciples were sleeping, near the garden's entrance. He roused them and then protectively stepped out in front to meet the soldiers. This is where the infamous kiss took place. The infamy is in this: the word used for "kiss" here is not the usual word (*phileo*), but an intensive form (*kataphileo*), which the Greek lexicon defines as "to kiss fervently, kiss affectionately."[1] The careful scholar Cranfield sees it as a prolonged kiss.[2] It is the kind of kiss one gives to someone one loves. Judas' kiss drips with horror, for it is a calloused prostitution of one of humanity's most sacred symbols. Judas' act was a deicide (a god-killer) and a suicide, for Judas was dying at his own hand. There was Hell there. George Herbert expresses the horror:

> Judas, doest thou betray me with a kisse?
> Canst thou find hell about my lips, and misse
> of life just at the gates of life and blisse?

Judas' infamous kiss showed how low a human heart can go.

Jesus' response was just the opposite, for it showed how high a heart can soar. The depth of Jesus' hurt was given prophetic expression by King David: "For it is not an enemy who taunts me—then I could bear it; it is not an adversary who deals insolently with me—then I could hide from him. But it is you, a man, my equal, my companion, my familiar friend. We used to take sweet counsel together; within God's house we walked in the throng" (Psalm 55:12–14). Betrayal is always terrible, but when it comes with a kiss, from a supposed friend, it is especially horrible. Yet there was no rejection from Jesus! No "You foul me, Judas! Get away!" Rather, Matthew tells us he said, "Friend, do what you came to do" (Matthew 26:50). Jesus did not just *say*, "Love your enemies and pray for those who persecute you" (Matthew 5:44)—he lived it.

This is what a life that has been steeled in prayer and submitted to the will of God can do. This betrayal was easily the most hurtful and grievous in human history, but Jesus was not conquered by it, nor was he taken captive by personal hatred. In fact, by calling Judas "friend," he was still reaching out to him. Here we must not be easy on ourselves with facile rationalizations about him being divine and us human. *We are called to do the same thing.* Have we ever been betrayed? Even worse, has it been with a kiss? Do we feel that we are entitled to hatred? *Jesus says we are not!* Moreover, his example teaches that if we steel ourselves in prayer and submission, we can even reach out to the offender.

Jesus' Sovereign Submission in Arrest (vv. 46–52)

And they laid hands on him and seized him. But one of those who stood by drew his sword and struck the servant of the high priest and cut off his ear. And Jesus said to them, "Have you come out as against a robber, with swords and clubs to capture me? Day after day I was with you in the temple teaching, and you did not seize me. But let the Scriptures be fulfilled." And they all left him and fled. (vv. 46–50)

The other Gospels give us supplementary details. After Judas' long fervent kiss, Jesus "came forward and said to them, 'Whom do you seek?' They answered him, 'Jesus of Nazareth.' Jesus said to them, 'I am he.' Judas, who betrayed him, was standing with them. When Jesus said to them, 'I am he,' they drew back and fell to the ground" (John 18:4–6).

I do not agree with those who say the mob fell to the ground as a result of Jesus' "moral force." The Roman soldiers knew nothing of Jesus and had no reason to fear or even respect him. Also note that they did not fall down when he asked what they wanted, but only when he said, "I am he," or literally, "I am." John represents this as a miracle. The fact is, Jesus answered in the style of Deity, using the divine predicate "I am," which goes back to the burning bush (Exodus 3) when God said, "I AM WHO I AM."

The message to the Church and to the world is that in Jesus' sovereign submission to arrest, *he was in charge!* The real arrestees were in the mob! For a few moments the action was fast and furious. The mob regained its footing and moved to take Jesus. This was too much for Peter. Out came his hidden sword, and he lunged at Malchus, the high priest's servant (John 18:10). His sword came down hard on Malchus' helmet and bounced down the right side, lopping off his right ear. Imagine the pounding tension as

Malchus stood wide-eyed, blood pouring through his fingers as a hundred steel blades rang from their scabbards in terrible symphony.

Peter's rash action had the potential for destroying the Church. Calvin comments: "No thanks to him that Christ was not kept from death and that His name was not a perpetual disgrace."[3] How easy it is to be out of step with Christ when we think we are serving him, even defending him.

This was the sad case in the dispute between two prominent nineteenth-century preachers, Newman Smith and Robert Hall. A controversy arose between the two on some religious point, and Rev. Smith wrote a bitter pamphlet denouncing Hall and his doctrine. Having finished the pamphlet, Smith was having trouble coming up with what he thought was a proper title. So he sent the book to a good friend (everyone needs a friend like this!) for a suggestion. Some time earlier Rev. Smith had written a widely read and helpful pamphlet entitled, *Come to Jesus*. When his friend read the new pamphlet against Hall, he sent the pamphlet back with this suggestion: "The title which I suggest for your pamphlet is this, 'Go to Hell' by the author of 'Come to Jesus.'"[4]

Chopped off any ears lately? Is there some blood on the ground due to a blow you have self-righteously (and wrongly!) inflicted? If so, then submit to Christ and do what he says. Dr. Luke tells us that Jesus answered Peter, "'No more of this!' And he touched [Malchus'] ear and healed him" (Luke 22:51). The Lord specializes in restoring lopped-off ears as we see our error and repent. Healing can come to the hurt we have caused.

Having healed Malchus, Jesus injected some spiritual reality into the situation. Matthew records his wisdom: "Put your sword back into its place. For all who take the sword will perish by the sword. Do you think that I cannot appeal to my Father, and he will at once send me more than twelve legions of angels?" (Matthew 26:52, 53). Since the full Roman legion was six thousand, he could have called six thousand for each of the eleven and six thousand for himself—seventy-two thousand angels.

This has vast personal application to all of us who are the Father's children and joint-heirs with Christ. As Calvin well said: "We turn our minds this way and that, as if there were no angels in heaven . . . thereby we lose their aid. Those who are forced by restlessness or excessive worry to put out their hands to forbidden measures against trouble are certainly renouncing the providence of God."[5] How many times have we thwarted the work of God on our behalf because of fleshly measures? May the Lord help us to learn to seek his will before we speak or act to solve a situation.

Our text ends with Jesus' arrest, his bowing to the word and will of God, and his abandonment.

And Jesus said to them, "Have you come out as against a robber, with swords and clubs to capture me? Day after day I was with you in the temple teaching, and you did not seize me. But let the Scriptures be fulfilled." And they all left him and fled. And a young man followed him, with nothing but a linen cloth about his body. And they seized him, but he left the linen cloth and ran away naked. (vv. 48–52)

Most scholars (all ten I consulted) believe that the young man was probably John Mark, the writer of this Gospel. They surmise that, as tradition suggests, the Passover meal had been eaten in the upper room of his family home, which became a prominent gathering-place for Jesus' followers (Acts 12:12). When Jesus and the Eleven went out to the Mount of Olives, Mark hastily dressed in only a linen garment. (Mark undoubtedly had been an eyewitness to Gethsemane. Hence the intimate details.) Poor Mark was almost grabbed by the mob, escaping *au naturel* in the night. But while there is much that can be said about John Mark, his point is simply this: *Jesus was absolutely alone as he submitted himself to the cross.*

The steeling of Jesus through prayer in Gethsemane wrought the most amazing results in his life.

> He went forth intrepidly to meet his end.
> He received the terrible kiss of betrayal, and responded with love.
> He submitted to the arrest of the mob.
> He refused the exercise of natural strength.
> He depended upon the Father and his angels.
> He did it all alone.

As partakers of the life of Christ, we must realize there is only one acceptable posture—submission to him who gave himself for us.

> Death and the curse were in that cup,
> Oh Christ, 'twas full for thee;
> But Thou hast drained the last dark dregs,
> 'Tis empty now for me.

But while we are not to drink that cup, we are to live in dependent submission to him, responding in love as he did. Are we loving those who have wronged us? Or has our sword been drawn, inflicting its own wrongful wounds? If so, we need to appropriate the mind of Christ.

50

The Two Rocks

MARK 14:53–72

STUDYING MARK'S WRITING CLOSELY brings an increasing appreciation of his theological artistry as we repeatedly observe the great skill with which he wove the events of Christ's life together to make his point and to minister to the suffering church at Rome, to which he was writing. Here Mark's Gospel is especially brilliant as he contrasts the failure of one man, Peter, with the steadfastness of the Son of Man, Christ, in order to teach the Early Church what was necessary to succeed in an inhospitable world. Mark first mentioned Peter in verse 54, then described Jesus' unflinching stand before the Sanhedrin in verses 55–65, and then turned back to Peter in verses 66–72 to record his failure. This is skillful writing.

The artistry is especially memorable because the contrast is between two rocks. Christ the Rock, "the spiritual Rock" that accompanied Israel in the wilderness (1 Corinthians 10:4) and is now the "foundation" of the Church (1 Corinthians 3:11), remains unmoved. The other rock is Peter, *Petros* (Rock), so named by Christ. For the moment he is seen crumbling under the pressures brought on by being identified as one of Jesus' followers. This provides an instructive contrast, a contrast that is relevant for anyone who is swimming against the tide of culture or who wishes to do so.

Mark framed the scene with a brief introduction: "And they led Jesus to the high priest. And all the chief priests and the elders and the scribes came together. And Peter had followed him at a distance, right into the courtyard of the high priest. And he was sitting with the guards and warming himself at the fire" (vv. 53, 54). When the disciples fled Gethsemane, Jesus was bound and led across the Passover-bloodstained Kidron back up to Jerusalem, where he was first taken to the home of the ex-high priest, Annas (John

18:13). After this, Jesus was led to the home of Caiaphas, the present high priest (Matthew 26:57).

It was already past midnight, but the Sanhedrin came flocking in by torchlight from every corner of the city. Jesus was placed in the middle of a sizable torch-lit hall. The Sanhedrin, seventy in number, took their places in an elevated semicircle around Jesus. To the left and the right were court clerks, prepared to take notes on the evidence submitted.

Presiding was Joseph Caiaphas, high priest and president of the Sanhedrin. He was an unusually powerful high priest who would serve for nineteen years, far beyond the average term of four years. His surname, "Caiaphas" or "inquisitor,"[1] fit him well, as he was now presiding over the most infamous inquisition in history. Though the assembly had all the trappings of a legal proceeding, it was not legal, for according to its own rules it was not to make final judgments at night, nor was it to do so outside its sacred chambers in the temple, nor was a capital offense to be determined during Passover—to name just a few illegalities. Nevertheless, they began their charade, looking first for the unanimous evidence from two witnesses that was necessary for conviction of a capital offense.

Meanwhile Peter, having sufficiently recovered from his humiliating dash from Gethsemane, had managed to enter Caiaphas' courtyard unnoticed among the flood of guests. We must note here that although he had fled the garden, Peter was still committed to making good his word that he would never forsake Jesus (Mark 14:29). Thus he was consciously in the courtyard at great risk. Just an hour before, he had drawn his sword before the whole mob and lopped off Malchus' ear. His face was well-known even before that event, but now it would be indelible in the memory of many. Peter was placing himself in great danger. He may have blown it, but no more.

Significantly, Mark tells us that he was "warming himself at the fire" (or literally, "toward the light"), so that his face was illumined by the dancing blaze. Peter would surely be recognized. Mark has set the stage for his brilliant contrast—essential teaching for the urban church in unfriendly Rome.

Christ: The Solid Rock (vv. 55–65)

The Sanhedrin began by trying to convict Jesus on the testimony of others. Mark records:

> Now the chief priests and the whole council were seeking testimony against Jesus to put him to death, but they found none. For many bore false witness against him, but their testimony did not agree. And some stood up and

bore false witness against him, saying, "We heard him say, 'I will destroy this temple that is made with hands, and in three days I will build another, not made with hands.'" Yet even about this their testimony did not agree. (vv. 55–59)

Early in Jesus' career, he said, "Destroy this temple, and in three days I will raise it up" (John 2:19). The Jews thought he was speaking of Herod's temple, when actually he was referring to his body. This misinterpretation could have earned him a capital conviction, for a mere threat against the temple appears to have been punishable by death. Years before, when Jeremiah had prophesied the destruction of the temple, he was arrested and brought before the royal court as a criminal deserving death (Jeremiah 26:1–19).

Even though they had the best witnesses money could buy, those who lied without a twinge of conscience, the testimonies were not in harmony. It is hard to lie in concert, much harder than telling the truth. They were getting nowhere. Jesus had not uttered a word, and he was winning. Anger and frustration darkened the Sanhedrin's already glowering faces. Some heads were going to roll.

Embarrassed and furious, the inquisitor, Caiaphas, approached the silent Lord. "'Have you no answer to make? What is it that these men testify against you?' But he remained silent and made no answer" (vv. 60, 61a). In regal silence Jesus refused to dignify the contradicting testimony with a response. "He was oppressed, and he was afflicted," said Isaiah, "yet he opened not his mouth; like a lamb that is led to the slaughter, and like a sheep that before its shearers is silent, so he opened not his mouth" (Isaiah 53:7).

Caiaphas was at his wit's end. Matthew says that he put Jesus under oath by the living God (Matthew 26:63) when he asked, "Are you the Christ, the Son of the Blessed?" (v. 61). Caiaphas was asking him two questions: if he was the Messiah, and if he was God, for "the Blessed" is used exclusively in the New Testament for God.[2]

Jesus did not have to answer, but now was the chosen time. "I am," said Jesus, and as their mouths dropped in surprised pleasure he said, "and you will see the Son of Man seated at the right hand of Power, and coming with the clouds of heaven" (v. 62). It was both a confession and a terrible warning, alluding to three Old Testament messianic passages to tell them that he was their coming Judge! Isaiah 52:8 says, "for eye to eye they see the return of the LORD to Zion." Psalm 110:1 adds, "The LORD says to my Lord: 'Sit at my right hand, until I make your enemies your footstool.'" Daniel 7:13 records, "I saw in the night visions, and behold, with the clouds of heaven there came one like a son of man, and he came to the Ancient of Days and was presented before him."

"You are judging me, but I will judge you," Jesus was saying. These were his only words to the leadership of Israel, and they were terrible. But the Sanhedrin did not have ears to hear.

In a contrived expression of horror and indignation, "the high priest [Caiaphas] tore his garments and said, 'What further witnesses do we need? You have heard his blasphemy. What is your decision?' And they all condemned him as deserving death. And some began to spit on him and to cover his face and to strike him, saying to him, 'Prophesy!' And the guards received him with blows" (vv. 63–65).

Souls were tumbling in darkness. There was damnation and Hell in that room. They condemned their Messiah to death. Some of the venerable body began to spit on him, the grossest of personal insults (Numbers 12:14; Deuteronomy 25:9). One of them threw a cloak over Jesus' head, and they repeatedly beat him with their knuckles.[3] Then they challenged him to prophesy who it was that did it in malignant mockery, using an ancient Talmudic misinterpretation of Isaiah 11:2–4 that the Messiah would be able to judge by smell alone.[4] Unwittingly they were fulfilling a real messianic prophecy: "I gave my back to those who strike, and my cheeks to those who pull out the beard; I hid not my face from disgrace and spitting" (Isaiah 50:6). Then in imitation of their religious leaders, the guards took Jesus and continued the beating. It was the earth's longest night, but as Peter would later say, "When he was reviled, he did not revile in return; when he suffered, he did not threaten, but continued entrusting himself to him who judges justly" (1 Peter 2:23).

The glory in all this is that through everything the Rock of our Salvation did not crack! He was the Rock of Israel: "[A]ll ate the same spiritual food, and all drank the same spiritual drink. For they drank from the spiritual Rock that followed them, and the Rock was Christ" (1 Corinthians 10:3, 4). He was the stone prophesied for the faithful: "Therefore thus says the Lord GOD, 'Behold, I am the one who has laid as a foundation in Zion, a stone, a tested stone, a precious cornerstone, of a sure foundation: 'Whoever believes will not be in haste'" (Isaiah 28:16). The stone suffered terrible rejection at the hands of the leaders of his people. He would become the foundation stone of the Church, just as was prophesied: "The stone that the builders rejected has become the cornerstone" (Psalm 118:22). The New Testament records the fulfillment of this, saying: "For it stands in Scripture: 'Behold, I am laying in Zion a stone, a cornerstone chosen and precious, and whoever believes in him will not be put to shame'" (1 Peter 2:6; cf. Ephesians 2:20).

He is the Rock that nourishes us as he did Israel of old. John's Gospel records that on the final day of the Feast of Tabernacles Jesus identified himself in the temple as the Rock that provides life for his people. "Jesus stood up and cried out, 'If anyone thirsts, let him come to me and drink. Whoever believes in me, as the Scripture has said, "Out of his heart will flow rivers of living water"'" (John 7:37, 38).

The question for us, as we view his rejection in the passages before us, is, how did he remain unmoved? How did he do this as a man, considering the weakness of human flesh? The answer is, Jesus stood rock-like before the Sanhedrin, then Pilate, and then the cross because he did not rely on his flesh, but on God the Father. Thus, he became the perfect example for all who seek to live out their faith in a hostile culture. Mark wanted us also to see that while Jesus was suffering abuse for his deliberate messianic claim, Peter was deliberately denying him.

Peter: The Cracked Rock (vv. 66–72)

Mark switched back to Peter in verse 66 and following:

> And as Peter was below in the courtyard, one of the servant girls of the high priest came, and seeing Peter warming himself, she looked at him and said, "You also were with the Nazarene, Jesus." But he denied it, saying, "I neither know nor understand what you mean." And he went out into the gateway and the rooster crowed. And the servant girl saw him and began again to say to the bystanders, "This man is one of them." But again he denied it. And after a little while the bystanders again said to Peter, "Certainly you are one of them, for you are a Galilean." But he began to invoke a curse on himself and to swear, "I do not know this man of whom you speak." (vv. 66–71)

The three denials are familiar ground. Suffice it to say that the final denial was a sweaty, sordid thing in which Peter cursed himself if he was lying and those present if they were lying about his being a disciple.[5] This was a nightmare for the apostle, the one to whom Jesus had said, "And I tell you, you are Peter [Petros/Rock], and on this rock [petra, referring to his great confession of faith] I will build my church . . ." (Matthew 16:18). Now Peter, the rock, had cracked and failed!

Unknown to Peter, because he was so caught up in the heat of his denial, the Lord was just then being led out from the chamber. Here Luke gives us a fuller explanation of verse 72: "But Peter said, 'Man, I do not know what you are talking about.' And immediately, while he was still speaking, the rooster crowed. And the Lord turned and looked at Peter. And Peter remembered the saying of the Lord, how he had said to him, 'Before the rooster crows today, you will deny me three times.' And he went out and wept bitterly" (Luke 22:60–62). Peter looked at the torn, bleeding visage of Jesus, and their eyes locked. Oh, the pain! The rooster began to crow for the next three to five minutes[6] over and over and over and over, and Peter remembered Christ's prophecy. He remembered and remembered and remembered.

Two rocks met their challenges as men. What made one stand and the other fall? The answer becomes crystal-clear when we see that Peter found it easy to be *self-dependent*. No disciple speaks as often as Peter. No disciple was reproved like Peter was, and he is the only disciple who thought he could reprove the Lord! He was impulsive. He was *numero uno* always. About the only time he was second was when he lost the footrace to the tomb with John. He had the great natural disadvantage of being the kind of person who always did it for himself somehow. When he became a follower of Christ, he naturally carried that style right into his service. He had the strength. He had the will. Whatever the cost, Peter would follow Jesus.

Jesus, on the other hand, knew that even perfect humanity apart from God the Father cannot succeed. Therefore, he lived in profound dependence upon the Father and remained the Rock!

It is this awareness of human weakness and the necessity of moment-by-moment dependence that Mark was urging on the Church. Paul capsulized it in these immortal words: "But he said to me, 'My grace is sufficient for you, for my power is made perfect in weakness.' Therefore I will boast all the more gladly of my weaknesses, so that the power of Christ may rest upon me. For the sake of Christ, then, I am content with weaknesses, insults, hardships, persecutions, and calamities. For when I am weak, then I am strong" (2 Corinthians 12:9, 10). Those who learn this become rock-solid for God.

Hudson Taylor said, "God chose me because I was weak enough. He trains somebody to be quiet enough, and little enough, and then uses him."[7] As the beloved Vance Havner put it: "The Lord had the strength and I had the weakness, so we teamed up! It was an unbeatable combination."[8]

Lloyd Ogilvie, master-preacher, testifies:

> I have learned this repeatedly in my own life. When my strength is depleted, when my rhetoric is unpolished by human talent, when I am weary, the Lord has a much better tool for empathetic, sensitive communication. The barriers are down. When I know I can do nothing by myself, my poverty becomes a channel of his power. More than that, often when I feel I have been least efficient, people have been helped most effectively. It's taken

me a long time to learn that the lower my resistances are and the less self-consciousness I have, the more the Word of God comes through.[9]

"But we have this treasure in jars of clay," says the Apostle Paul, "to show that the surpassing power belongs to God and not to us" (2 Corinthians 4:7).

God gives grace to those who renounce dependence upon self and depend upon him. How else did the Reformer Thomas Cranmer, who under duress was forced to write recantations of his faith, stand later in the Great St. Mary's Oxford and renounce his recantations, promising that if he must be burned, the hand that wrote them would burn first? And when he did die at the stake, he held his hand in the flames until his life was gone. How else did he do this but by dependence upon Christ?

Armando Valladares, who spent twenty-two years in Castro's prisons, records how Christian prisoners before firing squads regularly shout, *"Viva Cristo Rey!* (Long live Christ the King!)."* Officials have begun to gag their victims before execution lest the guards begin to think about what they were seeing and hearing.[10] Only dependence on God can accomplish this.

How else can a man or woman live out a consistent Christian life in the city or the suburbs except through the renunciation of self-dependence and the cultivation of conscious dependence upon God. It has always been the same. It was so when Gideon ritually divested himself of natural power and went on to defeat the Midianites (Judges 7). It was the same when King David announced his God-dependence to the doomed Goliath: "Then David said to the Philistine, 'You come to me with a sword and with a spear and with a javelin, but I come to you in the name of the LORD of hosts, the God of the armies of Israel, whom you have defied'" (1 Samuel 17:45).

51

Pilate before Christ

MARK 15:1–20

WHEN WILLIAM BOOTH began his mission work in 1865 among the poor in London's East End, he met tremendous opposition. The tent in which the work began was destroyed by a gang of toughs. When the work moved to a warehouse, hoodlum boys and drunks threw fireworks through the windows, and gangs frequently hurled stones and mud through as well.

Thus William Booth and his followers came to realize that they were at war, and in 1879 his Christian Mission became the Salvation Army with Booth as the General. Their paper became *The War Cry*. Persecution was fierce. In 1889 some 669 Salvation Army members were assaulted. Some were killed and maimed. It took years of persecution and sacrifice before the general public in ostensibly "Christian" England gave grudging recognition to the good of the Salvation Army's work—and then it was not so much for the evangelistic preaching of the gospel, but for its social service activities.[1]

General Booth and his followers lived out the repeated teaching of Scripture. "Indeed, all who desire to live a godly life in Christ Jesus will be persecuted," said Paul to Timothy (2 Timothy 3:12). Paul wrote to the Philippians while under arrest in Rome, "For it has been granted to you that for the sake of Christ you should not only believe in him but also suffer for his sake" (Philippians 1:29). To the Thessalonians he said, ". . . that no one be moved by these afflictions. For you yourselves know that we are destined for this. For when we were with you, we kept telling you beforehand that we were to suffer affliction, just as it has come to pass, and just as you know" (1 Thessalonians 3:3, 4). "Beloved," said Peter, "do not be surprised at the fiery trial when it comes upon you to test you, as though something strange were happening to you. But rejoice insofar as you share Christ's sufferings, that you may also rejoice and be glad when his glory is revealed" (1 Peter 4:12, 13).

Persecution has been the lot of the confessing, evangelical Church through the centuries. Sometimes the persecution is overt, as with the Salvationists. At other times it is subtle rejection. But it is always there. This is because Christianity is intrinsically countercultural.

David Niringiye, a man who endured the persecution of Idi Amin, emphasizes that if we are experiencing no opposition we are probably going the same direction as the culture—a sobering warning!

As we direct our thoughts to Mark 15, we must emphasize that it was written to an authentic, countercultural, persecuted church, the embattled church in Rome. Mark recorded the events of Jesus' rejection with an eye to encouraging that church and its particular trials. In 15:1–20 Jesus successively underwent four instances of rejection: 1) a *religiously* motivated rejection by the Sanhedrin, 2) a *socially* motivated rejection by Pilate, 3) a *politically* instigated rejection by the crowd, and 4) a *circumstantially* determined rejection by the soldiers. The Roman church was to understand that as followers of Christ they would undergo similarly motivated rejections. Reflecting on Jesus' example under persecution would give them wisdom and strength to endure victoriously. The benefits to us will not be less if we take this to heart.

The Sanhedrin: A Religiously Motivated Rejection of the King (v. 1)

The official religious rejection of Jesus had taken place only a few hours earlier at the torchlight interrogation of Jesus before the Sanhedrin, when the high priest, hearing Jesus' confession that he was the Messiah, tore his robes and shouted "blasphemy." They rejected him with their spittle and blows (14:61–65). Why such hate-filled rejection?

First, he was a threat to their power. The Seventy were the power-brokers of Israel. Jesus' ministry was loosening their grip on the people, and they could not allow that. Power is addicting, and the addicted will hate and kill to support their habit.

Second, he did not fit the expectations of their system. Their messianic expectations were martial—terrible armies with banners and blood making a way for the Jewish *imperium*—not a peasant king.

Third, Jesus showed them up for what they were, exposing their sin. He did this directly in such things as the cleansing of the temple and his devastating dialogues with their "big guns." He also exposed them by his person. Jesus had said earlier that very night in the upper room,

If I had not come and spoken to them, they would not have been guilty of sin, but now they have no excuse for their sin. Whoever hates me hates my Father also. If I had not done among them the works that no one else did, they would not be guilty of sin, but now they have seen and hated both me and my Father. But the word that is written in their Law must be fulfilled: "They hated me without a cause." (John 15:22–25)

Jesus' life and inner righteousness earned abiding hostility because it revealed the horrors of their sin and the shallowness of their goodness.

Once an African chief happened to visit a mission station. Hanging outside the missionary's hut on a tree was a little mirror. The chief happened to look into the mirror and saw her reflection, complete with terrifying paint and threatening features. She gazed at her own frightening countenance and started back in horror, exclaiming, "Who is that horrible-looking person inside that tree?" "Oh," the missionary said, "it is not in the tree. The glass is reflecting your own face." The African would not believe it until she held the mirror in her hand. She said, "I must have the glass. How much will you sell it for?" "Oh," said the missionary, "I don't want to sell it." But the woman begged until he capitulated, thinking it might be best to sell it to avoid trouble. So he named a price and she took the mirror. Exclaiming, "I will never have it making faces at me again," she threw it down and broke it to pieces. This is precisely what the religious establishment did to Jesus. They would dash this mirror of their souls! So they nailed him to a cross, only to find that this magnified the reflection.

This same syndrome was at the heart of the persecution that came to William Booth and the Salvation Army. English society, the exploiting slum landlords, the industrial buccaneers, the liquor magnates, and the uncaring Church were made to see themselves, and they hated it.

It is the same today. A Spirit-filled believer models Christ and shows life as it should be, and many recoil. Archbishop William Temple said, "The world . . . would not hate angels for being angelic; but it does hate men for being Christians. It grudges them their new character; it is tormented by their peace; it is infuriated by their joy."[2] Of course, the upside of this is that open hearts, like that of Nicodemus of the Sanhedrin, are ineluctably drawn to Christ.

There is nothing like the hatred of theologians. The mirror must not only be broken, but ground to powder.

"And as soon as it was morning, the chief priests held a consultation with the elders and scribes and the whole council. And they bound Jesus and led him away and delivered him over to Pilate" (v. 1). The reason the Sanhedrin met again very early in the morning was twofold. Most important, it was a legal necessity because their own regulations prohibited convicting criminals at night. Moreover, they had to decide on a political charge that Pilate would accept, because Jesus' claim to be Messiah was religious and of no interest to the state. So by twisting things just a little, they charged him with claiming to be king, a heinous offense in Roman eyes. They rushed through their deliberations, for Roman procurators always held court in the early morning, so as not to interfere with "the elaborately organized leisure of the Roman gentleman" that would occupy the bulk of Pilate's day.[3] So it was before mid-morning that Jesus was brought before Pilate, who was staying at Herod's Palace during the Passover celebration. Here Jesus' experience moves from religious rejection to a socially motivated rejection.

Pilate: A Socially Motivated Rejection of the King (vv. 2–15)

To understand the dynamics of this rejection, we must know something about Pilate. His career before coming to Judea as procurator is unknown, except that he undoubtedly served in a series of civil and military appointments. Some, on the basis of tradition, think that his marriage to Claudia Procula may have gained the position for him.[4] What we do know from ancient historians and Scripture is not inviting. He was an inept and heavy-handed administrator. He insulted the Jews by having his soldiers bring flags bearing images of Caesar into Jerusalem, almost causing open rebellion.[5]

Another time he raided the sacred *Corban* treasury of the temple (a treasure to be used only for service to God) to pay for building an aqueduct. Those who objected were beaten by plainclothes soldiers.[6] Again, he provoked the Jews over an alleged idolatry incident.[7] And ultimately he lost his job when he ordered his cavalry to attack Samaritans who were assembled at Mt. Gerizim in a religious quest.[8] The fourth-century historian Eusebius records that from there on life went so bad for Pilate, he took his own life.[9]

Pontius Pilate was a man who lusted for celebrity and status, who put his career before everything, including people and principle. When he finally lost his position, his life was not worth living. He lacked the traditional Roman virtues of honor and integrity. He lived for his career—in short, for self.

As Jesus stood before Pilate, the Sanhedrin's representatives made their charge of high treason—in effect, "This man would be King!" We observe an ascending curiosity on Pilate's part as the exchanges began: "And Pilate asked him, 'Are you the King of the Jews?' And he answered him, 'You have said so'" (v. 2). Jesus had responded affirmatively, but evidently the impersonal wording and his tone of voice conveyed, "Yes, but not the way you think." Then "the chief priests," says Mark, "accused him of many things" (v. 3). Luke explains more fully: "And they began to accuse him, saying, 'We found this man misleading our nation and forbidding us to give tribute to Caesar, and saying that he himself is Christ, a king'" (Luke 23:2). When they saw that Pilate was skeptical, Luke adds, "they were urgent, saying, 'He stirs up the people, teaching throughout all Judea'" (Luke 23:5). "And Pilate again asked him," says Mark in verses 4, 5, "'Have you no answer to make? See how many charges they bring against you.' But Jesus made no further answer, so that Pilate was amazed." Jesus' silence was a most eloquent answer. Pilate was used to loud protests, but now there was only silence. "He was oppressed, and he was afflicted, yet he opened not his mouth; like a lamb that is led to the slaughter, and like a sheep that before its shearers is silent, so he opened not his mouth" (Isaiah 53:7). *Pilate was convinced of his innocence.*

The other Gospels fill in the details. Luke says Pilate sent Jesus to Herod, where Jesus again kept his regal silence. Herod sent him back, saying that he had done nothing deserving death (Luke 23:15). John records that Pilate took Jesus back inside the palace and questioned him personally. Jesus told him, "My kingdom is not of this world" (John 18:36; cf. vv. 33–38). Pilate saw it all for what it was: Jesus was no bloodletting revolutionary. He was a victim of establishment envy. So, "[a]fter he had said this, he went back outside to the Jews and told them, 'I find no guilt in him'" (John 18:38).

The Sanhedrin was in an uproar, and Pilate was in a spot. He had been warned by Rome before about his heavy-handedness, and an insurrection would not look good on his record. Then came a great idea, he thought. There was a custom at Passover of granting amnesty to a prisoner of the people's choice. He had in custody a notorious criminal, who was a murderer and a bandit. He would give the crowd a choice. Of course they would choose to grant amnesty to this harmless Jesus.

Pilate was dumbfounded by their response:

> And he answered them, saying, "Do you want me to release for you the King of the Jews?" For he perceived that it was out of envy that the chief priests had delivered him up. But the chief priests stirred up the crowd to have him release for them Barabbas instead. And Pilate again said to them, "Then what shall I do with the man you call the King of the Jews?" And they cried out again, "Crucify him." And Pilate said to them, "Why, what evil has he done?" But they shouted all the more, "Crucify him." So Pilate, wishing to satisfy the crowd, released for them Barabbas, and having scourged Jesus . . . (vv. 9–15)

Pilate's tactical blunder left him no choice, for the riotous crowd was almost out of control. In order to placate them, he released Barabbas.

It looked like Pilate would have to condemn this innocent Jesus, but he had one remaining idea that would perhaps gain the sympathy of the people. To this end he delivered Jesus to be flogged. Though Mark places this at the end of the trial, it is really the penultimate event:

> And the soldiers led him away inside the palace (that is, the governor's headquarters), and they called together the whole battalion. And they clothed him in a purple cloak, and twisting together a crown of thorns, they put it on him. And they began to salute him, "Hail, King of the Jews!" And they were striking his head with a reed and spitting on him and kneeling down in homage to him. And when they had mocked him, they stripped him of the purple cloak and put his own clothes on him. And they led him out to crucify him. (vv. 16–20)

The scourging was done by the dread *flagellum* whip, consisting of thongs plaited with pieces of bone and lead. Eusebius tells of martyrs who "were torn by scourges down to deep seated veins and arteries, so that the hidden contents of the recesses of their bodies, their entrails and organs, were exposed to sight."[10] Josephus describes this in similar terms.[11] The *flagellum* left Jesus with bone and cartilage showing. ". . . his appearance was so marred, beyond human semblance, and his form beyond that of the children of mankind" (Isaiah 52:14). His brow wore the mocking crown of thorns. A faded purple robe, crimson with blood, hung dripping from his shoulders.

The horror completed, Pilate brought Jesus out and announced, "Behold the man [*Ecce Homo!*]!" (John 19:5). This is not the unmarked *Ecce Homo* by Richard Westall which hangs behind the pulpit of All Souls in London. The true scene, if reproduced here, would cause some of us to faint. Pilate was saying, "Behold the poor creature.[12] Have pity on him."

Was there any pity? "From then on Pilate sought to release him, but the Jews cried out, 'If you release this man, you are not Caesar's friend. Everyone who makes himself a king opposes Caesar'" (John 19:12). At this, Pontius Pilate, the one man who could have stopped it all, caved in! Why? Because his social position was everything to him. He had done his duty in the legions, and he was not going to take the chance of sacrificing his career for this Jesus.

What a type of the modern man Pilate is! Thousands have rejected Christ to protect position or promotion or scholarly respect. We may even be tempted ourselves. "Oh, you don't mean that you take the Bible literally? A tambourine-banger! I can't believe it!"

How many have gone only so far with Christ and then stepped back because of a sarcastic smile or a leering silence. We need to be Pauline before the world and shout: "For I am not ashamed of the gospel, for it is the power of God for salvation to everyone who believes, to the Jew first and also to the Greek. For in it the righteousness of God is revealed from faith for faith, as it is written, 'The righteous shall live by faith'" (Romans 1:16, 17). That's the way to face a hostile world!

The Crowd: A Politically Motivated Rejection of the King (vv. 6–15)

There is some grim poetry here. The surname "Barabbas" means "son of the Father," and some early manuscripts indicate that his given name was Jesus. In fact, the *New English Bible* translates Matthew 27:16, "Jesus Bar-Abbas"—"Jesus, son of the father." The crowd preferred Jesus Bar-Abbas to Jesus Bar-Joseph, the real son of the Father!

Why? Because Barabbas was a grotesque form of the Messiah that Israel wanted! He was a leading Zealot, a political activist who had taken to the bandit trail. He was a man of action who would even murder to reach his own ends (cf. Matthew 27:16; Luke 23:19; John 18:40; Acts 3:14). In the twisted thinking of some, he was a patriot. His vitality and élan appealed to the mob. Jesus, however, had disappointed them with his inaction. The people chose lawlessness instead of righteousness, violence instead of love, war instead of peace. The world is still the same. Marxism with its red flag seems so much more alive and full-blooded than the way of the cross. Revolution, not a King riding on a donkey!

Have you ever been disappointed with Jesus or with God? Have you ever expected him to act in a certain way, only to find he did not and will not?[13] Barabbas seems much more logical. But God says: "For my thoughts are not your thoughts, neither are your ways my ways, declares the LORD. For as the heavens are higher than the earth, so are my ways higher than your ways and my thoughts than your thoughts" (Isaiah 55:8, 9). Thank God that he does not fit into our little box! "Blessed are the poor in spirit, for theirs is the kingdom of heaven. Blessed are those who mourn, for they shall be comforted. Blessed are the meek, for they shall inherit the earth" (Matthew 5:3–5). Thank God he did not take the way of Barabbas.

The Soldiers: An Irrational, Circumstantial Rejection of the King (vv. 16–20)

The Roman soldiers had no vested interest in Jesus, yet fully participated in the rejection. Mark says that "the whole battalion" of soldiers (v. 16) played with Jesus like a cat plays with a mouse—in dispassionate, unblinking torture. Why? Because savagery begets savagery. It is like blood in the ocean sending sharks into a feeding frenzy. Some of those who so vilely mistreated General Booth and company were not doctrinaire anti-Christians, but simple people caught up by the carnival of persecution. Jesus experienced this, the Christians in Rome would experience it, and so has it been for Christians through the ages.

Mark was encouraging those in the beleaguered church in Rome by letting them see Jesus' rejection. The *religiously* motivated rejecters sought to crush Jesus because his life provided a dreadful mirror to their own souls. The *socially* motivated rejection by Pontus Pilate was an archetype of the hearts that would reject Christianity because it endangers status. The *politically* driven rejection wants a Christ who does things man's way. The *irrationally* motivated come along for the macabre ride.

The Scriptures say: "Indeed, all who desire to live a godly life in Christ Jesus will be persecuted" (2 Timothy 3:12). "For it has been granted to you that for the sake of Christ you should not only believe in him but also suffer for his sake" (Philippians 1:29). "Beloved, do not be surprised at the fiery trial when it comes upon you to test you, as though something strange were happening to you. But rejoice insofar as you share Christ's sufferings, that you may also rejoice and be glad when his glory is revealed" (1 Peter 4:12, 13).

Ships, like men, do poorly when the wind is directly behind, pushing them sloppily on their way so that no care is required in steering or in the management of sails. What is needed is a wind slightly opposed to the ship, for then tension can be maintained, and ideas can germinate.

We need to point our bows toward Christ and the contrary wind. This will mean vigilance and even danger. But we will be sailing as we were meant to, and there will be another countering wind in our sails—the wind of the Holy Spirit.

52

Revelations of the Cross, Part 1

MARK 15:21–32

GRAHAM GREENE, in his novel *The Heart of the Matter*, describes his principal character, Police Lieutenant Scobie, listening in on a dispassionate conversation about the suicide of an acquaintance. The men are discussing whether their deceased friend chose the best way to kill himself. As Lieutenant Scobie examines the man's few belongings and listens, he says to himself quietly, "Through two thousand years . . . we have discussed Christ's agony in just this disinterested way."[1]

Greene is right. It is so easy to become desensitized to reality. We daily view scenes of real violence—such as attacks on the Pope or the President—as we pass the potatoes and gravy. Crosses and crucifixes are so much a part of the landscape that we do not even see them, much less be moved by them.

As Christians, we must steel ourselves against such desensitization. Christ's passion was real. Granted, we should not be overcome by a morbid preoccupation with the gore of the cross or by shallow sentimentalism. At the same time, Christ's agony must never become a matter of dispassionate interest.

His physical sufferings have always been, and will remain, a window through which we see his heart—the heart of God. This is what we hope to see as we consider "Revelations of the Cross."

Martin Hengel, the celebrated German New Testament scholar, in his great work on the crucifixion ends with these words: "Reflection on the harsh reality of the crucifixion in antiquity may help us to overcome the acute loss of reality which is to be found so often in present theology and preaching."[2]

My hope for these chapters is to enhance the reality of this terribly real event. We will not linger unnecessarily upon the horror of Christ's physical suffering, nor will we understate it. We must keep in mind that Christ suffered greatly prior to the crucifixion. In Gethsemane he almost expired as he gazed with horrified amazement into the cup he must drink. In addition, Christ was first struck in Caiaphas' presence, then was subjected to a series of blows as the temple guards blindfolded him. They taunted him to identify them as they passed by, spitting upon him and striking him in the face. Next, he was scourged under Pilate. Scourging, nicknamed "the halfway death," meant the soldiers stripped Jesus naked, tied him down, and used the deadly *flagellum* to rip skin from the bone.

In their presentation of the "Comic King," the Roman soldiers again stripped Jesus, robed him in the Roman *chlemys* (short cloak) as a calculated affront to Jewish modesty, crowned him with thorns, and beat him on the face with a mock scepter until he was unrecognizable. It was then that Pilate presented him to the people, saying, *"Ecce Homo!*—Behold the man!"* Let us now behold the Incarnation and the love of God for us.

The Crucifixion's Revelation of His Love (vv. 21–24)

Jesus' final road to the cross began with his *Via Dolorosa*—"Road of Sorrows," as described in verses 21, 22: "And they compelled a passerby, Simon of Cyrene, who was coming in from the country, the father of Alexander and Rufus, to carry his cross. And they brought him to the place called Golgotha (which means Place of a Skull)."

Mark's Gospel, like the other Gospels, tells us very little about this, because everyone in the Roman Empire knew the familiar details all too well. Such marches were as common as today's funeral processions. Contemporary ancient history fills in the details. Jesus was placed in the center of a *quarternion*, a company of four Roman soldiers. The *patibulum*, the cross beam of the cross, weighing perhaps as much as one hundred pounds, was placed on his torn shoulders. St. Chrysostom saw prophetic fulfillment in this, seeing it as parallel to Isaac's bearing the wood for his own sacrifice to Mt. Moriah.[3]

Next, as Christ stumbled along the route to the cross, an officer preceded him carrying a wooden placard whitened with chalk and bearing the darkened inscription of Jesus' crime: "Jesus of Nazareth, the King of the Jews" (John 19:19).[4] Jesus was led on the longest route possible, so that proper fear would be bestowed throughout the city as a deterrent to crime.[5] As Christ tread his serpentine "Road of Sorrows," weakened from loss of blood, an innocent bystander, a *Diaspora* Jew from Cyrene in North Africa, was compelled to carry the *patibulum*. This was certainly not his idea of celebrating

Passover, though there is some evidence that this experience opened the way for grace into his family (cf. Acts 13:1; Romans 16:13).

At the place of execution, "they offered him [Jesus] wine mixed with myrrh, but he did not take it" (v. 23). The *Babylonian Talmud* (Sanhedrin 43a) says that respected women, in response to the merciful injunction of Proverbs 31:6 to "Give strong drink to the one who is perishing," appointed themselves to provide condemned victims with a narcotic, pain-reducing drink before execution.[6] But Jesus refused it (cf. Psalm 69:21; Matthew 27:34). Jesus rejected any form of relief for his sufferings because he wanted to maintain clarity of mind to the end, bearing the full weight of his suffering. He even maintained the lucidness to minister to the dying thief and pronounce the rest of his wondrous seven last words.

Simon, the Cyrenian, cast the loathsome *patibulum* to the ground in disgust. Jesus was thrown upon it, and spikes were driven through his hands. The *patibulum* was raised by the four soldiers with Jesus dangling from it and fastened to a standing post, the *crux simplex*. Then Jesus' feet were nailed, probably with a single spike, to the post. Jesus began his repeated genuflections as he struggled upward for breath and folded downward again in exhaustion.

This was the lowest form of degradation. Cultured Gentiles refrained as much as possible from even mentioning the word "cross."[7] Once when an upper-class Roman actor did a mime depiction of the crucifixion of a robber chief, the writer Juvenal was so repulsed that a member of the patrician class would so debase himself, he said he hoped the actor would end up on a real cross![8] Jesus' Jewish antagonists well remembered Deuteronomy 21:23 ("a hanged man is cursed by God") and gleefully misapplied it to Jesus. This was the lowest rung in the Lord's humiliation—"even death on a cross" (Philippians 2:8). He was indeed "a stumbling block to Jews" (1 Corinthians 1:23). To the Jews and Romans alike, it was madness to suppose that anyone crucified would pretend to be God.[9]

Jesus underwent limitless pain. The March 21, 1986 issue of the *Journal of the American Medical Association* carried the most complete medical review of Christ's crucifixion ever published in a medical journal. In it the authors detail the pain endured by the weight of the body hanging from nails that damage the medial nerves and tear at the tarsals, the respiratory torture, the cramping, and the pleural effusions, concluding that "Death by crucifixion was in every sense of the word excruciating, literally 'out of the cross.'"[10] Their assessment remarkably justifies C. S. Lewis's description and deduction made in 1960:

He creates the universe, already foreseeing—or should we say "seeing"? There are no tenses in God—the buzzing cloud of flies about the cross, the flayed back pressed against the uneven stake, the nails driven through the medial nerves, the repeated incipient suffocation as the body droops, the repeated torture of back and arms as it is time after time, for breath's sake hitched up. If I may dare the biological image, God is a "host" who deliberately creates His own parasites; causes us to be that we may exploit and "take advantage of" Him. Herein is love. This is the diagram of Love Himself, the inventor of all loves.[11]

The cross reveals the love of God as nothing else in the universe could! We must passionately weave this truth into the fibers of our consciousness for our soul's health. We must never fall into the delusion of thinking that the suffering was not as great for him because of the ontological fact that he was God. He did it as a man, among men, in total (and exemplary) dependence upon the Father. His pain was alleviated by nothing. If anything, it was heightened by his soul's health. And this says nothing of the ultimate pain, which we will speak of in the next chapter, as our sin-bearer. The realness of the cross says to us that *we are loved.*

Lewis Bayly's seventeenth-century devotional handbook, *Practice of Piety*, is largely unknown today. But at that time it was one of the two books that John Bunyan's wife brought to him for her wedding dowry. Near the end there is a dialogue between the soul and Christ in which Christ explains to the soul the meaning of the cross.

> *Soule.* Lord, why, wouldest Thou be taken, when Thou mightest have escaped Thine enemies?
> *Christ.* That thy spiritual enemies should not take thee, and cast thee into the prison of utter darkness.
> *Soule.* Lord, wherefore wouldest Thou be bound?
> *Christ.* That I might loose the cordes of thine iniquities.
> *Soule.* Lord, wherefore wouldest Thou be lift up upon a Crosse?
> *Christ.* That I might lift thee up with Me to heaven.
> *Soule.* Lord, wherefore were Thy hands and feet nayled to the Crosse?
> *Christ.* To enlarge thy hands to doe the works of righteousness and to set thy feete at libertie, to walke in the wayes of peace.
> *Soule.* Lord, why wouldest Thou have Thine arms nayled abroad?
> *Christ.* That I might embrace thee more lovingly, My sweet soule.
> *Soule.* Lord, wherefore was Thy side opened with a speare?
> *Christ.* That thou mightest have a way to come near to My heart.[12]

Fellow-believers, the cross is one place where sophistication and emotional detachment cannot be. It demands our passionate return of love.

God, I love Thee, I love Thee—
Not out of hope of heaven for me
Nor fearing not to love and be
In the everlasting burning.
Thou, Thou, my Jesus, after me
Didst reach Thine arms out dying,
For my sake sufferedst nails and lance,
Mocked and marred countenance,
Sorrows passing number
Sweat and care and cumber,
Yea and death, and this for me,
And Thou couldest see me sinning:
Then I, why should not I love Thee;
Jesus so much in love with me?
Not for heaven's sake; not to be
Out of hell by loving Thee;
Not for any gains I see;
But just that Thou didst me
I do and I will love Thee:
What must I love Thee, Lord, for then?—
For being my King and God. Amen.[13]

The Crucifixion's Revelation of His Lordship (vv. 25, 26)

Jesus' persecutors were not aware of the love that was being declared through the cross, but they were aware of the assertion of his Lordship. Verses 25, 26 tell us: "And it was the third hour when they crucified him. And the inscription of the charge against him read, 'The King of the Jews.'" Another Gospel fills in the details:

> Pilate also wrote an inscription and put it on the cross. It read, "Jesus of Nazareth, the King of the Jews." Many of the Jews read this inscription, for the place where Jesus was crucified was near the city, and it was written in Aramaic, in Latin, and in Greek. So the chief priests of the Jews said to Pilate, "Do not write, 'The King of the Jews,' but rather, 'This man said, I am King of the Jews.'" Pilate answered, "What I have written I have written." (John 19:19–22)

John's use of the imperfect verb tense suggests that the inscription galled Jesus' detractors, for while they gloated over his imminent death, the customary red or black letters stared back at them: "The King of the Jews." The Jews repeatedly asked Pilate to change the sign to read, "This man *claimed* to be King of the Jews." But Pilate would not change it and answered in the Greek perfect tense, "What I have written I have written." Or, more to the sense, "What I have written will always remain written." He was unwittingly stating an eternal truth. During Jesus' infancy Magi came from the East heralding him as King (Matthew 2:2). At the beginning of Passion Week the multitudes had cried, "Blessed is he who comes in the name of the Lord, even the King of Israel!" (John 12:13). Standing before Pilate, Jesus had borne witness to his kingdom (John 18:36, 37). Now his royal title is fixed to the cross, and the rulers of Israel could not get it removed!

Ultimately, he, the "Faithful and True," will come on a white horse, and those still present will see that:

> His eyes are like a flame of fire, and on his head are many diadems. . . . And the armies of heaven, arrayed in fine linen, white and pure, were following him on white horses. From his mouth comes a sharp sword with which to strike down the nations, and he will rule them with a rod of iron. He will tread the winepress of the fury of the wrath of God the Almighty. On his robe and on his thigh he has a name written, King of kings and Lord of lords. (Revelation 19:12–16)

The Aramaic, Latin, and Greek renderings of the inscription announce that his rule is not only regal but universal. Jesus rules from the cross. Virtually *every* New Testament reference to Jesus' rule is accompanied by a reference to his cross!

> Crown Him with many crowns,
> The Lamb upon His throne;
> Hark! how the heav'nly anthem drowns
> All music but its own!
>
> Awake, my soul, and sing
> Of Him who died for thee,
> And hail Him as thy matchless King
> Thro' all eternity.

The crucifixion not only proclaims Christ's love as nothing else could do, but it shouts his rule! What he did on the cross demands our obedience.

> Love so amazing, so divine
> Demands my soul, my life, my all.

If you see his love, you must see his demands. Christ on the cross is not a prayer-meeting Jesus Christ, nor a book Jesus Christ, but the New Testament Jesus Christ—God Incarnate. Jesus Christ wants absolute devotion to himself. The crucifixion reveals Jesus' love, then his Lordship, and now his atoning work.

The Crucifixion's Revelation of His
Substitutionary Atonement (vv. 27–32)

As though the crucifixion was not enough, Jesus was the object of cruel verbal violence.

> And with him they crucified two robbers, one on his right and one on his left. And those who passed by derided him, wagging their heads and saying, "Aha! You who would destroy the temple and rebuild it in three days, save yourself, and come down from the cross!" So also the chief priests with the scribes mocked him to one another, saying, "He saved others; he cannot save himself. Let the Christ, the King of Israel, come down now from the cross that we may see and believe." Those who were crucified with him also reviled him. (vv. 27–32)

Recently a man stood atop a building trying to get enough nerve to jump to his death, while a crowd dared him to jump. In another case a drunk man was killed while struggling to get out of the way of a commuter train as a crowd taunted him. There was a similar spirit in the average person who passed by Jesus. The chief priests and teachers did the same—but among themselves, lest they appear as crass as the mob.

Jesus was also mocked by his fellow-victims, the two terrorist bandits at his right and left. Even here there was grace, as Luke's Gospel records:

> One of the criminals who were hanged railed at him, saying, "Are you not the Christ? Save yourself and us!" But the other rebuked him, saying, "Do you not fear God, since you are under the same sentence of condemnation? And we indeed justly, for we are receiving the due reward of our deeds; but this man has done nothing wrong." And he said, "Jesus, remember me when you come into your kingdom." And he said to him, "Truly, I say to you, today you will be with me in Paradise." (Luke 23:39–43)

In a few hours Jesus was dead. The Jews, not wanting to leave the bodies there over the Sabbath, asked the soldiers to employ their iron *crucifragium* to break the bandits' legs, which they did, bringing death to one and life to the other! That thief saw Paradise and resides in glory today!

Here is something of unforgettable beauty, and it is this: if the cross teaches love, then the positioning of the crosses on Calvary teaches how Christ's love goes out to the world.

There is a beautiful, almost-dream-like story that comes from the life of Dr. Donald Grey Barnhouse. On a Saturday morning he was in his study working when the custodian came in and announced there was a man outside to see him, giving him the man's card. Dr. Barnhouse read the card, which indicated that the visitor was the captain of the *Mauritania*, the largest passenger vessel afloat.

Holding the card, Dr. Barnhouse went out to meet the man. The captain said, "You have a very beautiful church here." Dr. Barnhouse replied, "We are grateful for all that was done by our faithful predecessors a hundred years ago." The captain said, "It is very much like the Basilica at Ravenna in Italy." Dr. Barnhouse responded, "Well, it is an architectural duplication. In fact, years ago they brought workmen from Italy, and the tessellated ceilings and the marble columns and the mosaic were all done by Italian workmen. But that's not what you came to talk about. You didn't come to talk about architecture, did you?"

The man said, "No. Twenty-three times a year I sail the Atlantic. When I come down the bank of Newfoundland, I hear your broadcast out of Boston. And as I came this week I thought to myself, 'I've got twenty-four hours in New York. I'm going to get down and see Dr. Barnhouse.' So I took a train, hoping perhaps I would be able to meet you, and here I am." Dr. Barnhouse was very straightforward as he said, "Sir, have you been born again?" The captain replied, "That is what I came to see you about."

By this time they had reached a chalkboard in the prayer room, and Dr. Barnhouse drew three crosses. Underneath the first one he wrote the word "in." Underneath the third he wrote the word "in." Underneath the middle cross he wrote the words, "not in." He said, "Do you understand what I mean when I say those men who died with Jesus had sin within them?" The captain thought and said, "Yes, I do. Christ did not have sin within him." Then over the first cross and over the third cross Dr. Barnhouse wrote the word "on." He said, "Do you understand what that means?" The captain wrinkled his brow—he didn't quite understand. Dr. Barnhouse said, "Let me illustrate. Have you ever run through a red light?" "Yes." "Were you caught?" The man said, "No." "Well, in running that red light you had a sin in you. If you would have been caught, you would have had sin on you. So here the thieves bear the penalty of God."

Then he wrote another "on" over Jesus Christ and said, "The one thief's sins rested on Christ by virtue of his faith in Christ." Then he said, "Which one are you?" Well, the man was a very tall, distinguished man of British carriage, and as he stood for a moment Dr. Barnhouse could see that he was fighting back tears. He said to Dr. Barnhouse, "By the grace of God, I am the first man." Dr. Barnhouse said, "You mean your sins are on Jesus?" He said, "Yes, God says my sins are on Jesus!" He shot out his hand and said, "That's what I came to find out!" Dr. Barnhouse invited him to lunch and further shared with him, and the man went back to New York a glowing Christian.[14]

All of us, like the thieves, have sin *in* us. We are divided, as were the two thieves. Some of us have the penalty of sin resting on us, and others have by grace had it shifted over to Christ. Is your sin on you or on Christ in whom there is no sin? That is the great question.

If you want your sin to be on Christ, you must look closely at the cross. First, behold the man and his suffering. Observe how great his love for you is. Tell Jesus that you love him. Second, behold the King and his demands. Yield to his rule. Third, behold the crosses and ask Jesus to take your sins. "He himself bore our sins in his body on the tree, that we might die to sin and live to righteousness. By his wounds you have been healed" (1 Peter 2:24).

Now thank him with all your heart.

53

Revelations of the Cross, Part 2

MARK 15:33–41

Love's as hard as nails,
Love is nails:
Blunt, thick, hammered through
The medial nerves of One
Who, having made us, knew
The thing He had done,
Seeing (with all that is)
Our cross, and His.[1]

The crucified Christ is a divinely given diagram of God's love! We must therefore invite its raw horror to assault us. Its blood, its water and glistening bone ought to go to our hearts, and our hearts ought to repeatedly respond, "This is how I am loved!" There is no room in us for distant intellectualizing. The cross is for the Christian imagination and the health of our souls an object of *passionate* focus.

In the last chapter our focus was on the crucifixion itself—the revelations of the crucifixion. Here it is on the revelations of his death. The final events of Jesus' death reveal the unfathomable depths to which he went in atoning for our sins.

The Revelation of Love in Jesus' Death (vv. 33–37)

Jesus' death was dramatically emphasized by the darkness that engulfed the cross. Mark says simply, "And when the sixth hour had come, there was darkness over the whole land until the ninth hour" (v. 33). "The sixth hour" was noon when the sun was at its zenith. Darkness engulfed the cross at midday and remained for three terrible hours. Most likely the darkness was local, covering the Holy City and its countryside with a black blanket. Whatever the case, the Greek tenses indicate that it came suddenly, and all the Gospels regard it as a supernatural wonder.

In the preternatural darkness there was silence all around. The Gospels record no words from Christ or his antagonists in the eerie midday gloom. Thirty-three years earlier there had been brightness and music at midnight when Jesus was born. Now there is darkness and silence at noontide as he dies.

Why this darkness? To begin with, it was a sign of mourning. Amos prophesied there would be darkness at the time of the Day of the Lord, saying, "I will make the sun go down at noon and darken the earth in broad daylight. . . . I will make it like the mourning for an only son . . ." (Amos 8:9, 10). The cross is draped in the mourning sackcloth of darkness.

In concert with this, the darkness signified the curse of God. At the exodus, a plague of darkness spread over the land before the first Passover lamb was slain. Now before the death of the ultimate Passover Lamb, there again was darkness. God's judgment was being poured out in a midday night.

This takes us to the very center of what was happening, for in those three black hours, sin was poured upon Christ's soul until he became sin. This was in accord with the prophetic Scriptures:

> He was despised and rejected by men; a man of sorrows, and acquainted with grief; and as one from whom men hide their faces he was despised, and we esteemed him not. Surely he has borne our griefs and carried our sorrows; yet we esteemed him stricken, smitten by God, and afflicted. But he was pierced for our transgressions; he was crushed for our iniquities; upon him was the chastisement that brought us peace, and with his wounds we are healed. All we like sheep have gone astray; we have turned—every one—to his own way; and the LORD has laid on him the iniquity of us all. (Isaiah 53:3–6)

Peter makes what happened very clear: "He himself bore our sins in his body on the tree, that we might die to sin and live to righteousness. By his wounds you have been healed" (1 Peter 2:24).

Paul says: "For our sake [God] made him to be sin who knew no sin, so that in him we might become the righteousness of God" (2 Corinthians 5:21). Or as *The Living Bible* so meaningfully puts it, "For God took the sinless Christ and poured into him our sins. Then, in exchange, he poured God's goodness into us!"

Wave after wave of the world's sin was poured over Christ's sinless soul. Again and again during those three hours his soul recoiled and convulsed as all the lies of civilization, the murders of a thousand "Killing Fields," the whorings of the world's armies, and the noxious brew of hatreds, jealousies, and pride were poured on his purity. Finally he became a curse: "Christ redeemed us from the curse of the law by becoming a curse for us—for it is written, 'Cursed is everyone who is hanged on a tree'" (Galatians 3:13). In the darkness Jesus bore it all in silence. Not a word came from his lips. Can you see him writhing like a serpent in the gloom (see John 3:14, 15)?

Is there any analogy to this? Perhaps we can imagine a beautiful young girl, a virgin, who is raped by a terrible, perverted man and the horror she would experience in those moments. But this is only a dim shadow of Christ's agony.[2] And there is even more! Because he became sin for us, he had to undergo the cosmic trauma of separation from God who "is light, and in him is no darkness at all" (1 John 1:5). In the dark of the cross's night, Jesus was *alone*. His separation was not just *felt*; it was *real*. The ontological unity of the Trinity was not broken, but the separation of the Son from the Father and Spirit was fact.[3] This was possible because of the authenticity of the Incarnation. God's holy nature demanded separation as the Son became sin. Not even the most evil man, including Nero or Hitler, has ever known *in this life* the horror of being completely cut off from God. But Christ knew it.

He was experiencing that which he saw so clearly in the garden that he almost expired right then! The physical agony was nothing in comparison to the sin that caused him such agony—my sin and yours.

The black silence goes on for one hour, two hours. Wave upon wave comes to his convulsing soul. He who had never known a millisecond of separation from the Father and the Holy Spirit is alone. Then came the end of the third hour, and the silence is shattered: "And at the ninth hour Jesus cried with a loud voice, 'Eloi, Eloi, lema sabachthani?' which means, 'My God, my God, why have you forsaken me?'" (v. 34). Crucifixions were normally punctuated by intermittent raging or pleading or cursing by the crucified, and no doubt this is what the other two had done. But Jesus severed his silence with a great shout from Psalm 22:1. This undoubtedly reeled the onlookers with shock. Various attempts have been made to soften the force of this, the most popular being that the quoting of the first verse of a Psalm implies the content of the whole Psalm, and Psalm 22 ends on a triumphant note. But such explanations blunt God's Word.

Actually Jesus' cry expressed his unfathomable pain at his real abandonment. Clear-thinking John Calvin explains: "Jesus expressed this horror of great darkness, this God-forsakenness, by quoting the only verse of Scripture which actually described it, and which he had perfectly fulfilled."[4] With perfect integrity Jesus laid bare his soul and fulfilled prophecy. Moreover, by repeating, "My God, my God" he was affirming his trust in his Father.

I believe that with Jesus' ringing declaration of abandonment, the darkness began to lift, for he had emptied the cup to the dregs. Mark says, "And some of the bystanders hearing it said, 'Behold, he is calling Elijah'" (v. 35). Possibly they mistook, "Eloi, Eloi" as a reference to Elijah, or perhaps they pretended to do so in savage jest.[5] However that may be, St. John's account indicates that at this point Jesus said, "I thirst" (John 19:28). Then, as verse 36 of our text says, "And someone ran and filled a sponge with sour wine, put it on a reed and gave it to him to drink, saying, 'Wait, let us see whether Elijah will come to take him down.'"

Under the lowering sky, a soldier held the sponge up to Jesus' mouth as he sucked the refreshing wine vinegar.[6] Here again we must supplement what happened from the other Gospels, for Jesus lifted himself back up and pierced the gloom with another powerful cry—"It is finished [*Tetelestai!*]" (John 19:30). This was followed by a final loud burst: "'Father, into your hands I commit my spirit!' And having said this he breathed his last" (Luke 23:46; cf. Mark 15:37).

Two observations must be made. First, Jesus did not die an ordinary death by crucifixion. Normally the crucified, through progressive loss of strength, fell unconscious and died feebly. Jesus was conscious to his very last breath, just as he had determined to be in refusing the narcotic cordial. Jesus gave his life. It was not taken.

Second, *tetelestai*/finished means that he finished his mission, not that he was finished by his enemies. The sense of the perfect tense is, "It has been and it forever will be finished!" As the waking sun shone brighter on his still, hanging head, the greatest work ever performed was finished. Jesus had gone lower than any human had ever gone as your sins and mine poured over his wincing soul. He suffered a greater isolation from the Father than any living soul had ever undergone. And he conquered! Thus he could shout in victory, "Finished" and confidently yield his spirit to the Father.

You and I cannot top that! Salvation comes to us from his finished work on the cross. If any of us have the audacity to suppose that we can add to his work and thus earn our salvation, we heap on him a terrible insult! Salvation comes by trusting in his finished work—and nothing else. Are you trusting him alone? If so then you can sing:

Lifted up was He to die,
"It is finished," was His cry;

Now in Heav'n exalted high;
Hallelujah! What a Savior![7]

The death of Christ reveals to us the utter depths Jesus went to in order to procure our salvation. And having that, we now see the *effects* of his atoning death for us.

The Revelation of the Atonement's Effects in Jesus' Death (vv. 38–41)

Above all, its effect was liberating: "And the curtain of the temple was torn in two, from top to bottom" (v. 38). St. Matthew's version adds:

> And behold, the curtain of the temple was torn in two, from top to bottom. And the earth shook, and the rocks were split. The tombs also were opened. And many bodies of the saints who had fallen asleep were raised, and coming out of the tombs after his resurrection they went into the holy city and appeared to many. (Matthew 27:51–53)

The veil into the Holy of Holies was supernaturally slashed in two as if a great sword had fallen. The high priest could only go into the Holy of Holies once a year, but now the way is wide-open for all who are in Christ.

By Jesus' blood we no longer must stand outside, but can advance into the presence of God. The word is *access*! The writer of Hebrews says:

> We have this as a sure and steadfast anchor of the soul, a hope that enters into the inner place behind the curtain, where Jesus has gone as a forerunner on our behalf. (Hebrews 6:19, 20)

> Therefore, brothers, since we have confidence to enter the holy places by the blood of Jesus, by the new and living way that he opened for us through the curtain, that is, through his flesh, and since we have a great priest over the house of God, let us draw near with a true heart in full assurance of faith. (Hebrews 10:19–22)

As ministers of the gospel, "stewards of the mysteries of God" (1 Corinthians 4:1), we can invite others to Christ and the Holy of Holies, to be liberated to a new life. In demonstration of the freeing power of Christ's death, at the instant of his expiration some of Jerusalem's tombs cracked open, and out stepped believers who had been raised to life. Evidently their earthly stay was very short, just enough to establish the power of Christ and instill a grand appetite for what is to come at the resurrection at the end of time. As to how they returned to eternal life we do not know, but for them it was probably not soon enough!

The torn curtain and fractured tombs say it all. Christ's death liberates those who believe from the bonds of death. It gives them free access to God's holy presence. Full freedom is what the cross offers—spiritual liberty now that will eventuate once again in a grave-popping liberation at Christ's return. The word here is *freedom*, what Paul calls "the freedom of the glory of the children of God" (Romans 8:21). *Free access! Freedom from death!* Have you been liberated?

Not only did the cross have a liberating effect, it also had a revelational effect. The centurion who was charged with the execution had seen everything: the terrible scourging, Jesus' features beaten into anonymity, the *Via Dolorosa*. He had supervised Jesus' nailing to the *patibulum* and elevation on the *crux simplex*. He had seen Jesus' ministry to the co-crucified and his care for his mother. He had seen the midday darkness come. This centurion stood close to Jesus lest some foul play take place under its cover. Finally he saw Jesus' explosive, triumphant death! That is why Mark records, "And when the centurion, who stood facing him, saw that in this way he breathed his last, he said, 'Truly this man was the Son of God!'" (v. 39). We must not suppose that this declared the man's faith, but it was a responsive, momentary heralding of the deity of Christ. Possibly it became faith in the days ahead. We do not know. But the point is, Jesus' death, carefully considered, revealed who he was and is.

We who know the Lord see so much more than the soldier, for we see the depths Jesus went to in order to redeem us. We see him writhing under our sins as they were poured onto him. We see that he became a curse for us, that we might become righteous. We see him totally alone, undergoing the trauma of separation from the Father in darkness and silence.

We say with the deepest passion, "Truly this man was the Son of God!" Jesus said, "And I, when I am lifted up from the earth [he was speaking of his crucifixion], will draw all people to myself" (John 12:32). The cross draws us. The women who were watching from a distance were a figure of this (Mark 15:40, 41). With the Resurrection, the cross would become a great magnet drawing men and women and children from every culture and race.

We confess that we are so drawn—that the cross with its bone and blood and sweat is everything. There is no darkness over our heads who trust in Christ. The sun shines with the greatest intensity. In the darkness, our sins were poured on Jesus so that he became sin for us. In the darkness, he bore the penalty for our sins in his separation from God. He endured the wrath of God in our stead. His great shout—"It is finished"—at the end of the darkness meant that everything had been done by him to procure our salvation.

We can add nothing, and indeed must add nothing to it. The effects are: as we confess that he is God's Son, we are liberated to go into his holy presence and are freed from death itself.

> Guilty, vile and helpless, we;
> Spotless Lamb of God was He;
> "Full atonement!" can it be?
> Hallelujah! what a Savior![8]

54

Sunday's Children

MARK 15:42—16:8

The Effect of Christ's Death (15:42–47)

The death of Jesus was not without its immediate effects. Jesus' amazing love throughout the ordeal of the cross, the supernatural midday darkness in which he silently bore our sins, and Jesus' explosive cries of victory as he gave up his spirit left their marks on those who remained. As we have seen, Mark records the spontaneous response of a pagan centurion in verse 39: "And when the centurion, who stood facing him, saw that in this way he breathed his last, he said, 'Truly this man was the Son of God!'" This undoubtedly was a shadow of what would happen in the Gentile world in the following years.

Jesus' death also had its effect on the spiritually minded who had been following him. One such was Joseph of Arimathea, whom Mark spotlights in verses 43–46. He was a prominent member of the Sanhedrin (the Seventy), who ruled Israel. Mark describes him as "a respected member of the council, who was also himself looking for the kingdom of God" (v. 43). His hope for spiritual renewal and national repentance was probably long-established. He was "a good and righteous man" (Luke 23:50).

As such, he was drawn by the immense spirituality of Jesus and his teaching and was in fact, as John records, ". . . a disciple of Jesus, but secretly for fear of the Jews" (John 19:38). It was this fear, despite all his laudable qualities, that had rendered Joseph a moral failure in the closing hours of Jesus' life, for though he had not consented to the Sanhedrin's action (Luke 23:51), there is no evidence he did anything to save Jesus. However, after witnessing the amazing death of Jesus, he came "out of the closet," risking everything to obtain Jesus' body for burial.

The events of Joseph's coming out are like this: the Jews had already had an understanding with Pilate that the bodies of the crucified were to be taken down and buried before 6:00 p.m. when the Sabbath began (John 19:31, 32). Joseph knew this meant Jesus' corpse would be tossed into a common criminal's grave as an ultimate emblem of humiliation—and that, Joseph could not bear.

So he "took courage and went to Pilate and asked for the body of Jesus" (v. 43). This was an immensely dangerous move, for Pilate was smarting from being manipulated by the Sanhedrin into killing Jesus and could have easily implicated Joseph under the charge of treason. In addition, by making this request Joseph was running the risk of being expelled from the Sanhedrin and coming under the scorn of the common populace for identifying himself with this false, failed Messiah. What is more, he would himself be dressing a corpse during the hours of preparation for the Sabbath (cf. John 18:28) and would thus be ceremonially defiled. This was a huge act of courage! It was even more elevated because there was absolutely nothing in it for him now. Jesus was dead. The dream was over.

So as we see Joseph obtain permission, and then watch him and his colleague Nicodemus rush to take Jesus down from the cross as the shadows lengthen, quickly wash the blood from him, wrap him in linen with spices, and then place Jesus in Joseph's own tomb, we are seeing a remarkably noble act. *Jesus' death, properly contemplated, is elevating.* His courage begets our courage, his dedication our dedication, his sacrifice our sacrifice. There is no more elevating example in history.

If that was it, if after Joseph of Arimathea experienced his elevation of soul, giving Jesus an honorable burial, there was nothing else, the name of Jesus of Nazareth would be no more than a passing note in Josephus, if that! Why? Because Joseph of Arimathea, as well as the disciples, Mary, and the godly women at the cross, all went through the greatest despair and depression of their earthly existence, seemingly without a glimmer of hope. Without the Resurrection, that depression would never have lifted. That Saturday before the Resurrection was a day of desolation, shattered dreams, gloom, and inertia. Think how it was for Mary—a sword had pierced her soul. Think of Peter's paralyzing guilt, beloved John's heartache, and Mary Magdalene's despair.

All of us have experienced something of this feeling in our lives. The fact is, there are more people living today in the despair and darkness of dark Saturday "than have ever lived in the drama of Friday or the victory of Easter."[1] As Ray Stedman has written:

Someone has called our present generation "Saturday's children," and it is an apt term. Our great American cities are, for the most part, teeming with pools of human misery where people live out their days in a kind of ritual dance toward death with hope or illusion. In the midst of an increasingly godless world, despair grips people's hearts everywhere. Hopelessness and meaninglessness come crushing in on us from every side.[2]

Without the Resurrection, we are all Saturday's children. We may see that Christ has done a heroic thing on the cross. We may even see it as the consummate act of love in the universe. But there is no power in it! "But if there is no resurrection of the dead, then not even Christ has been raised. And if Christ has not been raised, then our preaching is in vain and your faith is in vain" (1 Corinthians 15:13, 14).

The Resurrection of Christ! (16:1–8)

No one in the world knew it, but an immutable law was at work in Christ—a spiritual axiom that he had established: *humiliation brings exaltation!* Jesus had said, "Whoever exalts himself will be humbled, and whoever humbles himself will be exalted" (Matthew 23:12). The Scriptures are consistent about the pattern of exaltation: "Humble yourselves, therefore, under the mighty hand of God so that at the proper time he may exalt you" (1 Peter 5:6).

Christ's humiliation was of cosmic dimensions. He had created everything in the universe—every speck of stellar dust, every color and hue, every texture, the firefly and the fires of Arcturus. He held (and holds) all things together. He was, and is, the atomic bond that the most sophisticated science labs explore. All the universe was created by him and is moving toward him in consummation (Colossians 1:15–18).

But though being this God, a God who is transcendentally pure and holy, he became a human child. At the pinnacle of his manhood, he allowed himself to suffer the lowest, most humiliating death possible. He became sin for us (a writhing serpent on the cross). Jesus suffered separation from the Father and Holy Spirit as he bore our sins alone. There could be no greater humiliation!

How are we to imagine this? When our family was young, we had a swimming pool in which I used to play a game with my boys. I would collect a handful of pennies and toss them into the deep end, and my boys would plunge in, both going after the lion's share. It was great fun. Two . . . four . . . ten . . . fifteen—greed would keep them down for a long time. But there came a moment when they simply could not stay at the bottom, and I would see them arch upward and shoot to the surface, bursting through the water into the air. So it was with Jesus, only a millionfold more!

Think of the infinite compulsion of this inexorable law as Jesus humbled himself. He had been pushed down, down, down, and finally in an explosive moment the grave could no longer hold him.

His humiliation set in motion his own irrefragable law of exaltation. In a brilliant moment on Sunday morning, says St. Matthew, "And behold, there was a great earthquake, for an angel of the Lord descended from heaven and came and rolled back the stone and sat on it. His appearance was like lightning, and his clothing white as snow. And for fear of him the guards trembled and became like dead men" (Matthew 28:2–4). Matthew here mentions one angel, Luke mentions two (Luke 24:4), but that is probably only those who elected to be seen. Many more, perhaps thousands more, watched, for as Peter says, these were "things into which angels long to look" (1 Peter 1:12). Jesus came right through his grave clothes, in his sacred human body, glorious and radiant, and the angels' cheers rose to the stars!

The Effects of the Resurrection (16:1–8)

Meanwhile, the godly women who had watched the cross were leaving their homes in the dark. "Sorrow wakes early."[3] They had a mission to perform—to wash and perfume his battered face. The impulse came from great love, because the lapse of time and the Middle Eastern heat would assure that the body was already in decay. Their action would be of no utility to their dead Master, but it was what their hearts needed.

Mark records that they were worried: "And very early on the first day of the week, when the sun had risen, they went to the tomb. And they were saying to one another, 'Who will roll away the stone for us from the entrance of the tomb?'" (16:2, 3). We see that there was not the slightest idea of the possibility of resurrection in their minds. One of them mentioned the stone, and they had a mutual fret. Why had they not thought of it? So true to human nature! But as they worried themselves along, Mark says, "And looking up, they saw that the stone had been rolled back—it was very large" (v. 4). Their hearts began to pound. Had someone stolen his body? What indignities now? Would they be denied this one last act of devotion? Little did they know!

They hurried to the tomb, and "entering the tomb, they saw a young man sitting on the right side, dressed in a white robe, and they were alarmed" (v. 5). The word for "alarmed" is used only here in the New Testament. It is a compound verb used to express strong fear and agitation. They were terrified! The "young man" was an angel whose clothing, Luke tells us, was "dazzling apparel" (Luke 24:4). They were whirling in emotion as he spoke.

"And he said to them, 'Do not be alarmed. You seek Jesus of Nazareth, who was crucified. He has risen; he is not here. See the place where they laid him. But go, tell his disciples and Peter that he is going before you to Galilee. There you will see him, just as he told you'" (vv. 6, 7).

"He has risen" is a one-word sentence in the original. This one brief word announces the greatest miracle ever wrought on earth. It is the door to understanding Jesus Christ. With this, the angel invites them to take a look: "[H]e is not here. See the place where they laid him." Every theory, ancient and modern, all objections about the validity of the Resurrection of Jesus, are shattered by this one question: "What became of Christ's body?"

Even the most extreme skeptics do not deny that the grave was empty, including the early Jewish polemicists.[4] Where was the body? The Jews did not have it, for they would have produced it post-haste. The disciples did not have it, for if they did, it would have been psychologically and spiritually impossible for them to live the dedicated martyrs' lives and deaths they did. If you believe Hugh Schonfield's *The Passover Plot*, you probably believe that Elvis lives! That the disciples were totally convinced that Jesus had risen is beyond doubt! When someone says, "I don't believe in the Resurrection," ask them, "What happened to the body of Jesus?"

The Gospel of Mark closes with the angel's charge and the women's electric response: "'But go, tell his disciples and Peter that he is going before you to Galilee. There you will see him, just as he told you.' . . . and they said nothing to anyone, for they were afraid" (vv. 7, 8). "Trembling" describes what was happening to their bodies—uncontrolled, continuing *tromos*. "Bewildered" (literally *ekstasis*) indicates their ecstasy of mind. They were swept beyond their normal selves. Their silence can only refer to their behavior as they fled. Can you see them explode from the tomb, racing toward where they think the disciples may be, their robes flying behind them? Matthew adds that it was a joyous flight (Matthew 28:8–10).

What a perfect ending for Mark's Gospel. William Lane says, "The . . . ending of Mark is thoroughly consistent with the motifs of astonishment and fear developed throughout the Gospel. These motifs express the manner in which Mark understands the events of Jesus' life."[5] An authentic encounter with the gospel is compelling.

They all had been Saturday's children a few moments before, depressed and despairing. But then they became Sunday's children, joyously flying along. When they told the disciples "and Peter"—especially Peter, the arch-offender—they *all* became Sunday's children. It was Sunday's children who took the gospel around the Mediterranean, into the steppes of Russia, to

Germany, to Spain, and to Ireland. It is Sunday's children who take it today to the tiny villages and great cities of the world.

To Sunday's children Jesus says, in the words composed by Bishop Melito of Sardis:

> I am your forgiveness,
> I am the passover of your salvation,
> I am the lamb which was sacrificed for you,
> I am your ransom,
> I am your light,
> I am your savior,
> I am your resurrection,
> I am your king,
> I am leading you up to the heights of heaven,
> I will show you the eternal Father,
> I will raise you up by my right hand.[6]

Sunday's children live in the historical, intellectual, and emotional reality of the Resurrection. Next to the empty tomb and the witness of God's Word, it is Sunday's children who form the greatest argument for the Resurrection.

Charles Colson tells of meeting an old friend, a Washington journalist who in the course of conversation interjected, "I'm not sure I can buy the deity of Christ . . . I mean, the resurrection." Colson says he

> . . . argued hard, reviewing many of the historical, scientific and psychological arguments for the case that Christ rose. Though we parted good friends, he was not persuaded.
>
> Ironically, only a few days after our luncheon, during an Easter trip to two Indiana institutions, I saw firsthand evidence that Christ did indeed rise from the tomb. It was not scientific proof, but the convincing demonstration of the lives of men and women—those locked in the hopelessness of prison—as well as those on the outside. Events in the life of former Judge William Bontrager serve as one very powerful illustration.
>
> Bill Bontrager's story is interwoven with that of Harry Fred Palmer, a young Vietnam veteran who accepted Christ in 1977 while in jail awaiting sentencing for a string of house burglaries. His offense carried a mandatory ten- to twenty-year sentence in Indiana, though that law, already acknowledged as harsh, was changed just eighteen days after his arrest. Judge Bontrager, who had himself been converted to Christ a year earlier, reviewed Palmer's case carefully. He realized the mandatory ten-year sentence would destroy rather than rehabilitate Palmer, so he declared it unconstitutional. Bontrager ordered him to serve one year in the state penitentiary and then, upon release, to reimburse those he had robbed and provide community service.

Palmer did just that. He was a model prisoner; after release he was reunited with his wife and family and began paying back his victims. The case seemed closed, a model of justice, restitution, and restoration.

But the Indiana Supreme Court swung into action; claiming that Judge Bontrager had erred, they ordered him to send Palmer back to prison—for at least nine more years!

For Bontrager, the order was clearly a case of choosing between the law of man and the law of God. He had been reading the Old Testament prophets; the words of Amos seared his conscience. He knew the Supreme Court's order did not meet God's standard of justice and righteousness, but would instead punish a man twice for the same crime, merely to satisfy a technicality of the law.

So Bontrager stepped aside, turning the case over to another judge. A nightmarish sequence of events followed. The Court slammed Palmer into Westville Correction Center, declared Bontrager in contempt, fined him $500, and sentenced him to thirty days in prison. Though that sentence was suspended, proceedings were begun to remove him from the bench. Rather than allow his own case to endanger Palmer's appeal for release, Judge Bontrager resigned.

His resignation was not without cost. Bill Bontrager gave up a comfortable salary, the judgeship he had always wanted, a position of respect. His radical talk about obeying God, not man, raised eyebrows in his community as well; it wasn't as if he left his post in a blaze of glory to open a lucrative law practice. In fact, clients for his small firm have been very scarce. But, as his wife told me, "We are waiting on the Lord to provide— so we're learning patience . . . if only we could encourage the phone company and a few other creditors to be patient too!"

So it was that I invited private citizen, ex-judge Bill Bontrager and his wife to accompany me to services at Westville on Easter morning. Bontrager said nothing as we waited for guards to unlock the entrance to the auditorium, but as the steel doors swung open he bolted ahead of me and made his way into the crowd of waiting inmates. Seconds later he found Harry Fred Palmer—and the tall, lanky ex-judge embraced the young ex-burglar in prison denims, as tears rolled down their cheeks.

As I watched their reunion, the witness was clear: a man giving up a respected, comfortable life to fight for what is right, against inexorable processes of an often hostile world, is evidence that Christ lives. . . .

Bill Bontrager is no saint. He's a country boy at heart who wears cowboy boots and string ties. He makes mistakes. But those who testify for Christ are not perfect people. If they were, one of His mightiest witnesses, a rough fisherman named Peter, would never have been called to serve. But Peter saw the resurrected Christ—and his life revealed that truth. . . .

I wish my novelist friend could have been with me on that Easter morning, for none of us who watched Bontrager and Palmer, brothers embracing in a modern-day tomb, could doubt that Jesus—the Prisoner who was executed—rose from His tomb and lives today.[7]

Sunday's children are arguments the world understands and needs. What is your day—Saturday with all its hopelessness and pessimism, or Sunday with its bounding life and irrepressible hope?

Soli Deo gloria!

Notes

Chapter One: The Purpose of Life

1. J. B. Phillips, *The Ring of Truth* (London: Macmillan, 1967), p. 74.
2. Kirsopp Lake, trans., *Eusebius the Ecclesiastical History*, vol. 1 (Cambridge, MA: Harvard University Press, 1965), p. 297 (III, XXXIX 15).
3. J. Sidlow Baxter, *Explore the Book, Six Volumes in One*, "Mark" (Grand Rapids, MI: Zondervan, 1975), p. 217.
4. William L. Lane, *The Gospel According to Mark* (Grand Rapids, MI: Eerdmans, 1975), pp. 15, 16. See Tacitus, *Annals*, XV, 35–38, 44.
5. Ibid., p. 25.
6. John G. Stackhouse, Jr., "The Gospel Song" (an unpublished parody).
7. Robert A. Raines, *Creative Brooding* (New York: Macmillan, 1966).
8. J. Armitage Robinson, *Unity in Christ* (London: Macmillan, 1903), pp. 69–73.
9. Richard Collier, *The General Next to God* (Glasgow: Collins, 1965), p. 72.

Chapter Two: The Effective Witness: John the Baptist

1. Charles Spurgeon, *The Metropolitan Tabernacle Pulpit*, vol. 10 (Pasadena, TX: Pilgrim Publications, 1973), p. 407.
2. Roland Bainton, *Here I Stand* (New York: Mentor Books, New American Library, 1950), p. 144.
3. William L. Lane, *The Gospel According to Mark* (Grand Rapids, MI: Eerdmans, 1975), pp. 50, 51.
4. Phillips Brooks, *Lectures on Preaching* (Manchester, UK: James Robinson, 1899), p. 9.
5. Haddon Robinson, *Biblical Preaching* (Grand Rapids, MI: Baker, 1980), p. 24.
6. Lane, *The Gospel According to Mark*, p. 49.
7. Ibid., p. 50.
8. Alexander Maclaren, *Expositions of Holy Scripture*, vol. 8, *St. Mark* (Grand Rapids, MI: Baker, 1974), p. 17.

Chapter Three: The Temptation of Christ

1. Charles Colson, *Who Speaks for God?* (Wheaton, IL: Crossway Books, 1985), pp. 27, 28.
2. William L. Lane, *The Gospel According to Mark* (Grand Rapids, MI: Eerdmans, 1975), p. 61.
3. Roger Worthington, *The Chicago Tribune*, February 16, 1982, Section 3, "Tempo."
4. John A. Broadus, *Commentary on the Gospel of Matthew* (Valley Forge, PA: American Baptist Publications Society, n.d.), p. 65.
5. William Hendriksen, *Exposition of the Gospel According to Matthew* (Grand Rapids, MI: Baker, 1973), p. 222.

6. Helmut Thielicke, *Between God and Satan* (Grand Rapids, MI: Eerdmans, 1973), pp. 51, 52.

7. This is a paraphrase of Thielicke's description given in ibid., p. 63.

Chapter Four: The Beginning of Christ's Ministry

1. David L. McKenna, *The Communicator's Commentary of Mark* (Waco, TX: Word, 1982), p. 46.

2. C. E. B. Cranfield, *The Gospel According to St. Mark* (Cambridge: Cambridge University Press, 1983), p. 42.

3. William L. Lane, *The Gospel According to Mark* (Grand Rapids, MI: Eerdmans, 1975), p. 69.

4. Lee Eisenberg and DeCourcey Taylor, eds. *The Ultimate Fishing Book* (Boston: Houghton Mifflin, 1981), p. 20.

Chapter Five: The Authority of Christ

1. Phillips Brooks, *Lectures in Preaching* (Manchester, UK: James Robinson, 1899), pp. 25, 26.

2. G. Abbott-Smith, *A Manual Greek Lexicon of the New Testament* (New York: Charles Scribner's Sons, n.d.), p. 141.

3. William Barclay, *The Gospel of Mark* (Philadelphia: Westminster, 1956), p. 25.

4. Joseph Bayly, *I Love to Tell The Story* (Elgin, IL: David C. Cook, 1978), p. 28.

5. William L. Lane, *The Gospel According to Mark* (Grand Rapids, MI: Eerdmans, 1975), p. 73.

6. Ibid.

7. Hugh Anderson, *The Gospel of Mark* (London: Oliphants, 1976), p. 91.

Chapter Six: The Heart of the Healer

1. William Barclay, *The Gospel of Mark* (Philadelphia: Westminster, 1956), p. 28.

2. Alexander Maclaren, *Exposition of Holy Scripture*, vol. 8, *St. Mark* (Grand Rapids, MI: Baker, 1974), p. 37.

3. E. Stanley Jones, *A Song of Ascents* (New York: Abingdon, 1979), p. 383.

4. William L. Lane, *The Gospel According to Mark* (Grand Rapids, MI: Eerdmans, 1975), p. 82.

Chapter Seven: The Master's Touch

1. Alexander Maclaren, *Expositions of Holy Scripture*, vol. 8, *St. Mark* (Grand Rapids, MI: Baker, 1974), pp. 39–60, which contains the sermons "A Parable in a Miracle" and "Christ's Touch," sources for the outline of this study and many of the insights.

2. Richard Chenevix Trench, *Notes on the Miracles of Our Lord* (Grand Rapids, MI: Baker, 1956), p. 135.

3. Philip Yancey, *Where Is God When It Hurts?* (Grand Rapids, MI: Zondervan, 1977), p. 32.

4. William Barclay, *The Gospel of Matthew*, vol. 2 (Philadelphia: Westminster, 1958), p. 301.

5. Arnold Dallimore, *George Whitefield*, vol. 1 (Edinburgh: Banner of Truth; Wheaton, IL: Crossway Books, 1975), p. 132.

6. Iain H. Murray, *David Martyn Lloyd-Jones, The First Forty Years, 1899– 1939* (Edinburgh: Banner of Truth, 1982), p. 207.

7. David L. McKenna, *Mark*, in The Communicator's Commentary Series, ed. Lloyd J. Ogilvie (Waco, TX: Word, 1982), p. 58.

8. Brooke Foss Westcott, *Christian Aspects of Life* (London: Macmillan, 1897), p. 354.

Chapter Eight: The Capernaum Caper

1. Francis Schaeffer, *The Church at the End of the 20th Century* (Downers Grove, IL: InterVarsity Press, 1970), n.p.

2. Charles Spurgeon, *The Metropolitan Tabernacle Pulpit*, vol. 17 (Pasadena, TX: Pilgrim Publications, 1971), p. 167.

Chapter Nine: Jesus, Friend of Sinners

1. According to Professor Brabanec the exact figures, based on simple calendar calculations (making no references to the exact date of Christ's birth), is $1,408,490 daily. His other calculations (for the fiscal year) are $32,376 per second, $1,942,542 per minute, and $114,552,520 per hour.

2. William Barclay, *The Gospel of Luke* (Philadelphia: Westminster, 1956), p. 61, where the author describes the two taxes in full.

3. William L. Lane, *The Gospel According to Mark* (Grand Rapids, MI: Eerdmans, 1975), p. 102.

4. Barclay, *The Gospel of Luke*, pp. 61, 62.

5. Lane, *The Gospel According to Mark*, p. 102.

6. Ibid., p. 103.

7. Vincent Taylor, *The Gospel According to St. Mark* (Grand Rapids, MI: Baker, 1981), p. 206.

8. Lane, *The Gospel According to Mark*, p. 104.

9. Ibid.

10. *Preaching*, vol. 1, no. 4, January/February 1986, p. 55.

Chapter Ten: The New Wine of Christ

1. Rebecca Manley Pippert, *Out of the Salt Shaker* (Downers Grove, IL: InterVarsity Press, 1980), p. 97ff.

2. William Barclay, *The Gospel of Mark* (Philadelphia: Westminster, 1956), p. 53.

3. W. E. Sangster, "Drunk and Mad," in Clyde E. Fant Jr. and William A. Pinson Jr., *Twenty Centuries of Great Preaching*, vol. 11 (Waco, TX: Word, 1971), pp. 341, 342.

4. Donald Grey Barnhouse, *Let Me Illustrate* (Old Tappan, NJ: Revell, 1967), p. 97.

5. Lloyd J. Ogilvie, *Life Without Limits* (Waco, TX: Word, 1975), p. 55.

6. Ibid., pp. 53, 54.

Chapter Eleven: Jesus, Pressured Jesus

1. Alexander Maclaren, *Expositions of Holy Scripture*, vol. 8, *St. Mark* (Grand Rapids, MI: Baker, 1974), p. 106.

2. Ray Stedman, *Expository Studies in Mark 1–8: The Servant Who Rules* (Waco, TX: Word, 1976), p. 84.

3. William L. Lane, *The Gospel According to Mark* (Grand Rapids, MI: Eerdmans, 1975), p. 130.

4. Ibid., p. 129.

5. Anne Morrow Lindbergh, *Gift from the Sea* (New York: Vintage Books, 1978), pp. 25, 26.

6. Ibid., pp. 49, 50.

7. Roland Hein, ed., *Creation in Christ* (Wheaton, IL: Harold Shaw, 1978), p. 317.

8. E. Stanley Jones, *A Song of Ascents* (New York: Abingdon, 1968), p. 383.

9. Maclaren, *Expositions of Holy Scripture*, p. 108.

10. Tim Hansel, *When I Relax I Feel Guilty* (Elgin, IL: David C. Cook, 1981), p. 19, quoting Hugh Prather's "Notes to Myself."

Chapter Twelve: A Third Opinion

1. Vincent Taylor, *The Gospel According to St. Mark* (Grand Rapids, MI: Baker, 1981), p. 236. Note that the word means "to arrest" in 6:17; 12:12; 13:1, 44, 46, 49, 51.

2. Ibid., p. 237. Cf. John 7:5 where we see that even his own brothers did not believe in him.

3. Albert Schweitzer, *The Quest for the Historical Jesus* (New York: Macmillan, 1959), pp. 370, 371, says:

> There is silence all around. The Baptist appears, and cries "Repent, for the kingdom of Heaven is at hand." Soon after that comes Jesus and in the knowledge that He is the coming Son of Man lays hold of the wheel of the world to set it moving on that last revolution which is to bring all ordinary history to a close. It refuses to turn, and He throws Himself upon it. Then it does turn; and crushes Him. Instead of bringing them eschatological conditions, He has destroyed them. The wheel rolls onward, and the mangled body of the one immeasurably great Man, who was strong enough to think of Himself as the spiritual ruler of mankind and to bend history to His purpose, is hanging upon it still. That is His victory and His reign.

4. R. C. Sproul, *The Holiness of God* (Wheaton, IL: Tyndale, 1986), pp. 101–26, where a chapter entitled "The Insanity of Luther" is devoted to demonstrating his supreme sanity.

5. William L. Lane, *The Gospel According to Mark* (Grand Rapids, MI: Eerdmans, 1975), p. 141.

6. Ibid.: "H. van der Loos . . . has suggested that the second charge entails an accusation that Jesus pronounced the name Beelzebub, perhaps softly, in the exorcism of demons."

7. Taylor, *The Gospel According to St. Mark*, p. 241 notes that the word for "property" or vessels or utensils or possessions is used of "body" in 2 Corinthians 4:7. Thus it naturally represents those enslaved by Satan.

8. The story is reported by Dr. David Walls of Bethany Bible Church, Phoenix, Arizona.

9. C. E. B. Cranfield, *The Gospel According to Mark* (Cambridge: Cambridge University Press, 1983), p. 143.

10. Ibid., p. 142.

11. Josh McDowell, *Evidence That Demands a Verdict* (San Bernardino, CA: Campus Crusade for Christ, 1972), p. 110, where he quotes Philip Schaff, *The Person of Christ*, American Tract Society, 1913, pp. 94, 95.

12. C. S. Lewis, *The Case for Christianity* (New York: Macmillan, 1944), p. 45.

13. C. E. B. Cranfield, *Romans*, vol. 1 (Edinburgh: T & T Clark, 1975), pp. 603–5 argues convincingly that "reasonable" (*logikos*) is a good translation, for the root idea of the word is *logical*.

Chapter Thirteen: Christ's Kinsmen

1. Vincent Taylor, *The Gospel According to St. Mark* (Grand Rapids, MI: Baker, 1981), p. 246.

2. George Arthur Buttrick, *Sermons Preached in a University Church* (New York: Abingdon, 1959), p. 125, where he quotes Renan's *Life of Jesus* (New York: Little, Brown, 1910), p. 313.

3. Alexander Maclaren, *Exposition of Holy Scripture,* vol. 8, *St. Mark* (Grand Rapids, MI: Baker, 1974), p. 133.

4. C. S. Lewis, *The Four Loves* (New York: Harcourt, Brace and Jovanovich, 1960), p. 55.

5. Amitai Etzioni, *An Immodest Agenda: Rebuilding America Before the 21st Century* (New York: McGraw-Hill, 1983), p. 110.

6. Lloyd Ogilvie, *Life Without Limits* (Waco, TX: Word, 1975), p. 79.

Chapter Fourteen: Authentic Hearing

1. Matthew 13:1 indicates that it was on the same day.

2. D. Edmond Hiebert, *Mark* (Chicago: Moody, 1974), p. 98, remarks that the "cove between Capernaum and the mouth of the Jordan, where the beach rises rather rapidly from the water which is quite deep within a few yards from shore, may have provided the needed natural amphitheater with acoustics adequate for the occasion."

3. William Barclay, *The Gospel of Mark* (Philadelphia: Westminster, 1956), pp. 91, 92.

4. C. S. Lewis, *Screwtape Letters* (London: Geoffrey Bles, 1942), pp. 12–14.

5. C. S. Lewis, *Surprised by Joy* (New York: Harcourt Brace & World, n.d.), p. 229.

6. Helmut Thielicke, *The Waiting Father* (New York: Harper and Row, 1975), p. 57.

7. Walter Underwood, *The Contemporary 12* (Nashville: Abingdon, 1984), pp. 86, 87.

Chapter Fifteen: Jesus Calming the Storm

1. I. M. Anderson, "When Sankey Sang the Shepherd Song," *Moody Monthly*, vol. 86, no. 6, February 1986, pp. 77, 78.

2. Vincent Taylor, *The Gospel According to Mark* (Grand Rapids, MI: Baker, 1981), p. 273, where the author says, "the subject . . . imparts a note of urgency."

3. Quoted by Harry Ironside, *Lectures on the Book of Acts* (Neptune, NJ: Loizeaux Brothers, 1975), p. 457.

4. Ruth Graham, *Sitting by My Laughing Fire* (Waco, TX: Word, 1977), p. 26.

5. A. T. Robertson, *Word Pictures in the New Testament*, vol. 1 (Nashville: Broadman, 1930), p. 293.

Chapter Sixteen: Jesus: Lord of the Spirits

1. Kenneth L. Woodward with David Gates, "Giving the Devil His Due," *Newsweek*, August 30, 1982, p. 74.

2. C. S. Lewis, *The Screwtape Letters* (London: Geoffrey Bles, 1942), p. 9.

3. Ray C. Stedman, *Expository Studies in Mark 1–8: The Servant Who Rules* (Waco, TX: Word, 1976), p. 131.

4. Gerhard Kittel, *Theological Dictionary of the New Testament*, vol. 2, trans. Geoffrey W. Bromiley (Grand Rapids, MI: Eerdmans, 1968), pp. 18, 19.

5. D. Edmond Hiebert, *Mark: A Portrait of the Servant* (Chicago: Moody Press, 1974), p. 119.

6. William L. Lane, *The Gospel According to Mark* (Grand Rapids, MI: Eerdmans, 1975), p. 185.

7. Karl Barth, *Church Dogmatics*, vol. 4, *The Doctrine of Reconciliation*, Part 2 (Edinburgh: T. & T. Clark, 1985), p. 231, who says:

> We have only to think of the story of the demoniac in Mark 5. Someone has described it as a burlesque. And why not? For all its final seriousness what happens to evil in its confrontation with Jesus is grotesque and (if we like) farcical. In Luke 10:18, for example, it tumbles down from heaven. And in this story it can only ask for permission to go, itself unclean, into the herd of unclean swine, to plunge with them over the cliff into the lake and to be drowned, thus perishing finally from the world. If only the community had let it rest at that, or learned again not merely to laugh, but genuinely to rejoice at this sign and what it so drastically signified!

8. V. Raymond Edman, *Storms and Starlight* (Wheaton, IL: Van Kampen Press, 1951), p. 124, who quotes John Oxenham, "Gadara, A.D. 31," *from Bees in Amber*.

Chapter Seventeen: Jesus' Power over Illness and Death

1. M. R. Vincent, *Word Studies in the New Testament* (Wilmington, DE: Associated Publishers and Authors, 1972), p. 103.

2. William Barclay, *The Gospel of Mark* (Philadelphia: Westminster, 1956), p. 128.

3. William L. Lane, *The Gospel According to Mark* (Grand Rapids, MI: Eerdmans, 1975), p. 190.

4. Barclay, *The Gospel of Mark*, p. 126.

Chapter Eighteen: Ministering Midst Unbelief

1. D. Edmond Hiebert, *Mark* (Chicago: Moody Press, 1974), p. 137, says:

The distinctness of the two visits seems established by the fact that Matthew clearly noted two separate visits to Nazareth. The rejection recorded by Luke coincides with the visit mentioned in Matthew 4:13 when He left Nazareth to establish headquarters in Capernaum. The visit recorded in Matthew 13:54–58 came later, agreeing with Mark's account. After this first visit, Jesus went to Capernaum to start His work there; after the second visit, He started on another tour of Galilee. Clearly, this visit seems later than that in Luke 4:16–31.

2. Vincent Taylor, *The Gospel According to St. Mark* (Grand Rapids, MI: Baker, 1981), p. 300.

3. Hiebert, *Mark*, p. 139 says:

It was the common practice among the Jews to use the father's name, whether he were alive or dead. A man was called the son of his mother only when his father was unknown. During His former visit to Nazareth, the people spoke of Him as "Joseph's son" (Lk 4:22). Stauffer holds that "the son of Mary" was now used as a deliberate insult, stamping Jesus as a bastard. He points out that custom required that so long as the sons of an adulteress lived "a life pleasing to God, nothing insulting shall be said about his birth," but if he becomes an apostate, "his illegitimate birth shall be spoken of publicly and unsparingly."

4. Arthur John Gossip, *From the Edge of the Crowd* (New York: Charles Scribner's Sons, n.d.), p. 22.

5. G. Campbell Morgan, *The Gospel According to Mark* (Old Tappan, NJ: Revell, 1927), pp. 135, 136.

6. Arthur John Gossip, *In Christ's Stead* (London: Hodder and Stoughton, 1925), p. 105.

7. William L. Lane, *The Gospel According to Mark* (Grand Rapids, MI: Eerdmans, 1975), p. 204, says: "By situating these two incidents at this point in his Gospel the evangelist shows that unbelief is the context in which the Christian mission advances and that rejection is an experience common to the Lord and the Church."

8. Taylor, *The Gospel According to St. Mark*, p. 303.

9. Lane, *The Gospel According to Mark*, pp. 206, 207 says: "The commissioning of the Twelve has a rich background in the juridical practice of Judaism, which recognized the official character of actions performed by authorized individuals. Reduced to its simplest form, the law acknowledged that 'the sent one is as the man who commissioned him.' . . ."

10. William Barclay, *The Gospel of Mark* (Philadelphia: Westminster, 1956), pp. 143, 144.

11. Lane, *The Gospel According to Mark*, pp. 208, 209.

12. Donald Grey Barnhouse, *Let Me Illustrate* (Old Tappan, NJ: Revell, 1967), pp. 358, 359.

Chapter Nineteen: Death of a Conscience

1. William L. Lane, *The Gospel According to Mark* (Grand Rapids, MI: Eerdmans, 1975), p. 219, says: "John's preaching was politically explosive. The powerful Nabatean forces across Herod's border posed a definite threat to his security, and the Tetrarch could not afford to have the provincials also inflamed against him."

2. Josephus, *Antiquities*, Book XVIII, V.2.

3. Alfred Edersheim, *The Life and Times of Jesus the Messiah*, vol. 1 (Grand Rapids, MI: Eerdmans, 1967), p. 659.

4. William Barclay, *The Gospel of Mark* (Philadelphia: Westminster, 1956), p. 150.

5. Lane, *The Gospel According to Mark*, p. 220, says: "The Herodians apparently celebrated their birthdays in this fashion regularly, for Josephus mentions a similar feast on a birthday of Agrippa (Ant. XIX, vii. l). l."

6. Josephus, *Antiquities*, XVIII, V.4.

7. William Shakespeare, *Macbeth*, act 5.

8. Alexander Maclaren, *Expositions of Holy Scripture*, vol. 8, *Mark* (Grand Rapids, MI: Baker, 1974), p. 249, where the original quotation is: "some hooked pole pushed at random into the sea, may bring up by the locks some pale drowned memory long plunged into the sea of oblivion."

Chapter Twenty: The Feeding of the Five Thousand

1. C. E. B. Cranfield, *The Gospel According to St. Mark* (Cambridge: Cambridge University Press, 1983), p. 222. Also William L. Lane, *The Gospel According to Mark* (Grand Rapids, MI: Eerdmans, 1975), p. 226.

2. Lane, *The Gospel According to Mark*, p. 231.

3. Ibid., p. 229.

4. Hugh Anderson, *The Gospel of Mark* (London: Oliphants, 1976), p. 173.

5. Alfred Edersheim, *The Life and Times of Jesus the Messiah*, vol. 1 (Grand Rapids, MI: Eerdmans, 1967), p. 666.

6. Nigel Turner, *Christian Words* (Nashville: Thomas Nelson, 1982), p. 78.

7. Cranfield, *The Gospel According to St. Mark*, p. 217.

8. Clarence Edward Macartney, *Macartney's Illustration* (New York: Abingdon, n.d.), p. 66.

9. Lane, *The Gospel According to Mark*, p. 229.

10. Edersheim, *The Life and Times of Jesus the Messiah*, p. 683. Also, Cranfield, *The Gospel According to St. Mark*, p. 218, who uses a rabbinical quotation: "when students sit arranged like garden-beds . . . and are engaged in studying the Torah."

11. Vincent Taylor, *The Gospel According to St. Mark* (Grand Rapids, MI: Baker, 1981), p. 324. Also see Edersheim, *The Life and Times of Jesus the Messiah*, p. 684 for more details.

12. Elizabeth Elliot, *Worldwide Challenge Magazine*, January 1978, pp. 39, 40.

13. Edersheim, *The Life and Times of Jesus the Messiah*, p. 679, says:

> There is at least in our view, no doubt that thoughts of the Passover and the Holy Supper, of their commanding and mystic meaning, were present to the Saviour, and that it is in this light the miraculous feeding of the multitude must be considered, if we are in any measure to understand it.

14. Cranfield, *The Gospel According to St. Mark*, pp. 222, 223.

Chapter Twenty-One: The Storms of Life

1. C. E. B. Cranfield, *The Gospel According to St. Mark* (Cambridge: Cambridge University Press, 1983), p. 175.

2. Ibid., p. 225.

3. James Hastings, ed. *The Speakers' Bible*, vol. 8 (Grand Rapids, MI: Baker, 1971), p. 138.

4. D. Edmond Hiebert, *Mark: A Portrait of the Servant* (Chicago: Moody Press, 1974), p. 166.

5. Alfred Edersheim, *The Life and Times of Jesus the Messiah*, vol. 1 (Grand Rapids, MI: Eerdmans, 1967), p. 692.

6. William L. Lane, *The Gospel According to Mark* (Grand Rapids, MI: Eerdmans, 1975), p. 238.

7. Edersheim, *The Life and Times of Jesus the Messiah*, p. 695, where he discusses the various conjectures as to why Peter's story was not included.

8. Alexander Maclaren, *Expositions of Holy Scripture*, vol. 10 (Grand Rapids, MI: Baker, 1974), p. 279.

Chapter Twenty-Two: Truly Clean

1. Herbert Danby, trans., *The Mishnah* (London: Oxford, 1974), p. 452.

2. Ibid., pp. 603–789.

3. Alfred Edersheim, *The Life and Times of Jesus the Messiah*, vol. 2 (Grand Rapids, MI: Eerdmans, 1967), pp. 11, 12.

4. William Barclay, *The Gospel of Mark* (Philadelphia: Westminster, 1956), p. 168.

5. *The Mishnah*, pp. 603–619.

6. Barclay, *The Gospel of Mark*, p. 167.

7. C. E. B. Cranfield, *The Gospel According to St. Mark* (Cambridge: Cambridge University Press, 1983), p. 236.

8. William Lane, *The Gospel According to Mark* (Grand Rapids, MI: Eerdmans, 1975), p. 251, says: "M. *Nedarim* V. 6, is particularly instructive because it shows that there were cases in which a son's vow which created a breach between father and son could not be set aside even with the best will on the part of the son."

9. Vincent Taylor, *The Gospel According to St. Mark* (Grand Rapids, MI: Baker, 1981), p. 342.

10. Barclay, *The Gospel of Mark*, p. 174.

11. Cranfield, *The Gospel According to St. Mark*, pp. 242, 243.

Chapter Twenty-Three: A Pleasing Faith

1. C. H. Spurgeon, *The Metropolitan Tabernacle Pulpit*, vol. 22 (Pasadena, TX: Pilgrim Publications, 1971), p. 458.

2. William L. Lane, *The Gospel According to Mark* (Grand Rapids, MI: Eerdmans, 1975), p. 258.

3. William Barclay, *The Gospel of John* (Philadelphia: Westminster, 1956), pp. 142, 143.

4. John Nicholas Lenker, ed., *Sermons of Martin Luther*, vol. 2 (Grand Rapids, MI: Baker, 1983), p. 150.

5. Helmut Thielicke, *The Silence of God* (Grand Rapids, MI: Eerdmans, 1962), p. 15.

6. A. Plummer, *An Exegetical Commentary on the Gospel According to St. Mark* (Cambridge: Cambridge University Press, 1926), p. 189.

7. Lenker, *Sermons of Martin Luther*, p. 152.

8. Thielicke, *The Silence of God*, p. 15.

Chapter Twenty-Four: Modeling Ministry

1. D. Edmond Hiebert, *Mark: A Portrait of a Servant* (Chicago: Moody Press, 1974), p. 188.

2. Vincent Taylor, *The Gospel According to St. Mark* (Grand Rapids, MI: Baker, 1966), p. 352.

3. Alfred Edersheim, *The Life and Times of Jesus the Messiah*, vol. 2 (Grand Rapids, MI: Eerdmans, 1967), pp. 45, 46, especially p. 46 where the author says: "But we mark that all here seems to be much more elaborate than in Israel. The reason of this must, of course, be sought in the moral condition of the person healed."

4. Alexander Maclaren, *Expositions of the Holy Scripture*, vol. 8, *Mark* (Grand Rapids, MI: Baker, 1974), pp. 273–301 provides the outline for this study.

5. Ibid., p. 278.

6. This story comes from Rev. Dave Walls, pastor at Bethany Bible Church, Phoenix, Arizona.

7. George Eliot, *Middlemarch*, Book 2, Chapter 20, Riverside edition, ed. Gordon S. Haight (Boston: Houghton Mifflin, 1956), p. 144.

8. Brooke Foss Westcott, *Christian Aspects of Life* (London: Macmillan, 1986), p. 354.

9. R. Kent Hughes, *Blessed Are the Born Again* (Wheaton, IL: Victor Books, 1986), pp. 99, 100.

10. Maclaren, *Expositions of the Holy Scripture*, p. 286, where he says:

> Let me remind you, too, that still more dangerous . . . is the pity which does not issue in strenuous work. It is easy to excite people's emotions; but it is perilous . . . unless they be excited through the understanding, and pass on the impulse to the will and the practical powers. The surest way to petrify a heart is to stimulate the feelings, and give them nothing to do. . . . Coldness, hypocrisy, spurious sentimentalism, and a whole train of affections and falsehoods follow the steps of an emotional religion, which divorces itself from active work. Pity is meant to impel, to help . . . let us remember that every time our compassion is stirred, and no action ensues, our hearts are in some measure indurated, and the sincerity of our religion in some degree impaired.

Chapter Twenty-Five: Nurturing Spiritual Understanding

1. Ezra P. Gould, *The Gospel According to St. Mark* (Edinburgh: T & T. Clark, 1948), p. 142.

2. William L. Lane, *The Gospel According to Mark* (Grand Rapids, MI: Eerdmans, 1975), p. 272.

3. Ibid., p. 274.

4. A. T. Robertson, *Word Pictures in the New Testament*, vol. 1 (Nashville: Broadman Press, 1930), p. 329, says: "Constative aorist followed the imperfect. They kept on."

5. D. Edmond Hiebert, *Mark: A Portrait of the Servant* (Chicago: Moody Press, 1974), p. 195.

6. Ibid., p. 197, explains:

Since leaven was strictly forbidden with certain offerings (Lev 2:11) and had to be removed during the Passover, it readily became a figure of evil or corruption. This was the meaning given it in rabbinical teaching and seems to be its uniform meaning in the New Testament. As producing a process of fermentation, leaven or yeast pictures a pervasive corrupting tendency that works invisibly. Christ's warning was thus "a pithy one-word parable for unseen pervasive influence."

Chapter Twenty-Six: Christ and Human Expectations

1. William L. Lane, *Commentary on the Gospel of Mark* (Grand Rapids, MI: Eerdmans, 1975), p. 285.

2. Vincent Taylor, *The Gospel According to St. Mark* (Grand Rapids, MI: Baker, 1981), p. 372.

3. Alfred Lord Tennyson, *In Memoriam, A.H.H.*

Chapter Twenty-Seven: What Confessing Christ Means

1. William L. Lane, *Commentary on the Gospel of Mark* (Grand Rapids, MI: Eerdmans, 1975), p. 289.

2. John 1:41 says that Andrew came and told Peter that he had found "the Messiah." Jesus was accepted as Messiah from the first.

3. The verb for "warned" is the same one Christ used in 1:25 in rebuking the demons.

4. Lane, *Commentary on the Gospel of Mark*, p. 303: "an outspokenness that conceals nothing."

5. Ray C. Stedman, *Expository Studies in Mark 1–8: The Servant Who Rules* (Waco, TX: Word, 1976), p. 221.

6. The *London Times*, April 9, 1978.

7. Paul Lee Tan, *Encyclopedia of 7700 Illustrations* (Rockville, MD: Assurance, 1979), p. 1213.

Chapter Twenty-Eight: The Midnight Son

1. William Barclay, *The Gospel of Mark* (Philadelphia: Westminster, 1956), p. 215, writes:

Tradition says that the Transfiguration took place on the top of Mount Tabor. The Eastern Church actually calls the Festival of the Transfiguration the *Taborion*. It may be that the choice of Mount Tabor is based on the mention of Mount Tabor in Psalm 89:12, but it is an unfortunate choice. Tabor is in the South of Galilee, and Caesarea Philippi is away to the north. Tabor is no more than 1,000 feet high, and, in the time of Jesus, there was a fortress on the top. It is much more likely that this happened amidst the eternal snows of Mount Hermon which is 9,200 feet high, which is much nearer Caesarea Philippi and where the solitude would be much more complete.

D. Edmond Hiebert, *Mark, A Portrait of the Servant* (Chicago: Moody Press, 1974), p. 212, adds:

The traditional identification of the place with Mt. Tabor is improbable, since it is too far south, was not a high mountain, and apparently had a fortification on it at the time. A southern spur of Mt. Hermon, which is truly a high mountain, is now generally accepted, but one of the three different mountains, each over four thousand feet high, southeast of Caesarea Philippi, is also possible.

2. Alfred Edersheim, *The Life and Times of Jesus the Messiah,* vol. 2 (Grand Rapids, MI: Eerdmans, 1967), who quotes from Henry Baker Tristram's *Land of Israel,* pp. 609–613.

3. William L. Lane, *The Gospel According to Mark* (Grand Rapids, MI: Eerdmans, 1975), p. 319.

4. *The Mishnah,* Sukkah 5:2–3, trans. Herbert Danby (London: Oxford University Press, 1974), p. 180

Chapter Twenty-Nine: Unbelieving Faith

1. Clarence Edward Macartney, *Great Interviews of Jesus* (New York: Abingdon-Cokesbury, 1944), p. 88.

2. Gerhard Kittel, ed., *Theological Dictionary of the New Testament,* vol. 1, trans. Geoffrey W. Bromiley (Grand Rapids, MI: Eerdmans, 1968), p. 415, says: "The man commissioned is always the representation of the man who gives the commission. He represents in his own person the person and rights of the others. The Rabbis summed up this . . . in the frequently quoted statement . . . 'the one sent by a man is the man himself'" (*Ber.,* 5, 5).

3. *Chicago Tribune,* January 13, 1988.

4. Ray C. Stedman, *Expository Studies in Mark 8–16: The Ruler Who Serves,* Waco, TX: Word, 1976, p. 32, writes:

They did not fail because they did not expect anything to happen. They were surprised when it did not happen. They expected the boy to be delivered. They had seen people delivered before from demons when they said the word in Jesus' name. But this time it did not happen. So faith is not merely a sense of expecting something to happen. That ought to be clear from this account.

5. William L. Lane, *The Gospel According to Mark* (Grand Rapids, MI: Eerdmans, 1975), p. 333, says:

Jesus seized upon the father's words at the point where they were most tempered with doubt: "if you can." Verse 23 can be paraphrased, "As regards your remark about my ability to help your son, I tell you everything depends upon your ability to believe, not on mine to act." By this reversal of intent, Jesus indicates that the release of the man's son from possession is not to be a response to the conditional "if you can," as if his power were something to be elicited through challenge.

6. Alexander Maclaren, *Expositions of Holy Scripture*, vol. 8 (Grand Rapids, MI: Baker, 1974), p. 31 is the source used to illuminate this truth about faith.

Chapter Thirty: Attitudes for Ministry

1. William L. Lane, *The Gospel According to Mark* (Grand Rapids, MI: Eerdmans, 1975), p. 339, who quotes A. Schlatter, *Der Evangelist Matthaus* (Stuttgart, 1935), p. 543.

2. Ibid., p. 340, who quotes from *ad Phil* 5:2.

3. Ibid.

4. Ibid.:

In the light of the experience of Jewish exorcists who misused Jesus' name, without understanding (Acts 19:13–16; cf. Mt. 7:21–23), it is necessary to affirm that the name of Jesus discloses its authentic power only when a man joins Jesus in faith and obedience to the will of God. The fact that Jesus' power was active in the man, bringing release to men who had been enslaved to demonic possession, marks him as a believer. His action was an effective witness to the imminent Kingdom of God.

5. William Barclay, *The Gospel of John*, vol. 1 (Philadelphia: Westminster), pp. 134, 135.

Chapter Thirty-One: The Demanding Requirements of Discipleship

1. Josephus, *Antiquities*, XIV.XV.10.

2. Suetonius, *De Via Caesarium*, 1.67.

3. A. J. Gossip, *The Hero in Thy Soul* (New York: Scribners, 1930), p. 140.

4. William Barclay, *The Gospel of Mark* (Philadelphia: Westminster, 1956), pp. 238, 239, says:

There are in this passage repeated references to Gehenna. Gehenna is spoken of in the New Testament in Matthew 5:22, 29, 30; 10:28; 18:9; 23:15, 33; Luke 12:5; James 3:6. The word is regularly translated Hell. It is a word with a history. It is a form of the word *Hinnom*. The valley of Hinnom was a ravine outside Jerusalem. It had an evil history. It was the valley in which Ahaz, in the old days, had instituted fire worship and the sacrifice of little children in the fire. "He burnt incense in the valley of the son of Hinnom, and burnt his children in the fire" (2 Chronicles 28:3). That terrible heathen worship was also followed by Manasseh (2 Chronicles 33:6). The valley of Hinnom, Gehenna, therefore, was the scene of one of Israel's most terrible lapses into heathen customs. In his reformations, Josiah declared the valley of Hinnom an unclean place. "He defiled Topheth, which is in the valley of Hinnom, that no man might make his son or his daughter pass through the fire to Molech" (2 Kings 23:10). When the valley had been so declared unclean and had been so desecrated it was set apart as the place where the refuse of Jerusalem was thrown to be burned. The consequence was that it was a foul, unclean place, where loathsome worms bred on the refuse, and where it smoked and smouldered at all times like some vast incinerator. The actual phrase about the worm which does not die, and the fire which is not quenched, comes from a description of the fate of Israel's evil enemies in Isaiah 66:24. Because of all this the valley of Hinnom, Gehenna, had become a kind of type of symbol of Hell, of the place where the souls of the wicked will be tortured and destroyed. It is so used in the Talmud. "The sinner who desists from the words of the Law will in the end inherit Gehenna." So then Gehenna stands for the place of punishment, and the word roused in the mind of every Israelite the grimmest and most terrible pictures.

5. C. E. B. Cranfield, *The Gospel According to Saint Mark* (London: Cambridge University Press, 1983), pp. 315, 316.

6. Dietrich Bonhoeffer, *The Cost of Discipleship* (New York: Macmillan, 1969), pp. 100, 101.

7. William L. Lane, *The Gospel According to Mark* (Grand Rapids: Eerdmans, 1975), p. 350, who quotes *Tractate Sopherim*, XV.8.

8. F. W. Boreham, *A Bunch of Everlastings* (Nashville: Abingdon, 1920), p. 186.

Chapter Thirty-Two: What Jesus Says about Divorce

1. John R. W. Stott, *Issues Facing Christians Today* (London: Marshall Morgan & Scott, 1984), p. 260.

2. Lawrence J. Crabb Jr., *The Marriage Builder* (Grand Rapids, MI: Zondervan, 1982), p. 10.

3. Ibid., p. 11. Crabb writes: "The issue of authority is really at stake here. To validate a plan of action by approaching to its potential for meeting needs is to replace the authority of an inerrant Bible with a humanistic value system."

4. William L. Lane, *The Gospel According to Mark*, (Grand Rapids, MI: Eerdmans, 1975), p. 363 lists the Jewish sources for such teaching, for example: M. *Gittin* IX.10; T.B. *Gittin* 90a; T.J. *Sotah* I.1.16b; Num. R. IX.30.

5. James B. Hurley, *Man and Woman in Biblical Perspective* (Grand Rapids, MI: Zondervan, 1981), pp. 99–102.

6. Stott, *Issues Facing Christians Today*, p. 278 remarks: "It is true that in Mark 10:3ff Jesus is recorded as having used the verb 'command,' but there it seems to have been referring either to Mosaic legislation in general or in particular to the issuing of the divorce certificate."

7. Hurley, *Man and Woman in Biblical Perspective*, pp. 102, 103.

8. John R. W. Stott, *Christian Counter Culture* (Downers Grove, IL: InterVarsity Press, 1979), pp. 96, 97.

9. John Murray, *Divorce* (Phillipsburg, NJ: Presbyterian and Reformed, 1972), p. 63.

10. Ibid., pp. 74, 75.

11. R. C. Trench, *Synonyms of the New Testament* (London: Kegan Paul, Trench, Trubner & Co., 1901), p. 206.

12. *The Wittenberg Door*, no. 65, February/March 1982, p. 24, quoting from an ad from *TV Guide*.

13. D. Martyn Lloyd-Jones, *Studies in the Sermon on the Mount*, vol. 1 (Grand Rapids, MI: Eerdmans, 1959), p. 261.

Chapter Thirty-Three: Like a Little Child

1. *The Oxyrhynchus Papyri*, IV. no. 744, cited by Adolf Deissmann, *Light from the Ancient East*, trans. Lionel R. M. Strachan (London: Hodder and Stoughton, 1911), pp. 154, 155.

2. Kirsopp Lake, trans., *The Apostolic Fathers*, vol. 2 in the Loeb Classical Library (Cambridge, MA: Harvard, 1965), p. 361: "They marry as all men, they bear children, but they do not expose their offspring."

3. N. G. L. Hammond and H. H. Scullard, eds., *The Oxford Classical Dictionary*, 2nd ed. (London: Oxford University Press, 1978), p. 789.

4. Ibid.

5. Benjamin B. Warfield, "Children," in James Hastings, ed., *Dictionary of Christ and the Gospels*, vol. 1 (Grand Rapids, MI: Baker, 1973), p. 31.

6. William L. Lane, *The Gospel According to Mark* (Grand Rapids, MI: Eerdmans, 1975), p. 360, says: "The suggestion of impatience and irritation is strengthened by the sharp staccato effect of the positive and negative commands, achieved by asyndeton: 'Let the children approach me; do not prevent them.'"

7. Hastings, *Dictionary of Christ and the Gospels*, p. 302, who quotes Irenaeus, *adv. Haer.*, II. XXII. 4, cf. III. XVIII. 4.

8. William Barclay, *The Gospel of Mark* (Philadelphia: Westminster, 1956), p. 250.

9. Charles Spurgeon, *The Metropolitan Tabernacle Pulpit*, vol. 32 (Pasadena, TX: Pilgrim Publications, 1974), p. 570, from the sermon "Jesus and the Children."

10. Lane, *The Gospel According to Mark*, p. 360.

11. *Pius fecit, quam rogatus erat.*

Chapter Thirty-Four: The Rich Young Man

1. William L. Lane, *The Gospel According to Mark* (Grand Rapids, MI: Eerdmans, 1975), p. 365.

2. Ibid., p. 366, who quotes the great Strack and Billerbeck, *Commentary on the New Testament and Talmud and Midrash*, vol. 1, p. 814: "That men possess the ability to fulfill the commandments of God perfectly was so firmly believed by the rabbis that they spoke in all seriousness of people who had kept the whole law from A to Z."

3. The verb *stugnasas* is an ingressive aorist, which denotes the beginning of an action of state.

4. Amy Wilson-Carmichael, *Things as They Are* (Old Tappan, NJ: Revell, 1903), p. 74.

5. James Hastings, ed., *The Speaker's Bible*, vol. 8 (Grand Rapids, MI: Baker, 1974), p. 20.

6. Roland Hein, ed., *Creation in Christ* (Wheaton, IL: Harold Shaw, 1976), p. 128.

7. D. Edmond Hiebert, *Mark: A Portrait of a Servant* (Chicago: Moody Press, 1974), p. 250. Cf. Lane's footnote, *The Gospel According to Mark*, pp. 369, 370:

> Rabbinic sources reflect a variant form of the image: "Perhaps you are from Pumbeditha, where they draw an elephant through the eye of a needle" (TB Baba Metzia 38b, refined in TB "Erubin 53a" . . . "through the eye of a fine

needle"); "This is proved by the fact that a man is never shown in a dream a date palm of gold or an elephant going through the eye of a needle," i.e. something absurd or impossible (TB Berachoth 55b).

8. Max Zerwick and Mary Grosvenor, *A Grammatical Analysis of the Greek New Testament* (Rome: Biblical Institute Press, 1981), p. 141.

9. Lane, *The Gospel According to Mark*, p. 369.

10. Tony Campolo, *The Success Fantasy* (Wheaton, IL: Victor, 1980), pp. 141, 142.

11. Ray C. Stedman, *Expository Studies in Mark 8–16: The Ruler Who Serves* (Waco, TX: Word, 1981), p. 71.

12. G. Campbell Morgan, *The Gospel According to Mark* (Old Tappan, NJ: Revell, 1927), p. 237.

Chapter Thirty-Five: Blind Sight

1. Vincent Taylor, *The Gospel According to St. Mark* (Grand Rapids, MI: Baker, 1981), p. 447: "His passage through the city bears the character of an ovation."

2. Clarence Edward Macartney, *Great Interviews of Jesus* (New York: Abingdon-Cokesbury, 1944), pp. 148–150. The preceding imaginative account is inspired by Dr. Macartney and is quoted in some places without quotation marks.

3. Charles Colson, *Who Speaks for God?* (Wheaton, IL: Crossway, 1985), pp. 136, 137.

4. Ibid., p. 138.

5. Macartney, *Great Interviews of Jesus*, p. 155.

Chapter Thirty-Six: Welcoming the King

1. William L. Lane, *The Gospel According to Mark* (Grand Rapids, MI: Eerdmans, 1975), p. 395 says:

The Attention given to this phase of the action and the explicit reference to "a colt tied," with its allusion to Gen. 49:11, points to a deeper significance supplied by the Oracle of Judah, Gen. 49:8–12. The allusion to Gen 49:11 confirms the messianic character which the animal bears in Ch. 11:1–10. It also indicates that the untying of the colt was itself a messianic sign, although it was not recognized as such at that time. In addition to the "colt of an ass," the oracle speaks of the enigmatic "Shiloh who is to come" (Gen. 49:10), and this reference was interpreted messianically in pre-Christian Jewish texts.

2. Merrill F. Unger, *Zechariah* (Grand Rapids, MI: Zondervan, 1972), pp. 163, 164.

3. G. K. Chesterton, *The Collected Poems of G. K. Chesterton* (London: Cecil Palmer, 1927), p. 297.

4. Albert Schweitzer, *The Quest for the Historical Jesus* (New York: Macmillan, 1959), pp. 370, 371.

5. Cf. 2 Kings 9:12, 13—"And they said, 'That is not true; tell us now.' And he said, 'Thus and so he spoke to me, saying, "Thus says the Lord, I anoint you king

over Israel.'" Then in haste every man of them took his garment and put it under him on the bare steps, and they blew the trumpet and proclaimed, 'Jehu is king.'"

6. Alfred Edersheim, *The Life and Times of Jesus the Messiah*, vol. 2 (Grand Rapids, MI: Eerdmans, 1967), p. 367.

7. Lane, *The Gospel According to Mark*, p. 397.

8. Note: Luke 19:38 replaces the "he" in Psalm 118:26 with "the King."

9. Edersheim, *The Life and Times of Jesus the Messiah*, p. 369.

10. Ibid.

11. Josephus, *Jewish War*, V. 12, 4.

12. Ibid., VII. 1.1.

13. G. Campbell Morgan, *The Gospel According to Luke* (Old Tappan, NJ: Revell, 1931), p. 221.

Chapter Thirty-Seven: The Wrath of Jesus

1. T. W. Manson, *The Sayings of Jesus* (London: SCM Press, 1975), p. 279.

2. William Barclay, *The Gospel of Mark* (Philadelphia: Westminster, 1956), p. 280.

3. James Hastings, ed., *The Speakers's Bible*, vol. 8 (Grand Rapids, MI: Baker, 1971), p. 50.

4. William L. Lane, *The Gospel According to Mark* (Grand Rapids, MI: Eerdmans, 1975), pp. 401, 402, says that the clause in verse 13, "'because it was not the season for figs'—should be interpretively translated, 'and the significant thing about this is that it was not even the season for figs'" (p. 401). Lane also says, "The parenthetical clause in verse 13 is thus a deliberate Marcan device, and rather than being a dissonant note to be removed from the score, it is the key to the primary theme" (p. 402).

5. J. D. Douglas, ed., *The Illustrated Bible Dictionary*, vol. 3 (Wheaton, IL: Tyndale, 1980), p. 1530. James Orr, ed., *The International Standard Bible Encyclopedia*, vol. 5 (Grand Rapids, MI: Eerdmans, 1939), p. 2937, says:

> Differences of opinion continue as to the sacred cubit. A.R.S. Kennedy thinks the cubit can be definitely fixed at 17.6 in. (Expos T, XX, 24 ff); G.A. Smith reckons it at 20.67 in. (Jerus, II, 504); T. Witton Davies estimates it at about 18 in. (H D B, IV, 713), etc. W.S. Caldecott takes the cubit of Jos and the Middoth to be 1 1/5 ft. It will suffice in this sketch to treat the cubit, as before, as approximately equivalent to 18 in. . . . Jos states that the area of Herod's temple was double that of its predecessor (BJ, I, xxi, 1). The Mish (Mid., ii.2) gives it as a stadium (about 600 Gr. ft.); but neither measure is quite exact.

6. Josephus, *The Jewish War*, Books IV—VII, trans. H. St. J. Thackeray, The Loeb Classical Library (Cambridge, MA: Harvard University Press, 1929), p. 499, VI. IX. 3, says:

> Accordingly, on the occasion of the feast called Passover, at which they sacrifice from the ninth to the eleventh hour, and a little fraternity, as it were, gathers round each sacrifice, of not fewer than ten persons (feasting alone not being permitted), while the companies often include as many as twenty, the victims were counted and amounted to two hundred and fifty-

five thousand six hundred; allowing an average of ten diners to each victim, we obtain a total of two million seven hundred thousand, all pure and holy.

Cf. *War* II, XIV, 3, Loeb Edition, p. 433:

So long as Cestius Gallus remained in Syria discharging his provincial duties, none dared even to send a deputation to him to complain of Florus; but when he visited Jerusalem on the occasion of the feast of unleavened bread, the people pressed round him, and a crowd of not less than three millions.

7. Herbert Danby, trans., *The Mishnah*, Berakoth 9:5 (London: Oxford University Press, 1974), p. 10 says: "He may not enter into the Temple Mount with his staff on, his sandal, or his wallet, or with dust on his feet, nor may he make of it a short by-path."

8. C. S. Lewis, *The Voyage of the Dawn Treader* (London: Collins, 1976), pp. 200, 221.

9. Warren W. Wiersbe, *Listening to the Giants* (Grand Rapids, MI: Baker, 1980), p. 19.

Chapter Thirty-Eight: A Warning to the Unreceptive

1. James E. Rosscup, *Abiding in Christ* (Grand Rapids, MI: Zondervan, 1973), p. 877, quotes *Calmet's Dictionary*.

2. Richard Chenevix Trench, *Notes on the Parables of Our Lord* (London: Society for Promoting Christian Knowledge, 1906), p. 199.

3. D. Edmond Hiebert, *Mark: A Portrait of a Servant* (Chicago: Moody Press, 1974), p. 289.

4. Alfred Edersheim, *The Life and Times of Jesus the Messiah*, vol. 2 (Grand Rapids, MI: Eerdmans, 1967), p. 423.

5. William L. Lane, *The Gospel According to Mark* (Grand Rapids, MI: Eerdmans, 1975), pp. 417, 418.

6. C. H. Spurgeon, *The Metropolitan Tabernacle Pulpit*, vol. 33, sermon 1,951, "The Pleading of the Last Messenger" (Pasadena, TX: Pilgrim Publications, 1975), p. 137.

7. Ibid. The quotation is modified from Elizabethan English, "Thou puttest thy finger into the very eye of God when Thou doest slight His Son."

8. Lane, *The Gospel According to Mark*, p. 420.

9. George A. Buttrick, *The Parables of Jesus* (Grand Rapids, MI: Baker, 1979), p. 221.

Chapter Thirty-Nine: Christians' Allegiances

1. Joseph A. Fitzmyer, S.J., *The Gospel According to Luke (X—XXIV)* (New York: Doubleday, 1985), p. 1296.

2. William L. Lane, *The Gospel According to Mark* (Grand Rapids, MI: Eerdmans, 1975), p. 424.

3. Ray C. Stedman, *Expository Studies in Mark 8–16: The Ruler Who Serves* (Waco, TX: Word, 1976), p. 114.

4. Richard Halvorsen, *Prologue to Prison* (Los Angeles: Cowman Publications, 1964), p. 223.

5. Fitzmeyer, *The Gospel According to Luke (X—XXIV)*, p. 1291, says:

They are to pay Caesar his due, but a fortiori God too. The pronouncement has nothing to do with Jesus himself; it is rather an instruction for his disciples' conduct. Further, his answer makes no reference to the coin or any specific tax. All of this suggests that the emphasis really falls on the second part of the pronouncement.

Chapter Forty: Resurrection? Yes!

1. Josephus, *Jewish Antiquities*, XVIII, 1.4.
2. Ibid., XIII, 10.6.
3. Josephus, *Jewish War*, II, 8.14.
4. Ibid., II, 8.14.
5. Josephus, *Jewish Antiquities*, XIII, 10.6.
6. C. E. B. Cranfield, *The Gospel According to Saint Mark* (London: Cambridge, 1983), p. 376, refers to "Origen, *Comment in Matt.*, Tom. XVII, 36, quoted by Swete: "It would be absurd to say that God, who said, 'He which is, that is my name,' is the God of men who have no existence at all. . . . So then Abraham and Isaac and Jacob are alive and are conscious of God and of his grace."
7. William L. Lane, *The Gospel According to Mark* (Grand Rapids, MI: Eerdmans, 1975), p. 430 summarizes the argument of French New Testament scholar F. Dreyfus, saying:

If God has assumed the task of protecting the patriarchs from misfortune during the course of their life, but fails to deliver them from that supreme misfortune which marks the definitive and absolute check upon their hopes, his protection is of little value. But it is inconceivable that God would provide for the patriarchs some partial tokens of deliverance and leave the final word to death, of which all the misfortunes and sufferings of human existence are only a foretaste. If the death of the patriarchs is the last word of their history, there has been a breach of the promises of God guaranteed by the covenant, and of which the formula "the God of Abraham, of Isaac and of Jacob" is the symbol. It is in fidelity to his covenant that God will resurrect the dead.

8. C. H. Spurgeon, *The Metropolitan Tabernacle Pulpit*, vol. 31, sermon number 1,863, "Departed Saints Yet Living" (Pasadena, TX: Pilgrim Publications, 1973), p. 544.
9. Ibid., p. 546.
10. Job 19:25–27; Psalm 73:24ff.; Isaiah 15:8; 26:19; Daniel 12:2.
11. Spurgeon, "Departed Saints Yet Living," p. 550.
12. Roland Hein, ed., *Creation in Christ* (Wheaton, IL: Shaw, 1978), p. 246, from George MacDonald's sermon, "The God of the Living."
13. Ibid., p. 247.

Chapter Forty-One: Not Far from the Kingdom

1. William L. Lane, *The Gospel According to Mark* (Grand Rapids, MI: Eerdmans, 1975), p. 432, quotes the *Babylonian Talmud, Sabbath* 31a; cf. also Tobit 4:15 and Strack-Billerbeck, vol. 1, p. 907.

2. The full *Shema* consisted of quotations from Deuteronomy 6:4–9; 11:13–21; and Numbers 16:37–41.

3. William Barclay, *The Gospel of Mark* (Philadelphia: Westminster, 1956), p. 308.

4. Lane, *The Gospel According to Mark*, p. 432, disagrees in footnote 49, but his listing of the antecedents demonstrates that they are not explicitly combinations of Deuteronomy 6:5 and Leviticus 19:18. Lane says:

> This combination of Deut. 6:5 and Lev. 19:18 has a number of antecedent parallels in Jewish material; e.g. Testament of Issachar 5:2 "Love the Lord and the neighbor"; 7:6 "I loved the Lord and every man with all my heart"; Testament of Dan. 5:3 "Love the Lord with all your life and one another with a true heart"; Testament of Zebulum 5:3; Testament of Gad 6:1, Sifre Deut. 3:29; Sifra Lev. 19:28. Cf J.B. Stern, "Jesus' Citation of Dt 6, 5 and Lv 19, 18 in the Light of Jewish Tradition," CBQ 28 (1966), pp. 312–316.

5. Barclay, *The Gospel of Mark*, p. 309.

6. C. E. B. Cranfield, *The Gospel According to Saint Mark* (London: Cambridge, 1983), p. 379, remarks:

> The command to love one's neighbor as oneself does not in any way legitimize self-love (as has sometimes been thought); but in it God addresses us as the men that we actually are, sinners who love ourselves, and claims us as such for love to our neighbors. (See further Barth, CD. 1/2, pp. 450f.)

7. Ibid.

8. F. W. Boreham, *A Bunch of Everlastings* (New York: Abingdon, 1920), p. 201, says:

> Susanna Wesley was a marvel of nature and a miracle of grace. To begin with, she was the twenty-fifth child of her father; and, to go on with, she had nineteen children of her own! And she found time for each of them. In one of her letters, she tells how deeply impressed she was reading the story of the evangelistic efforts of the Danish missionaries in India. "It came into my mind," she says, "that I might do more than I do. I resolved to begin with my own children. I take such proportion of time as I can best spare to discourse every night with each child by itself." Later on, people began to marvel at her remarkable influence over her children. "There is no mystery about the matter," she writes again, "I just took Molly alone with me into my own room every Monday night, Hetty every Tuesday night, Nancy every Wednesday night, Jacky every Thursday night, and so on, all through the week; that was all!"

9. James McGraw, *Great Evangelical Preachers of Yesterday* (New York: Abingdon, 1961), p. 57.

10. Boreham, *A Bunch of Everlastings*, p. 199.

11. McGraw, *Great Evangelical Preachers of Yesterday*, p. 57.

12. William Barclay, *The Letters to the Corinthians* (Philadelphia: Westminster, 1956), p. 289.

13. Boreham, *A Bunch of Everlastings*, p. 208.

14. Alexander Maclaren, *Exposition of Holy Scripture*, vol. 8, *Mark* (Grand Rapids, MI: Baker, 1974), p. 150.

Chapter Forty-Two: Whose Son Is the Christ?

1. William L. Lane, *The Gospel According to Mark* (Grand Rapids, MI: Eerdmans, 1975), pp. 439–449.

2. Joachim Jeremias, *Jerusalem in the Time of Jesus*, trans. F. H. and C. H. Cave (Philadelphia: Fortress, 1978), p. 244.

3. Other references to the Davidic sonship of Messiah are: 2 Samuel 2:8–29; Psalm 89:3, 4; 132:11; Isaiah 11:1–9; Jeremiah 30:9; 33:15, 17, 22; Ezekiel 23:13; Hosea 3:5; Amos 9:11.

4. Vincent Taylor, *The Gospel According to St. Mark* (Grand Rapids, MI: Baker, 1981), p. 492, says:

> The quotation shows that the Psalm was interpreted Messianically by Jesus and by the Rabbis of His day. It is true that this interpretation is not found in Rabbinic literature until much later; according to Billerbeck, iv. 1.452–65, not until the second half of the third century. In Justin's *Dialogue with Trypho*, 32f., 56, 83, for example, it is said that the Jews interpret the Psalm with reference to Hezekiah. Cf. Lohmeyer, 262f. Billerbeck argues that the silence is due to anti-Christian polemic stimulated by the freedom with which the Psalm was quoted in the primitive church.

5. Psalm 110 is quoted five times in the New Testament: Acts 2:34, 35; Hebrews 1:13; 5:6; 7:17, 20. There are also several New Testament allusions to it: 1 Corinthians 15:25; Ephesians 1:20–22; Philippians 2:9–11; Colossians 3:1; Hebrews 8:1; 10:12; 12:2; 1 Peter 3:22.

6. Walter A. Maier, *The Lutheran Hour* (St. Louis: Concordia, 1931), p. 101.

7. Arthur Bryant, *English Saga (1840–1940)* (London: Collins, 1945), pp. 51, 52.

8. Ibid., p. 59.

9. John G. Stackhouse, "The Gospel Song," an unpublished parody.

10. Clarence Macartney, *The Making of a Minister* (Great Neck, NY: Channel Press, 1961), p. 123.

11. Lane, *The Gospel According to Mark*, p. 440.

12. Warren W. Wiersbe, *The Integrity Crisis* (Nashville: Oliver-Nelson, 1988), p. 16.

13. Ibid., p. 17.

Chapter Forty-Three: Money Speaks

1. Rachael Field, "Art, Antiquities and Auction," *Pan Am Clipper*, vol. 18, no. 4, April 1988, p. 13.

2. *Psychology Today*, December 1986, p. 23, which quotes from "The Demographics of Gambling" by Brad Edmondson in *American Demographics*, vol. 8, no. 7.

3. James Hastings, ed., *Dictionary of Christ and the Gospels*, vol. 2 (Grand Rapids, Ml: Baker, 1973), p. 748.

4. *Mishnah*, Shekalim XI.5.

5. Ray C. Stedman, *Expository Studies in Mark 8–16: The Ruler Who Serves* (Waco, TX: Word, 1976), p. 130.

6. Merrill C. Tenney, ed., *The Zondervan Pictorial Encyclopedia of the Bible*, vol. 5 (Grand Rapids, MI: Zondervan, 1975), p. 928.

7. C. E. B. Cranfield, *The Gospel According to St. Mark* (Grand Rapids, MI: Baker, 1966), p. 386.

8. William L. Lane, *The Gospel According to Mark* (Grand Rapids, MI: Eerdmans, 1975), p. 442.

9. John Albert Bengel, *Bengel's New Testament Commentary*, vol. 1, trans. Charlton T. Lewis and Marvin R. Vincent (Grand Rapids, MI: Kregel, 1981), p. 362.

10. Frederick Louis Godet, *Commentary on the Gospel of Luke* (Grand Rapids, MI: Zondervan, n.d.), p. 256.

11. John Calvin, *A Harmony of the Gospels Matthew, Mark and Luke and the Epistles of James and Jude*, vol. 3, trans. A. W. Morrison (Grand Rapids, MI: Eerdmans, 1975), p. 72.

12. J. D. Jones, *The Greatest of These*, p. 51.

13. *Church News*, Diocese of Mississippi, Eastertide, AD, 1982, p. 33.

Chapter Forty-Four: Jesus' Farewell Prophecy

1. Josephus, *War*, V. 5.3.

2. Ibid., V. 5.6.

3. Josephus, *Ant.*, XV, 11.3, says: "The temple was built of hard, white stones, each of which was about twenty-five cubits in length, eight in height and twelve in width."

4. Josephus, *War*, VII. 1.1.

5. Will and Ariel Durant, *The Lessons of History* (New York: Simon and Schuster, 1968), p. 81.

6. Robertson McQuilkin, "Let Me Get Home Before Dark." Used by permission.

7. William L. Lane, *The Gospel According to Mark* (Grand Rapids, MI: Eerdmans, 1975), p. 466.

8. Ibid., p. 468, who refers to Josephus, *Ant.*, VIII. 8.2–9; Tacitus, *History*, V.9; and Philo, *Legatio ad Gaium*.

9. Josephus, *War*, IV. 3.8.

10. Eusebius, *Ecclesiastical History*, III. 5.4.

11. Josephus, *War*, II. 20.1.

12. Ibid., V. 12.3.

13. D. Edmond Hiebert, *Mark: A Portrait of a Servant* (Chicago: Moody Press, 1974), p. 327, says: ". . . the periphrastic form of the future tense here used stresses the duration, star after star falling."

Chapter Forty-Five: Love's Extravagance

1. Herbert Danby, trans., *The Mishnah* (London: Oxford University Press, 1974), *Pesahim*, 9.11; 10:1, p. 150.

2. John Calvin, *A Harmony of the Gospels Matthew, Mark and Luke and the Epistles of James and Jude*, vol. 3, trans. A. W. Morrison (Grand Rapids, MI: Eerdmans, 1975), p. 122.

3. William Barclay, *The Gospel of Mark* (Philadelphia: Westminster, 1956), p. 343, suggests this application, saying:

> Love can see that there are things the chance to do which only comes once. It is one of the tragedies of life that often we are moved to do something fine, and we do not do it. It may be that we are too shy to do it and that we feel awkward about it. It may be that second thoughts suggest a more prudent and common sense course. It comes in the simplest things—the impulse to send a letter to someone to thank them for something that they have done, the impulse to tell someone how much we love them and how grateful we are to them, the impulse to give some special gift or speak some special word. And the tragedy is that the impulse is so often strangled at birth. This would be a so much lovelier world if there were more people like this woman, who acted on her impulse of love, because she knew in her heart of hearts that if she did not do it then she would never do it at all. How that last extravagant, impulsive kindness must have uplifted Jesus' heart.

4. William L. Lane, *The Gospel According to Mark* (Grand Rapids, MI: Eerdmans, 1975), pp. 493, 494 says:

> F.W. Danker has shown that the meaning of the anointing may be understood in terms of the background provided by Ps. 42, which speaks of the poor but righteous sufferer and his ultimate triumph over his enemies. Like the psalmist, Jesus is the poor but righteous sufferer who, though betrayed by his closest friend, is confident that God will raise him up and vindicate him. The woman, unlike the dinner guests, perceived that Jesus is the poor man *par excellence* and her deed may be construed as an act of loving kindness toward the poor.

5. Alexander Maclaren, *Expositions of the Holy Scripture*, vol. 8, *Mark* (Grand Rapids, MI: Baker, 1974), p. 169.

6. William Wordsworth, *Ecclesiastical Sonnets*, Part 3, 43.

Chapter Forty-Six: The Master's Mastery

1. Albert Schweitzer, *The Quest for the Historical Jesus* (New York: Macmillan, 1959), pp. 370, 371.

2. William L. Lane, *The Gospel According to Mark* (Grand Rapids, MI: Eerdmans, 1975), p. 501, quotes the *Melkita* to Exodus 12:42, XIV. 20a.

3. Ibid., pp. 497, 498, who reconstructs the Passover meal's sequence relying on *Mishna Pesachim*, X2, 3, 4, 6 and *Mishna Berachoth*, VI.1.

4. *Chicago Tribune*, April 14, 1986, Section 1, p. 4.

5. D. Edmond Hiebert, *Mark: A Portrait of a Servant* (Chicago: Moody Press, 1974), p. 350.

6. Mark Wheeler, "Secure in the Storm," *Kindred Spirit*, Summer 1986, p. 10.

Chapter Forty-Seven: The Institution of the Lord's Supper

1. William L. Lane, *The Gospel According to Mark* (Grand Rapids, MI: Eerdmans, 1975), p. 505, who gives a fine reconstruction of Jesus' final Passover. The quotation is from *Mishna Berachoth*, 6.1.

2. Ibid., p. 506, who quotes from N. Glatzer, ed, *The Passover Haggadah* (New York: n.p., 1953), p. 27.

3. John T. McNeill, ed., *Calvin: Institutes of the Christian Religion*, vol. 2, trans. Lord Lewis Battles (Philadelphia: Westminster, 1975), p. 1371.

4. Rudolf Schnackenburg, *The Gospel According to St. John*, vol. 2 (New York: The Seabury Press, 1980), p. 62.

5. Leon Morris, *The Gospel of John* (Grand Rapids, MI: Zondervan, 1976), p. 379.

Chapter Forty-Eight: Steeling the Church

1. Vincent Taylor, *The Gospel According to St. Mark* (Grand Rapids, MI: Eerdmans, 1981), p. 552, says:

> With every desire to avoid unwarranted psychological interpretations, it is impossible to do any kind of justice to Mark's words without seeing in them something of the astonishment of the Son of Man who knows that He is also the Suffering Servant of Isaiah 53.

2. D. Edmond Hiebert, *Mark: A Portrait of a Servant* (Chicago, IL: Moody Press, 1974), p. 358.

3. Taylor, *The Gospel According to St. Mark*, p. 553.

4. Archibald Thomas Robertson, *Word Pictures in the New Testament*, vol. 1 (Nashville: 1930), p. 384, says "fell" is a "descriptive imperfect: 'See him falling.'"

5. John Calvin, *A Harmony of the Gospels Matthew, Mark and Luke and the Epistles of James and Jude*, vol. 3, trans. A. W. Morrison (Grand Rapids, MI: Eerdmans, 1975), p. 148.

6. William L. Lane, *The Gospel According to Mark* (Grand Rapids, MI: Eerdmans, 1975), p. 515.

7. David V. Erdman, ed., *The Complete Poetry and Prose of William Blake*, revised edition, "The Auguries of Innocence," lines 59–62 (Berkeley, CA: University of California Press, 1982), p. 491.

8. Excerpted from personal correspondence with J. Sidlow Baxter, September 8, 1987.

Chapter Forty-Nine: The Betrayal of Jesus

1. G. Abbot-Smith, *A Manual Greek Lexicon of the New Testament* (New York: Charles Scribner's & Sons, n.d.), p. 240.

2. C. E. B. Cranfield, *The Gospel According to St. Mark* (Cambridge, UK: Cambridge University Press, 1983), p. 437.

3. John Calvin, *The Gospel According to St. John 11–21 and the First Epistle of John*, trans. T. H. L. Parker (Grand Rapids, MI: Eerdmans, 1974), p. 156.

4. Clarence Edward Macartney, *The Woman of Tekoah and Other Sermons on Bible Characters* (New York: Abingdon Press, 1955), p. 128.

5. John Calvin, *A Harmony of the Gospels Matthew, Mark and Luke and the Epistles of James and Jude*, vol. 3, trans. A. W. Morrison (Grand Rapids, MI: Eerdmans, 1975), pp. 160, 161.

Chapter Fifty: The Two Rocks

1. William L. Lane, *The Gospel According to Mark* (Grand Rapids, MI: Eerdmans, 1975), p. 531, who says in note 119: "The surname 'Caiaphas' may have stood for something like 'inquisitor.'"

2. D. Edmond Hiebert, *Mark: A Portrait of the Servant* (Chicago: Moody Press, 1974), p. 372, says:

> The Christ points to His claim to be the promised Messiah, while the Son of the Blessed queries His claim to deity. The second title, used only here in the New Testament in this absolute sense, was a typical Jewish circumlocution to avoid the use of the name of God (cf. Mt. 26:63, "the Son of God"). The two titles are not synonymous and unite two aspects of the claim of Jesus. In Jewish thought, they were not always associated in the person of the Messiah. How far the combination was accepted in the first century is not clear. But it is clear from the gospels that Jesus united both ideas in Himself. While Jesus avoided the use of the term Messiah, apparently because of its political and materialistic implication in Jewish thought, He did not repudiate the title (Jn. 4:25–26). But it was His claim to be "the Son of God," variously expressed, that always aroused the fierce opposition of the Jewish leaders (Jn. 5:19–47; 8:16–19, 53–58; 10:28–39). It seems clear that the high priest now deliberately combined the two designations to attain his own purpose.

3. Vincent Taylor, *The Gospel According to St. Mark* (Grand Rapids, MI: Baker, 1981) p. 570.

4. Lane, *The Gospel According to Mark*, p. 540.

5. Ibid., pp. 542, 543: "The statement that he began to invoke a curse is intentionally left without an object in the Greek text to denote both that he cursed himself if he is lying and those present if they insist on asserting that he is a disciple."

6. Ibid., p. 543 says:

> It was the peculiar habit of the cock crowing, with comparative regularity, at three times during the period between midnight and 3:00 A.M. that accounts for the designation of the third watch of the night as "cock-crow" (cf. Ch 13:35b). An early rabbinic tradition speaks of people setting out upon a night journey, departing at the first cock-crow, or the second, or the third (TB Yoma 21a, Baraitha). Observation over a period of twelve years in Jerusalem has confirmed that the cock crows at three distinct times, first about a half hour after midnight, a second time about an hour later, and a third time an hour after the second. Each crowing lasts from 3–5 minutes, after which all is quiet again. Thus between the first crowing, noted in verse 69, and the second only an hour had passed, but Peter had been provoked to deny solemnly and emphatically his relationship to Jesus three times.

7. John Pollack, *Hudson Taylor and Maria* (Grand Rapids, MI: Zondervan) p. 125.

8. Vance Havner, *Threescore and Ten* (Old Tappan, NJ: Revell, 1973), p. 49.

9. Lloyd John Ogilvie, *Drumbeat of Love* (Waco, TX: Word Books, 1978), p. 224.

10. Armando Valladares, *Against All Hope, The Prison Memoirs of Armando Valladares* (New York: Alfred A. Knopf, 1986), pp. 16, 17, who writes:

> Those cries of the executed patriots—"Long live Christ the King! Down with Communism!"—had awakened me to a new life as they echoed through the two-hundred-year-old moats of the fortress. The cries became such a potent and stirring symbol that by 1963 the men condemned to death were gagged before being carried down to be shot. The jailors feared those shouts. They could not afford to allow even that last courageous cry from those about to die. That rebellious, defiant gesture at the supreme moment, that show of bravery and integrity by those who were about to die, could easily become a bad example for the soldiers. It might even make them think about what they were doing.

Chapter Fifty-One: Pilate before Christ

1. Clyde E. Fant, Jr. and William M. Pinson Jr., eds., *Twenty Centuries of Great Preaching*, vol. 5 (Waco, TX: Word, 1976), pp. 201–203, who reference Richard Collins, *The General Next to God* (New York: E. P. Button, 1965).

2. William Temple, *Readings in John's Gospel*, vol. 2 (London: Macmillan, 1945, 1950), p. 272.

3. A. N. Sherwin-White, *Roman Society and Roman Law in the New Testament* (Grand Rapids, MI: Baker, 1981), p. 45.

4. James M. Boice, *The Gospel of John* (Grand Rapids, MI: Zondervan, 1979), p. 91.

5. Josephus, *Ant.*, III, 1; *War*, II, IX, 2, 3.

6. Josephus, *Ant.*, XVIII, III, 2; *War*, II, IX, 4.

7. Philo, *Legatio ad Caium*, XXXVIII.

8. Josephus, *Ant.*, XXXVIII, IV, 1, 2.

9. Eusebius, *Ecclesiastical History*, II, VII.

10. Eusebius, *Ecclesiastical History*, IV, XV, 3–5.

11. Josephus, *War*, II, XXI.5, VI, V. 3.

12. Leon Morris, *The Gospel of John*, vol. 5 (Grand Rapids, MI: Eerdmans, 1971), p. 793.

13. Ray C. Stedman, *Expository Studies in Mark 8–16: The Ruler Who Serves* (Waco, TX: Word Books, 1981), p. 190, 191, says:

> We too, face the same decision these Jews had to make between Barabbas and Jesus. Have you ever been disappointed in Jesus, disappointed in God? Have you ever expected him to act in a certain way because of what you understood about him and his life and his nature—but he did not do it? Has that ever happened to you? It has to me. I have been angry and disappointed in God. I have been all but convinced that he did not live up to his promise, for I was sure that I knew what he was going to do, and God disappointed me.

Chapter Fifty-Two: Revelations of the Cross, Part 1

1. Graham Greene, *The Heart of the Matter* (New York: Viking Press, 1948), p. 211.

2. Martin Hengel, *Crucifixion* (Philadelphia: Fortress Press, 1978), p. 90.

3. Saint Chrysostom, "Homilies on the Gospel of St. John and the Epistle to the Hebrews," Homily LXXXV.1, *The Nicene and Post-Nicene Fathers*, vol. 14, ed. Philip Schaff (Grand Rapids, MI: Eerdmans, 1969), p. 317.

4. William L. Lane, *The Gospel According to Mark* (Grand Rapids, MI: Eerdmans, 1975), p. 567.

5. Hengel, *Crucifixion*, p. 50, says: "Quintillian could therefore praise the crucifixion as a good work: in his view the crosses ought to be set up on the busiest roads."

6. Lane, *The Gospel According to Mark*, p. 564, says: "In the first century A.D. the army physician, Dioscorides Pedarius, who made an intrinsic study of almost 600 plants and 1,000 drugs, observed the narcotic properties of myrrh (*Materia Medica* I, LXIV.3)."

7. Ibid., p. 561, cites Cicero, *Pro Rabirio*, V.16: "Even the mere word, cross, must remain far from the lips of citizens of Rome, but also from their thoughts, their eyes, their ears."

8. Hengel, *Crucifixion*, p. 35.

9. Ibid., p. 83.

10. William D. Edwards, M.D.; Wesley J. Gabel, M.Div.; Floyd E. Hosmer, M.S., AMI, "On the Physical Death of Jesus Christ," *Journal of the American Medical Association*, March 21, 1986, vol. 255, no. 11, pp. 1455–1463.

11. C. S. Lewis, *The Four Loves* (New York: Harcourt, Brace, Jovanovich, 1960), p. 176.

12. Lewis Bayly, *Practice of Piety: Directing a Christian how to walk that he may please God. Amplified by the Author* (London: Printed for Philip Chetwind, 1619), pp. 452–459.

13. Gerard Manley Hopkins, from St. Francis Xavier, "*O Deus Ego Amo Te,*" in Charles L.Wallis, ed., *A Treasury of Poems for Worship and Devotion* (New York: Harper & Brothers, 1959), pp. 98, 99.

14. Donald Grey Barnhouse, *The Love Life* (Glendale, CA: Regal Books, 1974), pp. 270–273).

Chapter Fifty-Three: Revelations of the Cross, Part 2

1. C. S. Lewis, *Poems*, "Love's As Warm As Tears" (New York and London: Harcourt Brace Jovanovich, 1964), pp. 123, 124.

2. Ray C. Stedman, *Expository Studies in Mark 8–16: The Ruler Who Serves* (Waco, TX: Word, 1981), p. 206, writes:

> I don't think it is possible for any of us to even remotely understand the agony that wrung this tremendous cry from the lips of Jesus. If you can imagine a beautiful young girl, an innocent virgin, being raped by an ugly, foul, rapacious man, and the horror that she would feel in that moment, you aren't even in the range of what was going through the soul of Jesus when he was made sin for us. You say, "I don't understand it." Well, join the club—I am way beyond my depth in trying to explain anything about these events to you.

3. C. E. B. Cranfield, *The Gospel According to St. Mark* (Cambridge: Cambridge University Press, 1983), p. 459, says: "It is, of course, theologically important to maintain the paradox that, while this God-forsakenness was utterly real, the unity of the Blessed Trinity was even then unbroken."

4. John Calvin, *A Harmony of the Gospels Matthew, Mark and Luke and the Epistles of James and Jude*, vol. 3, trans. A. W. Morrison (Grand Rapids, MI: Eerdmans, 1975), p. 81.

5. Cranfield, *The Gospel According to St. Mark*, p. 459, says: "On the idea of Elijah as helper in time of need see Jeremias in T.W.N.T. II, pp. 932ff. The present passage is the earliest evidence cited by Jeremias; but Elijah is often celebrated as helper in time of need in legends of a later date."

6. Some wine vinegar is mentioned in Numbers 16:13 and Ruth 2:14 as a refreshing drink. It was a kind of ancient Gatorade and was evidently from the soldiers' supplies.

7. Philip P. Bliss, "Man of Sorrows, What a Name," 1875.

8. Ibid.

Chapter Fifty-Four: Sunday's Children

1. Ray C. Stedman, *Expository Studies in Mark 8–12: The Ruler Who Serves* (Waco, TX: Word, 1981), p. 209, 210.

2. Ibid., p. 210.

3. Alexander Maclaren, *Expositions of the Holy Scripture*, vol. 8, *Mark* (Grand Rapids, MI: Eerdmans, 1975), p. 249.

4. William L. Lane, *The Gospel According to Mark* (Grand Rapids, MI: Eerdmans, 1975), p. 588.

5. Ibid., p. 591.

6. Gerald F. Hawthorne, *Current Issues in Biblical and Patristic Interpretation* (Grand Rapids, MI: Eerdmans, 1974), p. 174.

7. Charles Colson, *Who Speaks for God?* (Wheaton, IL: Crossway Books, 1985), pp. 54–57.

Scripture Index

General Index

Abraham, 251, 280, 295, 296, 297
Adam, John and Nancy Williamson, 231
Akiba, Rabbi, 234
allegiance, 229, 287–92 (ch. 39 *passim*)
Ames, William, 11
attitudes, 217–23 (ch. 30 *passim*)
Augustine, 99, 126, 348
authority, 16, 20
    of Christ *see* Jesus Christ—authority
    of goodness, 139
    resisting, 290–91

Babylonian Talmud, 252, 383, 425n1 (ch.
    41)
baptism, 22–25
Barabbas, 378, 379, 432n13
Barclay, William, 40, 162, 271
Barnhouse, Donald Grey, 41, 76, 387, 388
Bartimaeus, 191, 255–61 (ch. 35 *passim*),
    264
Bayly, Joe, 228
Bayly, Lewis, 384
Baxter, J. Sidlow, 356, 357
belief, 34–38, 40, 50, 59, 64, 80, 105,
    190, 193, 212, 296, 348
    Pharisaical, 71
Bengel, J. A., 163, 248, 317
Bitterman, Chet, 30
Bonhoeffer, Deitrich, 229
Booth, General William, 18, 76, 178, 373,
    375, 380
Boswell, James, 229
Bread of Life, 53, 147, 148, 149, 182,
    183, 187, 347, 348
Brengle, Samuel Logan, 18
bride of Christ, 76
Brooks, Phillips, 11, 21
Bryant, Sir Arthur, 310
busyness, 104, 334

Caiaphas, Joseph, 366, 367, 382, 431n1
Calvin, John, 318, 334, 348, 353, 362, 393
Carmichael, Amy, 251
Chesterton, G. K., 321
child, children, 35, 50, 57, 74, 97, 121,
    124, 126, 127, 175, 213, 223, 235,
    243–48 (ch. 33 *passim*), 326, 348, 356,
    396, 419n4 (ch. 31), 426n8
    abuse of, 310
    and Christ, 58, 210, 220
    Saturday's, 401, 403
    Sunday's, 399–406 (ch. 54 *passim*)
children of God, 97, 109, 132, 154, 349,
    356, 362
Christ *see* Jesus Christ
church,
    Body of Christ, 44, 132, 220, 265
    early, 15, 20, 35, 114, 133, 151, 219,
        243, 302, 309, 319, 326, 327, 365,
        366, 380
    as family, 96–97
    life, 144, 209
    modern, 31, 64, 134, 177–78, 218,
        253, 272, 310, 312
    priorities of, 44, 59, 71, 134, 174, 233,
        241, 307
    storm-tossed/suffering, 114, 151–57
        (ch. 21 *passim*), 229, 351–58 (ch.
        48 *passim*), 374
    triumphant, 354
    universal, 44, 64, 110, 128, 265, 272,
        276, 284, 289, 305, 306, 319, 323,
        327, 328, 334, 361, 362, 368, 370
cleannesses, in *Mishnah*, 150
Colson, Charles, 27, 257, 404
commandment(s),
    greatest, 300–2, 307
    ten, 162, 250, 251, 301
commitment, 38, 88, 96, 153, 154, 156,
    238, 241, 292, 324

Index of Sermon Illustrations

Church

The Church has been assaulted with a cultural perspective that sanctifies "winning." Being Number One is "American," and it is even thought to be "Christian." But to be "*Numero Uno*"—to want always to be served—is sub-Christian, 218

Jesus (along with the Father and the Spirit) resides in the children of God—in the wondrous mystery of Christ's Body, the Church. So practically speaking, when we welcome other children of God in Christ's name, there is a sense in which we receive and open ourselves further to Christ, because he indwells them and is identified with them, 220

The fig tree was meant to be a visual parable to Israel, and later to the Church (us). Just because we look good, because our leaves are large and shiny, does not mean that we are bearing fruit pleasing to God, 272

There are two disparate powers that can bind people together. One is love, and the other is hatred. Of course, love is to be preferred by far. Nevertheless, hatred, though ultimately destructive and fragmenting, can serve as a devilish cement among otherwise diverse people, 287

Dietrich Bonhoeffer: "Suffering, then, is the badge of true discipleship. Discipleship means allegiance to the suffering Christ, and it is therefore not at all surprising that Christians should be called upon to suffer. In fact, it is a joy and a token of His grace," 229

Conscience

We all do evil that we naturally put away from our conscience as if it never happened. Trivial incidents may awaken the suppressed conscience—a chance word, a sound, a scent, an expression on a face. Such an event is meant to call us to repentance and forgiveness, 141

A neglected conscience will suffer progressive desensitization to God so that we do not hear him when he speaks. We need to cultivate our conscience by filling our minds with God's Word and then obeying it, 142

Conversion

Renowned classics scholar Dr. E. V. Rieu's conversion while translating the Gospels, 13

Charles Colson's conversion, 258

Charles Wesley's conversion, 299–300

Evangelism

I am a good fisherman, but not great. To be great you have to fish and study so much that you mentally enter the great chain of life of the fish. You must read and study and fish and talk about fish. How much more difficult it is to be good fishers of men! How much more sensitivity and how much more tenacity is needed! But Christ is able to equip us for the task, 38

We must be careful never to box God in, because that results in limiting our usefulness. If we think he can work only along one of our experiential or cultural tracks, we will unconsciously resist him when he chooses to work in one of his mysterious ways, 190

malleable, and then presses his image, his character, into us, 292

Hopelessness

Ray Steadman writes of "Saturday's children" and the meaninglessness of the present generation, 401

Jesus

Christ is all action in Mark! Mark used the historical present tense 150 times. Jesus comes, Jesus says, and Jesus heals—all in the present tense. There are more miracles recorded in Mark than in the other Gospels, despite its being far shorter, 15

The logic is: if the One who created both the supernova and the firefly and holds them together by the word of his power (Colossians 1:15–17) became our servant, our waiter, how can we do less? 17–18

When Martin Luther was asked how he overcame the devil, he replied, "Well, when he comes knocking upon he door of my heart, and asks 'Who lives here?' the dear Lord Jesus goes to the door and says, 'Martin Luther used to live here, but he has moved out. Now I live here.'" When Christ fills our lives, Satan has no entrance, 32

Following Christ eliminates the trivial and expands our hearts, 38

Philip Schaff on the hypothesis that Jesus was a liar, 92

Jesus could not do miracles because he *would* not. Omnipotence is not omnipotence if it is bound by anything but its own will. Jesus was *morally* compelled not to show his power, 132

John Calvin's quote from Cyril of Alexandria about Christ's death, 353

The *religiously* motivated rejecters sought to crush Jesus because his life provided a dreadful mirror to their own souls. The *socially* motivated rejection by Pontus Pilate was an archetype of the hearts that would reject Christianity because it endangers status. The *politically* driven rejection wants a Christ who does things man's way. The *irrationally* motivated come along for the macabre ride, 380

C. S. Lewis comments on the love of God through the cross of Christ, 384

If you want your sin to be on Christ, you must look closely at the cross. First, behold the man and his suffering. Observe how great his love for you is. Tell Jesus that you love him. Second, behold the King and his demands. Yield to his rule. Third, behold the crosses and ask Jesus to take your sins, 390

John the Baptist

John's dress and lifestyle were a protest against the godlessness and self-serving materialism of his day. It amounted to a call to separate oneself from the sinful culture, repent, and live a life focused on God, 21

Why was John's witness so effective? First, because his character modeled his message. Therefore, what he said had the ring of truth. Second, his message was complete. It had both law and grace, and God's grace was (and is) infinite, 23

Joy

We are not just "guests of the bridegroom"—we are the bride of Christ! This is more than metaphorical language—it is reality. It speaks of the deepest intimacy and exchange. Therefore, we are to outdistance the attendants of the Bridegroom in the intensity and continuance of our joy, 76

Missions

Sometimes a touch, caring involvement, will do a thousand times more than our theology, 59

We cannot expect this to be only the job of missionaries because a church that does not regularly place its hand on the rotting humanity around it will not be sending missionaries to do so either, 59

Dr. Schaeffer on sacrificial faith in the work of L'Abri, 64

Obedience

External prosperity does not mean God approves of all we are doing. God approves obedience, 31

Never climb a mountain and you will never bruise your shins, but you will never stand on its peak exulting in victory in the alpine air. Never play baseball and you will never strike out, but you will never hit a home run either. Never obey Christ and you may miss some of life's contrary winds, but you will also never know the winds of the Holy Spirit in your sails bearing you on in service and power, 154

Number one: we must resist the climate of our soap-opera culture, which determines its commitments by what it is going to get (self-fulfillment). Rather, obedience to God's rule in our lives is more important than fulfillment. The truth is, obedience to God's Word will likely expose us to pains we could have avoided if we pursued self-fulfillment, 241

Prayer

E. Stanley Jones once described prayer as a "time exposure to God." He used the analogy of his life being like a photographic plate that, when exposed to God, progressively bore the image of God in keeping with the length of exposure, 49

If I have any sense of where the Christian culture is today, I would say our Number One sin is not sensuality or materialism (though they are close behind) but *prayerlessness*. So often

when busy, caring Christians get together and "let their hair down," they talk about the trouble with their prayer lives. We should be praying for our inner life: that our character will have grace to match our profession; that we will walk our talk, 175

The call to prayer is a call to discipline. Unfortunately, many reject this idea. They argue that such thinking promotes legalism. But there is an eternity of difference between legalism and discipline. Legalism has at its core the thought of becoming better and thus gaining merit through religious exercise. Discipline springs from a desire to please God, 356

Dr. J. Sidlow Baxter's diary entry that comments on a pastor's need for prayer, 356–57

George MacDonald: "What if He knows prayer to be the thing we need first and most? Communion with God is the one need of the soul beyond all other needs; prayer is the beginning of that communion, and some need is the motive of that prayer. Our wants are for the sake of our coming into communion with God, our eternal need," 83–84

Preaching

Hugh Latimer preaching the same sermon to Henry VIII even though it offended him, 19

Bishop Quail when answering the question "Is preaching the art of making a sermon and delivering it?" responded "Preaching is the art of making a preacher and delivering that," 22

There was and is radical "nowness" to Jesus' preaching. Now is the time to believe, and now is the time to repent," 36

Dr. Barnhouse compares teaching Scripture to whistling a tune of a symphony, 41–42

The Preaching the Word series is written
by pastors for pastors and their churches.

crossway.org/preachingtheword